Reporting and Writing the News

Reporting and Writing the News

Warren K. Agee
University of Georgia

Phillip H. Ault
South Bend *Tribune*

Edwin Emery
University of Minnesota

HARPER & ROW, PUBLISHERS, New York
Cambridge, Philadelphia, San Francisco,
London, Mexico City, São Paulo, Sydney

1817

Sponsoring Editor: Phillip Leininger
Project Editor: Pamela Landau
Designer: T. R. Funderburk
Production Manager: Marion Palen
Compositor: Haddon Craftsmen
Printer and Binder: R. R. Donnelley, & Sons Company

Reporting and Writing the News
Copyright © 1983 by Warren K. Agee, Phillip H. Ault, and Edwin Emery

All rights reserved. Printed in the United States of America. No part of this book may be used or reproduced in any manner whatsoever without written permission, except in the case of brief quotations embodied in critical articles and reviews. For information address Harper & Row, Publishers, Inc., 10 East 53d Street, New York, NY 10022.

Library of Congress Cataloging in Publication Data

Agee, Warren Kendall.
  Reporting and writing the news.

  1. Reporters and reporting.   I. Ault, Phillip H.,
1914-   .   II. Emery, Edwin.   III. Title.
PN4781.A34   1983   070.4'3   82-21305
ISBN   0-06-040173-7

Acknowledgments

PHOTOGRAPHS AND ILLUSTRATIONS

PART I
Page 1, Forsyth, Monkmeyer
Chapter 1
Page 6, © Anderson, 1981, Woodfin Camp
Chapter 2
Page 17, From National Geographic's *Romance of the Sea,* © 1980 National Geographic Society
Chapter 3
Page 25, Laffont, Sygma; p. 32, Ledru, Sygma; p. 53, Nogues, Sygma
Chapter 5
Page 57, UPI
Chapter 6
Page 62, Syndication International, Photo Trends

PART III
Page 83, © Griffiths, Magnum
Chapter 13
Page 152, Brucelle, Sygma

PART IV
Page 155, Forsyth, Monkmeyer
Chapter 18
Page 205, Grace, Sygma
Chapter 19
Page 219, Reprinted by permission from *presstime,* the journal of the American Newspaper Publishers Association

PART V
Page 211, UPI
Chapter 20
Page 233, Mingam, Liaison
Chapter 21
Page 249, UPI; p. 255, Tannenbaum, Sygma

PART VII
Page 297, Courtesy WNET/THIRTEEN
Chapter 26
Page 321, Don Black

Chapter 27
Page 332, Sygma; p. 339, Courtesy of Cox Communications, Inc.
Chapter 28
Page 343, Los Angeles *Herald Examiner*

TEXT

Chapter 4
Page 45, Associated Press story by Jan Carroll, published in the South Bend *Tribune*, July 2, 1981. Used with permission.
Pages 48–49, From The Goshen *News,* Goshen Indiana, May 16, 1979. Used with permission.
Chapter 8
Pages 79–80, From the San Luis Obispo County *Telegram-Tribune,* January 26, 1981. Used with permission.
Chapter 12
Pages 132–133, From the South Bend *Tribune,* February 11, 1981. Used with permission.
Page 135, From the San Francisco *Examiner,* April 5, 1981. Used with permission.
Pages 139–140, From the Santa Barbara *News-Press,* February 25, 1981, article entitled "Wonders of Life in Home of the Future" by James V. Healion. Reprinted by permission of United Press International.
Pages 141–142, From the Chicago *Tribune,* May 17, 1981. Copyrighted 1981, Chicago Tribune. Used with permission.
Page 149, From the Atlanta *Journal,* date unavailable. Used with permission.
Chapter 14
Pages 166–167, "Kim Novak Back after 11 years," by Judy Klemesrud, February 1981. © 1981 by The New York Times Company. Reprinted by permission.
Chapter 15
Pages 178–180, From the San Francisco *Chronicle,* February 6, 1981. Used with permission.
Chapter 25
Pages 301–303, From the Minneapolis *Star,* July 1981. Used with permission.
Pages 303–305, From the Washington *Post,* July 1981. Used with permission.
Pages 306–307, © 1981 by The New York Times Company. Reprinted by permission.
Pages 307–309, Reprinted by permission from *The Christian Science Monitor.* © 1981 The Christian Science Publishing Society. All rights reserved.
Appendix B
Pages 360–369, From the Associated Press *Stylebook,* 1980. Reprinted by permission.

Contents

Acknowledgments v
Preface xiii

PART I   THE SEARCH FOR NEWS   1

Chapter 1   THE NEWSROOM: DISCIPLINED BUSTLE   3
  A World of Deadlines   3
  The Role of the Reporter   7
  What a Good Reporter Needs   7
    A News Sense   8 • *An Ability to Search for Facts*   8 • *An Inquisitive Mind*   9 • *An Ability to Use Good English*   10 • *An Understanding of Newswriting Style*   10

Chapter 2   HISTORICAL ROLE OF THE REPORTER   13
  How Reporting Began   13
  The First Reporters   14
  Growth of Reporting Staffs   15
  Trends in Reportorial Standards   18
    Rise of Objectivity   18 • *Interpretive Reporting*   19 • *Investigative Reporting*   19 • *Alternative Journalism*   20

Chapter 3   WHAT IS NEWS?   23
  The Search for a Definition of News   23
  Hard and Soft News   26
  Explanations and Interpretations   28
  The Elements of News   30
    Proximity   30 • *Prominence*   31 • *Consequence*   31 • *Timeliness*   31 • *Human Interest*   31

Chapter 4 THE BASIC NEWS STORY 35
    Structure 35
    The Lead 38
    Different Ways to Write the Same Lead 41
    Delayed Identification 43
    Localizing 44
    Unity 44
    Chronological Treatment 46
    The Suspended Interest Story 47
    Rewriting a Story 48
    Tips on Newswriting 50
    Avoid Sexism in News Stories 51

PART II REPORTING THE STORY 53

Chapter 5 THE FOUR "MUSTS" 55
    Essential Story Elements 55
        Accuracy 55 • Attribution 56 • Fairness 56 • Objectivity 58

Chapter 6 PREPARING THE COPY 61
    The Changing Newsroom Scene 61
    The Traditional Method of Preparing Copy 62
    Editing Symbols 64

Chapter 7 THE FIRST ASSIGNMENT 67
    A Selective Process 67
    Taking Notes 68
    Using a Tape Recorder 70
    Planning the Story 71
    Tips on Covering a Speech 72

Chapter 8 WRITING THE SPEECH STORY 75
    Selection of a Lead 75
    Development of the Theme 77
    Use of Background Material 78
    Tips on Writing a Speech Story 79
    An Actual Example 79

PART III WRITING PROCESSES AND PROTOTYPES 83

Chapter 9 MORE ABOUT LEADS 85
    Varying the Lead 85
        Contrast 85 • Parody 86 • Literary Allusion 86 • The Astonisher 87 • Descriptive Lead 87 • Direct Address 87 • The Complex Story Lead 88 • Question 88 • Quotation 89 • Dialogue 90

Three Historic Leads 89
Leads to Avoid 90
The Say-Nothing Lead 90 • *The Abstract Language Lead* 91 • *The Foggy Lead* 92 • *The Flat, Dull Lead* 93 • *The Ungrammatical Lead* 93
Advice from an Editor 95

Chapter 10 BEDROCK ASSETS: GRAMMAR AND SPELLING 99
Emphasis on Basic Skills 99
Blunders in Print 100
Sentences 102
Usage 104
Spelling 109
The City Editor Says: Spell Those Names Correctly 109

Chapter 11 DEVELOPING A WRITING STYLE 113
Clarity Is the Primary Goal 113
Eight Guidelines to Improved Writing 114
Inject Details 114 • *Be Concise* 116 • *Use Vigorous Action Verbs and Nouns* 118 • *Avoid Overcrowding* 120 • *Strive for Tempo in Sentence Structure* 121 • *Seek Originality in Phraseology* 122 • *Use Quotations Frequently* 124 • *Set Scenes* 126

Chapter 12 THE FEATURE APPROACH 130
Varying the Writing 130
Ways to Use a "Soft Style" 132
An Example to Study 138
The Full-Dress Feature Story 139
An Example to Study 140

Chapter 13 THE DAILY GRIST: OBITUARIES, WEATHER, SECOND-DAY STORIES 145
The Necessary Routine 145
Obituaries 146
The Longer Obituary 148 • *Suicides* 150
Weather Stories 150
The Second-Day Story 151

PART IV INTERVIEWING AND PROBING 155

Chapter 14 THE ART OF INTERVIEWING 157
The Interviewer's Role 157
Preparation for the Interview 158
Tips for Effective Interviewing 159
Conducting the Interview 160
Taking Notes 165
The Tape Recorder 165
An Interview with Kim Novak 166

Chapter 15 WRITING THE INTERVIEW STORY 170
    Choosing a Lead 170
    Developing the Story 174
    Use of Quotations 177
    Tips on Writing the Interview 177
    A Breezy Interview 178

Chapter 16 A REPORTER'S RESEARCH TOOLS 182
    Where to Look 182
    Public Records 184
    Vital Statistics 184
        Ownership of Property 185 • Court Records 185 • Board Meetings 186 • Licenses and Permits 186 • Vehicle Ownership 186 • Other Public Record Sources 186
    General Research Sources 187
    Freedom of Information Act 188

Chapter 17 THE HANDOUT—TOOL AND TRAP 192
    Role of the News Release 192
    The Well-Prepared Release 194
    Handout Mentality 195
    Filling the Gaps 196
    From Handout to Pulitzer Prize 198
    A Press Release Debunked 200

Chapter 18 THE NEWS CONFERENCE 203
    An Opportunity for Reporters 203
    Presidents Meet the Press 205
    How to Seek Answers 206
    The Off-the-Record Problem 209

PART V LEGAL AND ETHICAL PROBLEMS 211

Chapter 19 DANGER! LIBEL AND INVASION OF PRIVACY 213
    Reputations Are Precious 213
    What Is Libel? 214
    Defenses Against Libel 216
        Truth 216 • Privilege 216 • Fair Comment 217 • Constitutional Defense 217 • Consent 218 • Mitigatory Defense 218
    The Constitutionalization of Libel Law 218
    "Red Flag Words" 222
    Guidelines for Reporters 223
    The Right of Privacy 223
        Commercial Use 224 • Intrusion 224 • Embarrassment 225 • False Light 225 • Federal Privacy Laws 226

Chapter 20   CONTEMPORARY ISSUES OF ETHICS AND TASTE   230
    Recent Ethical Problems   230
    Possible Causes of Improper Reporting   231
        The "New Journalism"   231 • The Influence of Television News   232 • The Increasing Use of Anonymous Quotations   232 • The Urge for Fame and Fortune   232 • Editor and Reporter Attitudes   232 • The Public's Need for Myths   233
    The Drive for Improved Professional Conduct   233
        Codes of Ethics   233
    A Newspaperman's Credo   236
        Conflicts of Interest   237 • Deceptive Practices   238 • Other Ethical Problems   239 • Self-Criticism   240
    Good Taste   240
        The Printed Word   240 • Photographs   241
    Guidelines for Reporters   242
        Gifts from News Sources   242 • Deception   242 • Cooperation with News Sources   243 • Personal Involvement   243

PART VI COVERING THE BEATS   245

Chapter 21   ON THE BEAT   247
    The Beat Structure   247
    What a Beat Reporter Seeks   250
    Breaking in on a Beat   253
    A Veteran Reporter Tells How   254
    Tips on Covering a Beat   257

Chapter 22   INSIDE THE POLICE WORLD   260
    The Police Reporter's Job   260
    How Police Are Organized   261
    Sources of Police News   262
    The Fire Department   267
    Guides to Writing Police Stories   268
    Ethical Problems on the Police Beat   269
    A Glossary of Common Police Terms   271

Chapter 23   THE COURSE OF JUSTICE   275
    Organization of Courts   275
    Criminal Case Procedures   276
        Attempts at Secrecy   278 • Juvenile Court Hearings   282
    Civil Court Cases   282
    A Glossary of Common Court Terms   283

Chapter 24   THE BIG STORY   287
    Assassination Attempt Against President Reagan   287

Unanswered Questions 289
America: A Giant Newsroom 291
Disaster in Midair 292

PART VII INTERPRETING THE NEWS 297

Chapter 25 INTERPRETIVE REPORTING 299
The Interpretive Dimension 299
Some Interpretive Reporting Examples 301
Washington: Political News Center 309
Covering the White House and Congress 310
Investigative Reporting 312
Assignment: Slum Cleanup 313
Health 314 • Property Ownership 314 • Crime Rate 314 • Racial Problems 315 • Education 315 • Recreation Facilities 315

Chapter 26 THE REPORTER AS PHOTOGRAPHER 319
A Supplementary Skill 319
Kinds of Photographs 320
Taking the Picture 322
Your Rights as a Photographer 323
Writing Cutlines 325

Chapter 27 REPORTING AND WRITING BROADCAST NEWS 330
Differences in Methods 330
Reporting for Radio 330
Writing News for Radio 333
Reporting for Television 336
Writing News for Television 339

Chapter 28 WHAT TO EXPECT ON THE JOB 342
Preparing for the Job 342
The Proper Attitude 344
What Kind of Salary? 345
The Beginner's Assignments 346

Appendix A WRITING ELECTRONICALLY 351
Appendix B EXCERPTS FROM THE ASSOCIATED PRESS STYLEBOOK 360
Appendix C THE LANGUAGE OF JOURNALISM 370

Index 377

Preface

The purpose of *Reporting and Writing the News* is to show how journalists work and to teach the skills required for careers in the news media. Although the book's approach is strongly utilitarian, with emphasis on "how to . . . ," the authors recognize that the acquisition of technical skills is only part of the education a young journalist needs in order to become a responsible professional. Therefore, we present the techniques of reporting and newswriting in a setting of the ethical problems a contemporary journalist encounters. We also include an historical perspective. Students should realize that the skills they are acquiring have been developed through trial and error by many generations of reporters and writers.

If a single word can characterize this book, that word is *realistic.* Among them, the three authors have combined practical journalistic experience of more than 50 years and a combined teaching experience of more than 65 years. To supplement this wealth of firsthand experience in the newsroom, the editor's chair, and the classroom, we obtained advice from prominent journalism educators, newspaper editors, and veteran reporters. Then we sought still another point of view: that of reporters a year or two out of college. In individual and group discussions, these young men and women told us about aspects of journalism that were inadequately learned in the classroom and about the problems they encountered on their first jobs as reporters. We have sought particularly to include material that covers these areas.

This book is structured to introduce the student to the techniques of reporting and to the craft of newswriting almost simultaneously, rather than as separate units. A young reporter on the job develops proficiency in reporting and newswriting at the same time while on daily assignments, so this unified approach is a logical way for classroom students to learn. Early in the course, students will go into the field, and they should be able to produce a basic story that is acceptable both in content and in writing style.

Instructors who use the Agee-Ault-Emery *Introduction to Mass Communica-*

tions, now in its seventh edition, and our *Perspectives on Mass Communications* will find the style of this book familiar. As in those textbooks, we have sought to present the material in an easily comprehended manner that is authoritative without being ponderous. A peppering of anecdotes that brighten the pages gives a taste of the "real-life" newspaper world.

In the teaching of reporting and newswriting, the use of examples to illustrate the points being explained is especially valuable. Students see theory turned into reality as they study how other reporters have written stories and solved problems. This book contains many contemporary news story examples taken from newspapers of all sizes, from metropolitan dailies to country weeklies. Students are asked to analyze these stories, to find their shortcomings as well as their strengths, and to determine how the poor stories should be rewritten.

The opening chapter of *Reporting and Writing the News* takes its readers on a tour of a 1980s electronic newsroom, explains the work of the various editors, and places the newsroom in relationship with other departments of a newspaper. It points out the differences between a large daily's news operations and those of a weekly newspaper. Then it describes the role of the reporter and discusses the five attributes of a good reporter.

In Chapter 2, the book describes the evolution of reporting and explains major trends in reporting styles, to give the student an understanding of how current journalistic practices came about.

With the background laid, the next four chapters introduce the student to the actual work of newswriting. Chapter 3 explores the question, "What Is News?" Chapter 4 explains the organization and writing of a basic news story; emphasis is placed on the inverted pyramid style, as the simplest form, but other story forms also are described. Chapter 5, "The Four 'Musts,' " stresses the need for accuracy, attribution, fairness, and objectivity in a news story. In Chapter 6, "Preparing the Copy," the student learns the fundamentals of editing copy for publication.

Next, the student advances into the "do-it-yourself" phase by being sent to cover a story. The assignment is to hear a speech and write a news story about it. Chapters 7 and 8 form a pair: "The First Assignment" and "Writing the Speech Story." One deals with the reporting techniques involved and the other with ways to write the story from notes the reporter has taken.

From this, the beginning reporter learns first-hand about the problems of writing a news story. The next three chapters concentrate on writing techniques, to make that part of the work better. In Chapter 9, "More About Leads," the student is shown many different ways in which a lead may be written, with good and bad examples of published leads. Because many students are weak in their use of English, Chapter 10, "Bedrock Assets: Grammar and Spelling," emphasizes the language tools every reporter needs. It illustrates its points with "howlers" collected from published stories. The third of these chapters about writing, "Developing a Writing Style," gives eight guidelines to improved writing.

A pair of chapters introduces the student to the techniques of interviewing. The first, "The Art of Interviewing," tells how to conduct an interview, and the second, "Writing the Interview Story," shows the reporter how to develop the interview notes into a bright and well-rounded story.

The emphasis switches next to reporting. Full of detail and examples, this group of chapters tells the student how to go about the tasks of newsgathering. "A Reporter's Research Tools" lists ways in which the reporter searches for information in public records and reference works. "The Handout—Tool and Trap" illustrates the function of news releases and demonstrates how a reporter should dig below the surface for revealing stories. "The News Conference" shows how to seek useful answers in group reporting situations.

"The Feature Approach" explains how a reporter can present the information he or she has gathered in distinctive and refreshing manner by varying the writing style with a "soft" news approach. After that, the student meets the bread-and-butter aspects of reporting in a chapter titled, "The Daily Grist: Obituaries, Weather, and Second-Day Stories."

Familiar by now with the fundamentals of news stories, the student at this point is introduced to the problems of libel and ethics that a reporter encounters. "Danger! Libel and Invasion of Privacy" explains the law and gives tips on avoiding trouble. Recent examples of ethical violations are cited in "Contemporary Issues of Ethics and Taste," together with codes of ethics for reporters to follow.

A cluster of four chapters then takes the student into the field as a reporter. "On the Beat" tells how a newspaper's beat structure is organized. "Inside the Police World" contains a detailed explanation of how to cover the police beat, as "The Course of Justice" does the court beat. In "The Big Story," young journalists see how a news staff works together when a major story breaks unexpectedly.

More complex forms of reporting are discussed in "Interpretive Reporting." Using published examples, this chapter explains the interpretive dimension and the function of investigative reporting. It describes how the Washington press corps functions.

The final three chapters cover topics that are important to a student planning to enter professional journalism but that are often ignored in other books. "The Reporter as Photographer" describes the fundamentals of the picture-taking responsibility that many beginning reporters find themselves required to handle. "Reporting and Writing Broadcast News" explains the basic techniques of processing news for the ear and of television news preparation. This is helpful to print reporters who may switch into the electronic media. Finally, "What to Expect on the Job" is a down-to-earth description of working conditions, attitudes, and salaries that a beginning reporter in professional journalism can expect to encounter.

Three appendixes provide additional guidance to students. The first gives instructions for using electronic equipment, the second contains excerpts from the Associated Press *Stylebook,* and the third is a glossary of journalism terms.

An instructor's manual is available providing guidance for the study projects in the textbook, examination questions, and other helpful information.

The authors wish to thank their academic and "working press" colleagues who have provided advice and information that has been incorporated in the text. We offer thanks particularly to Dr. Kent Middleton and Dr. Worth McDougald of the University of Georgia, James Risser of the Des Moines *Register,* Lewis Haber and Marchmont Kovas of the South Bend *Tribune,* and Don Brown of the Santa Maria *Times* for their special assistance. Our gratitude is extended also to the Associated Press, United Press International, and numerous newspapers whose stories, or story excerpts, are cited in the book as examples for study.

Warren K. Agee
Phillip H. Ault
Edwin Emery

PART I
The Search for News

COMING UP NEXT . . .

In this introductory chapter, we walk through a newsroom and watch production of a newspaper in progress. Blocks of words flash onto video display terminals (VDTs) as reporters tap their stories into the mysterious electronic jaws of a computer. We tell how a newspaper is organized and what each editor does.

We define the basic role of the reporter in this complex organization and discuss the special capabilities successful newspeople need. As an example of what can be achieved, we tell how a husband-and-wife pair of young journalists who possessed those qualities won a Pulitzer Prize with their weekly newspaper.

We see, too, how the news that journalists write and edit has changed, with more emphasis on magazine-style presentation and less on the wham-bam reporting of murders, "love triangles," and similar shockers that once delighted the souls of street-sale circulation managers.

Chapter 1
The Newsroom: Disciplined Bustle

A WORLD OF DEADLINES

Walking into the newsroom of a large city newspaper shortly before deadline time for the main edition, a visitor senses an atmosphere of intense energy. The room is quiet enough. No shouts of "Copy!" and scurrying office boys, the way old late-show movies portray it. Just a pervasive air of concentration. News from the city, the nation, and abroad is being written, compressed, and fashioned before the onlooker's eyes into the newspaper that will be delivered to thousands of readers within an hour or so.

It is an intricate, intriguing realm, this newsroom: a place where contemporary history is recorded by skilled professionals under severe limitations of time and space, and often despite obstacles placed by those who seek to suppress or manipulate the news through self-interest.

Men and women reporters working from notes tap out stories on rows of video display terminals, whose electronic screens glimmer with lines of words created by the writers. When a reporter finishes a story, he or she presses a button and dispatches it into the newsroom computer, to become part of the astounding amount of information accumulated in that machine's electronic memory.

The hub of the action, the generating and controlling force in the reporters' portion of the big room, is the city desk. Around it sit the city editor and the assistants. As the hands of the wall clock move inexorably toward the deadline hour—the moment when the final story must be finished in order to meet the production schedule—these editors work with high intensity. They call up reporters' stories from the computer and edit them on video terminals. If dissatisfied with the way a story has been written, the city editor summons the reporter for a hasty deskside conference. The insistent buzz of telephones interrupts this editing work; yet it is vital to the process, for every call carries the possibility of a late-breaking news story. News is an unpredictable, sometimes irrational, commodity that does not occur at the convenience of editors and reporters.

At the far end of the newsroom, a cluster of men and women scrutinizes stories on the screens of their video terminals. From time to time, they punch buttons to insert words, change punctuation, or correct a misspelling. Then they write headlines on the stories. This is the copydesk; here its members polish the work of the reporters that is forwarded from the city desk and give it a final examination for accuracy before dispatching the stories by another push of a button into the high-speed phototypesetter. Nearby, the news editor decides where stories should be placed on the various pages.

Crucial as it is, the city desk is only one part of a complex organization that each day produces a newspaper designed to inform, entertain, and influence readers of all ages and backgrounds.

At the head of the news organization is the *editor,* the man or woman responsible for the entire nonadvertising content. In the usual daily newspaper structure, under the editor is the *managing editor,* who has day-to-day responsibility for all sections of the news department. Also answering directly to the editor is the *associate editor,* who directs enunciation of the newspaper's editorial policy through the opinion pages.

Reporting to the managing editor are the *city editor,* who controls the staff of local reporters and is responsible for gathering news in the city and immediate environs; the *state editor,* whose duty usually is coverage of the outer portions of the circulation area; the *national* (sometimes called *telegraph*) *editor,* who chooses and edits stories from the wire services; and the *news editor,* whose primary responsibility is supervision of the copyediting process, headline writing, and placement of stories on the news pages. Editors of the *sports, business, family life,* and *entertainment* sections also report to the managing editor in the standard newsroom alignment. Some newspapers have variations in the chain of command and titles, including the position of *executive editor* above the managing editor.

Elsewhere in the newspaper plant are other departments whose work is essential to the creation and sale of each day's edition. These are *advertising,* which obtains and prepares the display and classified advertising that forms more than half of a newspaper's total content; *production,* which assembles the pages and prints the papers; and *circulation,* which distributes and sells the copies. Behind the scenes are other departments including personnel, promotion, purchasing, and bookkeeping. These function much like their counterparts in other industries.

In ultimate command of all business, production, and circulation functions, and of news and editorial content as well on many newspapers, is the *publisher*. On some newspapers that top position carries the joint title of editor and publisher.

The newspaper these men and women produce day after day is more than a mass of information recorded in ink on paper. In some mysterious way it takes on a personality of its own. Those who create the newspaper feel the mystique; so do those who read it. No other institution does so much to tie a community together as its newspaper. Arrival of the daily edition on the doorstep is part of the rhythm of family life. "Did you see in the paper that . . . ?" is an everyday expression. Somehow the newspaper is held responsible by many for the news it reports, although it is only the messenger. When the Weather Bureau forecasts sunshine and rain falls instead, readers grumble, "The paper was wrong again!" Like a close relative, it is alternately cheered and damned. From its pages readers learn the global news as well the local news; choose what movies to attend; get information about marriages, births, and deaths among their friends; find out about the baseball standings; and draw up food-shopping lists.

The newspaper being created in this quiet, carpeted newsroom differs from the ones that earlier generations of Americans read. Emphasis then was on brisk hard-news stories with little interpretation. Our parents and grandparents, especially if they lived in large cities, were fed a heavy dose of sensationalism: Murder stories full of blunt details over which the writer sprinkled flowery prose; raids on "love nests"—how old-time metropolitan city editors relished that phrase; tragedies of every kind imaginable; short page-one news bulletins set in boldface type; editions that carried the black label EXTRA!

Before radio and television news developed, newspapers brought the public its first news of events. Because many newspaper copies were sold on street corners by vendors, editors often stressed flashy appearance and excitement. Most stories were written in punchy, frequently cliché-ridden prose, which gave facts in such an order that paragraphs could be chopped off at any point under deadline pressure. Except for some political stories, relatively minor effort was made to put news situations in perspective.

Today's newspapers are less frantic. Aware that the electronic media usually are the first to break big news, often with at-the-scene coverage, newspaper editors stress the background and significance of stories, giving them depth that brief radio and television reports cannot achieve. In many newspapers, writing is more relaxed than in the past. Stress is placed on magazinelike presentation of information that helps readers with their daily living problems. The rigid formulas that governed the old-time approach to writing news have been broken down. The pressures of deadlines remain, but the scope of subject matter to be reported has been much broadened.

For newcomers to journalism, this change means greater opportunity for originality, creativity, and interpretation. They must, however, base their work on the fundamentals of sound journalism and operate under high ethical standards. This book will discuss both of these elements in detail.

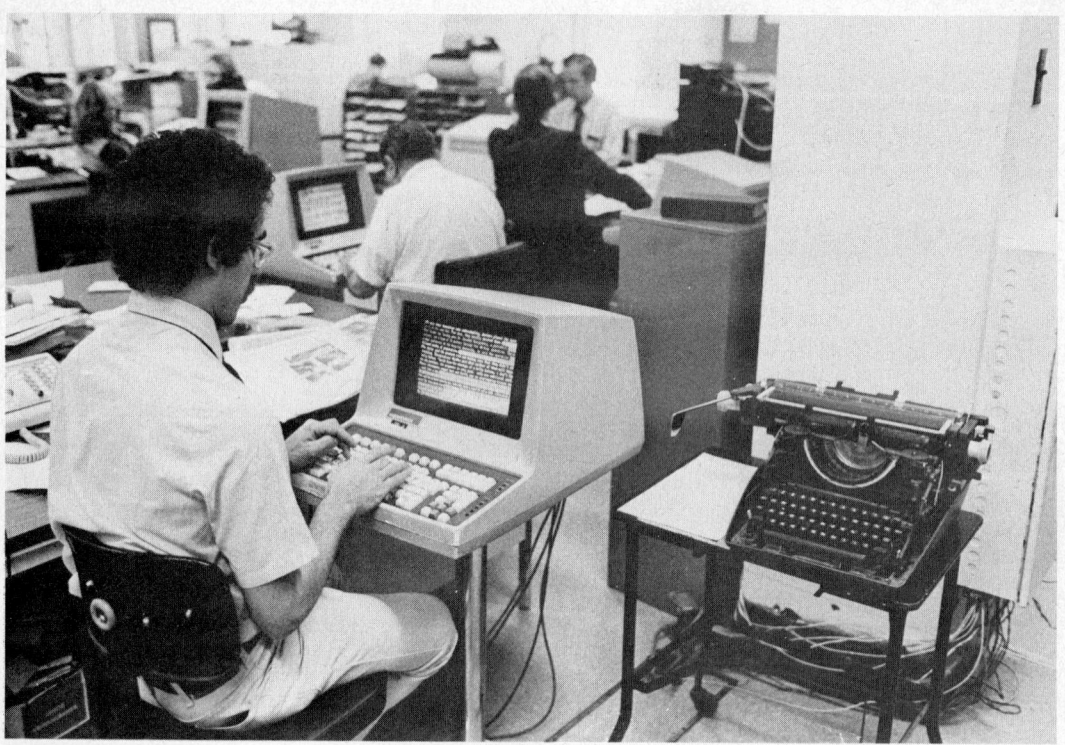

A reporter composes his story on a video display terminal while an outmoded manual typewriter, once a newsroom necessity, stands unused.

The newsrooms of weekly newspapers, on which many reporters begin their careers, are much smaller than those of the dailies, but they too have their moments of tenseness, especially on deadline day. Because weekly staffs are small, each member performs several duties, including reporting, copyediting, and page layout. Many weeklies are printed in central offset printing plants situated miles from their offices; their staffs prepare the news and the advertising material either in edited or camera-ready form to be delivered by messenger or staff member to the printing plant. Progressive weeklies frequently have video display terminals on which reporters write their copy, just like the dailies. Because weekly newspapers usually are published in smaller communities, they tend to have proportionately more drop-in visitors who wish to chat with editors and reporters than daily newspapers do. Thus, the members of weekly staffs have a more personal tie to their readers, many of whom they know socially as well.

Breaking into this world of newsgathering may seem formidable to the aspiring beginner, but it is a business with many aspects, and hundreds of young writers enter it every year. Although some may begin their careers in broadcasting, on small magazines, or in public relations, rather than on a newspaper, all persons working with news need a sound grounding in the principles of the reporter's craft.

THE ROLE OF THE REPORTER

At the center of the news business are the reporters. Without them, no need would exist for editors. Through their eyes readers see the day's events. Through their words the public learns the shape and meaning of what is happening. The reporter is a privileged observer whose task is to record lucidly and as objectively as possible. Being a human, not a machine, the reporter inevitably sees events subjectively based on personal experience and cultural background, no matter how strenuously he or she strives for a neutral posture. That is one reason for the editing process through which the reporter's stories pass—to strain out bias that the reporter may not recognize. Yet we would not want reporters to be machines. Their compassion for the suffering they see gives heart to the news; their anger at injustices and deceptions can drive them to extraordinary efforts to reveal the truth.

An exceptional example of this urge to find and print the truth occurred in the California community of Point Reyes Station, north of San Francisco. A youthful couple, David and Cathy Mitchell, published a small weekly paper there, the Point Reyes *Light*. They became puzzled about the behavior at Synanon, a wealthy drug and alcohol treatment center and alternative life-style society based nearby. They dug and dug for facts to prove their suspicion that Synanon had another, ugly face—that Synanon members had assaulted neighbors and ex-members, had engaged in child abuse, and had violated zoning and building laws while county officials blandly looked the other way. They sought to demonstrate in print that certain Synanon leaders had grown rich because the organization enjoyed tax-free privileges. Although the small weekly *Light* was in precarious financial position, the Mitchells had the courage to publish the information they uncovered, knowing that a retaliatory legal attack by Synanon's large staff of attorneys might bankrupt them. In the end, they triumphed. Synanon was shown in its true perspective, and the Mitchells achieved the rare prestige of receiving a Pulitzer Prize for Meritorious Public Service.

WHAT A GOOD REPORTER NEEDS

Reporting and writing news are frequently referred to as a single entity. In fact, they are quite separate skills. A person may be a reporter of enormous ingenuity and persistence, but, to use an old newsroom metaphor, "can't write his way out of a paper bag." Another person, blessed with a felicitous writing style, may lack those reportorial instincts. In the professional news world, the two functions usually are intermingled; relatively few persons are free to work solely in the reporting or the writing areas. A successful newsperson must become proficient in both skills, working hard to improve in the area in which he or she is weak. In this book, we introduce the beginner to newswriting and the techniques of reporting almost simultaneously, because that is the way a reporter on the job acquires the skills.

No mystery exists about what makes a successful reporter. Newswriting and reporting are not esoteric activities swathed in garments of abstract theory and high-flown rhetoric. They are practical arts, built around the practitioners' skill, perception, and understanding of the stories they are reporting.

To be a good reporter and writer of news, the individual needs these five kinds of knowledge and personal attributes:

1. A news sense—that is, an awareness of what makes news, of what readers need to know and would like to know, drawn from a wide spectrum of human knowledge.
2. An understanding of how to report: where to look for information and how to obtain it.
3. An inquisitive mind and willingness to search for details that make the difference between routine work and fine reporting.
4. The ability to write English in a simple, effective, and grammatical manner, and to spell correctly.
5. An understanding of newswriting techniques.

Some beginners have a natural aptitude for language, but are ill at ease about questioning sources for facts. Others possess an almost instinctive sense of what makes news, but find the mechanics of grammar menacing. A competent reporter needs all five of these tools. Study of good writing by others helps the beginner to overcome shortcomings, and experience brings confidence.

Let us look at those five qualifications a little more closely.

A NEWS SENSE

News is an ill-defined commodity. Nobody can say arbitrarily what all the characteristics of news are, because those characteristics shift as the interests and needs of readers change. Nevertheless, there are serviceable definitions that will guide beginners in their efforts to develop "news sense." Why does a newspaper carry certain stories on its front page, whereas others are placed far inside? Why does a news broadcast sometimes omit stories that draw high readership when published in a newspaper? We shall examine what news is, or what various experts believe it is, in Chapter 3.

AN ABILITY TO SEARCH FOR FACTS

Obtaining the information to write about is as important as developing an effective newswriting style. At times this is easy, because the facts are waiting on a platter to be picked up, as in the case of the fundamental facts about a traffic accident contained in a police report. But even these easy stories often require additional reporting effort and may be full of pitfalls as well. A careless reporter may misspell the name of a person involved, accidentally transpose an address, or omit a fact, any of which can show the circumstances of the accident in a false light. This leaves the reader confused and the newspaper possibly subject to a libel suit. Once the words of a news story are printed, no amount of prayer and pleading can call them back.

Accuracy! Accuracy! Accuracy!

Some editors post that admonition on their newsroom walls. The first time that beginning reporters see in print the errors in stories they have written, and are reprimanded by the city editor or an angry reader, that admonition is burned indelibly into their consciousness.

If easy stories contain such potential dangers, what about the difficult ones? Reporters must know the difference between legally privileged information that may be printed without fear of libel actions and statements for which the publication must take responsibility. They must learn how to verify controversial assertions, to use public records and standard reference works, to cultivate sources that will provide news tips, and to publish all sides of a dispute. A reporter never should be a special pleader in print, or be tricked into appearing like one. Common sense, a commitment to fairness, and a readiness to make that additional cross-checking telephone call will keep the writer out of most such difficulties. A reporter covering a story serves as the eyes and ears of the public. After the story is written, the reporter should reread it and ask, "Have I answered all the questions the readers might ask if they had been present?"

AN INQUISITIVE MIND

A good reporter approaches every news situation with the question "Why?" prominently in mind. Frequently the surface facts do not tell the real story. A sage old magazine editor once wrote that after decades of publishing investigative articles, he realized that a person often has two reasons for saying or doing something, a *good* reason and the *real* reason. Reporters should search for that real reason. Information for news stories usually comes from people, so newsgatherers must know how to get along with people and get them to talk. They should learn to be good listeners and to check the various versions of a situation that they hear against each other. They should be alert for nuances and contradictions. Examination of public records may help the reporter prove or disprove a story told by a news source. Stories are built by adding supporting detail, a little from one source and a little from another.

Such work can be tiresome and does not always pay rewards. When it does, however, the reporter feels the exultation of accomplishment for having contributed important knowledge to the public good that would have remained hidden otherwise.

AN ABILITY TO USE GOOD ENGLISH

A reporter whose stories are marred by grammatical errors and glaring blunders in spelling will not hold a professional job for long, or even get one. Editors know that when their pages are splattered with such mistakes, readers regard their publications as amateurish. Personnel directors often require applicants for news jobs to take spelling tests and automatically disqualify those who do poorly. Any reporter who commits careless errors, then says, "It doesn't matter, the copydesk will fix it," is headed for disaster.

The dictionary is the writer's best friend. Use it!

A well-written news publication presents information and ideas so clearly that readers can understand everything it contains. Sentences should be simple in construction and brief. The English language is a tool for communication, not a vehicle for showing off the writer's knowledge of obscure words and sophisticated slang that many readers may not recognize. As a mass communication medium, the newspaper must convey facts and ideas to persons with inadequate education as well as with high educational achievement. It should not be elitist or conversely pander to low tastes. Journalistic writing when well done is a model of concise, crystal-clear communication, often composed under the strain of time limits and space restrictions.

AN UNDERSTANDING OF NEWSWRITING STYLE

Writing an effective news story requires use of techniques that help the reader to grasp information in the least space possible. Because newspaper readers are frequently in a hurry, the newswriter should use an uncomplicated style that does not trap them in complex sentences and long, complicated paragraphs. Among the techniques we shall study are ways to write a lead—the opening paragraph, or sometimes two paragraphs—that tells the essence of the story swiftly. We shall examine methods of organizing news stories so that facts are presented in order of diminishing importance, to permit trimming the story if the allotted space is too short. Also, we shall illustrate use of direct quotations to brighten and strengthen the story; and shall explain ways to handle the fundamental questions that every news story should answer: *who, what, when, where, why,* and *how.*

The news story is different from an essay. First, the reporter's purpose is to describe an action or situation rather than to examine it in a critical sense; second, the reporter must write objectively, scrupulously avoiding any expression of personal opinion. Passing judgment on news developments that the reporter describes is left to the reader, to the editorial writers on the newspaper's opinion page, and to columnists whose work is clearly labeled as opinion.

Although today's reporters work with the aid of fascinating electronic technology, they carry on a tradition of recording human activities and natural disasters rooted deep in history. The journalistic rules and ethical standards that guide them have evolved through many generations of newsgatherers. It is important for beginners to understand the historical background before plunging into the technical aspects of becoming a reporter, so that the work they produce will meet these standards.

STUDY PROJECTS

1. Using an issue of a daily newspaper, determine what portion of the news and editorial content, or "news hole," including illustrations, is used for local news; for state, national, and foreign news (mostly from press associations); for family life, sports, entertainment, and opinion sections. Opinion includes the editorial page and any other signed columns of opinion in the edition.

2. Examine an issue of a weekly newspaper. Describe three important differences you found between it and the daily newspaper you analyzed.

3. Compare the presentation of a major news story from Washington or abroad by a daily newspaper, an evening network newscast, and *Time* or *Newsweek*. Among factors to be considered are length, interpretation, illustration, and background material.

READ MORE ABOUT IT . . .

Editor & Publisher is the weekly trade magazine of the newspaper industry.
Anthony Smith, *Goodbye Gutenberg, The Newspaper Revolution of the 1980s* (London: Oxford University Press, 1980).
Ben H. Bagdikian, *The Information Machines: Their Impact on Men and the Media* (New York: Harper & Row, 1971).

COMING UP NEXT . . .

Today's journalists did not invent their craft, although a few brash ones act as though they did. The ancient Athenians used reporting in their dramas. Roman scribes used it in their news posters. When regularly printed newspapers appeared in the early 1600s, the field for reporting in print broadened.

In order to give newcomers a comprehension of how today's journalism evolved, this chapter examines the historical role of the reporter. Famous names from the past, and what they contributed, are recalled—editors such as Joseph Pulitzer, Charles A. Dana, and Edward Wyllis Scripps, and reporters such as Richard Harding Davis, Margaret Fuller, and Ernie Pyle.

The styles of newswriting now in use have a history, too. Free-swinging first person journalism, excessively rigid objectivity, muckraking, and advocacy reporting—all had their heyday, then faded. Together, they contributed their bit to what is regarded as good journalism today. Understanding this background makes a better reporter.

Chapter 2
Historical Role of the Reporter

HOW REPORTING BEGAN

If the crucial contribution in the news process is that of the reporter, it would seem strange that there is no detailed, organized history of reporting and of the countless men and women of that craft. But there is not. There have been many published reminiscences of reporters, biographies, and collections of reporters' writings, and some descriptive and analytical studies of the news profession. A synthesis of the whole would be a truly massive undertaking! We should, however, gain an awareness of the historical procession of men and women who preceded us in the job of gathering information of interest to other people and presenting it to them in ways that made them understand it.

This historical procession includes, for example, the Athenian dramatists and the Roman news poster scribes; the medieval ballad singers, newshawkers, and town criers; the handwritten political newsletter "intelligencers," the Fugger business newsletter compilers, the Lloyds of London coffee house proprietors. Broadsheet printers, flourishing before the first regularly printed newspapers appeared in the early 1600s, ran off single sheets reporting a major world news event or, more likely, a murder, sex crime, hanging, or big fire. Some anonymous journalists called "penny-a-liners" did the writing in London.

The first newspapers were printed by men who had a sense of what interested people—news created newspapers, not the other way around. But few newspaper publishers were good enough writers to tell their stories in an interesting way, and fewer still had real reportorial instincts. Those who were good writers and editors found inadequate transportation and communication facilities tremendous handicaps. News came late and in dribbles. They made little effort to go out and find the news; they printed what came to them from letters, travelers, and other newspapers. There were no local news reporters by job designation until the nineteenth century—just 150 years ago.

THE FIRST REPORTERS

In America, the colonial weeklies ran brief accounts of fires, accidents, deaths, piracy, court trials, and governmental affairs, but their major fare was reprints taken from London papers. The colonial era did produce a few printer–editors with reportorial instincts, notably James and Benjamin Franklin. James introduced the element of entertainment to Boston journalism by imitating the "essay" papers of London, but he also printed news in his *New-England Courant* which stirred up political and religious controversy. Ben made his *Pennsylvania Gazette* a model of good printing, good editing, and better writing than that of his contemporaries.

Authorities on world news reporting such as Robert W. Desmond identify James Perry of the London *Morning Chronicle* as the first foreign correspondent. Perry, living in Paris in 1789, reported the opening year of the French Revolution. The *Times* of London sent Henry Crabb Robinson to the continent in 1807 to report about the political and economic impacts of the Napoleonic wars. However, there were no war correspondents with Nelson at Trafalgar, with Napoleon at Moscow, or at the climactic battle of Waterloo. London panicked for four days before news of Napoleon's final defeat came across the Channel.

The first identified local news reporter in England or America was John Wight of the London *Morning Herald,* who in 1823 began writing human-interest style reports from the Bow Street police court—ordinary stories about ordinary people, not scandalous crimes. The circulation of the *Herald* jumped from 1200 copies to 8000 by 1829, placing it second only to the *Times.* Wight, the first reporter to "make good" financially, was given a piece of the ownership to keep him on the staff.

In the United States, James Gordon Bennett is generally recognized as the first successful reporter. A transplanted Scotsman who was also a teacher, editor, and publisher, Bennett was at heart a writer and a reporter. He covered murder trials and the Congressional debates with equal skill. He was the first regularly established Washington correspondent before he founded the New York *Herald* in 1835. However, Bennett was not truly a local news reporter, employed as such. That honor in the United States apparently belongs to George Wisner, who was assigned the police court beat in 1833 by the New York *Sun's* founder, Benjamin

Day (a reader of Wight's stories from London). Wisner emulated Wight well enough also to win a share of ownership in his paper (which he sold in 1835 for $5000, a very substantial sum).

Note that the police and political beats remain now, as then, basic ones for reporters.

GROWTH OF REPORTING STAFFS

The dam was now breaking, and the art of reporting was being practiced steadily after the 1830s. Bennett's *Herald* led the way, excelling in reporting political news, court trials, financial affairs and markets, activities of society, and sporting events. Bennett also prized the important news coming from Washington and Europe, and led his contemporaries in using every available means of communication to speed it to the *Herald* office: successively, the pony express, railroad, telegraph, steamship, and underseas cable. The most romantic means was the carrier pigeon.

By the 1850s chief reporters were emerging on the big dailies, forerunners of the city editors. In 1854 Horace Greeley's New York *Tribune* boasted 14 reporters and 10 editors. Specialization was beginning and by the 1870s there were managing editors, city editors, telegraph news editors, business editors, drama critics, literary editors, and editorial writers. Henry Chadwick of the New York *Herald* became the first of a long line of baseball writers in 1862, in the midst of a civil war.

Greeley led in recognizing the abilities of women journalists, employing as Washington correspondents Margaret Fuller, who first attracted attention as editor of *The Dial,* and Jane Grey Swisshelm, first woman to occupy a seat in the Senate press gallery. Politics was also the forte of Henry J. Raymond, founder of the New York *Times* in 1851. Henry W. Grady of the Atlanta *Constitution* joined Greeley in demonstrating the use of the interview technique in reporting, thus adding zest to political coverage. Three great reporters of the period of reform called "muckraking" were Jacob Riis, Ida M. Tarbell, and Lincoln Steffens.

Wars have always given prominence to reporters, beginning with George Wilkins Kendall of the New Orleans *Picayune* in the United States-Mexican War. The American Civil War produced such great newsmen as Whitelaw Reid and Henry Villard of the North and Felix Gregory de Fontaine and Peter W. Alexander of the South. Some war reporters went on to cover the Indian wars or reported abroad, like Henry M. Stanley of the *Herald,* who became immortal by finding the missing Dr. Livingstone in Africa.

Charles A. Dana, editor of the New York *Sun* for three decades beginning in 1868, made his paper a training ground for reporters. He said the *Sun* should present "a daily photograph of the whole world's doings in the most luminous and lively manner." Reporters were prized for their writing skills, whether they reported a neighborhood quarrel, a new style in whiskers, or the skulduggery of the railroad magnates. Dana's *Sun* was less concerned, however, with the social and economic problems that arose in the urbanized and industrialized America of the 1880s and 1890s.

Joseph Pulitzer, whose New York *World* was the symbol of the liberal, aggressive "New Journalism" that spoke out on economic and social issues as the "people's champions," earned his newsman's spurs as a local reporter in St. Louis before founding the *Post-Dispatch* there in 1878. Two rivals of Pulitzer as people's champions were Edward Wyllis Scripps and William Randolph Hearst. Scripps espoused word economies in writing and editing the news, hard-hitting news reporting, and a low level of entertainment material in his newspaper group. Hearst, eager for human interest stories and emotion-producing writing, built up large staffs of men and women reporters on his big city dailies at the turn of the century.

Newspapers at the metropolitan level had expanded dramatically by 1900. The telephone and typewriter had changed reportorial practices. Rewrite men appeared to handle telephone calls from the beat reporters; desk men took over the chores of editing copy and writing headlines; the talented young men and women reporters were then free to search for news and features. The sports staff emerged, staking out its pages, as did the women's news staff dealing with fashions and social news. Men and women vied for positions on newspaper staffs, and the "romance of reporting" never seemed more attractive than it did to these eager, if largely untrained, newsmen and newswomen.

Those who gathered in the small hours of the morning from the various city staffs—in Doctor Perry's drugstore in New York or in the Whitechapel Club and Press Club in Chicago—admired the literary style and news skill of the leading reporters. They envied the "Van Bibber" stories of Richard Harding Davis and drank to the emotional "The City That Was" story written by Will Irwin in the wake of the San Francisco earthquake and fire.

Some of these reporters and editors were intelligent, perceptive journalists who were sensitive to the requirements of their craft. Many others, however, were less talented, more prone to seize upon the devices of sensationalism, or to substitute slovenly work for the disciplined journalism they should have produced. Although more were college educated, none had as yet had the opportunity to acquire professional training in journalism education. The professional standards that were being set were those of the best qualified practitioners of newspaper work. Those beginners fortunate to work with the best qualified were to become future leaders.

The autobiographies and biographies of reporters named in this section are instructive for young reporters and provide stimulating role models for students. A few names from the ranks of twentieth-century reporters might be added: Dorothy Thompson of the New York *Post* and Harrison Salisbury of the New York *Times* among foreign correspondents; columnist Ernie Pyle and Marguerite Higgins of the New York *Herald Tribune* among war correspondents; columnist

Front page of the New York *Times* shows a famous reporting and editing achievement.

Walter Lippmann, Helen Thomas of United Press International, and James B. Reston of the New York *Times* among Washington correspondents; Lowell Thomas and H. V. Kaltenborn, first radio newsmen; and television's Edward R. Murrow.

TRENDS IN REPORTORIAL STANDARDS

The colonial period produced two types of newspapers. One, called the mercantile press, was concerned primarily with relaying foreign news and business-related news to the merchants, traders, shippers, and professional people of the seaports. The other was the political press, the newspapers representing the interests of political parties or personalities within the parties. These commonly were subsidized by the political factions that benefited. By their nature, none of these papers experienced any semblance of mass readership appeal. The "penny press" era beginning in the 1830s produced dailies with wider appeal and substantial circulations cutting through varied levels of economic and political interests. They were better written and paid much more attention to local news and reader interests. Human interest stories vied with the better-presented important news. Obvious biases toward narrow economic and political interests were avoided.

All three types of newspapers continued to appear throughout the nineteenth century. However, rapid changes in American society that accompanied industrialization and the rise of great cities brought about another type of journalism by the 1880s. This was the "New Journalism" of Joseph Pulitzer and his contemporaries. The new dailies challenged conservative traditions, crusaded for improvements in wages and hours of workers, inveighed against political and economic corruption. To do this they sometimes used the news columns to advance causes or ideas, much as their business-oriented and political-organ rivals had done.

RISE OF OBJECTIVITY

There were, however, counterforces working to produce a standard of objective news reporting. One was the development of cooperative newsgathering or press associations similar to the present-day Associated Press and United Press International. These began in the 1840s to handle news from Europe arriving at the various seaports and to send one condensed version by telegraph to various subscribers in the interior. The telegraph also made possible the establishment of a common correspondent's office in Washington to handle the staple of news. By the close of the century the Associated Press was serving newspapers of all sizes and political outlooks across the country. It developed a factual, condensed style of presenting news that eschewed partisanship and viewpoints. Reporters used only facts stemming from eyewitness reporting of events or those attributed to sources. This objective style fitted the needs of papers appealing to a wide cross section of readers (also, it was appealing because every word cost money to send on the telegraph wires).

Old-style objectivity was designed to reduce reporter bias. Sources were not to be challenged by interjection of additional information about the facts or opinions offered. Reporters were to be neutral, quote both sides in a dispute, and refrain from presenting their opinions.

INTERPRETIVE REPORTING

Such "deadpan" objectivity was challenged by the growing belief that the reader needed to have a given event placed in its proper context if truth really was to be served. This concept of "fairness" argued that the reporter, rather than the source, was best qualified to shape the story objectively and accurately.

The changing environment of the 1930s and 1940s helped settle the issue in favor of interpretive reporting. The impact of the political-social-economic revolution of the New Deal years, the rise of modern scientific technology, and increasing interdependence in world power politics all dictated a new approach to the handling of news. "Why?" became important along with the traditional "who did or said what, when" of the objective era. Newspapers used interpretive reporting, both in breaking news stories and in background pieces. The news magazines, led by *Time,* and the radio commentators joined the movement. Reporter-specialists were further developed in politics, economics, foreign affairs, agriculture, and social work. Newsroom assumptions that difficult subjects like science and labor relations could not be made interesting were broken down. By the 1960s specialists in urban and environmental reporting were added to the list. (See Chapter 25 for a more detailed discussion of interpretive reporting and Washington correspondence.)

INVESTIGATIVE REPORTING

The traditions of crusading and muckraking of the turn of the century were continued, although they were at low level during and between the two great wars. By the 1960s the phrase "investigative reporting" came into widespread use and by the 1970s even the conservative Associated Press had its special investigative teams of reporters in action. Two leading investigative journalists were Carey McWilliams, longtime editor of the *Nation,* and I. F. Stone, publisher of *I. F. Stone's Weekly* from 1953 to 1971. Both journals ran depth analyses of McCarthyism, warned about the excesses of the FBI and CIA when both were sacrosanct institutions, and reported in depth on the tragedy of Vietnam. Seymour Hersh uncovered the story of the My Lai massacre in Vietnam, focusing attention on the investigative movement. But its great popularizers were Bob Woodward and Carl Bernstein of the Washington *Post,* whose investigative zeal triggered the resignation of President Richard Nixon. Television contributed such documentary investigative specials as "Hunger in America" and "The Selling of the Pentagon," as well as the top-ranked CBS News show "60 Minutes," starring Mike Wallace, Morley Safer, Dan Rather, and Harry Reasoner—all seasoned reporters. (Dan Rather has now been replaced by Ed Bradley.)

ALTERNATIVE JOURNALISM

The 1960s also brought other movements among the men and women of journalism. Rebellion against the status quo spawned the underground press movement, with its free-swinging papers that helped breathe new life into the established press. Alternative press is another way of describing the trend—alternative publications for young people, for minorities, for women. These gave new opportunities for reporting, both in terms of jobs and creative outlets. An extreme movement among the most zealous of the rebellious during the 1960s was called "advocacy reporting." Its proponents saw themselves as 100 percent advocates of a social goal (perhaps environmental reform) who would be employed by standard newspapers and be given freedom to write their stories as advocates in an all-black-or-white manner. Few city editors found the argument convincing and the movement waned. Stemming from all this turmoil was a slogan called "reporter power," which on some staffs won more representation for reporters in decision-making processes, better status, and substantially improved pay (a goal since 1933 of the Newspaper Guild). Women, who had largely been shunted to the women's news section by the 1920s after their good start in the New Journalism era, came back into prominence on most staffs as reporters, specialists, photographers, and editors. They became especially prominent in broadcast news.

STUDY PROJECTS

1. Read a biography or autobiography of a well-known reporter and submit a 500-word discussion of the subject's career.

2. Submit a 500-word commentary on the influence of either Joseph Pulitzer or William Randolph Hearst on American news reporting. Information about both men is available in libraries.

3. Read at least ten issues of a newspaper published before 1930 and in 500 words compare its reporting of sports, crime, and politics with that of a present-day newspaper. Many libraries have either microfilm or bound files of old newspapers.

READ MORE ABOUT IT . . .

Edwin and Michael Emery, *The Press and America: An Interpretive History of the Mass Media* (Englewood Cliffs, N.J.: Prentice-Hall, 1978) is a detailed study of American press history.

Warren K. Agee, Phillip H. Ault, and Edwin Emery, *Introduction to Mass*

Communications, 7th ed. (New York: Harper & Row, 1982) contains a more condensed account of the growth of the print media.

Calder M. Pickett, *Voices of the Past* (Columbus, Ohio: Grid Publishing, 1977). A storehouse of first-hand reporting.

Robert W. Desmond, *The Information Process: World News Reporting to the Twentieth Century* (Iowa City: University of Iowa Press, 1978)

John W. C. Johnstone, Edward J. Slawski, and William W. Bowman, *The News People* (Urbana: University of Illinois Press, 1976). A sociological study.

COMING UP NEXT . . .

Precisely what is this ephemeral thing called news? Seeking to define it, we are almost as frustrated as the blind men in the fable who try to describe an elephant. In this chapter, we examine several definitions that have been offered and ponder that elusive attribute called "news sense."

By general agreement, news falls into two broad categories—"hard" news and "soft" news. Citing examples, the chapter explains that hard news is event-centered. Its primary purpose is to tell what happened. Soft news is process-centered, with emphasis on explaining why an event occurred, or it may be fluffy change-of-pace entertainment about human foibles and quirky twists in the process of living.

We examine five principal factors that determine whether a set of facts constitutes a news story—proximity, prominence, consequence, timeliness, and human interest.

Chapter 3
What Is News?

THE SEARCH FOR A DEFINITION OF NEWS

Editors and educators have been trying in vain for more than a century to create an absolute definition of news by which a reporter may measure a set of facts. Finding such a guideline has proven about as difficult as locating the elusive Lost Dutchman gold mine in the desert mountains. Both quests may always be fruitless —for the mine, because it probably never existed, and for a foolproof definition, because news is an abstract concept whose shape changes as the interests of humans change.

News essentially is the report of an event, development, or opinion that reporters and editors, acting as agents for the public, believe will interest some or a great many of those who receive it. News, however, is never merely the event, development, or opinion itself. A forest fire is not news until someone reports it. Neither is a public official's expression of opinion that crime is increasing in a city nor the exodus of many persons from one community to another in search of jobs— until they are reported.

One difficulty in attempting to define news is that not all readers are interested in the same things, and reporters and editors, who serve as gatekeepers in deciding which stories are newsworthy enough to be published, vary astonishingly in their selections. Spread out the front pages of a half dozen newspapers in front of you and see how unlike in content they are. Perhaps two or three major national and international stories will appear in all of them; the rest of the front-page space is filled with different sets of stories that each editor believes to be significant or entertaining for his or her readers.

In our search for a definition, we must remember that news is relative. It is influenced in each newspaper by the size of the community; whether it is published in a daily or a weekly; the social makeup and economic base of the community; the emphasis or interpretation placed upon a story by the source of the information; and other factors. The report of a rural social event may be news in a small weekly, but such an account would never appear in the Tyler (Texas) *Telegram* and much less in the Chicago *Tribune.*

A hundred years ago John B. Bogart, city editor of the New York *Sun,* told a young reporter: "When a dog bites a man, that is not news; but when a man bites a dog, *that* is news" (when reported, of course). That is the most widely quoted definition of news ever given.

Charles A. Dana, the famous editor of the *Sun,* wrote that news is derived from "everything that occurs, everything which is of sufficient importance to arrest and absorb the attention of the public or of any considerable part of it." His newspaper was noted for its human interest stories.

Joseph Pulitzer, publisher of the New York *World* at the turn of the century, instructed his staff to look for stories that are "original, distinctive, dramatic, romantic, thrilling, unique, curious, quaint, humorous, odd, and apt-to-be-talked-about." Stories of this nature entertained the *World's* readers, many of whom were newly arrived immigrants with scant interest in public affairs. Today's editors must provide more solid fare.

Walter Williams, who founded the world's first school of journalism at the University of Missouri in 1908, wrote:

> . . . No matter how capable the reporter becomes in procuring information and in writing, if he does not learn to classify information; if he does not learn how to sift out and search for those things which are of value from the viewpoint of news, then he will lack what most editors say is a reporter's chief qualification.
>
> News, in its broadest sense, is that which is of interest to the readers—the public . . .

Stanley Walker, onetime great city editor of the New York *Herald Tribune,* said that news "is more unpredictable than the winds. Sometimes it is the repetition with new characters of tales as old as the pyramids, and again it may be almost outside the common experience."

In the opinion of Turner Catledge, former managing editor of the New York *Times,* news is "anything you can find out today that you didn't know before."

Because experience is the best teacher, perhaps the most apt definition, if a bit flippant, is that from an unidentified source: "News is anything a good city editor says it is."

Writes sociologist Tamotsu Shibutani:

> News is *information people urgently need* in getting their bearings in a rapidly changing world. Where the situation is ambiguous, or there are alternatives, or a

Forced to resign from office in the Watergate scandal, President Richard Nixon says farewell to the White House staff while Mrs. Nixon looks on in tears.

decision has to be made, any new information that might affect the outcome is news. News is information that is important to someone.

News is *perishable*. Once an event or situation is understood and the tension it has aroused eases, the accepted information becomes history. It is still interesting, but it no longer is pressing, no longer news.

Experience helps a reporter develop a news sense. As you practice the art of reporting and newswriting, study the content of newspapers. When you see a story that is somewhat out of the ordinary, ask yourself, "Why did they publish that?" News judgment is not absolute, as we have seen, but certain patterns will emerge as you observe the decisions editors have made. Some individuals may be born with an acute news instinct, but those who are not can still develop news judgment by a diligent study of how others do it.

Roy Peter Clark was a professor at Auburn University who became a writing coach for newspapers and joined the Modern Media Institute. At a recent convention of the American Society of Newspaper Editors, Clark described in a tongue-in-cheek manner what he learned about news judgment when he took a leave of absence from teaching writing and served a period as a general assignment reporter on the St. Petersburg (Florida) *Times*.

> I am sitting at my desk in the newsroom, the VDT thumping "pocketta, pocketta, pocketta"—I stole those "pockettas" from Walter Mitty—I dream of great investigative stories, of exposes, of Pulitzers. My city editor approaches.
>
> "Okay, Killer. We just heard over the police radio that a car has fallen on a man. Get out there, and don't come back without a story."
>
> I speed out to the accident, my car engine roaring, "pocketta, pocketta, pocketta." I am there for an hour taking notes, talking to witnesses, family members, paramedics. I return to the office a bit disappointed.
>
> "What did you get, Killer?"
>
> "Well, Mike, a car did fall on a man, but he's okay. It's not much of a story."
>
> "What do you mean, a car fell on a man?"
>
> "Well, the jack slipped and the frame pinned his head to the driveway."
>
> "A car fell on a man's head? How did they get the damn thing off him?"
>
> "Oh, some teenage boy was walking along the street and he heard this guy scream. He jumped over the fence and past a guard dog and lifted the car off the guy."
>
> I looked across the room at my city editor. I swear I could see his pupils dilating. I learned a lot that day. I learned I had no news judgment.

HARD AND SOFT NEWS

In discussions that go on in newsrooms, classrooms, and the offices of readership survey takers, news often is divided into two broad categories—*hard* and *soft*. Stories that fall into the hard-news category report specific, tangible events such as a fire, the death of a prominent person, and the passage of a bill by Congress. Such stories are event-centered. The following is an example of a straight hard-news story:

UNITED PRESS INTERNATIONAL

Tells what, when, where, why	Flames feeding on thickets of dry brush have blackened nearly 6,000 acres in California and Idaho, destroyed at least five homes and scorched many others in a holiday weekend of blazes, many caused by fireworks.	Damage was estimated in excess of $1 million.
Explains current status	Despite sweltering three-digit mercury readings, sun-parched brush and winds gusting to 50 mph, firefighters managed to control or contain most of the fires by nightfall yesterday. No deaths were reported.	Steady winds also whipped up a grass and sagebrush fire Saturday night near Boise, Idaho, but federal Bureau of Land Management firefighters managed to contain the blaze yesterday afternoon at 1,400 acres. *Begins summary of various fire scenes*
	In the most disastrous blaze, flames raced through 650 acres of brush and destroyed four homes in Vacaville, midway between San Francisco and Sacramento.	Six water tankers, one helicopter and three planes carrying fire retardant chemicals deluged the flames throughout yesterday in support of the 72 firefighters battling the flames and near-100-degree temperatures on the ground.
Describes role of winds	The fire, touched off by fireworks Saturday night, was fanned out of control by winds gusting to 50 mph. More than 150 firefighters controlled the blaze last night.	In Los Angeles County, a five-acre brush fire of undetermined origin erupted in the Silverlake area and quickly destroyed one home and scorched two others before firemen could extinguish the blaze in about 30 minutes . . .

For many decades, hard-news stories formed the bulk of newspaper content. Simple objectivity in reporting such occurrences was the goal. Editors strained for large headlines over sensational hard-news stories such as shootings; from the number of such fatal events available to them, metropolitan editors selected those with "class." In Los Angeles, for example, editors knew that a murder story containing the word *Pasadena* in the headline would sell more papers than a murder that happened in Compton, because Pasadena was regarded by readers as a suburb populated by the wealthy and influential.

Although every hard-news story in a newspaper edition might be accurate and interesting to at least some readers, taken as a whole these stories did not give a sufficiently rounded view of what was happening in a community, the country, and the world. Too many gaps were left, because much of the timely, significant information that readers needed and wanted did not conform to the traditional strictures of hard-news treatment. The sum of the parts in a newspaper did not add up to a whole picture of life.

EXPLANATIONS AND INTERPRETATIONS

This shortcoming brought into being a form of softer news stories intended to provide explanations and interpretations of what was happening in the world to fill the gaps left by hard-news stories. Such trend and background stories are process-centered rather than event-centered. Today's newspapers carry many such stories. Increased space was also given to stories pertaining to developments that affect the personal lives of readers, thus providing a service element in the newspaper's content.

An example of the process-centered news story is this front page article in the Atlanta *Constitution* concerning efforts to protect workers from diseases caused by asbestos:

By CAROLE ASHKINAZE

States the problem

A proposal to protect millions of American workers from asbestos-related diseases has been tossed like a hot potato from one federal agency to another for more than five years, and scientists fear it will now be buried by "cost-conscious" regulators who owe their jobs to President Reagan.

Defines current status

Dr. David Groth, chief of pathology for the National Institute for Occupational Safety and Health, said that after five years of trying unsuccessfully to persuade regulators to act, he has little hope that federal standards will be stiffened along the lines recommended by his agency.

Cites asserted cause of problem

"Industry pressures" have kept asbestos exposure standards at unsafe levels, he charged, despite repeated warnings by his agency that the risk to workers "is grave enough to warrant immediate action."

And reform now appears doomed by a new federal "philosophy, reverting back to the Depression philosophy of the '30s, that it's more important to have a job than not to get sick at your work," he said.

Quotation supports paragraph 2

"I'm afraid we went and elected some people last fall who are not likely to do anything about this," said Dr. Anthony Robbins, who was ousted by the new administration in March from his supposedly "non-political" job as NIOSH director. To an admittedly "embittered" Robbins, who says he "was given one hour to empty my desk and clear out" after serving only two years of a six-year term, it was a signal that government's "commitment to protecting workers was disappearing." . . .

Supports last portion of the lead

The story continued for several hundred words, listing further signs in support of the contention in the lead and balancing these with statements from a Reagan administration spokesman. Asbestos is the single largest cause of occupational disease, the story stated. The difference in approach between the fire story, which relates physical events, and the asbestos story, which discusses the difficulties of getting new safety controls adopted, is apparent. Yet both clearly are news.

Stories about personal welfare and health are an important part of the service function that contemporary newspapers stress. A conference on dental radiology probably would not have been covered by many newspapers 25 years ago, but a recent meeting produced this one of concern to all readers:

'Dental X-rays too Frequent'

By WARREN E. LEARY
Associated Press Science Writer

Reports fundamental news facts

WASHINGTON—X-rays of teeth are generally safe and useful but should not be taken routinely on every visit to the dentist, dental experts say.

Tells who reached the decision

The panel, drawn together at a three-day, government-sponsored conference on dental radiology, concluded Wednesday that X-rays should be taken only when there is an indication that exams are needed.

Background

The new recommendation springs from increasing public concern about the risk of radiation and the cost of health care, says Dr. Robert A. Goepp of the University of Chicago, who chaired the meeting.

But it runs counter to the practice of many dentists who have been taught to give X-rays routinely during the recommended yearly tooth examination.

"We have now refined the procedure," Goepp said. "The application of X-ray exams randomly probably is not a good thing. If there is no problem, X-rays are not recommended.". . .

Quotation expands the lead

Soft news of a fluffier nature has long existed in American newspapers to some extent, often in the form of brief offbeat, change-of-pace items of no particular significance that provide relief for readers from the burden of important but sometimes dull governmental stories. Called "brighteners," these entertaining bits serve the same function as those highly read, concise items in *Reader's Digest*. Feature stories are soft news, too.

Here is an example of the brief form of soft news with little significance to readers, but it tends to stick in the reader's mind, because in this case it is a switch from the old saying about carrying coals to Newcastle:

Stoneleigh, England (AP)—Prime Minister Thatcher, praising the efficiency of British farmers, said yesterday that Britain is now exporting brussels sprouts to Brussels.

She opened the annual royal agriculture show with word that Britain also is selling spaghetti to Italy, bulbs to Holland and sausages to Germany.

In an effort to attract new readers, especially a younger audience, newspapers in the 1960s and 1970s greatly increased their content of soft news and diminished the space devoted to hard news. Emphasis was given to stories about living styles, personal problems, trends in recreation, rock music, and personalities in the news. Readership surveys indicated that some readers desired even more of this non-event news than they were receiving.

Coverage of personalities became excessive in some instances, partly because newspapers attempted to keep pace with the exploitation of personalities on television. The cult of the "celebrity" and the "superstar" grew in print, at the expense of traditional straight news.

Eventually, editors sensed that they may have gone too far in their emphasis on soft news. They began to ask themselves questions such as: Who decides that a person is a celebrity—in addition to the person's publicity agent, that is? Precisely who promotes a "star" into a "superstar"? Was it really news when Farrah Fawcett-Majors, a minor actress who suddenly became a national figure after appearing in the TV show "Charley's Angels" and after posing for a sexy poster, lost a button from the front of her blouse?

A trend back to greater space for hard news and for the softer but still partially event-oriented interpretive stories of a significant nature began developing at the start of the 1980s. Today, newspaper editors, with some notable exceptions, seek a balance between straight news and softer stories of a background, personal service, and entertaining nature, with decreased emphasis on the so-called celebrity circuit. Personality stories will always have a place, however, because most people have an instinctive urge to know more about the lives of others. Many persons find satisfaction in relating vicariously to the supposedly glamorous lives of those in the public eye.

THE ELEMENTS OF NEWS

The newsworthiness of stories—how many persons read them and with what degree of interest—varies according to time, place, circumstance, and other factors. Research, however, has confirmed what editors have long known—that the principal qualities that determine the newsworthiness of a story are *proximity, prominence, consequence, timeliness,* and a variety of emotional appeals that may be lumped under the heading of *human interest.*

PROXIMITY

Most of the time the news of an occurrence in one's own neighborhood or city holds greater interest than an account of a similar happening farther away. Hence, editors will "play up" a local fire, but disregard a similar blaze in another town. A tornado killing two persons in or near the city of publication will be page-one news, whereas a typhoon in the South Seas killing 1000 persons likely will be carried on an inside page.

PROMINENCE

An automobile accident at Washington and College Streets in which two persons are slightly injured may be reported in only a paragraph or two. But if the occupants of one car are University of Georgia head football coach Vince Dooley and members of his family (as actually occurred), the story will be displayed prominently in the local newspapers and even run in other newspapers throughout the state. The maxim is: The more prominent the person or persons involved, the greater the news story.

CONSEQUENCE

One of the reasons people read newspapers is to conduct their lives in a more satisfactory way. Hence, the progress of a bill in Congress that promises tax relief is followed closely by many persons. Reports during 1982 that the Social Security system might soon be bankrupt caused extreme concern among older Americans whose monthly Social Security checks were their major source—in many cases, only source—of income. Any stories relating circumstances that possibly may affect our lives are read closely.

TIMELINESS

The more quickly an account of an event or development is communicated to readers, the stronger is its news value. That is one of the reasons that the press associations and individual media compete to be the first to tell the news. With the wire services there is a *Deadline Every Minute* (the title of a book about United Press by Joe Alex Morris). Once a story has been "broken," its news value rapidly diminishes unless important additional details are provided. Timeliness pertains only to the reporting of a happening, not to the time when the event occurred: An Egyptian pharaoh's tomb may have been stripped of its treasures centuries ago, but the theft becomes news only when an archaeologist discovers the fact.

HUMAN INTEREST

In a broad sense all news accounts are human interest stories or they would not be published. Stories containing one or more of the elements just described could be classified in such a broad category. The term *human interest,* however, generally is applied to stories that may or may not have a definite news peg, but all of which evoke an emotional response among readers and listeners.

Research has shown that the most widely read human interest stories concern animals, children, or the elderly. Other story elements also elicit a strong response: sex, humor, violence, conflict, pathos, drama, surprise, novelty, suspense, love, hate, curiosity, sympathy, anger, grief, nostalgia, irony—the list is almost endless.

A straight news story in which one or more of these elements is emphasized will receive much higher readership than otherwise. Most frequently, however, the presence of one or more of these human interest qualities will result in the publication of stories that contain virtually no news in the usual sense. These "brighteners" fulfill a dual purpose: They add zest and warmth to a page filled with hard-news accounts and, because of their usual brevity, they help make the page visually more attractive.

Story tellers in antiquity wove human interest elements into their oral accounts. Stories in fifteenth-century corantoes (news sheets) about beheadings, the birth of misshapen children or animals, and other such happenings were widely read,

Foreign correspondents reported a bizarre story from Jonestown, Guyana, when more than 700 followers of American cult leader Rev. Jim Jones committed suicide or were killed on his orders after a congressman visiting their community was assassinated.

as are stories about births of Siamese twins today. Because of the appealing style in which they were written and the human qualities present, insignificant stories about ordinary people attracted high readership in the newspapers of eighteenth-century England. Similar accounts were the grist of the popular "penny press" of midnineteenth century America. The previously discussed story about Coach Dooley's automobile accident attracted even greater attention because his car landed squarely on a large University of Georgia bulldog insignia freshly painted on the street—and the other automobile was painted in the red and black colors worn by the university's athletic teams. Such details add piquancy to a story.

Timeliness is a characteristic of all news stories. When an account also contains one or more of the other news determinants, its news value increases substantially. The ideal news story contains all these elements.

STUDY PROJECTS

1. Bring to class for discussion five hard-news stories and also five soft-news stories that are either process-centered or entertaining change-of-pace stories.

2. Submit five service-oriented stories from newspapers. Underline key sentences and paragraphs in them that deliver helpful information to readers.

3. List the stories and photographs on the front page of a daily newspaper. Indicate whether each item is of local, home state, national, or foreign origin. Select a story or picture on an inside page that you believe should have been on the front page, then tell which story or picture it should replace, and why.

READ MORE ABOUT IT . . .

Commission on Freedom of the Press, *A Free and Responsible Press* (Chicago: University of Chicago Press, 1947) is a landmark study.
Leo Bogart, *The Press and Public: Who Reads What, When, Where and Why in American Newspapers* (Hillsdale, N.J.: L. Erlbaum Associates, 1981).
Gaye Tuchman, *Making News* (New York: Free Press, 1978).

COMING UP NEXT...

The five Ws—who, what, when, where, and why—are the basic stuff of which news stories are made. The answer to "how" should be also included whenever possible. The way in which these elements are put together and supported with interesting details determines the effectiveness of a story.

In this chapter we examine first the traditional inverted pyramid style of writing a news story. This tells the essential facts in a summary lead and the remainder of the information in a descending order of importance. We see how leads can be formulated with emphasis on the different Ws. Examples illustrate the several ways in which the same lead can be written.

We then study other, less rigid ways to write a story that often can make it more attractive to the reader than the inverted pyramid approach. These include the chronological and suspended interest styles.

Chapter 4
The Basic News Story

STRUCTURE

A news story is organized differently from any other type of writing. For example, unlike an essay with its leisurely development, the news story quickly conveys the main facts of a happening—the climax—and then relates the other facts in the order of their diminishing importance.

It is easy to grasp this form of writing if you imagine how a friend would tell you about a bank robbery. Would the friend say this?: "I was standing in line at the First National Bank. I had been waiting about five minutes. Suddenly, three masked men rushed in with guns. . . ." Not likely. Anxious to share the news, the friend would get right to the point: "Three men just held up the First National Bank. They shot a teller, grabbed the money, and got away." Notice how the news story of this actual robbery began:

Three masked gunmen robbed the First National Bank about 10 a.m. Tuesday, escaping with an undetermined amount of money.
June Smith, a teller, was shot in the arm and taken to City Hospital.

In that lead (pronounced *lede*) are four of the five Ws found in most news stories: *who, what, where,* and *when.* The fifth W—*why*—is obvious. As the notorious criminal Willie Sutton responded when asked why he robbed banks: "That's where the money is." A sixth element often found in news stories—*how* —is partially answered with the words *masked* and *gunmen.*

A news lead must be written with accuracy, clarity, and brevity. Notice that no extra words clutter the bank robbery lead. The reader quickly learns the most important facts.

Here is the next part of the story:

```
The bank was crowded with customers when the three men darted in
with women's stockings covering their faces. One, brandishing a
shotgun, yelled:
     "This is a holdup. Everybody drop to the floor. Don't move or we'll
blow your brains out."
```

The first of these paragraphs (grafs in newsroom jargon) describes the scene and provides a transition, or bridge, to the rest of the story. Further details are provided: We learn how the men were masked and the nature of one of the weapons.

In both paragraphs note the short, declarative sentences and the use of colorful language—"darted in," "brandishing," and "yelled." A less experienced writer might have written "ran in," "holding," and "said."

Also observe the short paragraphs and the fact that the frightening command is set in its own paragraph for emphasis and as an "eye hook" to induce the reader to continue (such quotations should never be buried within a paragraph).

Read further:

```
The man with the shotgun stayed near the door. Pistols in their
hands, his partners leaped over the counter and filled paper sacks
with currency.
     When Smith failed to move out of the way, one man fired a warning
shot, grazing her left arm. She dropped to the floor.
     The men escaped in a late-model green sedan of an undetermined
make. Police, summoned by a silent alarm, arrived moments later.
```

These paragraphs complete the account of the action. Note that the lead has been retold and embellished. The story continues:

```
     "I was frozen—just couldn't move," Smith, of 8 Brookhaven St.,
told a reporter at the hospital. "He bumped into me, and then his gun
went off. It felt like fire. I guess I must have fainted."
```

Notice that Smith's address is given for the first time. Inserting it in the lead would have slowed the account. It is important that people involved in news stories be identified as fully as possible, including name, age, address, and occupation, when relevant. The story concludes:

The bank manager, Orville Jones, of 2220 W. University Ave., told police he would not know how much money was taken until later. He was at his desk on the main floor of the bank when the robbery occurred. He partially described the men.

"The fellow with the shotgun was about 6-feet tall," Jones said. "The others were shorter. All wore dark shirts and dungarees. I couldn't get any better description."

A customer, David Weatherford, of 210 E. Allen St., described the holdup:

"They came rushing in while I was waiting in line. When the big guy told us to drop, I did. I thought they might rob us too, so I slipped my billfold under me, just in case. But they didn't bother any of us."

The bank guard, William Hurst, of 104 W. Belknap St., also was taken by surprise and dropped to the floor with the others.

Teller Dolores Gomez, of 4416 Rosen Ave., said she was the one who tripped the alarm.

This was the bank's first robbery in about 10 years, according to Jones. Police searched highways leading from the city, but no sign of the getaway car was reported.

The story has been written in traditional *inverted pyramid* style, with each succeeding portion relating less important facts. A diagram of the story would look something like this:

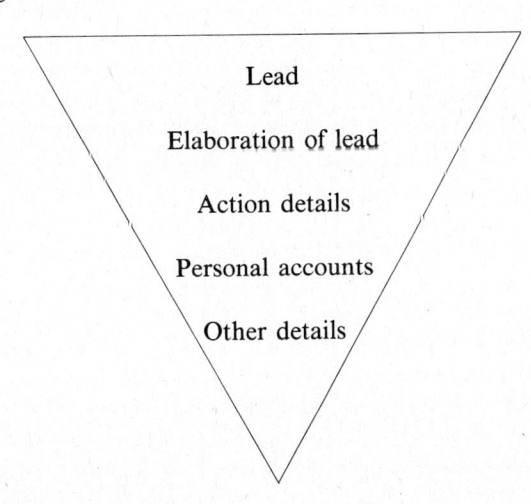

```
          Lead
    Elaboration of lead
      Action details
    Personal accounts
       Other details
```

The inverted pyramid style of news writing is said to have originated during the Civil War. Correspondents, fearful that the telegraph lines might be cut, began to report the most important facts in descending order. Press associations continued the practice.

This method relates the most important facts first so that readers need not continue unless they wish. It quickly satisfies curiosity. It enables newspaper makeup people to delete paragraphs from the bottom up to fit the story into available space without sacrificing more important information. And it helps the headline writer to grasp the essentials of the story quickly.

Notice that the story could end with almost any paragraph. This is known as *block paragraphing*. Thus any paragraph could be removed or additional information inserted without the necessity of rewriting.

Writing a story chronologically and in the suspended interest style will be discussed later in this chapter.

THE LEAD

The lead, whether it consists of one paragraph or more (the bank story has two), is the first unit of a news story. It must contain the *who* or *what* element as well as the *where* and *when,* at least in simple form to be elaborated upon later in the story if necessary. This enables the lead to stand on its own in a sense. In the bank story the essential elements are as follows:

- WHO—three masked and armed men.
- WHAT—robbed a bank and shot a teller.
- WHERE—First National Bank. (In large cities the address would be given.)
- WHEN—about 10 A.M. Tuesday.

A common mistake of beginning newswriting students is to omit one or more of these essential elements in the lead.

The *who* element often is the predominant feature of a lead:

```
Mayor Dorothy Allen was injured in an automobile accident on
Highway 78 east of the city Friday morning.
```

Because of the prominent position held by the woman, the story was run on page one. Had the mayor not been involved, the item likely would have been carried in a roundup report of automobile accidents and other mishaps.

Many stories emphasize the *what* element (often there is no *who*):

```
A tradition of long standing was ended Thursday when the City
Council voted that, because of lack of funds, the communitywide
Fourth of July fireworks display will no longer be held.
```

Where is the most important element of the following lead:

Standing on the 50-yard line in Owens Stadium at half-time of the Smith-Octagon football game Saturday, a Roseboro couple exchanged wedding vows.

The *when* element is the most important in this lead:

At midnight Thursday revelers in downtown Thibidoux ended their last-minute pre-Lenten celebration, and many walked to St. Joseph's Catholic Church for prayers.

Although emphasis on *when* is important in the examples such as those above, beginning newswriters frequently give *when* and *where* too much prominence in their leads when they are not the primary elements, as in this example:

Last night at the Civic Auditorium, Sen. James Philipson of Indiana warned that failure by students to repay their federal government loans on schedule has put the educational lending program in jeopardy.

The key factor here is the warning issued by Philipson, not the time and place of his speech. Thus these should be recorded in a less conspicuous manner. A better lead would have been:

Failure by students to repay their federal government loans on schedule has put the educational lending program in jeopardy, Sen. James Philipson of Indiana warned an audience at the Civic Auditorium last night.

At times the *why* element is most important and should be emphasized:

Because vandals had removed a traffic sign, two automobiles collided head-on at a highway construction site east of San José Thursday night.

How can be the most interesting aspect of a lead:

Their bodies slick with soap, two young prisoners squeezed through an air-conditioning opening in city jail Sunday night but were captured a block away.

Discerning reporters recognized the most important news values in these stories and composed their leads so as to emphasize the feature aspects. There was no thought of "writing a *when* lead or a *where* lead," for example, but simply of relating the story as attractively as possible. It is good practice never to bury a feature angle within a sentence, but to provide proper emphasis, normally with the first few words.

For decades, many newspaper reporters crowded as many of the five Ws and the *how* as possible into their leads. For example:

```
A band of about 12 to 15 men and women, some wearing colorful shawls
around their shoulders and others in plain attire but wearing
flashy costume jewelry, walked out of the Smithville Department
Store, 2222 S. Hudson St., with a dozen women's dresses, two
suitcases and three hair dryers shortly before the store closed
Wednesday night, Evelyn Nesbitt, manager, told police.
```

Such a lead is far too crowded and is seldom seen today. Instead the lead likely would have been written as follows:

```
About a dozen persons, described to police as "dressed like
gypsies," stole a dozen women's dresses, two suitcases and three
hair dryers from the Smithville Department Store Wednesday night.
```

A good lead provides the basic information that the reader needs to know and plays up the feature angle if there is one. In addition, the lead provides or implies the authority upon which the news is based and, if relevant, ties the story to previous ones with which it may be connected.

Examples of leads in which the attribution is stated:

```
The sudden hailstorm that struck Utica Monday broke windows in
three downtown stores and likely was responsible for two automobile
accidents, police reported.
The Westinghouse Electric Company plant in Salem will hire 200
more people by June 1, Helen Adams, plant manager, announced
Friday.
```

Examples of leads in which the authority is implied:

```
Firemen rescued three small children from a burning residence in
east Fort Worth Tuesday.
```

The source was the Fire Department, but adding "the Fire Department reported" would have been superfluous.

```
A 17-year-old youth drowned in Lake Wells Sunday while trying to
rescue his 3-year-old sister, who was saved when she grabbed a rope
thrown to her.
```

The sheriff's office, source for the report, was mentioned later in the story.

Note that in the first two stories the authority is provided *after* the news has been given because in neither instance was the attribution important enough to be placed at the beginning of the sentence. Doing so would have lessened the impact of the stories. At times, however, the source may be given first, as in the following example:

President Reagan announced Monday that a new arms treaty is being negotiated with Nicaragua.

In order to please their employers, many public relations people will submit stories to the press that begin with the name of the company or institution president. Reporters, after checking the facts, will rewrite the stories in customary news fashion.

Notice also that, in the fire and drowning stories, the names of the persons involved are not included. The names, however, must be given within the next paragraph or so. A good reporter always eliminates information from a lead that cannot be used by readers to assess whether they wish to proceed with the rest of the story. This criterion of "usefulness" can be applied to almost all leads.

When a story relates to one that has preceded it in the news, the lead will call readers' attention to that fact. Two examples follow:

A man convicted of murder in the slaying of a 32-year-old Itasca woman in February escaped from the Huntsville penitentiary early Saturday.

Romance has blossomed again for a 92-year-old woman whose sixth wedding in the last seven years made news recently.

Be certain that the time element in your lead does not appear in a clumsy place or alter the intended meaning.

Bad:

Winter's first storm is expected Wednesday to drop from 3 to 5 inches of snow, the Weather Bureau reported today.

Good:

Winter's first storm is expected to drop from 3 to 5 inches of snow Wednesday, the Weather Bureau reported today.

DIFFERENT WAYS TO WRITE THE SAME LEAD

Most leads may be written in a variety of ways. Unless the reporter wishes to rearrange the sentence for proper news emphasis, he or she will follow the simplest pattern: subject, active verb, and object.

Marlene Sanders, CBS-TV News correspondent, said here Monday night that the news business is still a "boys' club."

This form is ordinarily used when the name of the person speaking will attract readers as much, or more so, than what is said. The verb, "said," is most commonly employed. If called for, it could be replaced with "declared," "asserted," or another more forceful verb.

Here is another method, still beginning with the name:

Marlene Sanders, CBS-TV News correspondent, told Georgia broadcasters here Monday night that the news business is still a "boys' club."

If it is short, the identification can precede the name:

CBS-TV News correspondent Marlene Sanders said here Monday night that the news business is still a "boys' club."

CBS-TV News correspondent Marlene Sanders told Georgia broadcasters here Monday night that the news business is still a "boys' club."

In these leads the word *News,* is capitalized because CBS-TV News is the official name of that division of the network. If it were not, the word would be set lowercase (in small letters). The word *correspondent* begins with a lowercase letter because it is descriptive and not an official title, such as "CBS-TV News Vice-President." (Official titles preceding a name and not separated from it by a comma must be capitalized.)

Most often, however, what a person says holds greater reader interest than who is speaking. In those instances, the name should virtually never be given first.

The news business is still a "boys' club," Marlene Sanders, CBS-TV News correspondent, said here Monday night. (Or: told Georgia broadcasters here Monday night.)

Active voice is preferable to passive voice because the action moves forward rather than being twisted back upon the subject of the sentence.

If the reporter wishes to emphasize the audience, the lead could read:

Georgia broadcasters were told by Marlene Sanders, CBS-TV News correspondent, here Monday night that the news business is still a "boys' club."

The reporter could *paraphrase* the quotation:

Although more women are being employed than in previous years, the news business is still primarily a male occupation, a CBS-TV News correspondent said here Monday night.
"It's still a boys' club," Marlene Sanders told Georgia broadcasters in a meeting at the Georgia Center for Continuing Education.

Because few quotations are striking and often are long or prosaic, it is common practice for reporters to put such statements in their own words. Or they may extract a key phrase, such as "boys' club," for use in their paraphrased lead. In any event, actual quotations should be provided as soon as possible to support the indirect quotation.

In several of these examples, the phrase, "Georgia broadcasters," is substituted for the full name of the organization, which can be provided later in the story. Simply stating "here" in the lead also eliminates clutter by saving the five-word name of the location for use later in the account.

DELAYED IDENTIFICATION

Summarizing and emphasizing the key elements of a story in as few words as possible are the reporter's aims in writing most news leads. Meeting these requirements will force the reporter to use words and phrases that will be explained later and also to delay the identification of people and places unless they are so prominent that they must be identified immediately. An example is:

An 18-year-old Jonesboro woman was killed in a single-car accident near Murphreesboro Thursday night.
Jane Smith, of 1111 Old Orchard Road, was pinned under her car. . . .

Not naming the victim until the second paragraph enables the reporter to keep the lead short with maximum impact. The word *Jonesboro* also attracts the attention of readers in the community or nearby, providing just enough identification to sustain the lead. Including the woman's age in the lead adds human interest. A reporter might be inclined to begin the second paragraph with "She was . . . ," but would quickly realize that the two words are unnecessary.

Here is another example of a delayed identification lead:

Two Itasca men were shot to death and a Lakeville man was wounded at a Waukegan tavern early Sunday.
Police said Donald Smith and Alfred Jones, both of Itasca, were killed instantly during a fracas that broke out in the Good Times Tavern, 4441 Winston Highway, about 2 a.m.

Howard Wimbleton, of Lakeville, was treated for an arm wound and released from St. Joseph's Hospital.

The incorrect way to write the lead, unnecessarily crowding it with details, would be:

Donald Smith and Alfred Jones, both of Itasca, were killed and Howard Wimbleton of Lakeville was wounded in a shooting at the Good Times Tavern, 4441 Winston Highway, about 2 a.m. Sunday, police reported.

Although delaying the identification makes some stories more readable, the tactic cannot be employed in most timely stories, such as those involving elections and City Council meetings.

LOCALIZING

The wounding of a local man would cause the Lakeville newspaper to write the story with a different emphasis:

A Lakeville man was wounded early Sunday in a tavern shooting in Waukegan that left two other men dead.
Howard Wimbleton, 42, of 2121 E. Berry St., escaped with a minor arm wound and was released after treatment at a hospital.
Police identified the fatally wounded men as Donald Smith and Alfred Jones, both of Itasca. . . .

Note that the names of the tavern and the hospital are omitted as irrelevant because they are not local and that instead the Lakeville resident has been identified more fully. Reporters and editors must be constantly alert for local angles in the news reports they receive from press associations and correspondents. Fuller identification and additional angles may be developed, as necessary, through using city directories and telephone books, phone calls, and other interviews.

UNITY

A good news story is unified—that is, it is built around a dominant theme. The reporter, looking over notes, will ask: What is the most *significant* thing about this story? What is the most *interesting*? At times the important and interesting may be blended into an attractive lead; otherwise a choice must be made.

Once the central theme, or idea, has been determined, the reporter must focus upon it throughout the story. Secondary details will be used, but irrelevant material discarded. The use of transitional words and phrases will help tie together the various elements of the story.

In the following example, Associated Press writer Jan Carroll has achieved unity with a tightly knit dispatch:

By JAN CARROLL

Hard news lead	INDIANAPOLIS (AP)— Spring floods caused an estimated $1.225 billion in crop losses in Indiana, painting a picture of economic devastation unmatched in the state's history, Gov. Robert D. Orr said today.
Explains next step	As a result, the state will ask Agricultural Secretary John Block to declare Indiana an agricultural disaster area, triggering the availability of low interest loans to affected farmers.
Quotes support the lead	"It is important to understand the devastation this creates," Orr told reporters at a Statehouse news conference. "Economists usually multiply crop losses by three, giving an indication of the total impact on the economy."
	Using the economists' formula as a guide, the governor said, "Approximately $3 billion will not enter the stream of the economy. These are dollars that simply will not materialize."
Transition introduces new element	Aside from the financial hardship this creates for the farmers, the losses also will mean trouble for the state's sagging revenue picture.

"You extract the volume of economic activity from the volume of dollars being spent in this state, it's going to be a deterrent to the return to economic strength," Orr said.

Lt. Gov. John M. Mutz, who doubles as commissioner of agriculture, said the crop losses represent between one-fourth and one-third of the cash grain receipts in Indiana.

"These are dollars that can't be replanted. The growing season can't be repeated," Mutz said. "The impact on the economy as a whole is a tough one for us to take."

Most of the loss—$1.04 billion—involves crops which could not be planted or which were planted but then were damaged by flooding and rain. An additional loss of nearly $190 million in damage to croplands due to erosion pushed the total loss to $1,225,816,145, Orr said.

"This is the largest potential loss that anyone working in state or federal government in Indiana has ever seen," the governor said after the news conference concluded.

Supporting quotation

Cites additional source

Strong wrap-up quotation

Let us pick this story to pieces and see how the unity was achieved.

The lead presents the dominant theme: Governor Orr stated that $1.225 billion in crop losses from spring floods had created unprecedented economic devastation in Indiana. The lead answers the basic W questions: *who*—Governor Orr; *what*—crop losses; *when*—spring; *where*—Indiana; *why*—floods.

The second paragraph has a cause-and-effect link to the lead, with an important transitional phrase, *As a result*. Because of the losses, the state will ask the federal government to declare it an agricultural disaster area.

The reader now knows the basic content of the story. But these questions

46 PART I / THE SEARCH FOR NEWS

remain: How can the state's multifaceted economy be so devastated by loss of young crops in the spring? Who in addition to the farmers is hurt economically by their misfortune?

In the third and fourth paragraphs, the governor explains how economists multiply crop loss figures by three to find the total impact on the state's economy.

Then comes a transition paragraph in which the story switches from losses to the economy to the resultant losses in revenue that the state government will suffer. This transition is achieved with the phrase: *Aside from the financial hardship this creates for the farmers.*

In later paragraphs, the writer ties the story together with an explanation of how the figure of $1.225 billion in the lead was calculated and with a closing quotation from the governor reemphasizing the grim tone of his comment in the lead.

CHRONOLOGICAL TREATMENT

Some stories suggest chronological, rather than inverted pyramid, treatment. With so many readers learning the highlights of an event or disclosure from radio and television, reporters are increasingly using a narrative style to tell their stories.

In the following account, published in the Washington *Post,* the headline conveys the basic news with the reporter choosing the narrative style for maximum human-interest effect:

Md. Plane Crash Kills 3 on Way to a Wedding

Delayed lead

The two couples set out in a private plane from Neenah, Wis., at noon Friday, headed for a festive weekend in Riverdale to celebrate the wedding of Charlie Andreas, a hometown childhood friend now stationed at Andrews Air Force Base.

Narrative development

Even though no one had heard from the travelers by suppertime Friday, the wedding party remained calm. The pilot, Clark Anderson Jr., of Neenah, was an experienced and diligent flyer, they said; bad weather had probably forced him to land and wait for clear skies.

But at precisely that moment, Anderson was fighting for his life, caught in a blinding blanket of clouds in the northwest Maryland mountains. At 7 p.m., as Anderson tried to pilot his single-engine Beechcraft Bonanza to clear skies, the plane plunged into the Blue Ridge Mountains near Hagerstown.

Anderson and two passengers, Donald and Barbara Ann Abbey, were killed instantly. Vicki Anderson, the pilot's wife, survived.

The news reached the wedding party about three hours later, just as the family and friends of And-

Key fact of story: 3 killed in crash

More narrative

reas and his bride-to-be, Donna Colesanti, were leaving the Riverdale home of Frank Colesanti, the bride's father.

"The phone rang and the man said he was Clark Anderson. We thought, 'Oh great, they've arrived,'" Frank Colesanti recalled yesterday. But the caller was Clark Anderson Sr., the pilot's father, and the news transformed the joyous wedding party into a group of mourners.

"We're going ahead with the wedding on Sunday," the bride's father said. "We can pray for them and give them our bereavements, but life has to go on." About 200 guests are in town for the ceremony at St. Bernard's Catholic Church, he said.

Philosophical conclusion

THE SUSPENDED INTEREST STORY

The summary lead tells the main facts of the story immediately, as compactly as possible. As a result, readers may abandon a story after the first paragraph or two. The reverse of this lead is the suspended interest lead. This coaxes the reader into the story with an attractive opening, but holds back some essential facts until later in an effort to sustain interest. Here, side by side, are two stories published about the same news event. The one on the left carries a traditional summary lead; the other employs a delayed lead. Study them and decide which is more effective.

Extortion Trial Figure Flees, Later Retaken

THE LEBANON, KY. *DEMOCRAT*

A former Lebanon resident whose extortion trial began yesterday fled the courtroom during jury selection only to be captured a few hours later at his Davidson County home by a bail bondsman.

Jerry Wayne Summers, 27, arrested last February by Wilson County Sheriff Gwin King in the extortion of more than $400 from a Lebanon man, was discovered missing after nine jurors had been tentatively accepted to hear his case in criminal court.

Summers was apprehended later Wednesday by local bail bonds-

A Call of Nature Becomes Suspect's Call to Freedom

THE *TENNESSEAN*, NASHVILLE

Jerry Wayne Summers, 27, on trial in Wilson County Criminal Court for extortion, was granted permission to go to the men's room in the courthouse.

Summers kept on going.

The suspect's disappearance Wednesday morning took place while court was recessed and courtroom activities, to say the least, were relaxed.

After the recess, Assistant District Attorney General Bobby Capers asked the jury's indulgence, explaining that the accused was AWOL.

man Joe Jordan.

"He (Summers) just slipped right out of the courtroom after jury selection started," stated a court official, who asked not to be identified.

Assistant District Attorney General Bobby Capers said today the extortion trial has not been rescheduled yet.

"If his counsel thinks yesterday was not going to hurt his case, we'll try it as soon as we can. But, we gave him (Summers) his day in court and he ran out on us and he may end up sitting in jail a little longer for it," Capers said.

Summers is accused in the extortion of money from Bernest McCrary, whom he allegedly accused of attempting to date his wife, Rita, also charged, and with molesting the couple's young daughter.

He is back in custody today in the Wilson County Jail under $10,000 bond.

Bondsman Joe Jordan was summoned and promptly left for Summers' home in eastern Davidson County. Jordan determined the fugitive was in the house and radioed the sheriff's office for assistance.

A search of the residence at first turned up nothing, but then Summers was found beneath a pile of rags.

Judge Robert Bradshaw ordered Summers returned to the county jail, where he is being held without bond.

Summers' disappearing act, in effect, dissolved the jury which had been chosen temporarily but not sworn in.

Bradshaw ordered the jurors to return at 1 p.m. but later dismissed them when the prisoner was not returned at that time.

The case was postponed indefinitely.

Summers and his wife, Rita, 25, both formerly of Lebanon, are charged with extorting $400 and other items from Bernest McCrary, of Lebanon, earlier this year.

Other ways to write a news story, in addition to the inverted pyramid, chronological, and suspended interest styles discussed, will be examined in later chapters.

REWRITING A STORY

Now that we have analyzed how a basic straight news story should be written, let us examine a published story that fails to meet these standards and see how it might be rewritten into a lively, crisp article that will catch readers' attention. This is the story, as published in a midwestern newspaper:

SYRACUSE—It was learned during the Tuesday night town board meeting that six-year radio dispatcher Mrs. Ginny Gilbert has resigned and Steven Knispel has been appointed to the Syracuse Police Department.

Knispel was appointed May 1 to fill the vacancy created by the resignation of Town Marshal Ron Robinson, who left Dec. 31 to become captain in the county sheriff's department.

Knispel is 21 years old, unmarried, and is the son of Mr. and Mrs. Lorin Knispel, Syracuse. He graduated from Wawasee High School and has served four years with the National Guard.

According to Mrs. Gilbert's letter of resignation, "we have rules and regulations that are not carried out. When one operator cries on a shoulder, she always gets her way. This is unfair and should not be allowed." According to Mrs. Gilbert, "The town board should step in, take some responsibilities, and see what is going on."

Mrs. Gilbert said a dispatcher meeting had been held earlier in the day with Police Sergeant Louis Mediano and Fire Chief Kenneth Johnson. "Kenny is very helpful and is trying to get the other two dispatchers to do their share of the cleaning detail. However, Lou, on the other hand, does not wish to cooperate on the police end of it," she wrote. "He feels as though it is nothing but a gripe type of complaint and is not interested enough to take a hold and really look at things the way they are," continued Mrs. Gilbert.

Mrs. Gilbert concluded with, "I feel as though my past six years of faithful service should stand up against one who wants to just take over the office, sit on her fanny, and do all the typing, filing, totaling the log sheets and take charge of things, but does not help on the cleaning end of the job and she does (at least has) stick her nose in where it is not needed or wanted, and has been told about it by the police department heads." Mrs. Gilbert would be referring to Mrs. Deb Dull, the only other female dispatcher. Other radio dispatchers are Mrs. Gilbert's husband, Tom, and Don Blosser.

According to board discussion following the presentation of Mrs. Gilbert's resignation, which is effective May 15, authority of the radio dispatchers is the joint responsibility of the fire chief and police chief. Since Mrs. Gilbert did not request to talk with the board, and "unless there is some justification for Mrs. Gilbert's remarks," the board would be inclined to let the department heads handle the matter.

Further discussion indicated the board "might want to look into it."

The fundamental weakness of this story is that it buries a fascinating human-interest angle—a quarrel between two women radio dispatchers that was sure to set tongues clucking in a small community. By backing into the story, the writer obscures a set of intriguing quotations that expose the tense atmosphere existing in the office. The lead omits the *why,* which in this case is essential in understanding the story, and it is written in the passive voice, a weak form that diminishes its impact. The third weakness of the lead is that it is doublebarreled when it should not be, for it gives equal weight to the main element of the story, the resignation of the dispatcher, and a secondary element, the appointment of a new policeman. In fact, many editors probably would move the appointment information into a separate story to keep it from interfering with the flow of the resignation material.

Another shortcoming of the story, unrelated to writing technique but very important, is its failure to obtain rebuttal comment from the other female dispatcher who was criticized so roundly by Mrs. Gilbert in her letter of resignation.

Now let us examine another version of the story, in which Mrs. Gilbert's sense of outrage and her allegations are brought up to the top of the story, so the reader is immediately caught up in the dispute.

```
SYRACUSE  An angry Mrs. Ginny Gilbert resigned as one of the
community's two female radio dispatchers at the town board meeting
Tuesday night because, she claims, the other woman would rather
"sit on her fanny" than clean up the office.
   In a bitter letter of resignation, Mrs. Gilbert focused most of her
ire on what she perceived as favoritism toward her feminine
colleague.
   Although Mrs. Gilbert didn't use the other woman's name, she
obviously was referring to Mrs. Deb Dull, the only other female
dispatcher. Other radio dispatchers are Mrs. Gilbert's husband,
Tom, and Don Blosser.
   She wrote, "I feel as though my past six years of faithful service
should stand up against one who wants to just take over the office,
sit on her fanny, and do all the typing, filing, totaling the log
sheets, and take charge of things, but does not help on the cleaning
end of the job and she does (at least has) stick her nose in where it
is not needed or wanted, and has been told about it by the police
department heads."
```

Tips on Newswriting

In writing a news story, a reporter should use the following:

• **The active voice.** Write "Mrs. Fraser told the committee that she had donated . . ." rather than, "The committee was told by Mrs. Fraser that she had donated . . ."

• **Concise declarative sentences.** Choose the basic subject-object-verb sentence structure most of the time, because the reader grasps its meaning easily. Occasional sentences beginning with a dependent clause or other grammatical device give the prose rhythm and variety, but should be used sparingly.

• **Lively verbs.** "Action" verbs give a story a feeling of movement. Instead of writing that a crowd *left* the stadium, say that it *shuffled, dribbled,* or *crept* out. However, excessive straining for unusual verbs makes a story appear amateurish, and should be avoided.

• **Simple words.** You are seeking to convey information quickly and clearly, so avoid complex and obscure words that are roadblocks for many readers.

Avoid Sexism in News Stories

Care should be exercised in writing news stories to treat the sexes identically. Avoid stereotypes and such usages as "Jane Davis doesn't look the part, but she is an authority on, etc." Similarly, avoid the assumption of maleness when both sexes are involved, as in, "Carnes told newsmen, etc." Instead, use the neutral word *reporters*.

Usage of courtesy titles varies among newspapers. In the first use of a woman's name, do not include a courtesy title. Write "Elizabeth Buchanan" just as you would write "Warren Schultz."

In the second use of a woman's name, some papers print only her last name, precisely as is done with a man's, unless omission of a title creates confusion of identity. Others use Mrs. or Miss if her marital status is known. Use of the courtesy title Ms. is frequently restricted to women who indicate their desire to be known thus.

(Notice that this lead contains the *who,* Mrs. Gilbert; the *what,* her resignation; the *when,* Tuesday night; the *where,* at the town board meeting; and the *why,* because she believed that the other woman did not do her share of the cleaning. The second paragraph makes clear that Mrs. Gilbert made her allegations in a letter of resignation, and the third paragraph forms a transitional bridge. The action details, in this case quotations from her letter, follow in the next paragraph.)

Rules and regulations in the dispatcher's office were not being carried out, Mrs. Gilbert contended. She requested that the town board step into the situation and see what was going on.

"When one operator cries on a shoulder, she always gets her way," she complained. "This is unfair and should not be allowed."

(Notice that in this version the colorful quotation about crying on a shoulder has been placed in a separate paragraph for better visibility.)

Mrs. Gilbert also took a written swipe at Police Sergeant Louis Mediano for allegedly being insufficiently concerned about keeping the dispatch room clean. A meeting of dispatchers was held earlier in the day with Mediano and Fire Chief Kenneth Johnson, she reported.

"Kenny is very helpful and is trying to get the other two dispatchers to do their share of the cleaning detail," she stated. "However, Lou, on the other hand does not wish to cooperate on the police end of it. He feels as though this is nothing but a gripe type of complaint and is not interested enough to take a hold and really look at things the way they are."

52 PART I / THE SEARCH FOR NEWS

The rewritten story could then report the discussion that took place in the town board after presenting Mrs. Gilbert's letter, much as the original story did.

STUDY PROJECTS

1. Submit three news stories in which you have underlined the answers to the basic W news questions. Either use a different color to underline each element or number them 1. Who; 2. What; 3. When; 4. Where; 5. Why; 6. How (if given).

2. Submit examples of published stories that are written in the following styles:

- Inverted pyramid
- Chronological
- Suspended interest

3. Using the following facts, write a news story that includes a simple, effective lead and the essential news elements:

- Arrested: David J. Taylor, 821 Fremont Ave., age 25.
- Time: 2 A.M. today
- Location: McKinley Terrace, Hayward
- Casualties: Taylor shot in left leg. Two police officers suffered minor injuries.
- Charges: Assault on police officer. Other charges may be filed.
- Chronology: Police stopped Taylor for speeding on S. Main St. in what was believed to be a stolen van. Taylor drove away. Police pursued him for 30 miles at speeds sometimes more than 100 mph. He turned into a cul-de-sac. Six police cars trapped him. Trying to break out, Taylor crashed his car into three police cars. Two officers in cars slightly injured. When Taylor fled on foot, police fired, struck him in leg.
- Disposition: Taylor treated at Memorial Hospital, placed in county jail.

PART II
Reporting the Story

COMING UP NEXT . . .

Just as airline pilots have checklists to follow before takeoff, a reporter should use a mental checklist before turning in a story.

This chapter lists concisely, for easy reference, four fundamental requirements that every story should fulfill. Failure to satisfy any one of them may mislead the readers. It also may cause needless trouble for the individuals or organizations involved in the story, for the writer, or for both.

As a test of responsible journalism, a reporter should check each story for:

1. Accuracy
2. Attribution of sources
3. Fairness
4. Objectivity

Later chapters examine these requirements in greater detail.

Chapter 5
The Four "Musts"

ESSENTIAL STORY ELEMENTS

Every news story should contain four essential elements. Without them, the story should not be published, no matter how energetic its reporting and clever its writing. They are the factors that give credibility to a publication or a news broadcast and demonstrate a reporter's sense of responsibility.

ACCURACY

The facts in a story should be correct, down to the most minute detail. Get it right! Be precise! Spell names correctly, including the proper middle initials. Give the correct addresses of persons involved. Do not write "S. State St." if it should be "N. State St." If ages of story participants are used, make certain that these are accurate.

These may seem like petty details, but they are not petty to the persons involved. Readers tend to judge a newspaper's reliability by their own experiences with its coverage. Far too often, a reader is heard to say, "Every time I've been involved in a story published in that newspaper, they've messed up some of the facts. So I assume that all other stories in it are wrong too."

Inaccuracy in print can cause harmful results to innocent individuals. A journalism professor recalled an incident from his newspaper days when, as editor of a *Voters' Guide,* he failed to catch a transposition of a number so that a candidate was listed as 82 years old, not 28. "It may have cost him the election," the faculty member commented. "He had tears rolling down his face when he walked into the city room to bring the error to my attention."

When a story includes a sequence of events, double-check written reports and news sources to verify that you have the chronology correct.

If a story contains direct quotations, be positive that the words are what the speaker actually said.

Stories peppered with inaccuracies are a sign of a lazy reporter.

ATTRIBUTION

The sources from which a story's information is obtained must be clearly identified in print. Failure to do so makes a reporter's story suspect. The reader forms an opinion of a news situation from reading the stories about it. If the source of certain information in a story speaks from obvious self-interest—the attorney for a defendant, for example, or a candidate for office—proper identification of that source aids the reader in making a judgment.

Source identification should be as specific as possible. Use the person's name if possible, not merely "a spokesperson." Only under rare circumstances, with approval of a senior editor, should a news story attribute information to such a vague quarter as "an informed source" or "a confidential observer."

Reporters who seek literary effect at the expense of factual honesty and truthful attribution are headed for trouble. A reporter must not invent news sources or synthesize the experiences of several persons in the form of one hypothetical individual; that is the province of the fiction writer.

Two notorious instances within a few weeks of each other in 1981 demonstrate the peril. Janet Cooke of the Washington *Post* won a Pulitzer Prize for her story about an 8-year-old boy heroin addict. When the story later was proven to be false, she lost her job, the prize was withdrawn, and the newspaper was severely embarrassed. Michael Daly's column in the New York *Daily News* about an incident involving a British army patrol in Northern Ireland was discredited when the London *Daily Mail* established that the British soldier he quoted did not exist and the writer could not produce independent sources to substantiate his account. Daly resigned his job under pressure. In both instances the stories were colorful, emotional, and excellently written. But they were dishonest and misled the readers. (See Chapter 20 for further discussion of newspaper ethics.)

FAIRNESS

News stories should be scrupulously fair in their presentation of information. They never should serve as special pleadings for any group or individual. In stories reporting discussions at public meetings, the essential points made for and against all significant positions should be included and be evenly balanced.

When one person criticizes the behavior or opinions of another in a story, basic fairness requires that the person criticized must have an opportunity to respond. Sometimes that person is not immediately available; if so, a second-day story

Chapter 5 / The Four "Musts" 57

As a Washington *Post* reporter, Janet Cooke won a Pulitzer Prize for her story about a child heroin addict, but had to return the award and lost her job when the story was revealed as a fake. She is shown here with television talk show host Phil Donahue.

should be published containing the person's rebuttal. Whenever possible, however, the reply should be included in the original story.

If a reporter cannot reach the person under criticism, the story should state what efforts were made to obtain a reply.

In a memo to Associated Press editors and writers worldwide, Vice-President and Executive Editor Louis D. Boccardi gave these instructions about fairness:

> Too often, news stories in which a person or organization is attacked or criticized say only that the target "could not be reached" for comment. Or "There was no immediate comment . . . ," etc.
>
> That's not enough.
>
> We must be more specific. If two calls to the governor's office were not returned, say so. If we left six messages with three lawyers for the defendant, say so. If the public relations representative promised to call back and didn't, identify him or her and say so. If the duty officer at the State Department at midnight said he could not reach anyone, say so and name him.
>
> The reader is entitled to know what we did and how we tried to obtain comment.

OBJECTIVITY

Writers should strive to keep their personal opinions out of a news story. Ideally, a perceptive reader should be unable to detect the reporter's political beliefs and religious or social attitudes. This is not as easy as it may seem.

None of us lives in a vacuum. We all have personal beliefs, interests, and involvements. At times a reporter will cover events that run contrary to those personal concerns. In that case, the reporter should work especially hard to achieve evenhandedness.

Lack of objectivity is frequently unintentional rather than calculated slanting. For example, a reporter covers a city council budget meeting at which a heavy reduction in municipal funding of fine arts programs is under discussion. Her husband plays in the chamber music orchestra that will lose half its payroll subsidy if the cut is made. Without intending to, but subtly influenced by her desire to see the subsidy remain intact, the reporter may give greater emphasis in her story to arguments against the reduction than to those supporting it.

An excellent reporter in a northern city was removed from a story on his regular beat because he was accused of not being objective. A local hospital sought to build a parking lot on land it owned. This land adjoined a quiet residential street whose residents had a property owners association in which the reporter was active. The association opposed the parking lot project, because it feared that excessive traffic and night lighting would disturb residents. After the reporter covered the first public hearing on the issue, hospital officials claimed to the editor that the reporter's story was slanted. The reporter denied the charge. The issue was a matter of semantics. Nevertheless, another reporter was assigned to the story, to the regular man's disgust and embarrassment, so that the proponents, even if unjustified, no longer could claim that the newspaper was biased.

Signed columns and properly labeled articles of opinion provide a writer freedom to inject personal beliefs. News stories do not. Their mission is to deliver the factual base from which readers and opinion writers may draw conclusions.

> *Before you submit a story, read through it one more time and ask yourself: "Is it accurate? Does it have proper attribution? Is it fair? Is it objective?"*

STUDY PROJECTS

1. Underline the sources cited in each story published on the first three pages of a daily newspaper. (Remember that some stories may include attribution from several sources.)

2. Bring to class (a) a published news story in which proper attribution is lacking; or (b) a story that lacks fairness or objectivity. Be prepared to discuss the shortcomings.

3. Study the main news section of a daily newspaper—the content and positioning of the stories and the size and wording of the headlines. Then describe in 300 words how well or poorly the newspaper meets the standards of attribution, fairness, and objectivity. Cite examples to support your conclusion.

READ MORE ABOUT IT . . .

Valuable sources of professional commentary on news story handling are:
   The weekly *AP Log*.
   The weekly *United Press International Log*.
   APME News, published by the Associated Press Managing Editors Association, and its annual *APME Red Book*.
   ASNE Bulletin, published by the American Society of Newspaper Editors.
      A 138-page paperback book, *Improving Newswriting*, was published in 1982 by ASNE. It contains "the best" recent articles printed in the *Bulletin*.

COMING UP NEXT . . .

After a story has been written, it must be edited before being put into type. In the preelectronic era when all stories were typed onto paper, standard copy preparation methods were in use for generations. Every new journalist must learn the traditional methods and editing symbols, because numerous needs for them continue to exist.

In this chapter we explain the rules for preparing typed copy and demonstrate the copyediting symbols. The student learns the symbols with which an editor gives instructions for such steps as abbreviating a word, inserting an apostrophe, and marking a paragraph.

Appendix A explains how to edit copy that is written on a video display terminal. It also describes preparation and marking of copy intended to be run through an optical character recognition (OCR) machine, often called a "scanner."

Chapter 6
Preparing the Copy

THE CHANGING NEWSROOM SCENE

Writing stories on copy paper is a thing of the past in all-electronic newsrooms, where reporters compose their stories directly on video display terminals (VDTs).

In many newspaper offices, everything is electronic except the reporters' stations, where copy is typed on special sheets for optical character recognition (OCR or "scanner") reproduction.

In a dwindling number of newsrooms and in most journalism school laboratories, however, stories are still composed on copy paper with the use of electric or manual typewriters.

No matter where reporters work, they must still know the traditional method of copy preparation and editing. Even in all-electronic newsrooms, stories are occasionally received on paper, or must be written and edited by typewriter and pencil before they are placed in the computer system. Articles submitted to magazine or book publishers and to broadcasting stations, as well as those written in public information offices or by individuals, are prepared by the traditional method. Consequently, all journalists must learn how to write and edit copy for publication.

Rows of video display terminals are the most prominent feature of a metropolitan paper's newsroom.

THE TRADITIONAL METHOD OF PREPARING COPY

Practices vary somewhat from newspaper to newspaper, but the following rules generally are followed for copy written on paper:

1. Type copy double spaced or triple spaced on soft-finish paper.
2. Observe 1-inch or greater margins, but do not divide words line to line and do not run paragraphs over from one page to another. (Both of these stipulations aid the printer in setting copy.)
3. In the upper left-hand corner, type your last name and a "slugline" of one or two words that identifies the story. Thus:
   Jones
   robbery
4. Begin typing about a third of the way down the page, leaving room for headlines, a new slugline, or typographical instructions.

Chapter 6 / Preparing the Copy 63

Nine indictments alleging a plot to transport more than one hundred stolen automobiles and trucks from San Diego to South America were made public yesterday in United States District court.

Nine persons, including a former San Diego police officer, were named as defendants.

Three of the defendants, along with 4 other men, also were charged in separate indictments with hijacking truck loads of shoes, clothing, stereo and camera equipment, brass, tires, and orange juice.

Late model Toyota cars and pick up trucks and Jeep wagoneers allegedly were stolen and stored in San Diego and driven individually to Los Angeles, where they were altered to appear new and then shipped to South America. FBI agents reportedly recovered more than one hundred cars in Los Angeles warehouses during a three year investigation.

Charged with participating in the alleged ring in 1981 and 1982 were John Millett, 35, a former San Diego police officer; Mark Millett, 44, his brother, unemployed for ten years; William Autono, 28, of 444 Chase street; Rafael Martinez, address not given, an unemployed nightclub manager; Vincent Riccardo, 45, of E. First street; Jon Wildman, 26, an unemployed boat repairman; Moses Ritterdam, 38, and Sidney Overman, 40, both of Los Angeles; and George Auden, 52, of Chico.

more

A page of a news story, after copyediting

5. Avoid strikeovers (example: 6̸). Simply "x" out words or phrases that contain typing errors or that otherwise must be deleted, and continue writing.
6. On each succeeding page, write your last name, the slugline, and the page number in the extreme upper left-hand corner. Thus:

      Jones   Jones—robbery—2
                     or
      robbery—2

7. Begin your copy on page 2 and the succeeding pages about 1 inch below the slugline.
8. At the bottom of each continuing page type the word: *more*. At the end of the story type: XXX or -30-.
9. Edit your story with a soft-lead copy pencil *after* you have finished, not, of course, while the sheet is still in the typewriter. Adding or deleting words and punctuation is acceptable. If, however, the finished copy is messy, retype it.

Your intention throughout is to make everything clearly legible to those who will read it, especially the person who will set the story into type.

EDITING SYMBOLS

Before copy is put into print, it is edited internally, as contrasted with proofreading marks that are placed in the margins of printed copy. The following copyediting symbols are commonly used:

- paragraph   ⌐In the coffee houses
- capital letter   w̳estern world
- small letter   W̸estern world
- abbreviate   (Street)
- spell out   (Ft.) Worth
- separate   end|product
- delete word and close up   a ~~good~~ second-place finish
- delete letter and close up   too many lette̸rs
- remove space   awk⌒ward
- insert apostrophe   woman⌄s
- transpose words   a (green ⌒woman's) purse
- transpose letters   a gre⌒en purse

Chapter 6 / Preparing the Copy **65**

- insert dash   forces just as quickly
- insert hyphen   long haired dog
- no paragraph   Suddenly it was over
- insert comma   Suddenly it was over
- add period   Suddenly it was over
- use numerals   fourteen
- spell out numeral   8
- flush left   [By June Pritchard
- flush right   ]By June Pritchard
- center   ]By June Pritchard[
- ignore correction; let it stand   the quick decision
- spelling is correct; do not change   it was Smyth
- run in   but the fact remained that the game was over and Duke won
- clarify copy   Duke won
- italics   it was all over
- boldface   Duke 30, East Carolina 16
- overline longhand o, m, n; underline a, w, u   the base was submerged
- end mark   XXX (or -30-)

READ MORE ABOUT IT . . .

The Associated Press Stylebook and Libel Manual (New York: Associated Press, 1980). Excerpts from the manual are in the appendix of this book.
Bruce Westley, *News Editing* (Boston: Houghton Mifflin, 1980).
Martin L. Gibson, *Editing in the Electronic Era* (Ames: Iowa State University Press, 1979).

COMING UP NEXT . . .

You have studied how to write a news story. The time has now come to do it yourself.

For your first assignment, you will cover a speech and write a news story about what was said.

This chapter and the following one discuss that assignment from two aspects.

This chapter tells what to look for in the speech, how to use the power of selection, how to take effective notes, the importance of obtaining full-sentence direct quotations, the advantages and possible dangers of using a tape recorder, and how to plan your story.

In the chapter that follows, we shall examine actual writing of the story from the notes and impressions you have gathered. The better the job a reporter does in gathering the material, the easier the writing part of the assignment will be.

Chapter 7
The First Assignment

A SELECTIVE PROCESS

Studying the principles involved in writing a news story has provided you with the groundwork for becoming a reporter. The time has come to put that knowledge to work. You have been given your first assignment—to attend a meeting and write a news story about a speech to be given there. The speaker may be a prominent figure who has been brought to the campus by the student body organization, or perhaps a faculty member discussing an important development in his or her special field. Even a sermon at a nearby church might be suitable.

The task may seem a little formidable. What, precisely, does the reporter covering a speech look for? With so much being said, how does the reporter pick out the material to record in notes and put into the story?

It really is not especially difficult, if you approach the assignment with two guidelines in mind.

First, concentrate on writing a story about the most interesting and newsworthy points the speaker said. Do not try to produce a chronological summary of the speech in the way an organization's secretary might record the official minutes of the meeting. Your job is not to take down a stenographic transcript, but to choose from the speech those portions you consider to be important. Use your power of selection. Let your reporter's mind serve as a filter to catch the speaker's significant thoughts and statements while the rest of the verbiage drains away. Even the most profound speaker usually devotes part of a speech to making introductory comments, inserting humor (or attempted humor), and using oratorical devices to establish rapport with the audience. Although these are valuable tools for the speaker, they can be easily winnowed out by the reporter as being of little consequence in a news story.

The reporter represents hundreds of readers who were not present; they have the right to expect a story that catches the essence of the speaker's message. Meanwhile, over the writer's shoulder the editor says, "Keep it tight!"

Second, be certain that the story is accurate and balanced.

Direct quotations used by the reporter should correctly represent what the speaker actually said, in the context in which they were intended. Although sensational "quotes" taken out of context make eye-catching headlines, they constitute irresponsible journalism. Both speaker and readers depend on the reporter to write a fair and evenhanded report of what was said. If the speaker makes a statement that sounds extreme but later qualifies it with exceptions or limitations, those qualifications should be included in the story. The reporter's personal opinions concerning what the speaker said have no place in the news article.

TAKING NOTES

Experience in taking notes during class lectures helps to prepare the reporter for covering a speech. In some classes, an astute student soon perceives the form of the outline from which the professor is lecturing and can anticipate points still to come. Although this is sometimes true in public speeches, often it is not. Even speakers who have carefully organized their material frequently get carried away and stray up verbose sidepaths. Relatively few speakers are professionally trained; many have a tendency to fumble and to toss in a handful of "and-uhs" to fill the gaps. While listening and taking notes, the reporter should attempt to recognize the speaker's pattern; this ability helps in organizing the written story.

In recording direct quotations, it is important to take down complete sentences whenever possible. These are blocks with which the writer builds the story. Occasional use of fragmentary quotations—that is, two or three key words plucked out of a sentence—is permissible. Sometimes such a stray phrase is sufficiently striking to be used in the lead of the story. However, excessive use of fragmentary quotes produces a rather jerky story and may leave the impression that the reporter was scrambling to keep up with the speaker.

Putting down complete sentence quotations in your notes is not always easy. While a reporter is writing one sentence, the speaker may start another that also seems important, and indeed may be more valuable than the first one. This requires a reporter's concentration and perhaps a quick decision. The reporter must either get down the first quotation in full, letting the other go unrecorded, or quickly abandon the first quotation and switch to the second. The danger is in ending up with several partial scribbles that provide nothing sufficiently rounded to incorporate in the story. Leave sufficient space in your notes so that when the speaker reaches a "soft" spot—a transition, an aside, or a joke, for example—you can seize the breathing spell to go back and fill in the missing words that, with luck, you have stored in your memory. Practice being a disciplined listener; try listening closely as your friends talk and see if you can mentally pluck whole sentences from their conversation.

Few American reporters take shorthand, although it is a commonplace skill among British reporters and one to be envied. American reporters usually develop a personal semishorthand consisting of abbreviations, initials, and symbols. For example, an experienced reporter's notes may show such contractions as "pox" for police, "trou" for trousers, "pix" for pictures, and "tt" for that. Any device that saves time and is easily recognizable later is helpful. When the speaker uses a name frequently, merely write the initial of it after the first time or two. Another time saver is to omit the articles "a," "an," and "the." These fall into place automatically when reporters transcribe their notes. Often this can be done as well with the verb forms "are," "to be," "is," and "was," and with the conjunctions such as "and" and "if."

As a brief example of these time-saving techniques in note taking, this sentence occurred in a politician's speech: "What we are seeing is the release of pent-up frustrations which have been accumulating for the past four years."

Listening to this, a reporter might write: "What we seeing is release pent-up frusts which accumulating past 4 yrs."

The following excerpt from notes made by Merriman Smith, United Press reporter at the White House, during a press conference held by President Franklin D. Roosevelt in 1944 shows the extreme condensation used by a skilled reporter working under pressure.

> tnk be gud tng sy smtg re ILO NA 20 Apl—34 cntrs—vry impt mtg bcs undbtly whn we come to devise UNs org, ILO will be ind but afflt cum new org of UNs.

To get down the President's statement in a hurry, the reporter used condensations without vowels, initials, parts of words, an old United Press telegraphic code symbol (NA stands for Philadelphia), and Latin words, *re* meaning "about" and *cum* meaning "with." When Smith wrote his story later, the President's words came out like this:

| I think it would be a good thing to say something about the meeting of the International Labor Organization in Philadelphia on the 20th | of April. Thirty-four countries will be represented. It will be a very important meeting because when we come to devise the United Nations |

| organization, the I.L.O. will be independent, but affiliated with the | new organization of the United Nations. |

Always put quotation marks around direct quotations in notes to identify them as such. When a reporter's notes paraphrase something a speaker has said and the reporter carelessly puts direct quotation marks around the paraphrased material in a published story, the speaker may complain properly of being misquoted: "That isn't the way I said it!"

Eventually every speaker utters those awaited words, "And finally . . ." or their equivalent. This may be followed by a concise, significant conclusion. Or, having signaled that the end is near, an uneasy speaker may not know how to quit and merely runs down like a tired clock, rather than striking a sharp final note. Whichever is the case, the reporter has a notebook full of scribbles that must be transformed into a story.

As quickly as possible, expand these notes with pen or pencil. Then get to a typewriter or video terminal and type out your notes in full while they are fresh in your mind. "Cold" notes are as unpalatable as cold coffee. Not only does this practice of expanding notes while they are fresh prevent uncertainty about what the condensed words and sentence fragments mean, but it also helps the reader to perceive the speech as a whole.

USING A TAPE RECORDER

Using a tape recorder to preserve the entire speech is obviously a much easier method than the handwritten note system just described. It captures the speaker's statements accurately and in full. When a speaker complains of being misquoted in a story, the reporter finds immense satisfaction in being able to play back the tape and prove the story's accuracy. Existence of such tapes has prevented many politicians from weaseling out of statements they made but wish they had not. For these reasons, a large percentage of reporters carry tape recorders as standard tools of their craft.

A shrewd reporter, however, uses the tape recorder as a safety backup device, not as the primary source for the story's raw material. Being mechanical instruments, recorders do not always function properly. Extraneous noise can blot out or distort vital portions of a speech. The reporter may not be seated in a position where the recorder can be used effectively. Even with a tape recorder running, a good reporter takes written notes from which he or she can write a satisfactory story even if the tape proves to be blank.

Another factor that works against excessive dependence upon the tape recorder is time. Playing back a tape and taking notes from the playback double the time a reporter spends in gathering information for the story. When the story must be written for an early deadline, the reporter frequently does not have time; even hunting back through the tape for specific portions takes minutes that may not be available. When you hear the speaker make an especially quotable statement, jot down the footage number so that later you can quickly find the quotation in the tape. Handwritten notes, of course, are ready for instant use. It is best, then, to use the tape recorder for double-checking and expanding handwritten notes. As such, it is a boon that reporters of earlier generations never dreamed of having.

Too much reliance on a tape recorder creates a psychological peril as well. Reporters may tend to listen to a speaker less attentively when they know they have the backup protection of a recording. Then when they go back to the tape for quotations, they may pick out the best ones without regard for the context in which these were spoken, thus creating a distortion of the speaker's intent. Rarely, a speaker may request that no tapes be made of the speech—a request that has scant justification if the speech is a public performance. If this happens, reporters should courteously advise the speaker that they are using recorders.

When the speaker is an important government official or an officer of a large corporation, the speaker may distribute copies of the speech in advance, frequently with a specific hour of release noted at the top. This helps the reporter, of course, but complete dependence upon the handout has its perils. Speakers often stray from their printed texts, either injecting timely and significant new material or omitting a portion of the advance release. If the portion that has been left out is newsworthy, accepted practice is for reporters to include it in their stories with a notation to readers that it was in the prepared text, but was not actually delivered.

If the reporter can talk to the speaker after the meeting, this is an opportunity to check on the accuracy of notes and to ask the speaker for elaboration on certain points. Request a copy of the speech if you do not have one already. Be sure to identify yourself as a reporter. Such after-the-meeting personal contacts may develop into interviews that produce provocative additional material. When well-wishers crowd around the speaker, it may be wise to make an appointment for 15 minutes later or to stand in the background until the handshakers depart.

PLANNING THE STORY

The speaker talked for 30 minutes; the reporter has 400 to 500 words in which to cover what was said. Thus careful organization of the raw material in the reporter's notes is necessary.

The first, and most important, step is to select a focal point for the story—that is, the most striking and significant point the speaker made. Around this point, the writer constructs the lead paragraph. Sometimes this decision is easy, because the speaker stressed one theme so emphatically that it almost automatically becomes the lead. Another speaker may present greater difficulties because he or she makes several points of approximately even weight, thus forcing the writer into making a choice.

Tips on Covering a Speech

1. Select the most interesting and significant material contained in the speech.
2. Strive for accuracy and balance.
3. Include full-sentence direct quotations in your notes.
4. Develop a personal semishorthand that includes abbreviations, symbols, and initials.
5. Use a tape recorder if possible as a safety backup, but do not depend upon it excessively.
6. If possible, talk to the speaker after the meeting for additional material.
7. Plan your lead around the most important statement the speaker made.

Some of this planning can be done while the speaker is talking. When writing down each main point spoken, the reporter can test it against previous statements as potential lead material, then do the same with subsequent points. Thus, when the speech ends, the reporter may already have a fairly clear idea of what the best potential lead is. This idea can be either confirmed later, with supporting detail, as the reporter goes over his or her expanded notes, or can be replaced by another "angle" when the reporter has had time for reflection. The filtering process in the reporter's mind should be going on, almost subconsciously, the entire time the speech is in progress.

J. Montgomery Curtis, a retired vice-president of Knight-Ridder Newspapers, Inc., and former director of the American Press Institute, recalls advice he was given during his cub reporter days about 1920. His editor at the Wheeling (West Virginia) *Daily News* sent him to interview Tim McCoy, a member of one of the feuding Hatfield and McCoy mountain clans, shortly before he was to be executed. Curtis had to get his story done in a hurry, and in those days transportation was slow.

"The editor told me to write the first four paragraphs of the story in my head as I rode the streetcar back to the paper," Curtis told *Editor & Publisher* in a retirement interview. "It's a good trick and I've written that way ever since."

What Curtis recommends is an extension of the testing process used during the speech, so that the reporter mentally shapes the main course of the story before sitting down at a keyboard.

STUDY PROJECTS

1. Bring to class a published news story reporting a speech. Be prepared to discuss the writer's choice of a lead angle and how well the writer supported the lead with direct quotations.

2. Listen to a radio commentator or a broadcast speech and write a 100-word opening segment of a news story based on what you heard.

3. Using notes taken in one of your college course lectures, list four major points that should be included in a news story about the lecture; include quotations to support them. Then write a lead for the story.

COMING UP NEXT . . .

That blank sheet of paper or empty video display terminal screen confronts you. How do you turn your speech notes into a story?

First, the reporter must decide upon a lead. Everything that follows depends upon it. What type of approach should it be—a hard-news lead or a feature lead that concentrates either on what the speaker said or on the speaker's personality?

This chapter emphasizes the hard-news lead approach because it is the easiest to write. Once reporters feel comfortable in handling this method, they should then experiment with other approaches. Later chapters on leads and on feature writing will be helpful.

After selecting a lead, the writer must focus on the principal theme with supporting quotations, then develop secondary points and background material.

Plunge right in. It is like learning to ride a bicycle. Once you get the hang of it, you realize that it was easier than you expected.

Chapter 8
Writing the Speech Story

SELECTION OF A LEAD

Next comes the most difficult part: getting the story onto paper or into the video display terminal. A news report of a speech may be a straightforward account with a hard-news lead. It may also be written in a featurized style that focuses either on what the speaker said or on the personality of the speaker rather than the message itself. As an example of the latter form, a national political reporter covering a presidential candidate, having heard the politician give his standard formula speech for the fortieth time, may write a story not specifically about what the candidate says but about how and why he says it: his gestures, the way he manages to put a sob in his voice at the same patriotic paragraph every time he delivers it, and how he weaves in calculated appeals to identifiable blocs of voters. Such featurized treatment requires unusual skill and long experience. Our concern at this point is with mastering the straight news form.

The first problem is selecting a lead that catches the reader's attention and states a key point made by the speaker, as discussed in the preceding chapter. A helpful device is for the writer to ask oneself, when drafting a lead, "What kind of headline can the copydesk write from this?" The better focused the lead is, the more appealing the headline can be, and that is what attracts the reader to the story.

Too often the beginning reporter, anxious not to "miss the lead," tries to crowd several elements into the opening paragraph. Combining two news elements in a lead is acceptable and indeed common, but to introduce more than that may confuse the reader. Another mistake inexperienced reporters often make is attempting to answer too many of the who-what-when, and so on, questions in the lead. A brief, tersely worded and provocative lead is best. Skillful writers weave in the essential answers fairly high in the story, but do not permit them to intrude upon the flow of the account. Remember that in speech coverage, *when* and *where* are usually minor information.

Once the lead has been chosen, the writer decides upon the order in which the remaining material is to be introduced. Also, the writer should decide where to work in background information about the speaker and the meeting, in order to put the event in perspective.

Although a substantial amount of supporting material should be given to the "angle" stressed in the lead, some secondary points may be reported in only a few words; because of the space limit that the city editor assigns and the average reader's limited span of interest in most stories such condensation is required. Here is where the reporter's news judgment comes into play.

An effective method is to place a summary paragraph early in the story that lists additional major points the speaker made. These can then be developed in detail as space permits in the order they were listed.

Here is a lead typical of those written by beginning reporters.

```
Last night at the Student Center, Dr. Mildred Robinson, president
of the Feminine Freedom Organization, urged members of the
Associated Woman Students not to avoid confrontations for their
rights, to campaign for more scholarships for woman athletes, and
asked them to work for adoption of the Equal Rights Amendment.
```

Quite a handful, that lead—and not even grammatical! It embodies several common errors. Let us see what is wrong.

First, the speech lead should be couched in positive terms, not negative ones. Only under rare circumstances should a lead contain the word *not*. The *not* may be dropped out accidentally during the typesetting process so that the intended meaning is reversed, and its use places an extra burden on the reader's ability to grasp the content quickly. A much better form would be: "... urged members of the Associated Woman Students to fight for their rights," and so on.

Grammatically, the lead violates the rule that a sentence should be parallel in construction: that is, its multiple elements should be identical in form. The speaker urged her listeners *to avoid* and *to campaign*. Therefore, the final portion of the sentence should read *and to work for adoption,* and so on, omitting "asked them."

The third major fault of the lead is overcrowding. Because the writer failed to exercise the power of selection, the reader must grasp three concepts in a single sentence.

Which lead angle should the writer have emphasized? By using a process of elimination, we find that the Equal Rights Amendment is the least important because the appeal has been made so frequently. Although having the virtue of being specific, Dr. Robinson's support for more scholarships for woman athletes is part of her broader appeal for woman students to fight for their rights.

Thus a more effective lead would have been:

> Dr. Mildred Robinson, president of the Feminine Freedom Organization, wants woman students to fight harder for their rights by challenging university administrators face-to-face with demands.
> "Don't be afraid of confrontations," the peppery, diminutive feminist advised members of the Associated Woman Students here last night. "When you believe that men on the campus are being given unfair advantages, speak up. March into the dean's office and demand equality."
> "Challenge the president himself."
> Her advice drew cheers from a predominantly female audience at the Student Center.

In this simpler version, the lead is built around the single most important point; a copydesk editor could easily write a headline from it, such as:

'Demand Rights on Campus,' Women Told

A strong direct quotation from the speaker supports the lead. Time and place are stated inconspicuously. The speaker is identified and described, and the reason for her statements, an appearance before the Associated Woman Students, is given, all within the first 90 words.

A lead stating or implying physical action, if justified by the facts, is usually stronger than one involving abstract concepts.

DEVELOPMENT OF THE THEME

The stage is now set for the writer to move from the speaker's general theme to a specific example of it—her proposal that more scholarships should be granted to woman athletes. The handling of this point forms the second segment of the story. A transition is needed to hold the story together. It could be written thus:

As an example of what she perceived as sexual inequality on the campus, Robinson pointed to the small number of athletic scholarships given to women as compared with those received by male students. Only 32 women hold athletic grants here at Southwest University, she reported, whereas 208 men receive such financial assistance.

"The coaches of the men's teams spend thousands of dollars on recruiting trips to coax high school athletes to attend the university so the coaches can have winning teams," she said, pounding the lectern angrily with her fist. "Why aren't woman coaches permitted to do the same thing?

"More than half the students on campus are women, yet most of the intercollegiate sports are for men only. And I don't mean having women play football either. Men have a cross-country team. Why don't women? They can run, too, you know."

USE OF BACKGROUND MATERIAL

At this point the reader may wonder who is this Dr. Mildred Robinson? What is her background and why does she speak with such vehemence? The reporter anticipates these questions by including a paragraph or two here, describing her career. She is a member of a national speakers' bureau for the Equal Rights Amendment; by listing that fact, the writer eliminates the need to include a paragraph about the ERA appeal in her speech. Perhaps the career information is available from advance publicity material. If not, the reporter should ask the speaker for it after the meeting. She may be listed in *Who's Who in America,* too.

In the remaining space available, the writer summarizes the speaker's suggestions of methods by which the women students can apply pressure to attain their goals—making aggressive calls on university officials and trustees, carrying placards outside the football stadium, writing letters to the editor of the student newspaper, appearing on the university radio station, and organizing their male friends into a support group. If there is space, this listing can be accompanied by more of Dr. Robinson's pungent quotes.

Valuable as they are in making a story sparkle, direct quotations are a little bit like fudge: too much at one time makes a person choke. The best method is to alternate direct quotations with paragraphs paraphrasing some of the speaker's statements. Direct quotations not interrupted with paraphrasing should contain no more than 100 words. Seldom, if ever, should long direct quotations be given in the body of a paragraph. An example is: She said, "The coaches of the men's teams . . . " The "she said" element should either precede the quotation or be buried within it in an appropriate fashion after the first phrase or sentence—*never* at the end of two or more quoted sentences, and *never* repeated during a series of quotations uninterrupted with indirect quotes (paraphrasing). The reader,

Tips on Writing a Speech Story

1. Keep the lead terse, built upon one or two elements in the speech.
2. As you compose a lead, ask yourself, "What kind of headline can be written from this?"
3. Support the lead with a full sentence or more of direct quotation.
4. Include a summary paragraph early in the story telling the other important points the speaker made, then develop them one by one.
5. Include background information about the speaker.
6. Work in answers to the basic five W questions inconspicuously.
7. Alternate direct quotations with paragraphs of paraphrased speech material, limiting direct quotations to maximum segments of 100 words at a time.

---

scanning the story, will see the quotation marks as "eye hooks," evidence that someone is being quoted. Readability is enhanced when a personal, not an abstract, statement is made in a story.

AN ACTUAL EXAMPLE

The speech we have just reported is an imaginary example. The following is an actual newspaper story covering a speech delivered by Earl Butz, the controversial former Secretary of Agriculture, at California Polytechnical State University. It was published in the San Luis Obispo County *Telegram-Tribune*. The reporter approached the assignment in a standard hard-news manner. Before you write your assigned speech story, study this one to see how it was put together and analyze its strengths and weaknesses.

Butz Speaks at Poly; Says Pesticide Use Worth Risk

Former Secretary of Agriculture Earl Butz urged Cal Poly alumni and farm management students Saturday to become more politically involved because the profit motive in agriculture is "under siege."

In a wide-ranging speech to nearly 250 on the Cal Poly campus, Butz predicted increased uses of pesticides, warned against the threats of urban sprawl and alerted agriculturalists to pressures for price controls of farm goods.

And in talking to a reporter after his speech, Butz said he hopes President Ronald Reagan will not lift the grain embargo against the Soviet Union until "we get something in return."

Butz, who spent five years as secretary of the Agriculture Department under Presidents Richard Nixon and Gerald Ford, made a strong plea for agriculturalists to begin tilling the field of politics.

Food and fiber producers "have a stake in politics," Butz told the crowd, which included Republican Assemblywoman Carol Hallett of Atascadero, a strong proponent of agricultural interests.

Butz praised private enterprise as "the wellspring of innovation, of cost cuts, of affluence."

Profit, he said, "is in ill repute in this country" because "demagogues in this country" like to attack the rising prices of food.

Butz insisted the price of food is actually "America's No. 1 success story" because "we now feed ourselves with only 17 per cent of our take-home pay."

In order to provide low-cost food for an ever-increasing population, he said, farmers are going to have to use more insecticides and herbicides.

"Sure, we're going to have to take a little risk when we drop some chemicals on the melon crop in California to kill the bugs," he said. "But the benefits outweigh the risks."

During an interview after the speech, Butz said he had heard that Reagan was considering lifting the grain embargo against the Soviet Union.

"I don't think it should be lifted unless we move to get something in return," Butz said. "That something might be a pledge (by the Russians) to tell the truth about the way our hostages were treated in Iran" or as a concession to slow the Russian military buildup.

Although Butz's speech decried trends of increased government controls on business, he said he favored local controls to stop urban sprawl in agricultural areas.

[*The reporter should have written the present tense, "favors."*]

He said some regulations are needed if America is to preserve its prime farm land from highway and residential developments.

"I don't know of any other way to produce the food we need without land," he said.

Butz, 71, is dean emeritus of agriculture at Purdue University.

He resigned from the Ford administration in October of 1976, after a furor raised by a disparaging racial remark he made as a joke.

He was Nixon's agriculture secretary during the Watergate era and described Watergate as "an incredibly stupid incident."

Butz's humor peppered his speech and included this one about Watergate:

"Someone has said that Watergate was just a little like someone from GM sneaking into the Ford offices to steal the Edsel plans."

STUDY PROJECTS

1. Bring to class three published leads that are overcrowded with information and your rewritten, simplified versions of them.

2. Paste a published news report of a speech on one or more sheets of paper. Underline the major points made in the story, marking them A, B, C, and so on. Then circle and mark with the appropriate letter the direct and the indirect quotations the writer used to support each point.

3. Analyze the strengths and the weaknesses of the published Butz story appearing in this chapter. Discuss them in a report of 250 words.

PART III
Writing Processes and Prototypes

COMING UP NEXT . . .

A newspaper in which almost every story has a hard-news summary lead becomes monotonous. Therefore a reporter should find ways to begin stories that will whet the reader's curiosity and provide a stimulating change of pace. As this chapter demonstrates, there are many ways to do this.

You will find here examples of alternative leads to try—leads based on contrast, parody, literary allusion, an "astonisher," description, direct address, question, quotation, and dialogue. Also, there is the 1-2-3 lead for the complex story. With such a varied arsenal available, any writer can achieve freshness and originality.

Along with these positive suggestions, the chapter offers a chamber of horrors—types of leads to be avoided under all circumstances. It closes with advice from the general news editor of the Associated Press.

Chapter 9
More About Leads

VARYING THE LEAD

Composing a lead for the story is the trickiest part of the newswriting craft. As you probably discovered while doing your first assignment, the rest of the material begins to fall into place once you have found a satisfactory beginning paragraph.

So far we have dealt with the summary news lead, the form most commonly used in newspapers. Numerous other ways of starting a news story exist, some of them alluring to the reader when used properly and others so faulty that they always should be avoided. Editors seek variations in lead style because they know that a newspaper whose every story opens with a hard-news lead in declarative sentence form bores its readers. By using the variations in lead writing that we shall examine in this chapter, we show that a clever writer also can inject zest into a spot news story.

CONTRAST

A lead that develops contrasting elements, such as time and purpose, is a frequently used device for whetting the reader's interest.

For 50 years during the 1800s the Trimborn Farm was one of southeastern Wisconsin's most important sources of lime.

85

Now a new chapter in the old, picturesque farm's history is beginning.

Milwaukee County has purchased 7.5 acres of the original farm at 800 W. Grange Ave. to be developed into a park.

PARODY

In this form, the lead mimics a familiar song, statement, or expression, as in this example:

Pepsi-Cola hit the spot for burglars who broke into the bottling plant on South Main St. last night.

They got $500 (and that's a lot), said Detective Sam Howerton.

They might have got twice as much for their money too, but they couldn't break into a smaller safe inside the big one, Howerton added.

(Adapted by a reporter from an old jingle: "Pepsi Cola hits the spot; 12 full ounces, that's a lot! twice as much for your money too: Pepsi Cola is the drink for you.")

The parody lead is tricky to handle, but can be entertaining if done cleverly. However, unless the original material it mimics is widely known among readers, the parody can leave many of them confused.

LITERARY ALLUSION

Like the parody, a lead based on an allusion to a literary figure from the past treads on dangerous ground unless the source of the allusion is commonly known. The writer can reduce the risk by explaining the allusion, but that may slow the flow of the lead. Also, highly literate readers may regard the explanation as a little bit patronizing. Here is an example:

He probably never heard of the beautiful Atalanta of Greek mythology, who dropped golden apples in order to outrun her suitors. But the results were the same.

A man grabbed a handful of bills from the cash register at Lala's Service Station, 200 E. Broadway, Thursday afternoon, police reported.

Running across a field, the thief dropped some of the currency every 20 feet or so.

As owner Carl Lala stopped to recover the cash, the thief jumped into a pickup truck and escaped.

Because few readers, however, are acquainted with Greek mythology, the story probably should be told in a straight narrative fashion, that is, in suspended interest style, told in the sequence in which it happened. The *Tennessean's* version of the suspect's flight from a courtroom, quoted in Chapter 4, uses the narrative style.

Shorn of its literary allusion, the filling station robbery might be told thus:

```
A thief grabbed a handful of bills from the cash register at Lala's
Service Station, 200 E. Broadway, Thursday afternoon.
  Running across a field with owner Carl Lala in close pursuit, the
thief dropped some of the bills every 20 feet or so.
  While Lala was picking up his stolen cash, the thief jumped into a
pickup truck and escaped.
  Lala told police he lost $180.
```

THE ASTONISHER

Usually told in few words, this lead seeks to intrigue the reader with an amazing or seemingly unbelievable statement.

```
  It rained frogs.
  Picked up by a small cyclone that swept nearby swamplands, dozens
of the green creatures fell on a city block near the end of Old
Hill's Road about 2:30 p.m. Sunday.
```

DESCRIPTIVE LEAD

Entirely unlike the summary lead, which tells readers immediately the essential facts, the descriptive lead drops them into the middle of the action in progress. Having thus caught the readers' attention, the writer proceeds to explain what the situation is all about.

```
  The performance charged to an increasingly feverish pitch. A sense
of passion and grandeur tore through the music.
  Yet, as the opening act on Summerfest's Main Stage, the Allman
Brothers Band's inflamed concert Thursday night suited the
festival's trend toward softer acts.
  These pioneers of Southern rock weren't soft in an insipid or
syrupy way. Indeed, their sweeping arrangements of blues, rock and
country sounds, combined with impeccable musicianship, offered a
more sophisticated 110-minute show than most rock acts are capable
of producing.
```

DIRECT ADDRESS

Here the writer speaks to the reader on a direct person-to-person basis, or has the primary figure in the news story do so to someone else. Bob Considine's lead about the Louis-Schmeling fight, quoted in this chapter, is in direct address: "Listen to this, buddy, etc." Here is another example:

Forget those sexy movie roles and the suggestive jeans commercials. The real Brooke Shields is a clean-cut girl who hates cigarettes.

That's what the 16-year-old actress told a House subcommittee Thursday, protesting the dropping of antismoking ads she had done free for the Department of Health and Human Services.

THE COMPLEX STORY LEAD

At times the reporter faces the problem of handling a complex story containing several elements of almost equal weight. Instead of cramming all these elements into the opening paragraph, the writer can list these and use a handy typographical device called a bullet (a dot) at the beginning of several paragraphs. Some newspapers use the numerals 1, 2, 3 instead of the bullets for the same purpose.

Here is an example illustrating use of the bullet:

A redevelopment plan that will give downtown a contemporary concrete-and-glass look in place of its musty brick image was adopted by the city council last night.

The plan includes these major features, whose initial cost will exceed $30 million:

- A five-block pedestrian mall along S. Broadway.
- A riverfront convention center.
- A nine-story hotel linked by an overpass to the convention center.

QUESTION

Asking a question will draw the reader quickly into the story. This technique is used more often in writing a feature story than a straight news account. It is a favorite of reporters who must write a follow-up story about an event or development that contains one or more unanswered questions.

Who killed 18-year-old Susan Smith while she was baby-sitting for a South Side couple last week?

Detectives today continued their search for clues in the case that has spread apprehension throughout the city.

The question lead is used more frequently as an enticing way to begin stories that explore complex social, political, and economic conditions.

How does heavy drinking by parents affect their children?

"The damage to kids is just unbelievable," Charles Englehart, director of the Ozaukee County Council on Alcoholism, said yesterday.

QUOTATION

Including a quotation in the lead paragraph is an effective method, provided the quotation is brief and simple. A complex quotation in the opening paragraph may confuse the reader and it also tends to make the lead sentence too long. Some

Three Historic Leads

Colorful leads such as these examples have a life of their own, becoming a part of the folklore of journalism. The first, by Jack Lait of the old International News Service, reported the shooting of gangster John Dillinger by FBI agents in Chicago in 1934:

> John Dillinger, ace bad man of the world, got his last night—two slugs through the heart and one through his head.
> He was tough and he was shrewd, but he wasn't as tough and shrewd as the Federals, who never close a case until the end, and their strength came through his weakness—a woman.

Although this lead by Meyer Berger of the New York *Times* is long by contemporary standards, it carries emotional power:

> Jack (Legs) Diamond, human ammunition dump for the underworld, was killed in a cheap rooming house at 67 Dove Street here this morning, a few minutes after he had dropped off in a drunken sleep, following celebration of his acquittal in Troy last night on the charges of kidnapping.

By using the direct address style, sportswriter Bob Considine created dramatic impact in this 1938 lead:

> Listen to this, buddy, for it comes from a guy whose palms are still wet, whose throat is still dry and whose jaw is still agape from the utter shock of watching Joe Louis knock out Max Schmeling.

newswriting instructors, observing that many students adopt this method as an "easy way out" of writing a lead, forbid the practice until other styles of lead writing have been mastered.

```
"You're lucky I didn't throw the book at you," Judge William
Fisher told a Springfield ex-convict yesterday as he sentenced
him to 10 years in state prison for his fourth offense in as many
years.
```

(For a more detailed discussion of quotation use, see Chapter 11, "Developing a Writing Style.")

DIALOGUE

This is an extension of the quotation lead, in which the quotation in the opening paragraph is followed by further quotations from one or more persons to pull the reader into the story.

```
"I think there's a silver dollar in that pool," Maria Ramirez
remarked to her friend.
 "Why don't you find out?" Celestine Lopez challenged her.
 Thrusting her hand deep into the pool, Ramirez lost her balance and
tumbled in. She struggled out moments later clutching a soda pop
top.
 Ramirez, of 210 Hillcrest Apartments, told this story Sunday to a
policeman who arrested her for wading in a Hillside Park pool.
```

LEADS TO AVOID

We have been examining numerous ways in which a lead can be written, all of them effective if done properly. Now we shall look at five types of leads that should be avoided under all circumstances. They can be avoided with a little effort, but far too many of them creep into print because the writers are careless or lazy.

THE SAY-NOTHING LEAD

Some reporters fail to stress the news element of a story; the result is a say-nothing, or label, lead.

```
President Reagan spoke to the Congress Thursday about his tax
reduction plan.
```

Rewritten as a do-something lead:

President Reagan urged the Congress Thursday to pass his tax reduction plan with no changes.

. . .

The Kiwanis Club heard an address at its luncheon Tuesday by John Koppinger, chief of the Montana Bureau of Investigation.

Better:

Car thefts in the state have "got out of hand," John Koppinger, chief of the Montana Bureau of Investigation, told the Kiwanis Club at its luncheon Thursday at the Holiday Inn.

. . .

Saturday, May 10, the Santa Maria Arts Council announced the award winners of their annual grants at an 11 a.m. luncheon.

Rewritten:

Fourteen winners of the annual grants of the Santa Maria Arts Council were announced at the council's luncheon Thursday at the Ramada Inn.

Note the multiple errors in the original lead of the arts council story: lack of news emphasis, beginning the story unnecessarily with the date, using "their" instead of "its" and giving the time of the luncheon (important only in a story printed *before* the luncheon is held).

THE ABSTRACT LANGUAGE LEAD

When writing leads, the reporter should pay particular heed to that precept for all good writing: "Be specific." Avoid vagueness by using precise words and phrases rather than generalities. Instead of stating that a politician urges a broader housing policy for the city, write that he or she advocates construction of 800 low-cost apartments. Do not report that the school board discussed low attendance on days before holidays; instead, write that members were dismayed to find the rate of absenteeism three times as high on days before a holiday as on an ordinary schoolday.

Observe the difference in impact between this lead couched in abstract language and the rewritten version that provides specific information.

The House voted sweeping changes in the food stamp program Friday, carrying out wishes of the Reagan administration to reduce the government's cost of the program.

92 PART III / WRITING PROCESSES AND PROTOTYPES

Rewritten to include definite aspects of the changes:

The House voted rules changes today that will take away food stamps from more than 1 million of the present 23 million recipients and reduce benefits for millions of others.

Here are two leads that avoid abstraction and create a sharp picture in the reader's mind:

Some consumers have been getting finely ground bits of bone in their hot dogs for more than a year without realizing it.

If the No. 2 pencil you buy at the corner stationery is good enough for the American public, it should be good enough for the federal bureaucracy, the government has decided.

THE FOGGY LEAD

A reader trying to find the way through an obscure lead like the following feels like a man beating his way through the jungle:

Valley Cities Investment Corporation of Van Nuys, owner of the Rancho Los Alamos Mobile Home Park, has filed suit in Superior Court here that asks the county's Fifth District Mobile Home Rent Control Board to set aside its decision of Jan. 22 that imposes a rent ceiling at Rancho Los Alamos.

How's that again? Why not the following?

Lifting the recently imposed rent ceiling at Rancho Los Alamos is the aim of a suit filed in Superior Court by the Valley Cities Investment Corporation of Van Nuys.

Here is another foggy lead:

By a vote of 3 to 2, directors of the Solvang Municipal Improvement District last Thursday night rescinded an ordinance calling for a substantial hike in sewer connection charges for residential and commercial properties after hearing requests from representatives of the business sector for additional time to study the proposal.

The reader who struggles through to the end of that lead must be thoroughly confused. The reporter could lift the fog by simply writing:

Solvang residents won't have to pay higher sewer connection charges, at least for a while.

THE FLAT, DULL LEAD

Too many leads fall into this category. When a man with a gun, wearing a surgical mask over his nose and mouth, robbed a store, the reporter missed the human interest element in the story by writing:

> An armed robbery occurred at the Cass Dairy store at 101 New York Ave. last night around 9 p.m. According to police reports, a lone white male walked into the store, pulled a revolver and demanded all of the cash in the register....

Four paragraphs later the reader learns about the surgical mask. Robberies occur daily in most communities, so the alert reporter must play up anything out of the ordinary to make such accounts more attractive. The lead on this story could well have been:

A gunman wearing a surgical mask over his nose and mouth robbed the Cass Dairy Store, 101 New York Ave., about 9 p.m. yesterday.

Notice that the redundancy—9 P.M. last night—has been eliminated in the rewritten lead.

THE UNGRAMMATICAL LEAD

Errors in grammar can creep into a hastily written and unedited lead, making the story seem sloppy and amateurish.

Police Lt. Charles Hurley said the stocking-masked pair who robbed Mr. and Mrs. William Grounds Jr., of 3933 Greenmont, of $900 after forcing their way into the home and tying up the couple about 11 p.m. Monday apparently was a case of mistaken identity.
Lt. Hurley said that from the statements made by the intruders during the 30 minutes in the residence and from the background of the Grounds, it appears the assailants were looking for drugs and mistakenly went to the Grounds' home.

It is obvious that "the stocking-masked pair . . . apparently was a case of mistaken identity" represents poor, ungrammatical writing. And the plural of the proper name, "Grounds," is "Groundses." The lead might have been written:

94 PART III / WRITING PROCESSES AND PROTOTYPES

An apparent case of mistaken identity. That's how Police Lt. Charles Hurley describes the home robbery of a local couple Monday night.

Here are a half dozen poor leads on stories published in daily and weekly newspapers. Read them carefully, analyze their weaknesses, and think how you would rewrite them.

Results of the state Assessment Program tests held last spring were announced at Wednesday night's meeting of the Lakeview Elementary School District Board of Directors, which showed local third and fourth graders to be above the expectancy band in reading ability and within the ideal range in math and language.

Anyone willing to give up their seat in a computer science course at Northern Illinois University could find themselves $300 richer.

Saturday certainly didn't go right for the vacationing Hamptons of Lawndale, as she was cited on suspicion of petty theft of gasoline in Buellton, he fell out of their house trailer as it was speeding north on U.S. 101 and was cited for riding in a trailer, and the family dog bit a sheriff's deputy and was locked up by Animal Control.

Leonard F. Trew and Dorothy H. Brown, doing business as "Hi Liners," a co-partnership, filed an application in May with the Public Utilities Commission, requesting a certificate of public convenience and necessity to establish a passenger stage service for the transportation of scenic tour passengers between Fort Bragg and Mendocino; one tour to operate between Fort Bragg and Moyo Harbor, and a second to operate between Fort Bragg and Mendocino.

One of the most significant statistics coming from the Nov. 3 election is that less than a third of the registered voters in the county bothered casting ballots, with the poorest showing going to the Carpinteria Sanitary District and the best to the Mission Hills Community Services District in Lompoc Valley.

> On November 17th at 11:30 a.m. the Valley Republican Women's Federation will have as their guest speaker Mr. Brooks Firestone, founder of the Firestone Winery. The meeting will be held at the Firestone Winery in Los Olivos at the invitation of Mr. and Mrs. Brooks Firestone.

ADVICE FROM AN EDITOR

Jack Cappon, general news editor of the Associated Press, recently offered the following advice in a newsletter to the AP staff:

> ### DON'T SAY TOO MUCH IN LEADS—OR TOO LITTLE
> The purpose of the lead is to usher readers into the story—with a little shove, maybe, but anyway by pointing them in the right direction.
> The old five Ws school did it brutally, by trying to cram everything into the opening paragraph.
> That approach is mercifully obsolete. Such leads are seldom readable. The trend is the other way: toward highlighting one overriding news element and deferring subsidiary detail, toward stressing a human angle and focusing on people.
> Fine, but pendulums notoriously can swing too far and at times this seems like an era of the pointless lead—not so much in the hard-news stories but in the softer sort.
> Anecdotal and vignette leads can be compelling if they lead straight into the story. When they fail to do this they just drift, wandering lonely as a cloud high above the story.
> Here are some examples from our report:
> *His graying hair seems just a trifle grayer in recent weeks. He appears a touch more nervous.*
> Who he? the reader asks. And so what? Three grafs down, assuming the reader soldiers on, he finds the story is about a legislator ostracized by his peers.
> *When this 90-year-old farm was young, the dairy cows were as good as any in Kent County.*
> Yawn. The point was this:
> Twice in the past three years a dairy farmer has seen his cherished Holstein cows die. Now he's $400,000 in debt . . . etc.
> *They say they are prisoners in their own apartments, and not even safe there.*
> Three more "they say" grafs follow while the reader yearns to get to the point. The fourth graf finally comes out with it: "These are Washington's elderly. . . ."
> And finally:
> *It's been years since the Abenaki Indians hunted and fished where they pleased, but the Indians say times really haven't changed that much. They want to wander freely again.*
> The point? The Indians are petitioning for the right to hunt and fish anywhere in the state. Would you guess from the lead?

Now consider two other feature leads:

NEW ORLEANS (AP)—If they can ever get alligator tails untangled from the government red tape, there'll be a new kind of meat in the grocery stores. (By Tony Donina.)

SEATTLE (AP)—Doug Poth is one 13-year-old who doesn't come to the door selling baseball raffle tickets or asking if he can mow the lawn. He's more likely to be looking for a stolen television set or serving a subpoena. (By Wendy Walker, about a youthful licensed private detective.)

These are soft leads too, but they work. They take the reader directly into the story.

There are rare occasions when the central point can be deferred—for example, when the lead builds up genuine suspense.

But on the whole the rule of thumb should be: When your first graf, standing alone, makes no strong point, rewrite it.

Loaded down with so many options, good and bad, and so much advice, the beginner may feel a bit overwhelmed. With practice, this sense of uncertainty will go away. Leads will emerge from the keyboard more easily. Before long, the writer will produce opening paragraphs that say precisely what he or she wants them to say. One way to achieve a sense of ease is to clip leads from newspapers and rewrite them, trying out the variations described in this chapter.

STUDY PROJECTS

1. Bring to class published examples of the following types of lead:

   - Direct quotation
   - Contrast
   - Direct address
   - Question

2. Clip three newspaper stories whose leads you find to be unsatisfactory and rewrite them in more effective form.

3. Rewrite the following story, which appeared in a weekly newspaper, with a lead that points up the tensions and maneuvering among board members:

Culver's school board voted 4-2 Monday evening to hold election of officers. Mrs. Peggy Clark, Phil Mallory, Howard Hildebrand and Paul Snyder, Jr., were in favor of the election while Marvin Good and Don Keller voted against.

Keller, the board's vice president, opened the meeting in the absence of President Paul Davidson. Mrs. Clark then nominated Snyder for president, but Snyder declined the nomination. Snyder nominated Hildebrand and the vote passed 5–1 with Good voting against. Keller then turned the meeting over to the new president. Hildebrand continued with the election of officers by nominating Good as vice president. Good said, "Since I voted against the reelection of officers in the middle of the year, I will not accept any nominations for any offices."

Mallory nominated Mrs. Clark and the vote was 3-3 with Good, Keller and Mrs. Clark voting against her appointment. Mrs. Clark then nominated Keller and he declined any office. Mrs. Clark then nominated Snyder and he was voted in as vice president with a 4-2 vote. Keller and Good voted against. Mallory was voted in as secretary with a 4-2 vote.

COMING UP NEXT . . .

Students who have trouble with spelling and grammatical construction should not despair. They have ample company. If they hope to land good jobs in journalism, however, they should concentrate on overcoming this weakness, because many employers in the media judge applicants in part on these basic skills.

Citing dozens of embarrassing bloopers that have found their way into print, this chapter shows how even the best newspapers commit errors in use of the English language.

To help students polish up their usage of the language, the chapter includes a list of common errors in newspaper writing, compiled by the Associated Press Managing Editors Association for its members. In a section on sentences, the chapter explains how to achieve unity, clarity, and emphasis.

Finally, there is a 50-word spelling test that one newspaper gives to its newsroom applicants.

Chapter 10
Bedrock Assets: Grammar and Spelling

EMPHASIS ON BASIC SKILLS

A person who wants to be a reporter should have a good command of language. The best writer in the world would fail miserably as a reporter if the person lacked news sense, reportorial judgment, and the desire to go out and get the news. But even the best reporters in the world are going to be in trouble if they mix agreement of subjects and verbs, produce murky sentences, and are weak on spelling.

Writing skill, of course, is a prerequisite throughout the journalistic world. Executives of newspapers, magazines, broadcast stations, publishing houses, and advertising agencies all very early ask questions about the writing abilities of job candidates. They are really asking two questions. First, they want to know if the candidate possesses the imaginative qualities that are so necessary in journalism and that distinguish a good writer from a dull one. Second, they also want to know if the candidate has mastered the essentials of grammar and spelling.

Good journalistic writing is simply good writing. There is no such thing as *journalese,* a term of scorn sometimes applied to the work of the reporter. Writing sometimes labeled "journalese" is simply bad writing; the faults might include careless organization, sloppy sentences, incorrect usage, poor word choices (slang and clichés), and incomplete coverage. Neither the journalism professor nor the newspaper editor tolerates bad writing, any more than does the English composition teacher.

Attention to those bedrock assets of effective writing, grammar, and spelling waned during recent decades of challenge to social conventions, customs, and authority. Insistence upon niceties of word usage, spelling accuracy, and sentence clarity seemed impositions upon individual freedoms. The methodical study of grammar and holding of spelling drills declined in schoolrooms. So did the language ability scores of high school graduates. The result was rising concern among newspaper editors, expressed in their conventions and in trade journals. A flood of bad grammar, misspellings, mixed metaphors, redundancies, misused words, and jargon was impeding readers' ability to grasp the facts, offending sensibilities of educated subscribers and horrifying true language buffs.

Some of those buffs started coming to the rescue. The New York *Times* had begun distributing a publication called *Winners & Sinners* to its staff in 1951, started by the late Theodore Bernstein and continued by Allan Siegal. William Safire wrote a book about the problem and also his weekly column in the New York *Times* concerns grammar. NBC newscaster Edwin Newman also qualifies as a buff with his book, as does David Shaw, media critic of the Los Angeles *Times.*

Among newspapers distributing reports on writing, grammar, and spelling to their staffs by 1981 were the Washington *Post,* Boston *Globe,* San Jose *Mercury-News,* Miami *Herald,* and Milwaukee *Journal.* The St. Petersburg *Times* established a Modern Media Institute under the direction of Roy Peter Clark, an English professor and writing coach, to which newspapers throughout the country send reporters and editors. Knight-Ridder Newspapers, Inc., developed a comprehensive 3-hour test for copy desk applicants. Many newspapers give job candidates a spelling test—proper spelling is still a "thing" for many an editor (see elsewhere in this chapter the South Bend *Tribune*'s 50-word spelling quiz).

Here are some examples of what these concerned editors—and their unhappy readers—see in newspapers daily and weekly, large and small. The offending words in each example are set in italics.

BLUNDERS IN PRINT

- **Improper word usage:** "He was arraigned on charges of *negligible* homicide" (Boston *Globe*); "As the author of the column on federal benefits that has *illicited* such a volume of letters to the editor" (Indio, California *Daily News*); "efforts to keep Northern Virginia's *principle* reservoir from drying up" (Washington *Post*); "Dr. Russell G. Mawby will be the *principle* speaker" (South Bend *Tribune* joins in); "Charles argued that the two men should be tried for all three felonies *irregardless* of which one did which act" (Gallup, New Mexico *Independent*).

- **Agreement of pronouns:** "Dunn said this could be settled like gentlemen between *he* and Wright" (San Jose *Mercury-News*); "Gates' original statement, which caused a confrontation between *he* and Commissioner Joan Wells" (Santa Maria, California *Times*); "Yager opposed because he thought each supervisor would appoint *their* own members" (same *Times* staff member).
- **It's and its:** "Each company is able to make a deal on *it's* own" (Milford, Utah *Beaver County News*); "Work on the Tellico Dam had been halted when it was claimed *it's* completion could lead to the extinction of the fish" (Santa Barbara *News-Press*).
- **Subject and verb agreement:** "While the primary fear is that the uranium could fall into the hands of terrorists, NRC officials said the chances of the 265-plus pounds of uranium being cached in one place at one time *is* slim" (UPI story in Ventura, California *Star-Free Press*); "He said he didn't take a count, but there *was* 'quite a few' people in the bank, 'a line-up' " (Santa Maria, California *Times*).
- **Misleading sentence construction.** "A 30-year-old St. Petersburg man was found murdered by his parents in his home late Saturday" (St. Petersburg *Times*). His parents found his body. David Shaw reports that a Los Angeles *Times* copyeditor came across the phrase "He died in his home, Post Office Box 320-A."
- **Redundancy.** "The explosion occurred at 12:15 A.M. Sunday *morning*" (Cassopolis, Michigan *Vigilant*); "They celebrated their *50th* Golden Wedding Anniversary" (Santa Maria *Times,* which, it should be noted, is the hometown paper of one of the authors of this book and thus becomes especially vulnerable).

Lest you think that the elite organizations do not sin in matters of grammar and spelling, here are some examples from press associations:

- **The Associated Press.** "Kissinger also discloses in his memoirs that he tried to stop Time magazine from naming both *he* and Nixon . . . "; "Johnson *wracked* up several other awards"; "He said the official was not Brezhnev, *whom* a State Department official said is ill"; "Borg, the one-time boy wonder *whom* they say is made of ice and steel, won . . . "
- **The United Press International.** "Neither Newton nor Boilermakers' coach Lee Rose *are* particularly happy . . . "; "Scymanky survived because he may have *drank* more water than the others . . . "
- **The Copley News Service.** "Call her soon and invite her. This way, you are in control of the situation, not *her*" (a she-her error, but also a misleading sentence by the advice columnist).

The Los Angeles *Times,* according to David Shaw, during one week misused he for him, whom for who, was for were, were for was, would for will, and which for that. The New York *Times* was charged with misusing such words as refute, dilemma, barrage, ironically, who, and whom. And finally, the weekly trade journal, *Editor & Publisher,* printed among its too-frequent slipups this sentence about a food editors' convention where there was a speaker from the Tupperware company: "After a *Tupperwar* executive pitched the company's new product line, a food editor stood up and asked if *her's* was the only paper in which *t*upperware does not advertise."

Many of the blunders cited above would have been avoided had the reporters involved been more observant in their studies of the basic rules for writing and for word usage. Let us review briefly the precepts for writing acceptable sentences that are vital in the mastery of grammar.

SENTENCES

Good sentences have unity; they achieve clarity; and they transmit to the reader the emphasis that the writer intended. In concert, they have sufficient variety to be attractive to the reader.

Unity means the state of being one, or singleness. A properly written sentence containing a single statement that represents a complete thought is obviously unified. But unity also means the reference of all the elements to a single main idea. Complex and compound sentences containing two or more statements achieve unity only when they are written so that the reader is able to grasp a single main idea.

If, for example, two statements in a sentence are not closely related, sentence unity is violated and the reader is confused: "The natives of the country wear wooden shoes and are naturally hospitable." Not many would-be reporters make such an obvious error. But a good many have trouble with some aspect of the principle of subordination. When two statements are coordinate in importance, they are written in a coordinate form; but when one statement is less important, it must be subordinated if the reader is to grasp the main idea easily. The worst sin, of course, is to put the main idea in a subordinate construction, either as a dependent clause or as a participial phrase.

An example of incorrect subordination of a coordinate idea would be writing "Educated at Harvard, he became a professor at California in 1980" instead of "He was educated at Harvard and became a professor at California in 1980." An example of failure to subordinate a less important statement is: "The school board meeting ended at 9 P.M., but none of the members would discuss the decision reached." A better version would be: "None of the school board members would discuss the decision reached at the meeting, which ended at 9 P.M." An example of improper subordination of the main idea would be: "He was walking through the alley behind the house when he saw the body of the dead girl." The "when" should open the sentence, or the two parts should be reversed.

Clarity is lost when the writer changes the pattern of a sentence by failing to observe rules of grammar. The literate reader expects to find parallel construction within a sentence. And the reader does not expect to find dangling modifiers, inconsistent enumerations, or widely separated subjects and verbs.

Parallel construction means that for a like meaning there must be a like construction; the same grammatical forms and parts of speech must be used in pairs or series. Some examples of errors are italicized in the following sentences:

- "Johnson denied the *murder* and *dumping* the body in the ditch." Noun and gerund are not parallel.
- "The dean said he would appoint a committee *to review* the salary scale and another *for studying* promotion policies." Infinitive and gerund are not parallel.

A dangling modifier is a modifier that cannot be connected immediately and unmistakably with an antecedent in the same sentence. Dangling participles, gerunds, and infinitives create some of the "slips that pass in the dark" in newspapers; they also annoy the reader. The most usual mistake is to open a sentence with a modifier that implies a subject and then not to follow with the subject. Some typical danglers are:

- "After considering the problem, a vote was taken." The subject of the modifier, "they," is missing.
- "To hold the paper in place, the thumb must be placed against it." The subject of the modifier, "you," is missing.

A sports reporter ruined an otherwise good baseball story for sensitive readers by managing to combine a dangling modifier and nonagreement of subject and verb in a single sentence:

> But that last Spartan effort had the fans on their feet. After disposing of the first two batters in easy fashion, an infield error and a hit batsman was followed by a single by pinchhitter Ron Bietz.

This atrocity appeared in a metropolitan newspaper. The reporter meant to say something like this:

```
But that last Spartan effort had the fans on their feet. After
Roberts had disposed of the first two batters in easy fashion, one
Spartan was safe on an infield error and another was hit by a pitched
ball. Pinchhitter Ron Bietz then hit a single.
```

Inconsistent enumeration occurs when a necessary "and" or "or" is omitted. "The new journalism building has offices, reporting and editing rooms." The sentence needs an "and" after "offices" instead of a comma.

Wide separation of subject and verb is not an outright error, but it can be confusing to the reader. Rules of good writing call for the verb to follow the subject as closely as possible. Long sentences that open with a subject and close with a verb are always suspect. This is especially true if the intervening clauses are set apart by commas: "Johnson, who had been following the debate closely, and who had encouraged Smith to speak after speaking himself earlier on the motion, now again rose to answer." Two sentences would be better.

USAGE

A study committee of the Associated Press Managing Editors Association has compiled, for the benefit of its members, a list of "Common Errors in Newspaper Writing." This is a good, but by no means complete, catalogue of common errors in usage. It provides a useful checklist not only for newspaper people, but for anyone who writes.

Want to test your own accuracy in using the language? Here's the list:

1. *Affect, effect.* Generally, *affect* is the verb; *effect* is the noun. "The letter had a significant *effect.*" BUT *effect* is also a verb meaning *to bring about.* Thus: "*It is almost impossible to effect change.*"
2. *Afterward, afterwards.* Use *afterward.* The dictionary allows use of *afterwards* only as a second form.
    The same thinking applies to *toward* and *towards.* Use *toward.*
3. *All right.* That's the way to spell it. The dictionary may list *alright* as a legitimate word but it is not acceptable in standard usage, says Random House.
4. *Allude, elude.* You *allude to* (or mention) a book. You *elude* (or escape) a pursuer.
5. *Annual.* Don't use *first* with it. If it's the first time, it can't be annual.
6. *Averse, adverse.* If you don't like something, you are *averse* (or opposed) to it. *Adverse* is an adjective: Adverse (bad) weather, *adverse* conditions.
7. *Block, bloc.* A *bloc* is a coalition of persons or a group with the same purpose or goal. Do not call it a *block,* which has some 40 dictionary definitions.
8. *Compose, comprise.* Remember that the parts *compose* the whole and the whole *comprises* the parts. You *compose* things by putting them together. Once the parts are put together, the object *comprises* the parts.
9. *Couple of.* You need the *of.* It's never "a couple tomatoes."
10. *Demolish, destroy.* They mean to do away with *completely.* You can't partially demolish or destroy something, nor is there any need to say *totally destroyed.*
11. *Different from.* Things and people are different *from* each other. Don't write that they are different *than* each other.
12. *Drown.* Don't say someone was *drowned* unless an assailant held the victim's head under water. Just say the victim drowned.
13. *Due to, owing to, because of.* We prefer the last.

- Wrong: The game was canceled *due to* rain.
- Stilted: *Owing to* rain, the game was canceled.
- Right: The game was canceled *because of* rain.

14. *Ecology, environment.* They are not synonymous. *Ecology* is the study of the relationship between organisms and their *environment.*
    - Right: The laboratory is studying the *ecology* of man and the desert.
    - Right: There is much interest in animal *ecology* these days.
    - Wrong: Even so simple an undertaking as maintaining a lawn affects our *environment.*
15. *Either.* It means one or the other, not both.
    - Wrong: There were lions on *either* side of the door.
    - Right: There were lions on *each* side of the door.
16. *Fliers, flyers.* Airmen are *fliers.* Handbills are *flyers.*
17. *Flout, flaunt.* They aren't the same words: they mean completely different things and they're very commonly confused. *Flout* means to mock, to scoff or to show disdain for. *Flaunt* means to display ostentatiously.
18. *Funeral service.* A redundant expression. A funeral *is* a service.
19. *Head up.* People don't *head up* committees. They *head* them.
20. *Hopefully.* One of the most commonly misused words, in spite of what the dictionary may say. *Hopefully* should describe the way the subject *feels.*

    For instance:

    Hopefully, I shall present the plan to the president. (This means I will be hopeful when I do it.)

    But it is something else again when you attribute hope to a non-person. You may write: Hopefully, the war will end soon. This means you hope the war will end soon, but it is not what you are writing. What you mean is: I hope the war will end soon.

21. *Imply* and *infer.* The speaker implies. The hearer infers.
22. *In advance* or *prior to.* Use before; it sounds more natural.
23. *It's, its. Its* is the possessive; *it's* is the contraction of it is.
    - Wrong: What is *it's* name?
    - Right: What is *its* name? *Its* name is Fido.
    - Right: *It's* the first time he's scored tonight.
    - Right: *It's* my coat.
24. *Lay, lie. Lay* is the action word: *lie* is the state of being.
    - Wrong: The body will *lay* in state until Wednesday.
    - Right: The body will *lie* in state until Wednesday.
    - Right: The prosecutor tried to *lay* the blame on him.

    However, the past tense of *lie* is *lay.*
    - Right: The body *lay* in state from Tuesday until Wednesday.
    - Wrong: The body *laid* in state from Tuesday until Wednesday.

    The past participle and the plain past tense of *lay* is *laid.*
    - Right: He *laid* the pencil on the pad.
    - Right: He *had laid* the pencil on the pad.
    - Right: The hen *laid* an egg.
25. *Leave, let. Leave alone* means to depart from or cause to be in solitude. *Let alone* means to be undisturbed.
    - Wrong: The man had pulled a gun on her but Mr. Jones intervened and talked him into *leaving her alone.*

- Right: The man had pulled a gun on her but Mr. Jones intervened and talked him into *letting her alone.*
- Right: When I entered the room I saw that Jim and Mary were sleeping so I decided to *leave them alone.*

26. *Less, fewer.* If you can separate items in the quantities being compared, use *fewer.* If not, use *less.*
    - Wrong: The Rams are inferior to the Vikings because they have *less* good linemen.
    - Right: The Rams are inferior to the Vikings because they have *fewer* good linemen.
    - Right: The Rams are inferior to the Vikings because they have *less* experience.

27. *Like, as.* Don't use *like* for *as* or *as if.* In general, use *like* to compare with nouns and pronouns; use *as* when comparing with phrases and clauses that contain a verb.
    - Wrong: Jim blocks the linebacker *like* he should.
    - Right: Jim blocks the linebacker *as* he should.
    - Right: Jim blocks *like* a pro.

28. *Marshall, marshal.* Generally, the first form is correct only when the word is a proper noun: John *Marshall.* The second form is the verb form: Marilyn will *marshal* her forces.

    And the second form is the one to use for a title: *Fire Marshal* Stan Anderson, *Field Marshal* Erwin Rommel.

29. *Mean, average, median:* Use *mean* as synonymous with *average.* Each word refers to the sum of all components divided by the number of components. *Median* is the number that has as many components above it as below it.

30. *Nouns.* There's a growing trend toward using them as verbs. Resist it. *Host, headquarters,* and *author,* for instance, are nouns, even though the dictionary may acknowledge they can be used as verbs. If you do, you'll come up with a monstrosity like: "Headquartered at his country home, John Doe hosted a party to celebrate the book he had authored."

31. *Oral, verbal.* Use *oral* when use of the mouth is central to the thought: the word emphasizes the idea of human utterance. *Verbal* may apply to spoken or written words; it connotes the process of reducing ideas to writing. Usually, it's a *verbal* contract, not an *oral* one, if it's in writing.

32. *Over* and *more than.* They aren't interchangeable. *Over* refers to spatial relationships: The plane flew over the city. *More than* is used with figures: In the crowd were more than 1,000 fans.

33. *Peddle, pedal.* When selling something, you *peddle* it. When riding a bicycle or similar form of locomotion, you *pedal* it.

34. *Pretense, pretext.* They're different, but it's a tough distinction. A *pretext* is that which is put forward to conceal a truth.

    He was discharged for tardiness, but this was only a *pretext* for general incompetence.

    A *pretense* is a "false show": a more overt act intended to conceal personal feelings.

    My profuse compliments were all *pretense.*

35. *Principle, principal.* A guiding rule or basic truth is a principle. The first,

dominant, or leading thing is *principal*. *Principle* is a noun: *principal* may be a noun or an adjective.
- Right: It's the *principle* of the thing.
- Right: Liberty and justice are two *principles* on which our nation is founded.
- Right: Hitting and fielding are the *principal* activities in baseball.
- Right: Robert Jamieson is the school *principal*.

36. *Refute*. The word connotes success in argument and almost always implies an editorial judgment.
    - Wrong: Father Bury *refuted* the arguments of the pro-abortion faction.
    - Right: Father Bury responded to the arguments of the pro-abortion faction.

37. *Reluctant, reticent*. If he doesn't want to act, he is *reluctant*. If he doesn't want to speak, he is *reticent*.

38. *Temperatures*. They may get higher or lower, but they don't get warmer or cooler.

39. *That, which*. *That* tends to restrict the reader's thought and direct it the way you want it to go: *which* is non-restrictive, introducing a bit of subsidiary information. For instance:

    The lawnmower that is in the garage needs sharpening. (Meaning: We have more than one lawnmower. The one in the garage needs sharpening.)
    The lawnmower, which is in the garage, needs sharpening. (Meaning: Our lawnmower needs sharpening. It's in the garage.)

    Note that *which* clauses take commas, signaling they are not essential to the meaning of the sentence.

40. *Under way,* not underway. But don't say something got under way. Say it *started* or *began*.

41. *Unique*. Something that is unique is the only one of its kind. It can't be very unique or quite unique or somewhat unique or rather unique. Don't use it unless you really mean unique.

42. *Up*. Don't use it as a verb.
    - Wrong: The manager said he would *up* the price next week.

43. *Who, whom*. A tough one, but generally you're safe to use *whom* to refer to someone who has been the object of an action. *Who* is the word when the somebody has been the actor:

    A 19-year-old woman, to *whom* the room was rented, left the window open.
    A 19-year-old woman, *who* rented the room, left the window open.

44. *Who's, whose*. Though it incorporates an apostrophe, *who's* is not a possessive. It's a contraction for *who is*. *Whose* is the possessive.
    - Wrong: I don't know *who's* coat it is.
    - Right: I don't know *whose* coat it is.
    - Right: Find out *who's* there.

45. *Would*. Be careful about using *would* when constructing a conditional past tense.
    - Wrong: If Soderholm *would not have had* an injured foot, Thompson wouldn't have been in the lineup.
    - Right: If Soderholm *had not had* an injured foot, Thompson wouldn't have been in the lineup.

For a final drill on usage, the following two lists are vouched for by David Shaw of the Los Angeles *Times.* You may want to check in your dictionary!

Here are the dozen words that newspaper editors say their papers most often use incorrectly: *dilemma, egregious, enormity, fortuitous, fulsome, hopefully, ironically, penultimate, portentous, presently, quintessential,* and *unique.*

Here are the pairs of words that newspapers most often mix up and misuse:

- *abdicate* and *abrogate*
- *adverse* and *averse*
- *affect* and *effect*
- *alleged* and *intended*
- *allude* and *elude*
- *allusion* and *illusion*
- *breach* and *breech*
- *composed* and *comprised*
- *convince* and *persuade*
- *continually* and *continuously*
- *disinterested* and *uninterested*
- *flaunt* and *flout*
- *gantlet* and *gauntlet*
- *imply* and *infer*
- *lay* and *lie*
- *lectern* and *podium*
- *nauseated* and *nauseous*
- *noisy* and *noisome*
- *pore* and *pour*
- *precipitate* and *precipitous*
- *prostate* and *prostrate*
- *rebut* and *refute*
- *who* and *whom*

1. Circle any word improperly spelled:

playwright	accomodate	committment
embarrass	hemmorhage	permissable
ambivalance	decongestant	barbituate
lien	mispell	supercede
exhorbitant	ecstasy	impostor
excell	omission	sustenance
metalic	nonchalant	permissible
judgment	attorneys	liason
defendant	gauge	harassment
		questionaire

2. Delete the incorrect form within the parentheses:

The man spent his day off just (laying, lying) around the apartment.

This country needs (fewer, less) critics and (fewer, less) criticism.

The tramp took only a (couple, couple of) apples and tangerines.

He found his companions to be (alright, all right).

Let's not forget the (affect, effect) this will have on our neighbors.

An excerpt from a language knowledge and usage test given to job applicants by members of the Associated Press Managing Editors.

The City Editor Says: Spell Those Names Correctly

Misspelled names and wrong addresses are among the most frequent and irritating mistakes in news stories. It is the reporter's responsibility to get them right. Make an extra effort to check a name and address when it is given to you.

For example, you are interviewing an eyewitness to an accident and ask his name and address.

He replies hurriedly, "Ed MacNeil, 642 Grand." Those simple words are full of traps for the careless reporter. Does Ed stand for Edward, Edwin, or Edgar? Which of the six frequent spellings of his last name does he use—MacNeil, McNeil, McNeill, McNiel, McNeal, or Macneil? Is that 642 address on South, North, East, or West Grand? And is it a street, avenue, place, or boulevard?

Or perhaps the name he gives sounds like Meyer. It might also be Myer, Meier, or Mayer, and it may possibly have an "s" at the end. The optional "O" and "E" in Scandinavian names is a source of trouble. Is it Peterson or Petersen? Other typical and rather common name difficulties include Stuart or Stewart, Philip or Phillip, Francis or Frances, Marian or Marion. There are many others. Every city desk has its own danger list of unusual spellings of local names frequently in the news.

SPELLING

Fortunate is the young reporter who has been drilled in spelling, who has learned the "i before e except . . . " routine and other aids to learning spelling patterns, who has been trained never to guess but to look the word up in the dictionary, and who finally has mastered some of the "spelling demons" that veteran news editors love to spring upon unsuspecting colleagues and friends. The former publisher of the Hartford *Courant* kept a list of 50 such elusive words in his pocket to pull out at after-dinner drinking sessions to harass (harrass?) or embarrass (embarass?) those who were willing to accommodate (accomodate?) his idiosyncrasy (idiosincracy?). If you are wondering, the first spelling is the correct one in each case.

Part of a test given applicants for reporting jobs at the South Bend *Tribune* is a spelling test. Applicants are given 10 minutes to run through a list of 50 words. The instructions read: "Some words are spelled correctly, others are not. In the space after each word, place a check mark if the word is spelled correctly. If it is not, print the correct spelling in the proper space. A space left blank is considered an incorrect answer."

Here is the *Tribune's* list of words. Write down the numbers of the misspelled words. Afterward, do some practicing with memorizing such commonly misspelled words as "accommodate." You will have many opportunities to put the extra "m" into another's copy.

1. assessment
2. sherriff
3. synonomous
4. phenomenon
5. hemorrhage
6. guage
7. observent
8. abreviate
9. permanant
10. rarified
11. occassion
12. questionarie
13. accomodate
14. occurrence
15. comparatively
16. exhorbitant
17. subpoena
18. preponderence
19. proceedure
20. diptheria
21. arraignment
22. disastrous
23. municiple
24. indictment
25. separately
26. embarass
27. coroner
28. misspell
29. committment
30. recommend
31. sizible
32. seize
33. subsidary
34. conscience
35. liaison
36. rhumba
37. naptha
38. comparable
39. weild
40. infallable
41. resurrection
42. deductable
43. possession
44. restaurateur
45. weird
46. sargeant
47. barrel
48. perennial
49. incredable
50. parallel

STUDY PROJECTS

1. Circle any word in the following list that is spelled incorrectly:

- playwright
- embarrass
- ambivalance
- lien
- exhorbitant
- excell
- metalic
- judgment
- defendant

- accomodate
- hemmorhage
- decongestant
- mispell
- ecstasy
- omission
- nonchalant
- attorneys
- gauge

- committment
- permissable
- barbituate
- supercede
- impostor
- sustenance
- permissible
- liason
- harassment
- questionaire

2. Delete the incorrect form within the parentheses in each of the following sentences:

- The man spent his day off just (laying, lying) around the apartment.
- This country needs (fewer, less) critics and (fewer, less) criticism.
- The tramp took only a (couple, couple of) apples and tangerines.
- He found his companions to be (alright, all right).
- Let's not forget the (affect, effect) this will have on our neighbors.
- The game was canceled (because of, due to) rain.
- The small town was (ravaged, ravished) by the rampaging river.
- I didn't mean to (imply, infer) you are a crook.
- I am (eager, anxious) to go.
- His appearance was different (than, from) the mayor's.

- Wilson was (hung, hanged) for murder despite his appeal.
- Lettuce Inn will soon be the oldest place in town that has been (continuously, continually) in business.
- I went to the store to buy some (stationary, stationery).
- Our (principal, principle) business is to pass the law.
- It might have an (adverse, averse) (affect, effect) on our sales.
- The candidate was (convinced, persuaded) to change his position.
- The smell left him (nauseous, nauseated).
- Let us not (flount, flaunt) our superiority.
- The reason given was only a (pretense, pretext) for general incompetence.
- He was (censored, censured) for his failure to follow through.

The lists in Projects 1 and 2 were published in the *APME News*.

3. Bring to class three stories from newspapers that contain a misspelled word or a grammatical error.

READ MORE ABOUT IT . . .

R. Thomas Berner, *Language Skills for Journalists* (Boston: Houghton Mifflin, 1978).

E. L. Callihan, *Grammar for Journalists* (Radnor, Pa.: Chilton, 1979).

Robert Gilboy, *Spell It Fast: The Quick Way to Spell Using 60 Stimulating Word Lists* (Washington, D.C.: Acropolis, 1981).

COMING UP NEXT . . .

The primary objective of effective writing is clarity. When news stories stagger along with inept phraseology and vague, loosely constructed sentences, the writers fail in their assigned mission to communicate information and ideas. Every reporter should attempt to develop a writing style in which clarity of expression and gracefulness of phraseology are evident.

This chapter offers eight guidelines that will improve your writing. Each point is explained carefully and illustrated with examples from stories published in newspapers.

As you study this chapter, observe how successful writers achieve effects by including descriptive details, how they tell a story with vigorous verbs rather than adjectives, and how they trim out unnecessary words and phrases. Notice too how they vary their sentence structure and brighten their copy with colorful figures of speech.

Chapter 11
Developing a Writing Style

CLARITY IS THE PRIMARY GOAL

When readers find themselves wading through a bog of muddled phraseology, they frequently abandon an ill-conceived story in frustration, thereby depriving themselves of important information. This need not happen if reporters use the relatively easy techniques available to help them develop an attractive writing style. Writing for newspapers and the other news media involves certain restrictions on reporters, primarily those of space, time, and objectivity. Yet within those boundaries the writer of journalistic prose can develop an individual style that shines with clarity, punches with vigor, and charms with grace.

Development of a writing style is an intensely personal matter. Style evolves from practice and reflects the personality of the writer. Ernest Hemingway's writing is terse, staccato. Charles Dickens wrote in a leisurely nineteenth-century style that seems elaborate today. William Faulkner's fiction is intricate and at times obscure. Yet each won literary renown. Although the young writer can profit from studying the styles of these and other eminent writers, attempts to imitate them make the beginner's work stilted and artificial.

Working under the strictures of newswriting, a reporter cannot indulge in all of the devices that novelists use to create their styles. A newswriter can, however, learn to deliver information and interpretation to the reader in a style that is flexible, easy to absorb, and touched with individuality.

Clarity is the primary goal. To achieve this, writing must be simple, specific, and uncluttered. Crispness, vigor, and illuminating detail are essential elements of good style. When clarity is further supplemented by vivid figures of speech and turns of phrase, the writing becomes not only a transmission conveyance for information, but also a source of pleasure in itself.

Many reporters stumble along on a plateau of monotony in their writing because they do not make the necessary effort to improve their style. Others, exhilarated by the heady wine of words, succumb to the sin of "fancy writing" that besets those who strain too hard for effect. Successful writing is never pompous or overstated.

EIGHT GUIDELINES TO IMPROVED WRITING

In this chapter we offer the following eight guidelines to help you improve your writing:

- **Inject details.** This gives the story texture. Help the reader to see, hear, and sniff what you are describing.
- **Be concise.** Trim the needless words from your sentences. Write in the active voice, only rarely in the passive. Lean writing makes strong reading.
- **Use vigorous action verbs and nouns.** Use adjectives sparingly; use only when they clarify a statement or supply a needed descriptive or limiting touch.
- **Avoid overcrowding.** Do not jam too much information into a single sentence. The clutter confuses the reader.
- **Strive for tempo in sentence structure.** Emphasize short declarative sentences, but judiciously mix in a few longer and inverted ones for variety and pace.
- **Seek originality in phraseology.** Apt figures of speech and clever turns of phrase give writing flair and zest. But avoid clichés.
- **Use quotations frequently.** Be certain that those you include are significant additions to the story, not just "puff" words.
- **Set scenes.** Especially when writing a long, complex article, establish scenes the way a novelist or dramatist does. This helps the reader to "see" a situation.

Let us examine each of these guidelines more carefully to see precisely how its use will produce better writing.

INJECT DETAILS

Search for and use the little touches that define personality and bring a situation alive. Be specific. Instead of writing, "She waved her hand," say which hand. And how did she wave it? "She waved her left hand with a flutter of fingers."

A beginning reporter working for a tough city editor who demands the telling detail soon finds himself or herself observing people and surroundings more keenly than previously. Stuart Dim of the Charlotte *Observer* has a revealing story about how he had the need for detail hammered home in his youthful reporting years at *Newsday*. The anecdote was repeated by Roy Peter Clark to the American Society of Newspaper Editors.

> About 20 years ago, I learned a great reporting lesson from Al Marlens, my managing editor at *Newsday*. He taught me about detail.
>
> I was covering a gangster's trial. I took pains to describe his gray sharkskin suit, his white-on-white shirt, his blue silk tie, his stickpin, his pinky ring. I was proud of the word picture I had painted, and I turned in my story.
>
> About three hours later—by now it was about midnight—Al came over and said, "Stu, not a bad story, but what about the handkerchief?"
>
> Handkerchief? Al told me he wondered whether the gangster also wore a handkerchief in his breast pocket. "Gee, Al, I don't think he wore a handkerchief."
>
> Al told me to call the man and ask him. Call a gangster at midnight to ask about his handkerchief? He had to be kidding. He wasn't. So I called.
>
> The gangster answered the telephone. I did some sweet fast-talking. Incredibly, the gangster agreed to walk to his closet and look at his suit jacket.
>
> "Yeah," he said, he had a handkerchief in his pocket.
>
> "What color?"
>
> "White."
>
> "How many points?"
>
> "Five."
>
> I went back to my typewriter and inserted the handkerchief information. Al Marlens stopped by my desk again and said, "Stu, now that's reporting."

Here are examples of how judiciously chosen detail can put color into a story. An Associated Press reporter covering a fatal shooting spree by a gunman at Rochester, New York, talked with an eyewitness who was narrowly missed by one of the gunman's bullets. The writer might merely have recorded that the eyewitness was making a delivery when the shots rang out. Instead, he specified "... who was delivering potato chips to a bar across the street from the bank." To describe the narrow escape, the writer quoted the deliveryman's words: "... felt wind go by my pants like an airgun. I looked down and there was a hole in my pants. After that, I ran."

Readers could readily identify with the deliveryman, visualizing themselves trapped in the same situation.

Notice the descriptive touches in this quick sketch of a California politician in an AP report from Sacramento:

> The Republican state senator from Arcadia with the *short gray hair, boyish grin* and *ample girth* favors *loose-fitting sweaters, suspenders* and *baggy pants* ...

Even better is this description by Jules Loh of the AP, writer of the popular "Elsewhere in America" feature stories. After a perceptive description of a woman that lets us visualize her, Loh comments with a striking figure of speech that makes us hear her as well:

> Her notion of senior citizenship, however, is premature. In appearance, she's *a slender 40* with *beauty-parlored hair high and wide, wet brown eyes, a chain talker* given to *dangly earrings* and *sparkly hand and wrist baubles.* She's a calliope in the oboe section.

Such a summary observation, supplementing straight physical description, adds a dimension of depth to feature reporting when done with the freshness of style Loh displays.

BE CONCISE

Good writing means tight writing, from which the fat of needless words has been pared. Even experienced writers find upon rereading their copy that it frequently contains excess baggage. With this trimmed out, the story is more concise and stronger.

The trimming process requires a little extra time and a willingness to impose self-criticism. If you do not tighten your story, a copydesk editor probably will do it for you, with loss of time for everyone concerned. A reputation in the newsroom for producing crisp copy that does not require laborious editing serves a reporter well when time for promotion comes along.

In Strunk and White's handbook, *The Elements of Style,* a gem that every writer should study, the point is made succinctly:

> Vigorous writing is concise. A sentence should contain no unnecessary words, a paragraph no unnecessary sentences, for the same reason that a drawing should have no unnecessary lines and a machine no unnecessary parts. This requires not that the writer make all his sentences short, or that he avoid all detail and treat his subjects only in outline, but that every word tell.

These are a few ways to remove waste wordage from your sentences:

- *Find single words* to replace phrases. Write "now" for "at this time" and "later" for "at a later day."
- *Write in the active voice,* not the passive, except in rare instances in which the passive voice makes the point more effectively.
- *Eliminate phrases containing clusters of prepositions,* such as "with the exception of." Use "except for" instead.
- *Strike empty, windy phrases* such as "needless to say" (if so, why say it?) and "It goes without saying."

- *Hold to a minimum* phrases beginning with "which," "who," and "that."
- *Beware of phrases that say the same thing twice.* For example, "future planning" (who ever heard of past planning?), "old adage" (all adages are old), and "Both parties met at the conference table" (it takes more than one party to hold a meeting, so, "The parties met at the conference table").

In the following sentences, observe how eliminating unnecessary words produces leaner prose.

"It was believed by police that the burglars in all probability forced their way through the rear door of the store with a crowbar." When the sentence is recast in the active voice and the excess baggage is removed, it is much stronger: "Police said that the burglars probably forced the rear door with a crowbar."

"The horses ~~that were~~ grazing in the field walked ~~in the direction of~~ toward the fence."

"~~A host of~~ city police and fire officers, aided by county, state, and federal investigators, are attempting ~~to gain~~ seeking additional evidence."

"Harold Powers, ~~who has been~~ a weatherwatcher here for three years, has been transferred . . ."

"~~In the event that it starts raining~~ If it rains during commencement services on the lawn, the ceremony will be moved into the gymnasium."

The power of brief, evocative sentences is demonstrated in the advertisement published in *The Wall Street Journal* by United Technologies under the headline "Keep it simple."

- Strike three.
- Get your hand off my knee.
- You're overdrawn.
- Your horse won.
- Yes.
- No.
- You have the account.
- Walk.
- Don't walk.
- Mother's dead.
- Basic events require simple language.
- Idiosyncratically euphuistic eccentricities are the promulgators of triturable obfuscation.
- What did you do last night?
- Enter into a meaningful

- romantic involvement or fall in love?
- What did you have for breakfast this morning?
- The upper part of a hog's hind leg with two oval bodies encased in a shell laid by a female bird or ham and eggs?
- David Belasco, the great American theatrical producer, once said, "If you can't write your idea on the back of my calling card, you don't have a clear idea."

USE VIGOROUS ACTION VERBS AND NOUNS

Writers whose prose is vigorous build their sentences on verbs and nouns. These make a sentence move. Three descriptive adjectives piled onto the back of a noun will not accomplish nearly as much as a vivid verb.

Mark Twain wrote, "Whenever you see an adjective, kill it." Although he exaggerated, because adjectives used sparingly are essential at times, the tendency of beginning writers to employ adjectives excessively muddles their writing. If the chosen verb does not seem to give quite the impact you desire, try to supplement it with an adverb rather than tacking adjectives onto a noun in the sentence.

In this passage from *Life on the Mississippi,* in which Twain describes a steamboat crossing a sandbar in low water, see how he follows his own precept:

> We touched bottom! Instantly Mr. Bixby set a lot of *bells ringing, shouted* through the tube, "Now, let her have it—every ounce you've got!" then to his partner, "Put her hard down! *Snatch* her! *Snatch* her!" The boat *rasped* and *ground* her way through the sand, *hung* upon the *apex of disaster* a single tremendous instant, and then over she went! And such a shout as went up at Mr. Bixby's back never *loosened* the roof of a pilot-house before.

When Samuel Clemens as Mark Twain wrote *Life on the Mississippi,* he was a literary figure not concerned with the pressures of daily deadlines. Writing in a hurry, we often fall into wordiness and trite word patterns that might be avoided if we had more time. At least, that is the excuse some writers use. So, let us look at a splendid example of writing done under extreme pressure that sings with action and intensity. This is an excerpt from Merriman Smith's memorable story on the assassination of President John F. Kennedy in Dallas on November 22, 1963. The United Press International White House correspondent won a Pulitzer

Prize for the dispatch. Smith was riding in the pool press car behind Kennedy's car in the cavalcade moments before the shooting.

> Everybody in our car began *shouting* at the driver to pull up closer to the President's car. But at the moment, we saw the big bubbletop and a motorcycle escort *roar* away at high speed.
>
> We *screamed* at the driver, "Get going, get going!" We *careened* around the Johnson car and its escort and set out down the highway, barely able to keep in sight of the President's car and the accompanying Secret Service follow-up car.
>
> They *vanished* around a curve. When we *cleared* the same curve, we could see where we were heading—Parkland Hospital, a large brick structure to the left of the arterial highway. We *skidded* around a sharp left turn and *spilled* out of the pool car as it entered the hospital driveway.
>
> I *ran* to the side of the bubbletop.
>
> The President was face-down on the back seat.

Here is reporting with immense impact, yet almost stark in its simplicity.

Smith's story described a moment of historical crisis, laden with physical action. Richard Ben Cramer of the Philadelphia *Inquirer* won a Pulitzer Prize for his report of a walk in 1978 through the no-man's land of southern Lebanon, between the Israeli and Palestine Liberation Organization lines. Action was loud in the background, but immediately around him were silence and fear. In this excerpt, observe how Cramer, like Smith, uses short words, brief sentences, and lively verbs, with hardly an adjective to be found:

> Here, everything *is frozen* in time, like a Pompeii without the lava. Crates of oranges *are stacked*, unattended, next to empty houses. Telephone wires *dangle* broken and useless from their poles. An open spigot *pours* an endless stream of water onto a swamp that once was a garden.
>
> Here, the mere *whoosh* of a breeze through the leaves can make you *sprint* for cover, *scanning* the sky for warplanes until you *dive* into the orange groves . . . only to emerge later feeling foolish and shaky from the rush of adrenaline.
>
> To be sure, there is noise and plenty of it. There are real planes and antiaircraft guns nearby. Artillery blasts *thudding* on the hillsides make the sheep *bleat* and the frogs *wail* in the ditches.
>
> But it takes man's noise to break the stillness—a *child's cry,* an engine, or a laugh. And without man, the *eeriness* is unrelieved in this world between two worlds.

A word of caution: When seeking distinctive verbs, avoid those the saboteurs of the language have created from nouns. This is one of the sins of computer talk; users write such things as "First, access the data bank" and "The new software will impact the programming techniques." Equally, a reporter writing for general readership must shun the jargon of special groups, which abounds in such obscure terminology as the sociologist's "typology of adaptive modes" and the educationist's "input of meaningful experience."

AVOID OVERCROWDING

Sentences that contain too many ideas are difficult for the reader to digest. They should be thinned out, much as a shrub is pruned. Elements that are removed because they are extraneous to the main thrust of the sentence can be recast in additional sentences.

One bad habit that causes overcrowding is using a "which" clause. Using "which" as a peg, either within a sentence or at its end, the writer introduces subsidiary material that obstructs the flow of the main idea. This is especially deadly when used to jam more information into a lead.

In this example, the "which" tacks a trailer onto the end of the sentence:

> Sailing around the world every 90 minutes, astronauts John W. Young and Robert L. Crippen today prepare the Columbia for the demanding and potentially hazardous ride home on Tuesday, which will be the first time in 20 years of manned space flight that a spaceship has returned from space and landed like an airplane.

Better style would be to end the sentence after "Tuesday." Then substitute "This" for "which" and we have a new sentence that delivers the second idea in easily digestible form.

Here is an instance, cited by Jack Cappon, general news editor of the Associated Press, in the *AP Log,* where the "which" clause occurs in midsentence with equally confusing results:

> The survey, which zeroed in on operations of the community college system and drug abuse programs, pointed out the need for improved financial management, particularly in the preparation of accurate financial statements and improved billing procedures.

Again, as Cappon points out, breaking the long sentence into two short ones makes the material more easily comprehended. He suggests this form:

> The survey focused on the community college system and drug abuse program. It pointed out the need for improved financial management, particularly in the preparation of financial statements and in billing procedures.

Further illustrating the perils of overcrowding, Cappon quotes this mouthful from an AP story:

The records show that the recruiter made calls from his Austin, Tex. office to the police department and the Angelina County district attorney's office in Lufkin, Tex.,	Nov. 12, 1975, according to the Marines, who also say a third call was made to the county sheriff's office but there is no telephone receipt to prove it.

Get out your blue pencil and chop that one down to size!

Two seductive little enemies in the fight against overloaded sentences are the conjunctions *and* and *but*. Whenever you see one of them tying together two thoughts in a sentence, ask yourself, "Is that word really necessary?" Most times it is not. End the sentence where the "and" or "but" occurs and start a new sentence.

A third bad habit that produces overcrowding is using the non sequitur; that is, linking illogical and unrelated facts in a sentence. This happens usually when a writer tries to work in background material inconspicuously, only to end up with a contrived and clumsy sentence. For example:

```
Born in Denver, Ross scored 20 points or more in eight games this
season.
```

Each of these facts is relevant to the player's biography, but they do not belong together.

STRIVE FOR TEMPO IN SENTENCE STRUCTURE

The declarative sentence is the foundation of good writing: direct, compact, and easily comprehended. When you analyze a well-written news story, you will find a large number of sentences of this type. Yet, if the story were composed only of sentences that start with the subject, then have a verb and an object, the copy would seem flat and monotonous. A change of pace is needed to give the writing rhythm.

This can be achieved by varying the length of the sentences, as well as using an occasional sentence that opens with a dependent clause. If you write a long sentence, follow it as soon as possible with a crisp one of less than ten words. Be careful not to fall into a repetitious pattern of sentences that run about 30 or 35 words each.

Transitional devices are needed at times for paragraph and sentence openings, and they also give variety to the story. In the following excerpt from a dispatch reporting a Senate subcommittee hearing on regulation of labor unions, two transitions, indicated by italics, turn the story in new directions:

> Hardenbrook, vice president of Union Bag-Camp Paper Corp., said regulation of union internal affairs—proposed in several bills before the subcommittee—might become less necessary if his far-reaching proposals were adopted.
>
> *Another witness,* Theodore Iserman, New York attorney specializing in labor relations matters, also urged action in the three fields cited by Hardenbrook.
>
> Iserman, who said he had represented many employers in labor cases, asserted "the need for the reforms I favor has been clear for years."
>
> *However,* the subcommittee has indicated it is not going into some of the major issues raised by Hardenbrook and Iserman. . . .

Compound and complex sentences occur naturally in all writing and provide change of pace in stories composed mainly of simple sentences. Sentences containing semicolons offer variety, but are used less often in newswriting than in essay writing. The dash often is used instead. Interrogative sentences sometimes fit the subject matter of a story; imperative and exclamatory sentences are suitable less often. When they are used, they offer deviations from the declarative sentence pattern.

Some editors attempt to enforce a maximum word limit on sentences, posting an edict that no sentence in a news story should be more than 30 words long, or some similar arbitrary length. Their purpose is commendable, but the limit is not entirely realistic. Occasionally, a long sentence, when simply constructed, is the best way to handle a set of facts such as a list of participants in an event. Sentences of 20 words or fewer give a story punch.

When you describe an action such as a police pursuit or a tense moment in a basketball game, use a staccato series of short sentences. Sprinkle in some phrases. This gives the feeling of fast movement. Film directors use the same principle in showing a chase sequence by fast cuts from one participant to another.

Here is an example from a story of a tense basketball game:

> Only 12 seconds remained. Trailing by one point, the Lions had the ball under their own basket. Clark lofted a pass over the fingertips of a Warrior defender to McGowan in midcourt. McGowan flicked it to Sanders. Back to McGowan. Over to Leonard in the far corner. As the clock showed 2 seconds, Leonard dribbled once, pivoted and arched a soft 15-footer that slid through the net without touching the rim. Then the gun. The Lions had won, 78–77.

SEEK ORIGINALITY IN PHRASEOLOGY

By using figures of speech, similes, and allusions, a resourceful writer adds zest to copy. Comparison of the thing you are describing with something readers know well helps them to visualize the object or scene.

- "And lodgings, as they once were referred to in these parts, are harder to find than a gold nugget." (San Francisco *Chronicle* story about a murder trial in a little Mother Lode town.)
- "A row of tents stretched like a finger from the village into the rolling brown desert dunes." (William Mullen in the Chicago *Tribune*.)
- "The defendants came on like Chinese wrestlers bellowing and making hideous faces as if to frighten the prosecutors to death." (Mary McGrory in the Washington *Star* about the Watergate trial.)

Allusions to Biblical and ancient historical events are a favorite device of some writers, especially those anxious to display their erudition. Danger, however, lurks here. Alluding to Las Vegas as a modern Sodom and Gomorrah may seem apt to some readers of a newspaper story, but others will wonder, "What are they?" Be sure that when you use an allusion, it refers to something that readers at varying educational levels will understand. If you are in doubt, add some explanatory words.

Here is a cleverly conceived indirect allusion that has a lilt of its own, even if some readers fail to realize that it paraphrases a nursery rhyme. Gregory Jensen of United Press International, writing from London, described the unusual jobs done by behind-the-scenes workers in preparation for the wedding of Prince Charles and Lady Diana Spencer. One sentence read:

| In a downstairs room of a 440-year-old stately home, Robert Gooden and Janice Rushen cod- | dled the worms that spun the thread that wove the silk that went into the dress that Di wears. |

At the other end of the spectrum from such fresh writing lies that menace, the cliché. In their search for figures of speech, careless writers turn to phrases made trite by overuse. Although effective when new, these weary phrases weaken a story rather than strengthen it. If you are tempted to write the following, don't!

"As comfortable as an old shoe . . . hailstones the size of golfballs . . . struck like a bolt of lightning . . . leave no stone unturned . . . as American as apple pie . . . quick as an arrow . . . turned a cold shoulder . . . let the chips fall where they may."

Also in the rogue's gallery of clichés are such grossly overworked terms as *high-speed chase, long black limousine, ill-fated journey, beautiful blonde,* and *sultry brunette,* as well as the words *dramatic, spectacular, thrilling, marvelous,* and *historic.*

Be careful, too, that the figures of speech you use make sense, that they do not misfire like this classic blunder: "A lot of people are running around with their heads in the sand."

USE QUOTATIONS FREQUENTLY

Direct quotations scattered through a story help to move it along and make it attractive to the eye. They should be used judiciously, however. To merit inclusion, a quotation should accomplish a purpose. It may describe an action, express an opinion, show a person's state of mind, define a situation, or shed light on a personality. If the quotation repeats in fuller form what already has been stated in the lead, it should be omitted because it wastes space. For example:

```
  Police said today the bomb explosion that destroyed a car parked on
a West Side residential street Monday night probably was
drug-related.
  No suspects have been arrested in the bombing outside 751 W.
Woodridge Ave. shortly before midnight, but police seek one man for
questioning.
  "We are almost certain that the blast was related to the drug
situation in the city," Sgt. Robert Slater said.
```

In this case, the quotation in the third paragraph adds nothing to the lead and should have been left out. Had the sergeant told what he thought the relationship was—a double cross in a marijuana deal, for example—that would have been a valuable quotation to include.

For emphasis, we repeat some of the advice given in earlier chapters about the use of quotations.

Quotations in news stories should be brief, preferably only a sentence or two at a time. The best way to cover an extensive amount of copy containing quotable material is to alternate paragraphs that have quotes with paragraphs that paraphrase. Frequently, a thought can be presented more concisely in paraphrased form than in direct quotation.

The practice of using partial quotations—a few words lifted from a sentence—is commonplace, but should be followed sparingly. When too many fragmentary quotes appear in a story, a jerky, incomplete effect results. Beginning writers in particular tend to use fragments inside quotation marks when the words could be written as effectively without the marks. A partial quotation should be used in a lead only when it is sufficiently distinctive to enhance the impact of the sentence.

Should a direct quotation ever be used alone as the entire lead of a story? Some editors reject such leads; they consider them a weak form that leaves readers puzzled until they read on far enough to discover who said the words and why. On rare occasions, however, this method is justified because of the shock effect it has on the reader. For example:

```
  "He leaned over me with the gun and pretended to pull the trigger."
Nancy Miller gasped with remembered terror as she told how an
```

escaped convict who invaded her home threatened to kill her unless she gave him the keys to her car.

Starting a story with that vivid quotation grabs the reader's attention far more intensely than a straight lead such as this:

Nancy Miller told today how an escaped convict who invaded her home threatened to kill her unless she gave him the keys to her car.

Attribution of quotations can be a problem. Either the writer does not do it clearly enough for the reader to be certain who is speaking or does it excessively, thereby impeding the flow of the story. The first quoted sentence must carry an attribution. If a further quote follows immediately and clearly is a continuation of statements made by the same speaker, the attribution may be omitted, as in this example:

"Unless the council permits construction of high rise apartments, this city will be unable to provide housing for the workers we need to employ in our new electronics plant," Mayor George Drewes said.
"The environmental purists who don't want tall buildings because they will obstruct the view of the mountains are being unrealistic."

Excessive attribution is frequently found in police stories by beginning writers, who put "police said" or "police reports showed" in every paragraph of an account of a crime. Instead, phrase the story so that subsequent paragraphs describing what happened are tied clearly to the first attribution showing the police as the source.

The basic verb used in attributing quotations is "said." Because excessive use of the same verb in a long story may become monotonous, some writers look for alternatives such as "stated," "declared," "asserted," "contended." Other verbs showing the manner in which words were spoken include "drawled," "stuttered," and "sputtered." Use of such alternatives can spice up a story, but the writer must be certain that the verb chosen is accurate. "Said" is neutral; "contended" implies an argumentive posture; "sputtered" records anger. Straining for an unusual verb of attribution results in exaggerated writing.

A useful technique when a story contains quotations from two or more individuals, especially when they are participating in a discussion, is to use a colon in place of a verb of attribution. Thus, after early paragraphs in which the speakers have been identified, the writer can do this:

Pritchard: "The practice of recruiting football players for college teams and giving them benefits other students don't receive cheapens the university that does it."

Harvey: "But the alumni want winning teams, and happy alumni make big gifts to the school."

Far too often, the quotations found in stories are too stilted or too polished to seem real. When reporters record direct statements from a speech or a document, they have no choice. In interviews, however, they should select from the mass of spoken material quotations that have a natural flavor, zest, and descriptive power. Such quotations as these give a story vigor:

- "The time that we think we can respond to cannons by pelting marshmallows is over."
- "I am not the most easy guy to get along with. If I don't like what a guy's done, I'll tell him. Unfortunately, my colleagues don't like that . . . I'm a very direct guy in an indirect world."
- "Most people don't intentionally invite intruders to ransack their homes, but they might as well have hung up a sign saying, 'Burglars welcome.'"
- "If I had the difference between what people think I have and what I actually have, I would be a rich man."

SET SCENES

One way to show the reader what you are reporting, rather than merely stating it, is to create scenes. These are the blocks with which a long story is built. The reader moves with you from scene to scene, watching a drama unfold or a problem being solved. When a scene is drawn with detail, including bits of irony or contrast, the reader is pulled inside the picture.

Hugh Mulligan of the Associated Press has a knack for keen observation that enables him to create sharply etched scenes in his stories. Discussing his technique in the *AP Log,* he asked other writers:

> If the hearing on your school budget is held in the high school gym do your readers see the board members at the tables under the backboards? Do they see the taxpayers up in the stands? The opposition rising near the foul line? Do they smell the varnish? What does the scoreboard say? Zero?—a nice touch if the budget is defeated. Did the reporters use all their powers of observation or did they just repeat the quotes?

Mulligan drew from his own experience this example—a story he wrote about the visit of Pope John Paul II to Ireland:

In Ireland the pope said Mass at a youth rally on the Galway Race Track. For the writer, as reporter, it wasn't enough to say the kids camped out all night in the rain. Did the readers see the glow of the Coleman stoves in that chilling fog, the huddle of sleeping bags in the track infield, the rucksacks and knapsacks garnished with buttons, "I peeked at the Pope"?

The pope at a race track, fancy that. I got there early, we all did, and had one of the race track stewards—not one of the bishops or priests—show me around. The helicopter pad where John Paul II would land was rimmed with flowers. I asked the steward what the area normally was. "The winner's circle," he replied. Wow, the pope in the winner's circle! Woo woo woo, as we say in Polish.

I asked where the tote board was. He said they had built the altar up over it. Not only that, but the pope put on his vestments in the jockeys' weighing-in room. The bishops vested in the paddock stables, which now had a different aroma: incense from the altar boys warming up their thuribles. The New York *Daily News,* which had two reporters at Galway, used my AP story under the heading: "Pope Wins, Places and Shows." Here the reporter had looked, listened, sniffed.

STUDY PROJECTS

1. Bring to class four published news stories in which you have underlined specific details the writer used to help the reader visualize an individual involved.

2. Edit the following sentences to remove needless words:

   a. The general concensus of opinion was that the new school building was the most unique in the city.
   b. What we need is more advance planning.
   c. Funeral services will be held at 2 P.M. tomorrow afternoon.
   d. He promised that all the proposals would be subjected to examination at a later date.
   e. His automobile was completely demolished.
   f. I want to take this opportunity to express my thanks to neighbors who painted my house when I was bedridden and unable to get around.
   g. Those who attend will receive free gifts.
   h. None of the suggestions that were offered from the audience, with the exception of one by John Leonard, won approval from the board.
   i. She was strangled to death in her bed.
   j. Each year an annual dinner is held to give honors to those who perform outstanding community service.

3. Alongside each of the following verbs and phrases, write a verb that is stronger or more colorful:

   a. Said loudly
   b. Walked slowly

    c. Defeated by a large score
    d. Flew high
    e. Moved briskly
    f. Criticized severely
    g. Deceived
    h. Moved unevenly
    i. Fell heavily
    j. Tossed lightly

READ MORE ABOUT IT . . .

William Strunk and E. B. White, *The Elements of Style,* 3rd ed. (New York: Macmillan, 1978).

William Zinsser, *On Writing Well,* 2nd ed. (New York: Harper & Row, 1980).

Rudolf Flesch, *The Art of Readable Writing,* 25th anniversary ed. (New York: Harper & Row, 1974).

COMING UP NEXT . . .

Using the feature approach in writing is like coming in the side door. The hard spot news story charges in head-on, whereas the feature story sidles in obliquely, "hooking" the reader with a clever angle. This chapter explains when a straight news approach is best and when a feature approach works well.

The soft style can be used either for featurized treatment of spot news or for a feature "situationer" or interview that contains no current news elements at all. We examine both types of feature treatment by studying published examples. These illustrate how a story written in flat news style can be brought to life and vastly improved when given a feature treatment.

Scene-setting is an effective feature opening under some circumstances. Developing an unusual point of view is another. A detailed analysis of a successful feature story shows how it was organized.

Chapter 12
The Feature Approach

VARYING THE WRITING

A major league baseball pitcher wins by keeping the batters on edge with a tantalizing mixture of pitches. Successful newspapers do much the same thing. Instead of delivering all the day's news content to their readers in taut straight news style—call it the equivalent of the pitcher's high, hard fastball—wise editors mix up their presentation with stories written in a softer, featurized style. This prevents monotony and gets the reader's attention, like a dash of tabasco in the stew. For the skilled reporter, feature writing is an invitation to creative ingenuity.

When interviewed for jobs, young reporters usually say, "I want to write feature stories." To which veterans of the newsroom reply, "Who doesn't?" Before attempting the feature approach, however, a reporter should master the straight-news style, because the basic information must be included in a feature story just as in a straightaway treatment. The facts are merely presented more obliquely in a feature. Reporters striving for a distinctive approach to a story sometimes forget this; sports writers attempting to compose nonroutine reports of football games have been known to omit the most fundamental fact of all, the score.

The soft approach has two aspects:

1. **The feature story.** This need not contain current news elements. Often it is a look at a provocative personality. It may be a story about an unusual set of circumstances or a report on a trend that informs or entertains readers. Spot news is not essential in a full-dress feature story.
2. **The featurized treatment of spot news.** This means delivering hard-news information in an unorthodox form as a change of pace. As seen in earlier chapters, a featurized lead gives a story a tangy flavor. But more is involved in applying a featurized treatment to a current news situation than writing an attractive lead.

In this chapter we shall first look at the featurized treatment of a spot news situation and then at the less timely full-dress feature story.

First, the reporter must decide whether a news development should be told "straight" or featurized. Breaking news stories should be reported in the traditional straightaway pyramid style with a concise hard-news lead, that is, to deliver the facts in the quickest way with the greatest possible impact. The opportunity for a featurized approach to a news situation such as the firing of the football coach or a fire in a campus dormitory lies in second-day or "overnight" stories and sidebars. Newspapers, radio, and television have already delivered the basic facts of the event; follow-up stories for the next day's newspapers and news broadcasts should put the news in perspective and build up interesting angles that could not be covered in the first rush to deliver the breaking news. Here a featurized approach often is best.

The featurized follow-up is especially useful in sports stories, such as next-day roundups of college basketball games. By noon, the results of the previous day's games are known to many fans from morning paper stories and broadcasts. Yet the afternoon newspaper must report them, so it hunts for a fresh approach.

In this well-done example of a second-day featurized lead by the Associated Press, observe that a news fact—that relief pitcher Kent Tekulve won the game for the Pittsburgh Pirates by pitching two scoreless innings—is not mentioned until the end of the fourth paragraph.

Narrative lead	Two years ago, Kent Tekulve of the Pittsburgh Pirates was one of the hottest relief pitchers in baseball.	the start of this year. That all ended Tuesday when the skinny, bespectacled reliever pitched two scoreless innings in a 6–4 victory over the Chicago Cubs.	
Narrative continues	But something snapped near the end of the 1980 season, and he couldn't win for losing. "There were times I was wondering if I would ever stop losing," he says.	"It's a good feeling," said Tekulve, who had 31 saves and 10 victories in 1979 and 21 saves and 8 victories before going into his horrendous slump beginning last Aug. 8 . . .	Reaction to news
2nd sentence gives hard news	Tekulve dropped seven games at the end of 1980 and three more at		

From this point, the story is a straightaway account of how Tekulve won his comeback victory.

Featurized treatment often creates high readership for minor news stories that might pass almost unnoticed if written in a flat who-what-when, and so on, style. An alert reporter keeps an eye open for such opportunities. Although the facts of a situation sometimes are so offbeat that they beg for special treatment, often only a writer with a perceptive eye and a flexible mind can see the possibility in them. Excessively verbose or complicated story openings, used to achieve a feature effect, should be avoided because they weary rather than beckon the reader. So do feature attempts that are excessively "cute."

WAYS TO USE A "SOFT" STYLE

Telling a story from the point of view of a participant is one method of featurizing the news.

The routine way of writing a story from a police report on file in a small Michigan city concerning a minor incident would have been about as follows:

```
CASSOPOLIS—James Lee, 22, was arrested Tuesday for shooting up
John's Bar at 135 S. Broadway, after he broke two of the tavern's
windows, entered the barroom and fired six shots at random. No one
was struck by the bullets.
   Village Police Chief Frank Williams and Captain Paul Parrish of
the Cass County Sheriff's Department arrested Lee, who fought so
strenuously that three police officers were injured while subduing
him.
   Lee was lodged in the Cass County jail on charges of assaulting a
police officer, careless use of a firearm and malicious destruction
of property. Police listed his address as the Hilton Street
Apartments, Cassopolis.
```

Instead of using this flat approach, the South Bend *Tribune* reporter wrote the story from the point of view of a tavern customer, supplementing information on the police report with facts and quotations obtained by interviewing persons present during the shootup. The result was this lively, detailed account:

By JOEL THURTELL
Tribune Cass County Bureau

CASSOPOLIS—Marvin Burns took a look out the window of his home here Tuesday morning and decided the snow was falling too heavily to drive a truck to Grand Rapids.

Instead, Burns walked over to John's Bar at 135 S. Broadway and sat down for a quiet beer. The coast-to-coast truck driver never finished that drink.

Out front, a man, later identified by Cassopolis village police as James Lee, 22, of Hilton Street Apartments, Cassopolis, swung a .38-caliber revolver at the thermopane windows of the tavern, breaking two panes before he entered the building.

Burns said that moments after entering the bar, Lee fired six shots from a .38-caliber revolver. Nobody was hit by the bullets, but three police officers were hurt while trying to wrestle the gun from Lee's hands. Burns, who was one of the few people who remained in the bar during the incident, recalls that a waitress shouted, "He's got a gun!" Many of the bar's patrons quickly ran out the front door.

Waitresses estimate about 65 customers were having lunch at 1:10 p.m. when James Lee entered the bar.

Lee came to Burns' table, and, recalls the trucker, "He asked me what I was looking at."

Burns said nothing, and Lee turned over his table. "I didn't even get a chance to finish my beer," said Burns. Burns rose and stood in a corner opposite the bar's shuffleboard game. He was the only one who remained in the rear area of the bar.

Burns said Lee then tipped over the shuffleboard game one-handed and began firing the revolver across the bar.

"I thought he had just went on the nut," said Burns. Burns said Lee was not aiming at anyone in the bar.

A waitress said Lee tried to force open a door leading to a rear room where she and others were hiding.

A police witness, Captain Paul Parrish of the Cass County Sheriff's Department, said he heard four shots, a pause, then another pair of shots.

From inside, Burns said a waitress shouted that the gun was empty.

Parrish and Cassopolis Village Police Chief Frank Williams ran into the bar and rushed Lee. Parrish said he and Williams wrestled Lee to the floor and disarmed him, although both officers were struck in the head as Lee fought with them. Several policemen then carried a kicking and cursing Lee to a police cruiser.

The episode lasted about 25 minutes, according to a sheriff's department dispatcher.

Lee was lodged in the Cass County Jail on charges of assaulting a police officer, careless use of a firearm and malicious destruction of property.

The headline was a teaser, in the same mood as the story: "He sat down for a quiet beer and . . ."

The only important element missing from the story is the arrested man's motive. He was in jail and not available for an interview, however, and had given no clue while the incident was in progress.

Here is another example of the personalized approach to a news story, this one about an airplane crash. In this instance, the Associated Press dispatch is a second-day report for afternoon newspapers. The opening portion of the story follows:

Suspended interest lead	SOLANA BEACH (AP)—Kathy McAuley was having lunch in her kitchen when she heard something that sounded like an earthquake.	Hard news told
Quotation builds up suspense	"It shook the whole house and I heard a bunch of glass breaking. I opened the door and there was a dead body right in the front yard," she said, only then realizing that a single-engine plane had crashed into two cars in a driveway only a few feet from her door. Two men died in the Saturday morning crash, but luckily no one on the ground was injured. Witnesses told authorities the two-seater Grumman aircraft apparently lost power as it made a low left turn over this coastal community . . .	Switch to inverted pyramid style

The story continues in an orthodox style with details of the plane's last minutes, its flight plan, and the names of the victims.

A second useful device for featurizing a story based on hard-news elements is to play up an analogy between an aspect of the story and a situation familiar to readers. This was done cleverly by Peter King, a San Francisco *Examiner* reporter, in his story about the plan to refund $12.25 million to California consumers who purchased Levi Strauss & Co. jeans at an excessive price.

In a straight-news approach, however, the lead might have been something like this:

```
  With one day left to file, the state attorney general's office
reported today that it has received 1,263,150 claims for refunds
from persons who purchased Levi Strauss & Co. jeans at excessive
prices in the early 1970s.
  Chet Horne, the deputy attorney general handling the case, said a
sampling of the claims indicates that they represent 4.1 million
individuals seeking refunds for the purchase of 31 million pairs of
jeans.
  The manufacturer agreed to make the refund in an out-of-court
settlement of an antitrust suit filed against it.
  Because of the heavy response to Attorney General George
Deukmejian's invitation for purchasers to file claims, individual
refund payments will be less than the figure of "up to two dollars a
pair" Deukmejian forecast last year.
```

That treatment is accurate, concisely stated—and dull.

Using an approach that compared a pair of the controversial jeans to the promised refund, King produced a story with high reader interest. He did so by expanding upon the official press release with arithmetic of his own, research in the newspaper files, and interviews with persons involved in the refund project officially and unofficially. His story, in part:

Chapter 12 / The Feature Approach 135

By PETER H. KING
Examiner Staff Writer

Suspended interest lead using comparison

Just like a pair of your basic shrink-to-fit Levi's, the refunds promised to California consumers who purchased pairs of overpriced Levi Strauss & Co. jeans may have to be shrunk to fit an unexpectedly heavy demand.

Material from newspaper files

When the San Francisco-based firm agreed last year to set aside $12.25 million for those who purchased overpriced Levi's in the early 1970s, state Attorney General George Deukmejian heralded the proposed settlement as "a major victory for consumers in California."

A letter sent to every California residence announcing the proposed refund plan—it still must pass a court challenge this month—promised "a cash refund of up to two dollars per pair."

Reporter's arithmetic

But it now appears that "major victory" for consumers actually will provide a refund of only 33 cents for each pair purchased—roughly double what it cost for the stamp needed to mail in the necessary form.

Government statement

The low return is the result of a huge response to the attorney general's controversial call for Californians who bought Levi's between 1972 and 1975. The refunds were the product of an out-of-court settlement of an antitrust suit filed against the company.

With only one day left to file, 1,263,250 claims for refunds have been received by the state attorney general's office. Chet Horn Jr., the deputy attorney general handling the case, said a sampling of the claims indicates they represent 4.1 million individuals seeking refunds for the purchase of 31 million pairs of Levi's.

"When we went to court with this plan," Horn said, "the best estimate was that we would get around a million claims. We've done just a little bit better than that."

Interview with government source

Before any pennies filter into the pockets of consumers, however, the proposed refund plan must be approved in San Francisco Superior Court. A hearing is scheduled for April 27 before Judge Ira Brown Jr.

It will pit the attorney general against, among others, a public-interest law firm that contends the refunds won't help consumers. Levi Strauss plans to maintain a neutral position in the ensuing court battle over how to best redistribute the settlement money.

Conflict established

Each side offers a jarringly different assessment of the refund proposal.

Transition

Pointing to the heavy response, Horn called the drive to round up eligible consumers—a campaign that included mailings and television spots by actor Michael Landon —"far and away the most successful consumer distribution in history."

Government's contention

But an attorney with Public Advocates Inc., which is representing eight organizations and 11 individuals opposed to the plan, called the very same drive "the largest consumer fraud ever sanctioned . . ."

Opponent's contention

Simple scene-setting is a third approach to giving a news story a featurized look. This style uses the opening paragraph to establish a situation, then unfolds the events that followed in chronological order, and saves the crucial facts for the end. Such suspended resolution pulls the reader along, just as a short fiction story usually does. Here we have the exact reverse of the fundamental news story approach in which the most important facts are summarized in the lead and the rest of the story explains and expands them. British newspapers frequently use the scene-setting technique. Although it is seen less commonly in American newspapers, it can deliver strong impact under certain circumstances.

The following story from the London *Sunday Express* by its correspondent in New York, Caroline Law, exemplifies this method.

NEW YORK—The four men sat down to their weekly poker game, just as they had been doing for the past six years. They opened a few beers and dealt the first hand.

For two hours the game carried on as usual at the New Jersey home of 54-year-old James Lewis. But the double-glazing fitter became increasingly agitated as, even with good cards, he just could not seem to win.

Then, with the pot standing at £30 and rising, a card fell to the floor and there was an awkward silence as the players saw it was the ace of spades . . . an identical card lay on the table.

James Lewis leapt to his feet, took a revolver from a nearby sideboard and fired at the man who had dropped the card . . . his friend Arthur Ellison. Shots rang out five times—"one for each ace," snarled James—and Arthur slumped to the floor.

He was rushed to hospital, but was dead on arrival. Lewis has been charged with murder.

Now let us see how these different techniques may be applied to circumstances so odd that a quirk-in-the-news treatment is obviously in order. A reporter for a large midwestern newspaper had in hand these condensed notes obtained from a fire report and follow-up interviews:

Hank Marshman was repairing his 1974 Volkswagen on driveway outside his detached garage at 55555 Brink. About 8 P.M., after dark, he finished job and was cleaning up with gasoline-soaked rags. Rag touched hot trouble lamp and set car on fire. He ran 100 feet to his house, called fire department. He and family waited on porch for fire trucks, watching car burn. As they waited, strange things happened. Car's lights went on. Its horn honked. Then to family's surprise its starter engaged. Volkswagen moved by itself 15 feet forward through open doors into two-car garage. There it stopped. Flames from it spread to Pontiac GTO in other space, gardening equipment, and garage itself.

Marshman quote: "We were just waiting in front of the house. We didn't want to get any closer because the whole front of the car was in flames. And then it was just like it turned its key on. Freaky. Real freaky."

Firemen from two trucks worked 45 minutes to put out flames in cars and garage. Total estimated damage $6000. Fire Capt. Dave Pedzinski believed

Volkswagen odd behavior resulted when fire disturbed wiring system. Ron Nicklas, Volkswagen agency mechanic, agreed wires could have melted from heat, crossed and produced short circuit necessary to start car.

In writing the story, the reporter could have used the *personalized approach,* the *analogy,* or the *scene-setting* opening. The reporter chose to use the analogy, beginning the story thus:

> If Disney Studios wants to make a film about "Herbie the Torch" or "The Love Bug Goes Kamikaze," Hank Marshman has a car that has a shot at the lead role.
> Disney made millions of dollars from movies starring a mischievous Volkswagen with a mind of its own. But all Marshman has gotten out of his little bug is about $6000 worth of fire damage and a bunch of neighbors who think he is cuckoo . . .

If the lead had been written from the personalized angle, it would have focused on Marshman's surprised reaction to his Volkswagen's antics, rather than on the car itself. The lead might have been something like this:

```
Hank Marshman watched with amazement as his burning Volkswagen
turned on its lights, honked its horn and drove itself up the
driveway into the family garage.
  Soon the garage and its contents were ablaze, too.
  "Freaky," Marshman exclaimed later. "Real freaky."
```

Suppose the reporter had chosen the third, or scene-setting, approach and withheld key facts until late in the story. The opening paragraph might then have been along these lines:

```
Darkness had fallen by the time Hank Marshman finished repairing
his six-year-old Volkswagen on the driveway outside the family
garage, and he was hurrying to get his mess cleaned up. A
gasoline-soaked rag he was using touched a hot trouble lamp and
caught fire.
```

Which method is most effective? Or could a more provocative approach be made?

Opening a feature story with a question is another tactic. This may be an attention-getting literary device with the answer given almost immediately, or the reply may be postponed until later in the story to hold interest. The question lead with the answer briefly withheld is used in this brief story from *Newsday*.

NEW YORK—What's in a name?

Don't ask the producer of the new ABC comedy-adventure show that premiered two weeks ago, "The Greatest American Hero."

The hour-long program is meant to be a lighthearted fantasy. An average American high school teacher is chosen by aliens from another world to combat crime and corruption with the aid of a superpower suit. It's like Superman with the Clark Kent character, played by actor William Katt, named Ralph Hinkley.

On Tuesday ABC spokesman Charles Franke said the show's producer, Stephen Cannell, agreed to change the lead character's name because of its similarity to John W. Hinckley Jr., the name of the man accused of shooting President Reagan. The similarity, Franke said, was an "unfortunate coincidence."

The Hinkley character will be called "Mr. H" and all Hinkley references will be erased from the sound track.

"Look, if a character named Ralph Hinkley was part of, let's say, 'Three's Company,' I don't think there would be any problem," said Franke. "But because of the show's name, I guess everyone thought a change was appropriate."

AN EXAMPLE TO STUDY

Here is an example of a feature story opportunity missed. The weekly *Sun* in Julian, a California mountain community, deserves credit for digging up this unusual story and illustrating it, but it failed to tell the story in an appealing manner. As you read the story, think how it could be reworked into a lively featurized account of an innovative teacher's methods and what additional questions you would like to see answered.

In last week's *Sun* it was reported that 4th grade teacher David Stone participates in some out-of-the-ordinary incentive programs with his students.

The students were given a spelling test of 121 words. The words were checked not only for correct spelling but also proper penmanship. Some of the words were given by definition only. The students were required to match the spelling list word with the correct definition. The students scoring 100 per cent are allowed to throw a pie at the teacher.

This sort of teaching tool is great fun and all are encouraged to study hard so that they may have the privilege of throwing the pie, according to Mr. Stone. He also stated that this provides the motivation for each child to strive for his or her best. In addition it helps raise grades. Sixteen kids out of 28 scored 93 per cent or better on the test.

Only one person, Tim Morey, got 100 per cent on the test and had the opportunity to pie the teacher.

A quotation from the boy who tossed the pie is badly needed. So is one from the teacher telling how the pie felt. What kind of pie was it? The story would have had a much crisper touch if some of the teacher's comments about the value of the stunt had been in direct quotations. What other innovative teaching methods has David Stone tried?

THE FULL-DRESS FEATURE STORY

We have been discussing ways to dress current news facts in feature garb. The stories examined so far in this chapter have a common characteristic: They report events that have an element of timeliness and therefore are spot news stories.

Many articles published in newspapers lack such a news peg. Nothing has just happened, or is about to happen, to give them a sense of urgency. Yet they may be among the best read in any day's edition and frequently are the best written. If the subject, either an individual or a situation, has potential general interest and the writer presents the material in a stimulating manner, the full-dress feature story does not need spot news facts to command readership.

Techniques used to featurize hard-news stories may be used equally well in writing the nonspot feature story. Because the writer of the latter usually has more flexibility in the amount of space available, and frequently more time in which to develop the story, he or she has a better opportunity to build up the personality angles that help so much to enliven a story.

For example, James V. Healion of United Press International was assigned to write a story about a new type of solar home in Greenwich, Connecticut. The topic was of much concern to architects, builders, and environmentalists, but how could he coax others to spend time reading about an inanimate object, a house built by a trade association? What kind of lead could he contrive that would catch readers long enough for him to tell them about the computerized, sun-powered wonders of the structure?

Healion solved his problem by focusing the lead of the story not on the house, but on the husband and wife who lived in it. The lead paragraph does not even mention the structure, which is the reason the story was written. Readers relate much more easily to other humans than to a computer. He opened his story this way:

By JAMES V. HEALION

Teaser lead— who, what, when, where

Tells why

GREENWICH, Conn. (UPI)— Some people don't want to be millionaires. They just want to live like them. Molly and Dean Hendrickson are doing just that.

They are living in the house of tomorrow until somebody pays the asking price of $1 million. It is a third generation solar home built as a new product showcase by the Copper Development Association and 20 companies, the who's who of the building industry.

The other houses built in Houston and Tucson, Ariz., are like it in concept, but not design. Between

Supports lead — its active and passive solar systems, the new "Sun Tronic" house produces 60 percent of the home's heat and hot water.

Interview with Molly — The Hendricksons manage the house, sort of put it through its paces, welcome visiting professionals, and make an occasional women's group feel right at home.

At first, Molly Hendrickson didn't think the idea of living in a house other than her own was such a good one, even though the furnishings were selected by W & J Sloane.

"Then we decided why pass up an opportunity like this. We rented our house in New Canaan, Conn., and we're here under contract for six months or maybe a year."

Mrs. Hendrickson was the curator for several years of an historical house. Dean Hendrickson is a retired executive who is convalescing from hip joint surgery.

Interview with builder — "We wanted to put together a total package demonstration home that would be of interest to the building community across the board, not just architects but interior designers and so on," said Paul A. Anderson, an association vice president.

The 5,400-square foot house with its sloping copper roof and exterior of California redwood, slate and copper metals settles snugly into the earth to shield it from north winds on a three-acre wooded site overlooking a pond.

The multi-level house has three bedrooms, 2½ baths, living room, dining room, family room, laundry, mechanical room, two-story combination greenhouse and solarium plus a spacious kitchen. Mrs. Hendrickson had 80 guests recently and some of them gravitated to the kitchen.

More Molly interview — "You know that old saying, 'No matter where I serve my guests they always seem to like my kitchen best'? I think that works out in this lovely, gorgeous home," she said . . .

While telling readers about Molly and Dean Hendrickson, the reporter worked in such essential facts as the name of the builder; the name of the house, "Sun Tronic"; the name of the decorator, W & J Sloane; the size of the house, 5,400 square feet; and its price tag and the materials of which it was constructed. Summarized in one paragraph, these facts would have been dull reading. The ability to weave them into the story without letting them protrude exemplifies good feature writing.

AN EXAMPLE TO STUDY

Now that we have examined the elements of a feature story and methods of writing such material, here in full is a successful story that achieves its goal of informing the reader in an entertaining way. The dispatch is by Jim Gallagher, Moscow correspondent of the Chicago Tribune Press Service. As you study the story's structure, observe that it contains no hard news, but discusses a significant trend. Gallagher wove facts, interpretive commentary, and supporting quotations from Soviet and Western sources into a cohesive whole.

Soviets Use Disco to Limit Discontent

By JIM GALLAGHER
Moscow correspondent
Chicago Tribune Press Service

Interpretive comment by reporter

MOSCOW—Guess who's helping the Communist Party here keep the kids in line? Donna Summer, the Bee Gees, the Village People and a host of other Western disco stars.

With many young Soviets apathetic and bored and a growing number drifting into drunkenness and crime, officials are finding that disco music hath charms to soothe the restless discontent.

Factual summary

More than 1,000 Soviet discotheques now exist, although most are open only one night a week. Sponsored by the Komsomol (Young Communist League), trade organizations, and cultural groups, they allow young folks to get it out of their system inside the system.

Recently, a national Komsomol conference was held to encourage the opening of many more discos and to discuss ways of making them appealing to youth. Seminars were held in selection of stereo equipment, training of disk jockeys and use of strobe lights.

Quotation from Soviet leader supports the writer's comment

"YOUNG PEOPLE need a place to get together and have fun," said Aleksandr Lazarev, a 26-year-old Komsomol worker who helped set up one of Moscow's more than 320 disco clubs.

"It used to be that there weren't many places to meet new people, to get to know new girls," he said. "But the discotheques have changed all that. Now we can go someplace every night if we want."

Description of disco club scene

This was Thursday night, so Lazarev was living it up at his own club's weekly disco in the Teachers Cultural Hall, just a short walk from the Kremlin.

Strobe lights blinked and a Beatles record played: "Oooooh, I get by with a little help from my friends . . . oooooh, I get high with a little help from my friends." Still, by Western standards, it seemed pretty tame, and the only alcohol available was warm beer.

A young grade school teacher, Alexei Karavlov, was attending his fourth disco that week. "Without them my life would be boring," he said, looking very Western in a brown body shirt and a pair of tight tan jeans.

BOREDOM is a common complaint among Soviet youth, even in the biggest and busiest cities. In many, it had given rise to a ritual called the "stometorovka," in which young people promenade back and forth along a downtown street in the evening. In Moscow, this is sometimes called "walking Broadway," although the common routes are Gorky Street and Kalinin Prospekt.

The ritual once inspired a Pravda writer to note: "How empty and uninteresting it must be in the dance halls, the factory clubs, the palaces of culture, and even the town theaters if they are incapable of filling the spiritual vacuum, and if they have nothing to offer the hearts and minds of young people."

But boredom is the least of the social problems besetting young people here today, although it may be at the root of several others. The post-Stalin generation of Soviet

Interpretive section, examining boredom of Soviet youth

youth seems to be inordinately dispirited and disaffected.

Soviet officials complain about sharp increases in crime, alcoholism and divorce among the young. Among workers in their 20s, absenteeism and job turnover have reached alarming rates.

NOT SURPRISINGLY these problems have arisen hand-in-hand with improvement in the standard of living. In material terms, Soviet youth today is the most blessed generation since the toppling of the czar.

But many young people want even more, and despite rash promises by Leonid Brezhnev and other Soviet leaders, the system is not equipped to supply it. As a result, political cynicism is deep-seated among the young, who find Communist rhetoric increasingly irrelevant.

Quotation from Soviet scholar supporting reporter's interpretation

"The values of many of our young people are out of synch with those of their leaders and their elders," a Soviet scholar claims. "As a result, they don't read Soviet newspapers, they find Soviet television boring, they turn up their noses at Soviet movies.

"What many of them care most about comes from the West—Western music, Western clothes, Western books."

Description of official efforts

FINALLY, youth officials are trying to fight fire with fire, and the disco drive is only one of the steps they have taken. A full-scale effort is under way to create a credible rock industry that can compete with Western stars for the attention of Soviet youth. To date, a few first-rate groups have emerged, the best of which is Time Machine, which won the gold medal at the first Soviet Rock festival held in Ibilisi last spring.

And in grade school gym classes, boys and girls are being taught to dance the latest rock and disco steps.

"The party is trying to preempt the rock phenomenon," one Western cultural attache assigned here said. "The leaders recognize how dangerous it is to have so many young people deeply interested in something they associate pure and simple with the West. They want to show that Soviets, too, can produce good rock music. They want to use Soviet rock music to bring some of the lost lambs back into the fold."

Interpretive quotation from a Western cultural attaché

LAZAREV'S disco club is a case in point. The idea originated with a group of friends who often got together in one another's flats to listen to Western music, he said.

Factual account of disco club's growth

"We went to the regional Komsomol organization to ask for help in getting equipment and space," he explained. "Now they're looking for a bigger ballroom for us, and we hope to have discos several nights a week soon."

Still, it seems unlikely that discos such as this one will make life much more interesting for the ordinary Soviet youth, since tickets are not sold openly but distributed within Komsomol groups.

Interpretive summary

"It's just like everything else here," a disgruntled young Soviet woman said. "Tickets go to those with connections, or the goody-goodies who do party work. The only way I could get a ticket is to buy one on the black market."

Gallagher set out to report a social phenomenon in the Soviet Union—growing boredom and disenchantment among Soviet youth—even though, as he said, "Soviet youth today is the most blessed generation since the toppling of the czar." He might have written a profound politico–sociological dispatch, but, remembering that he was reporting for a general newspaper audience, he focused on one easily visualized portion of the Soviet government's campaign to stimulate its youth—officially sponsored disco dance halls. He built his lead on a question, then answered it immediately, and in so doing established from the start that the Communist Party is borrowing from the West.

While describing colorfully how Soviet disco functions, Gallagher worked in the background, which gives his dispatch depth and political meaning. He ended his feature story with a cynical twist, not in his own words but in those of a young Soviet woman. This is an excellent example of how to present serious material in a lively manner.

STUDY PROJECTS

1. Submit five examples of nonspot news feature stories and three stories employing featurized treatment of spot news.

2. From a Sunday newspaper sports section, clip three major stories reporting games played the previous day—football, baseball, or basketball, for example. Determine whether each was written in hard spot news or featurized style; then prepare a lead for each one written in the opposite style.

3. Paste up a full-length nonspot feature story; then analyze its structure with comments at the side, as was done in this chapter with the Jim Gallagher story on Soviet disco.

READ MORE ABOUT IT . . .

William Ruehlmann, *Stalking the Feature Story* (Cincinnati: Writer's Digest, 1978).
Neale Copple, *Depth Reporting* (Englewood Cliffs, N.J.: Prentice-Hall, 1964).
Lee Miller, *The Story of Ernie Pyle* (New York: Viking, 1950).

COMING UP NEXT . . .

In every life a little rain must fall, and in every reporter's career many hours must be spent in writing unexciting but essential routine stories.

This daily grist includes obituaries. These reports of deaths usually appear toward the back of the newspaper, but have high readership and demand extreme accuracy. Errors of fact in an obituary distress the family and friends of the deceased and injure a newspaper's reputation.

Writing weather stories is another routine task. Here again accuracy is the first requirement, but when unusual conditions occur, the weather writer has an opportunity for innovative approaches. In stories about major storms that cause extensive damage, the writer's ability to organize is on display.

The third area examined in this chapter is second-day stories: how to find fresh angles for stories whose basic facts have already been published and broadcast.

Chapter 13
The Daily Grist: Obituaries, Weather, Second-Day Stories

THE NECESSARY ROUTINE

Under the watchful eye of the city editor, the beginning reporter, if not assigned to a beat, generally will be directed to handle routine stories that fulfill the newspaper's everyday needs, such as obituaries, the weather, and the updating of previously printed stories. Once the reporter has demonstrated proficiency and speed in writing these often minor but well-read stories, bigger assignments will follow.

OBITUARIES

Studies have shown that obituaries are among the most heavily read items in a newspaper. Most of them, of course, concern persons who have never been prominent in the news; it is a truism that most people "get their names in the paper" only three times—when they are born, when they marry, and when they die. However boring they may be to write day after day, these stories are important not only for their news value, but because they generally are clipped and kept by family members.

The first requisite in writing "obits," as they are called, is *accuracy*. Every fact, especially the spelling of names, must be checked. The second requisite is *thoroughness*. All must contain the name, occupation, and date and place of death. Other information, such as the person's age and the cause of death, should be provided if possible.

Every newspaper has its own style in reporting deaths of a routine nature. Before beginning the assignment, the beginning reporter should study the form in which previous obituaries have been printed and follow that formula unless time is available for a different approach. Does the newspaper permit the age to follow the name? Some editors believe this practice indicates present tense and insist on a separate sentence, such as, "He was 62 years of age." In most papers it is correct to write, "Survivors include. . . ." In others, that paragraph may begin, "He leaves. . . ." Some permit the use of "widow," but most insist on "wife." The style varies with different newspapers. In almost all, however, Mr. and Mrs. precede the names of married persons on second usage.

A typical obituary provides the following information in the order given:

1. Name, age, address, occupation, date and place of death and, if known, the cause of death.

    Ralph Smith, 64, of 1624 West Ave., a retired carpenter, died in a local hospital Wednesday.

2. Facts about the person's life.

    A native of Tennessee, Mr. Smith was a graduate of the University of Tennessee at Knoxville. He was a member of Sigma Phi fraternity and Haygood Memorial United Methodist Church. He was an Army veteran of World War II and a former member of the Buckhead Exchange Club.

Chapter 13 / The Daily Grist: Obituaries, Weather, Second-Day Stories 147

3. Survivors.

> Mr. Smith is survived by his wife, the former Lorene Adams; two daughters, Mrs. Irene Jones of Rocky Mount, N.C., and Mrs. Elizabeth Wooley of Elberton, Ga.; a brother, James Smith of Westville, Tenn.; and five grandchildren.

4. Time and place of funeral services and burial.

> Services will be conducted at 10 a.m. Wednesday at Haygood Memorial United Methodist Church with the Rev. Albert Dallmeyer officiating. Burial will be in Evergreen Cemetery.

5. Often the name of an organization to which memorial contributions may be made will be provided.

> In lieu of flowers, the family requests that contributions be made to the American Diabetes Association, 2 Park Ave., New York, N. Y. 10016.

Here are some tips about the handling of each of these items:

1. The lead should be brief, but complete. For space reasons, metropolitan newspapers likely would not provide the street address, because it would be included in the accompanying column of death notices prepared by funeral homes and paid for as a part of funeral expenses. In fact, this story would not appear in a large metropolitan paper since Smith was not prominent. Some newspapers would give the name of the hospital in which Smith died. Others would not, for reasons of policy or in deference to continued good news relations with community hospitals. (Administrators dislike continuing publicity about deaths in their hospitals; when a hospital fails to cooperate in reporting necessary information about persons injured in accidents, newspapers have been known to insert the name of the hospital prominently in obituaries.)
2. Biographical information should be given succinctly. A common fault in such paragraphs is implying cause and effect: "A native of Tennessee, Mr. Smith was a former member of the Buckhead Exchange Club."
3. Survivors usually are listed in the following order: spouse, parents, children, brothers and sisters, and grandchildren. (The number of grandchildren is given but not the names.) If they are locally known, the names of other relatives such as aunts and uncles, nephews and nieces, are often provided. Some newspapers print the given name of a married woman: "Mrs. Henry W. (Irene) Jones." Mr. and Miss are not used in listing the names of survivors.
4. Some newspapers omit the word *funeral* before *services* and the words,

conducted or *held*. Others shorten the form even further. Officiating clergy should be identified with their churches or synagogues. The reporter must remember that priests celebrate or say masses and ministers and rabbis officiate at or conduct services. Metropolitan papers generally report funeral services only in the paid notices.

5. Frequently, a statement about memorial contributions provides a clue as to cause of death. In all events, the cause of death should be given if it can be learned; readers are intensely interested in this fact. It is a reader aid to provide the complete address to which contributions may be sent. A simple phrase such as "in lieu of flowers" will avoid the use of awkward or imperative sentences such as "Flowers should not be sent; instead . . ." and "Send memorial tributes to. . . ."

At times another sentence will be included to let mourners know that they may call on the family at a certain time: "The family will be at Harveson-Cole Funeral Home from 7 to 9 p.m. Wednesday." Many newspapers reserve the phrase, "will lie in state," for use in connection with the deaths of persons of great importance, such as the president or a member of Congress.

Euphemisms such as "passed away" and "went to an eternal reward" must be avoided; "succumbed" occasionally is used as a substitute for "died." Bodies are buried, not interred. Cremation takes place at a crematorium.

Follow-up, or second-day, routine obituaries generally begin with the announcement of time and place of funeral services.

Reporters learn about deaths in written information received from funeral establishments or by telephone calls to or from funeral homes and relatives and friends. Hoaxes have been perpetrated by pranksters erroneously reporting a death. Mark Twain's statement that "The report of my death has been greatly exaggerated" evoked a chuckle, but such reports are no laughing matter. Every death must be verified by a funeral home, the coroner or a medical examiner, an attending physician, a hospital, or the police. Some newspapers require that reporters make telephone call-backs to confirm all obituaries unless they have clearly come from a well-identified funeral home.

Funeral homes fill out detailed obituary blanks about each deceased person. Some newspapers prepare stories from forms delivered to the classified advertising department. Obtaining information by telephone should be avoided if possible because names may be misspelled.

THE LONGER OBITUARY

By gathering information from relatives, friends, the newspaper library, and other sources, a reporter can write an interesting story about any person; there are facts in all our lives that merit telling. Few newsrooms, however, are sufficiently well staffed to permit writing human interest stories about the lives of nonprominent people who have died.

Chapter 13 / The Daily Grist: Obituaries, Weather, Second-Day Stories   149

Reporter Anne C. Valdes wrote the following story, published in the Atlanta *Journal:*

Attorney O'Boyle Dies of Leukemia

Suspended interest lead

Thomas A. O'Boyle Jr. had many ambitions—to be the best tax attorney in Augusta, to run in the Peachtree Road Race, to see his last child born. At the end, that last ambition took precedence.

Supports the lead

"His major wish was that he would live to see the child," said his wife, Rose Mary O'Boyle. The baby, a daughter named Regan, was born a month early. That was two weeks ago, and he saw her every day from her birth until he died Sunday at the age of 34.

Hard news facts

O'Boyle succumbed at the Fred Hutchinson Research Center for Adult Leukemia in Seattle after an almost two-year battle against leukemia.

Interview with widow

His three eldest children had visited him every day during his hospitalization in Seattle, which began March 3. "They wanted to know if it hurt when he got his wings," Mrs. O'Boyle said. "It really taught my children that birth and death are part of it."

Shortly after O'Boyle moved to Augusta from Atlanta in September 1977, he found out he was suffering from leukemia. He was hospitalized the following December for treatment of a virus and pneumonia and was later admitted to the Talmadge Memorial Hospital for chemotherapy treatment.

Interview with attorney

"He continued to remain very optimistic, though, that he would be cured," said Wyck Knox of the law firm of Knox & Zachs, where O'Boyle was an associate. "He tried his best to continue his work until the end and was active in the practice of law until December 1978."

O'Boyle, described by friends and associates as a physical fitness buff, jogged up to 12 miles a day during his early months with the Augusta law firm. He even trained for last year's Peachtree Road Race, although his illness prevented him from competing.

Interview with friend

"Tom never gave up, he just kept trying," said a close friend, Stephen McLaughlin.

"Tom's ambition was to become the best tax attorney in Augusta, and we had great hopes that he would be," said Knox. "He's going to be greatly missed."

The story continues with a quotation from a onetime law associate, Carl Sanders, former Governor of Georgia, and much more career information as well as insights into O'Boyle's other hobbies, such as playing guitar with a rock band and restoring an old Chevrolet.

Most newspapers as well as the press associations maintain files containing scores or hundreds of stories about prominent people, ready for use upon their death or involvement in another major story. Reporters frequently are assigned to prepare such advance copy at times when other duties are not pressing. Stories such as that about O'Boyle, however, usually result from sheer enterprise on the reporter's part.

Covering the funeral of a prominent person represents another challenge for a reporter. In these instances the delivered eulogies normally provide the lead. Obtaining the names of newsworthy mourners present and estimating the number of people in attendance often are other requirements.

SUICIDES

Most real or apparent suicide stories are handled routinely along with other news obtained from the police blotter or from other sources. The reporter must be careful not to state that death was self-inflicted until that fact has been ascertained by the coroner or the medical examiner, or determined in an autopsy or inquest. Most of these stories contain such phrases as "was found in a gas-filled room" or "was found hanged in a jail cell," and readers draw their own conclusions.

These spot news stories generally are more explicit about the probable cause of death than the obituaries that follow. In deference to the family, obituaries seldom indicate in what way the person died.

News values, such as prominence and human interest, come into play with the real or apparent suicide of a person well known in the community or nation. The death of former Secretary of the Navy James Forrestal in a plunge from a tall building drew worldwide attention.

In order not to precipitate other suicide attempts by despondent or mentally unbalanced persons, the reporter should not provide explicit details about how a suicide was accomplished, such as identifying a specific poison.

WEATHER STORIES

"Everybody talks about the weather, but no one does anything about it," Dudley Warner wrote in an editorial in the Hartford (Conn.) *Courant* about 1890. We may be able to do little if anything about the weather, but it affects us all and ranks as not only the most universal subject of conversation, but one of the most widely read features in newspapers. Even during periods when the weather is virtually unchanging, readers want to reassure themselves of that fact and learn what the weather is likely to be tomorrow, next week, and even during the coming year. Weather is important in how we feel; how to protect ourselves from heat, cold, rain, and more violent manifestations; how crops and grocery buying are apt to be affected; how to plan travel and attendance at outdoor events; how delicate machinery may be affected; and many other eventualities.

Except for complex storm roundups, at which time a more experienced newsperson may be assigned, the beginning reporter may be called upon to write weather stories with great frequency. These augment the page-one weather briefs and the meteorological maps and other data carried on inside pages, obtained from the wire services or one of the offices of the National Weather Service of the National Oceanic and Atmosphere Administration, a part of the Department of Commerce.

The reporter may strain his or her imagination and vocabulary in seeking new leads for essentially old or repeated stories. Each story, however, will include temperature extremes compared with records that have been set, amount of precipitation, tomorrow's forecast, and anything else of possible interest to readers in the newspaper's circulation area.

When extreme weather conditions prevail, the reporter, often aided by others on the staff and by correspondents, must gather all sorts of information, usually by telephone. This information may include human casualties and injuries; property damage, transportation, communication, and utility problems; police and volunteer group activities and warnings; and reports from eyewitnesses and other persons who may have been affected.

The reporter will find it necessary to learn precise weather definitions. For example, the Weather Bureau defines a gale as consisting of winds ranging between 39 and 46 mph, a storm as winds between 55–63 mph, a violent storm as winds between 64–73 mph and a hurricane as winds exceeding 75 mph (called a typhoon in the western Pacific). Winds rotating at 200 mph or more comprise a tornado. A blizzard consists of snow blown by winds in excess of 35 mph, temperatures falling below 20 degrees Fahrenheit, and visibility of less than one-fourth of a mile. There are dozens of such definitions.

Becoming a weather specialist is a fairly certain road to advancement in the newsroom. In a national survey conducted in late 1980, media critic David Shaw of the Los Angeles *Times* learned that, despite extreme weather conditions in recent years, no daily newspaper in the United States had assigned a reporter fulltime to cover weather. This despite the fact that broadcast stations have employed large numbers of meteorologists in recent years.

THE SECOND-DAY STORY

The beginning reporter often is assigned the task of rewriting and updating stories that have appeared in competing newspapers or those printed in the previous day's edition of his or her own newspaper that are not the purview of a beat reporter. Giving the story a new, updated lead and as much additional content as possible, if justified, requires ingenuity.

The first requirement is to check the basic facts to insure that they are correct. The second is to develop new information or to provide a fresh angle that will make the story appealing. The lazy or frustrated reporter often will take the easy way out, such as:

Searchers today continued to look for clues. . . .
Investigation resumed today into the circumstances. . . .

Arab leaders of the Organization of Petroleum Exporting Countries (OPEC) discuss another increase in world oil prices. Soaring OPEC prices during the 1970s and early 1980s contributed heavily to inflation in the United States and other importing countries.

The Associated Press, in one of its handbooks, wrote:

> Falsely updated second-day leads constantly employ such contrivances as x x x prepared today for another effort, x x x headed back into x x x today, x x x kept a close watch today on x x x, x x x turned attention today to x x x, x x x was set today, x x x two (or three)-pronged investigation under way today.

In one of its handbooks, United Press International (UPI) told its staff members to discontinue the use of such crutches in second-day story writing as "continued," "planned," "scheduled," "resumed," "began," "opened," "investigated," "pondered," "searched," and any form of the verb "to be." The UPI editor wrote: "They are used when reporters fail to give the desk fresh material and the desk fails to give the reporters fresh angles to explore."

Professors Douglas P. Starr and J. Roy Moses of North Texas State University, in an article published in *Journalism Educator* in April 1976, advised reporters to:

Chapter 13 / The Daily Grist: Obituaries, Weather, Second-Day Stories   153

1. Double-check all details, using every available source.
2. Check for new information as time permits, obtain additional or later information, developments, or corrections from the original sources, or ask appropriate persons for reaction and opinion.
3. If there is no time for checking, "rely upon the initial story and cause-effect logic to provide quasi-new information. For example, a death always results in funeral plans, a prison escape always results in a search, a denial of bail bond always results in imprisonment, a crime always results in a search for the criminal. . . ."
4. Commit the facts to memory, then write a new story without referring to the original until completion.
5. If there is no "today" lead, subordinate the time element.

Jack Cappon, general news editor, told Associated Press staff members how to "escape those second-day doldrums" in an article in the *AP Log:*

> Significant stories that break in one cycle have to be carried over to the next. Sometimes the overnighters arrive on stretchers:
> *Investigators were looking today for the cause of a train derailment. . . .*
> *Karl Thomas was out over the Atlantic today in his try to become the first person to reach Europe by balloon. . . .*
> *Final arguments are scheduled today for the court martial of a Marine drill sergeant. . . .*
> It's sound technique to build the PMs intro on what comes next, but these leads are too obvious and perfunctory. What's the central issue in the sergeant's trial that the final arguments will have to deal with? What new perils loom in the intrepid balloonist's path? What theory do the investigators work on?
> And there's small profit in proclaiming that something that was bound to be continuing is in fact continuing. The classic version of this non-lead is, of course, *"The hearing . . . went into its fifth day today."* Never!
> A resounding never, also, to a lead like this:
> *Negotiations resume at 1 p.m. today in the four-day-old strike by 1,300 Columbus non uniformed employees as the city continued dumping raw sewage. . . .*
> That won't look enticing to a reader settling down to his afternoon paper long past 1 p.m.
> How to escape the second-day quandary? As always, digging up fresh information is best—reaction, a different perspective from sources, and the like. But even when you draw a blank, there's no need to declare bankruptcy.
> An angle submerged or slighted in yesterday's story can be lifted up. The consequences of an event can be developed. A crisp, readable summary of what's changed in a given situation offers another approach.
> When possible, the PMs redo should look ahead to something that makes a difference:
> CHARLESTON, W. Va. (AP)—Normal production from the nation's coal mines isn't expected until next week although thousands of miners who walked off their jobs in recent weeks have returned to work.

Or:

Increased unemployment benefits will go out to the state's jobless within two weeks. The governor signed yesterday. . . .

Here is an effective overnighter on the verdict in one newsworthy trial:

The state of California spent 16 months and more than $2 million to convict three men who were already in prison, two with life sentences. . . .

One of the best ways to enliven a second-day story is the human interest narrative: Instead of *"bone-weary firefighters continued their battle today against the worst forest fire in a decade,"* it could go like this:

Forest ranger Joe Smith hadn't slept in 30 hours. Sitting with his 10th mug of coffee, he looked out the window at the dark sky.

"If the wind shifts north," he said, "we'll lose another 1,000 acres."

STUDY PROJECTS

1. Bring to class an example of a news story based on obituary material, one of a second-day news story built around an individual, and one of a second-day story built around a situation.

2. Clip a front-page spot news story from a morning newspaper. Write a second-day lead on the material, up to 100 words, in such a manner that the story will appear fresh to readers of an afternoon newspaper at 5 P.M.

3. Write a weather news story from the following forecast for northern Indiana issued by the National Weather Service:

NORTHERN INDIANA—Tonight a few rain showers. Otherwise, cloudy and cold. Lows in the mid-30s. Thursday cloudy and cold with a chance of rain. Highs in the mid- to upper 40s. Southeast winds 10 to 15 miles per hour, becoming 10 miles per hour tonight. Chance of rain, less than 20 percent tonight, increasing to 40 percent Thursday.

EXTENDED OUTLOOK—Friday through Sunday: Chance of showers Friday. Fair Saturday and Sunday. Unseasonably cold Friday and Saturday. Warmer Sunday. Highs Friday and Saturday in the 40s, and in the 50s Sunday. Lows Friday and Saturday in the mid- to upper 20s, and in the 30s Sunday.

High temperature recorded at the National Weather Service Station at the Michiana Regional Airport for the period from noon to midnight Tuesday: 69 at 3:30 p.m. Low for the period from midnight to 7 a.m. today: 48 at 7 a.m.

Precipitation recorded at the airport for the 24-hour period ending at 7 a.m. today: none. October total: 1.18 inches. October normal: 3.06 inches. Total since Jan. 1, 1981: 33.52 inches, 3.56 inches above normal.

One year ago today, the high was 55, the low was 40. Record temperatures for this date were 85 in 1953 and 23 in 1952.

Oct. 22: sun rises, 7:05 a.m.; sets, 5:54 p.m.

PART IV
Interviewing and Probing

COMING UP NEXT . . .

A reporter sent on an interview assignment needs to be a psychologist who knows how to establish rapport with the person interviewed, what questions to ask and when to ask them. This chapter discusses these aspects of the interviewing art and other problems as well.

We define the difference between the spot news interview, in person or by telephone, and the more leisurely feature interview. Then we discuss the steps involved in an interview:

- **Preparation.** This includes drawing up questions to ask.
- **Conducting the interview.** How to break down barriers in conversation, when to slip in tough questions, when to use the soft approach.
- **Taking notes.** Use of a tape recorder. Ways to avoid having a person being interviewed "freeze up."

The chapter closes with analysis of a successful interview with actress Kim Novak.

Chapter 14
The Art of Interviewing

THE INTERVIEWER'S ROLE

Conducting an interview is an exercise in personal relationships—a one-to-one interplay of mind and personality between the person being interviewed and the one asking the questions. An effective interviewer does more than pose a series of prepared questions in a rigid, formal manner. He or she seeks to develop a rapport with the subject to get the person loosened up and talking easily. For a successful interview, a reporter needs to prepare well and to use psychological strategies that will encourage a flow of information and opinion.

Interviews take two forms. The *spot news interview* in person or by telephone seeks to obtain specific factual information for a news story, often in a hurry with a deadline approaching. The more leisurely *feature interview,* conducted in person after being arranged by appointment, tries to portray the subject's personality and opinions. A feature interview provides the reporter with one of the most challenging yet enjoyable opportunities that journalism has to offer.

The spot news interview usually is limited in scope and should be conducted briskly and straight to the point, especially if done by telephone. In such quick fact-gathering conversations, the person being questioned may be in a hurry, may have been interrupted by the ringing telephone in the midst of important business, and may indeed be hesitant to talk to a reporter.

For instance, a sports writer approaches the coach of the school basketball team in the locker room just after a game and asks his opinion about what happened. If the home team has won, the coach may be jovial and expansive. If it has just lost by one point in overtime, he may be curt and uncommunicative. A financial reporter reaches the president of a local bank by telephone to inform him that the county grand jury has just indicted him for fraud. The banker's answer may be a brusque "No comment" delivered in a frigid tone, or he may respond with an elaborate assertion of innocence and blame the trouble on the plotting of his business rivals. Although most people are helpful, the reporter should be prepared for reluctance, even unfriendliness, on the telephone, yet be ready to push ahead politely and persistently in pursuit of the needed information.

The feature interview is a conversation directed toward a goal. Usually it is conducted in relaxed circumstances, perhaps at lunch, in the subject's home, or over a cup of coffee in a newspaper conference room. It is a challenge to the reporter's curiosity: What is this person like? What does she have to say that will interest my readers? Also, it tests the reporter's powers of observation and ability to convey these impressions on paper. Several steps are involved in conducting an effective interview.

PREPARATION FOR THE INTERVIEW

Beginning reporters are often shy about approaching people in interviews for fear of appearing ignorant or bothering the person. Such hesitancy is usually unnecessary. No matter how much they protest, most interview subjects are secretly flattered by the attention. They may be tense and uneasy, however, unless they are professionals experienced in dealing with the press. The interviewer must seek to put the subject at ease and, in order to achieve that, must approach the assignment with confidence.

One key to a successful interview is good preparation. If the subject is a public figure, refer to the newspaper files and reference books. Find out in advance, if possible, relevant biographical facts about the subject, so you do not have to waste time during the interview on such fact-gathering.

Write down a set of questions to ask during the interview. These provide a framework for the interview, but need not be asked in a rigid sequence. Be flexible in using them. Often it is more effective to work them in casually as the conversation flows. If necessary, amend them or discard some of them if the interview goes off in an unexpected direction more stimulating than your prepared questions.

Perhaps the person to be interviewed is an authority on earthquakes, a topic about which the reporter knows little. Half an hour spent reading an encyclopedia article and recent clippings on the subject should enable the interviewer to speak intelligently, and the knowledge displayed in the questions will encourage the interviewee to talk more freely. Conversely, if the interviewer asks a question that shows lack of even rudimentary nontechnical knowledge, he or she may alienate the person being interviewed. Who can blame an earthquake expert for disdaining an interviewer who asks how earthquakes are measured and obviously does not know about the Richter scale? Of course, reporters cannot be expected to possess expert knowledge on all scientific topics, but they should try to have a basic layperson's understanding of the topic involved. Surely the person granting an interview deserves that much.

When given an assignment to interview a specialist in a complex field—a Nobel Prize winner in physics, for example—some reporters take the reverse approach. They say to the scientist, "I don't know anything about nuclear physics, so please explain your work to me in simple terms." This is risky, like throwing yourself onto the mercy of the court. Those who use this approach contend that if they do not know anything about a technical topic, most of their readers will not either, and the scientist will be forced to explain the material in layperson's terms. Some scientists with strong teaching instincts will do precisely what the reporter asks. Others will resent the tactic and give minimum responses; they fear that an ill-informed reporter will write an erroneous story and make them look foolish in the eyes of their colleagues.

Faced with such an assignment, a reporter might obtain a better story for general readership by talking to the physicist not about the scientific details of his Nobel Prize-winning research but about what happened when he won the prize. The backstage mechanics of this prestigious award must be interesting. Who nominated him? Did the candidate have to submit masses of material about his work, as though applying for a fellowship? Did a screening committee from the Nobel organization question him? Did the physicist know he was a finalist? How has the award affected the winner's life, professionally and personally? What tangible impact on everyday life will the prize-winning research eventually have? What does the physicist do for relaxation—read mysteries, do jigsaw puzzles, rebuild antique automobiles? Readers will enjoy seeing the informal "human" side of a Nobel laureate.

Tips for Effective Interviewing

1. Find out as much as possible in advance about the person to be interviewed.
2. Prepare a set of questions as a framework for the interview.
3. Approach the interview with confidence.
4. Watch for news lead angles as you talk.
5. Ask direct, searching questions, but try to do so without arousing antagonism.
6. Take ample but not excessive notes. Use a tape recorder as a backup if possible.
7. Add power to the interview by noting frequent direct quotations.
8. Seek to catch the interview subject's personality and physical characteristics.

The city editor may assign a reporter to do an interview for which advance research is almost impossible. If you are told to interview a woman who is observing her 90th birthday, how can you prepare? She never has been a public figure. The only justification for the interview is her advanced age and a report from relatives that she is spry and alert. A light, sympathetic touch is in order. What can you ask her?

Here is where the reporter's ingenuity comes into play. Analyze the problem for a moment. Presumably the most interesting information she can provide is from her memories. So focus on them, but add zest by playing off those memories against her opinions of current trends. The reporter might ask:

Did women ever wear pants when you were young instead of those long, billowing skirts? "Good Lord, no!" Do you think the tight-fitting jeans girls wear now are immodest? (The answers from some elderly interviewees are surprisingly uninhibited; they relish the opportunity to be "on stage.") What would have happened if your mother had caught you going out of the house in pants? "She would have grabbed me by the hair and whacked me!"

Two or three such questions may open the way for tart comments on other aspects of life today. What does she think about so many women holding jobs when in her youth women stayed home? "Yes, stayed home and slaved in the kitchen. Have you ever tried washing clothes in a tin tub and hanging them on the line to dry? Women today don't know how easy they have it. When I was young, any husband would laugh at his wife if she asked him to do half the cooking."

By now the 90-year-old is warmed up and enjoying herself. So toss in a challenging question: "What do you wish you had done when you were young but didn't have the courage to try?"

In interviews of this type, a bright "kicker" to close the story is valuable in addition to a sprightly lead. Frame a question or two that might produce a humorous quotation. If you can intersperse the conversation with discussion of foods, pose the whimsical query, "Are frozen pies as good as those your grandmother used to make?" That ought to spark a useful quote, one way or the other.

Armed with a set of such questions, the interviewer can approach the appointment confident that an interesting story will emerge.

CONDUCTING THE INTERVIEW

When the reporter and the person being interviewed—strangers to each other—sit down together, a psychological cat-and-mouse game begins. Each is sizing up the other. These opening minutes may be vital to the success of the interview, because the reporter must decide after receiving a first impression of the subject what kind of approach to use. If the subject makes clear that time is short and that the appointment has been squeezed in between others, the interviewer should get down to business after only a few introductory remarks. If the circumstances and the subject's manner indicate that there is no rush, a bit of casual preliminary chitchat usually is advisable. The interviewer needs to get the subject conversing, not merely answering questions.

The subject in turn is judging the interviewer. If the reporter gives an impression of brashness or aggressiveness, the subject may "freeze up" or turn antagonistic. Thus the reporter should present a low-key image—neat in dress and discreet, but quietly self-assured. Winning the subject's trust is the first goal of the interviewer; after that comes gaining information.

In most interviews, the original barrier erodes as the two persons get the "feel" of each other. By asking a few easy, general questions first, the interviewer seeks to put the subject at ease. An alert interviewer senses quickly whether the subject will take the initiative in the conversation, guided by a few questions, or whether the interviewer will need to prompt, cajole, and pull out usable answers. Sometimes the subject is genuinely shy and fearful of this unfamiliar exposure to the press. Even the shy ones who profess reluctance secretly are flattered at being interviewed. The late A. J. Liebling, whose interviews and profiles in *The New Yorker* were brilliant, once said, "There is almost no circumstance under which an American doesn't like to be interviewed. We are an articulate people, pleased by attention, covetous of being singled out."

A fundamental rule of interviewing is to let the subject talk. Do not interrupt once the conversational tap has been turned on. Let the subject see that you really are interested in what he or she is saying. Make eye contact frequently. An occasional response such as "Yes, I see" or even a noncommittal "mm'hmm" shows the speaker that you are following closely.

To draw out a difficult subject, some interviewers in trying to probe in depth abandon the role of listener and become talkers by discussing their own affairs. This practice is more suitable for lengthy magazine interviews than for newspaper stories. By using this psychological device, the interviewer hopes to coax the subject into a reciprocal burst of personal frankness. In writing the story later, the interviewer uses only the subject's personal admissions, not the interviewer's. Obviously, this tricky and rather questionable technique must be used sparingly; some subjects will resent wasting their time listening to the interviewer's personal affairs. Yet under certain circumstances, skillfully done, this ploy may produce surprising results.

When Truman Capote interviewed Marlon Brando on a film set in Japan, the frankness of Brando's statements in the resulting story surprised readers. Brando even talked about his mother's alcoholism in these blunt words: ". . . I didn't care any more. She was there. In a room. Holding on to me. And I let her fall. Because I couldn't take it any more—watching her breaking apart, like a piece of porcelain. I stepped right over her. I walked right out. I was indifferent. Since then, I've been indifferent."

Harsh stuff, that. How did Capote draw such quotations from the actor, a man experienced in dealing with the press?

As Bob Thomas, a biographer of Brando, tells the story, Brando explained later, "Well, the little bastard spent half the night telling me all his problems. I figured the least I could do was tell him a few of mine."

At times the person being interviewed, although having agreed to the interview, is openly hostile. Saul Pett of the Associated Press encountered this attitude when he interviewed the controversial labor leader, James Hoffa, who later disappeared and was believed murdered. Pett's brief, blunt lead reported not what Hoffa said, but his manner:

> It was an unusual interview. In tone, it ran the gamut from frigidity to mere coldness.

A United Press International reporter who interviewed the eminent composer Virgil Thomson built his lead on a similar theme, the subject's attitude toward the reporter. Thus:

> The word on Pulitzer Prize-winner Virgil Thomson was that he was a tough interview, sometimes snoozing instead of answering questions and coldly cutting off questioners who said something ignorant.
>
> "I take naps," deadpanned the composer, conductor, author and critic, who turned 84 on Thanksgiving Day . . .
>
> Instead of viewing his interviewer with suspicion, the round little man wearing a checkered jacket was ebullient when speaking of his hometown.
>
> "I love to breathe the western air, the clean Missouri air," Thomson says. "I'm a Kansas City boy."

A warning to the interviewer: Do not fire your heaviest ammunition at the beginning. If you have a harsh, potentially embarrassing question to pose, try to drop it into the conversation when the mood is fairly relaxed. When the interviewee has the hard fastball thrown at him or her without sensing a danger signal in advance, the response is more likely to come with some candor. If the answer is unsatisfactory, it sometimes is good technique to veer away from the touchy point for an easy question or two, then return to it with a lead-in such as, "Going back a bit, you didn't quite make yourself clear when I asked about, etc." This may elicit a better response, or may produce such a belligerent retort that the interviewer knows the door is shut tight on that issue.

In some interviews, the reporter must become an adversary rather than play the role of respectful listener or chatty friend. This is especially true when the subject is suspected of improper activity. The interview becomes a duel of wits: the reporter boring in with demanding questions, the subject giving evasive answers. Tension develops. In such an atmosphere, an adroit reporter may obtain admissions the subject did not intend to make. Goaded by repeated antagonistic questions, the subject may explode with angry but revealing statements. Arguing with the subject may produce the same result. Or if the reporter uses the technique of a trial cross-examiner, pinning down specific details, then confronting the subject with the contradictions in them, newsworthy admissions may result.

Cold persistence under cover of formal politeness is the best method. If the subject accuses you of invasion of privacy, remind him that you represent the public. The reporter, however, has no legal power to force an individual to answer a question. Even when under oath in a legal procedure, a person may refuse to reply by claiming protection of the Fifth Amendment of the Constitution against self-incrimination, known colloquially as "taking the Fifth."

Feature interviews may produce hard-news leads, so keep your ears open for them. If the interviewee says something newsworthy, develop the point with follow-up questions. Be sure to obtain full-sentence quotations to substantiate and expand the news angle. For example, the earthquake expert may volunteer the opinion that Southern California probably will suffer a temblor of major proportions, with high casualties, within the next ten years. There's a headline! Logical follow-up questions would include asking for steps the population can take to get ready for the anticipated disaster and keep down the casualty toll. If no hard-news lead emerges, be on the lookout for an opening feature angle that will attract the reader's attention.

Interviewers need to protect themselves against later charges of having misquoted the person interviewed. An effective way to do this, as the conversation closes, is to turn back in your notes to the most controversial comments and say, "Before I go, I'd like to check a couple of these quotes with you, just to be sure I have them right." Read them to the subject, who may correct them, if necessary, and in doing so perhaps add useful new material. The same device can be used if the reporter, in the haste of note taking, failed to get down all the words in a key statement. Rechecking is especially important when a scientist or other specialist is being interviewed.

Occasionally, the interviewer's problem is not getting the subject to start talking, but getting the person to stop. Many personalities who make news, especially in politics and entertainment, are extroverts and frequently are self-centered. Keeping them on the track is not always easy. They are accustomed to dominating conversations while their admirers listen. The interviewer must find ways to break in tactfully with specific questions; if this is not done, the interviewer may find the allotted time gone and little accomplished. On the other hand, reporters may become so intrigued with the personalities of gracious, chattering interviewees that they remain too long. Do not overstay your welcome! An hour should be ample for all but the rarest interview, and many can be done satisfactorily in less than that.

The subject of an interview, unfamiliar with newspaper practice, may ask to be shown a copy of the writer's story before it is published. Should this happen, the reporter must refuse politely but firmly, explaining that standard policy among newspapers forbids this practice. Editors look upon submitting a story to anyone for approval before publication as a potential form of censorship. When the subject matter is complex, however, the reporter may wish to read back to the interviewee crucial portions of the story to check their accuracy.

A device sometimes useful when interviewing a person whom the reporter suspects of holding back information is to imply that you know more about the situation than you actually do. If the subject believes that you are informed about the basic facts, he or she may let the barriers down and talk rather freely about the details, thus providing confirmation of a story that the reporter only suspected. By skillful backtracking in questioning, the reporter can pin down the complete story from the reluctant source. Keeping a secret is not easy for many people. Sometimes they actually welcome the opportunity to discuss their big news with a caller, once they believe the story has been, or will be made, public. "Fishing" for information is a tricky game, however, best played by an experienced and quick-witted interviewer. A beginner who through clumsy questioning lets the subject feel that he or she has been misled may be deeply embarrassed. Skillful "fishing" has produced many news beats.

One entertaining example, from the hard-fought street sale circulation war days of an earlier journalistic era, concerns the flamboyant white-robed evangelist, Aimee Semple McPherson. Her dramatic platform style and erratic personal behavior made her a spectacular evangelistic figure even in those pretelevision days. A rumor circulated that she planned to be married, but none of the reporters in Los Angeles, her home city, could obtain confirmation. Finally a reporter who had covered her activities in the past telephoned her and began the conversation by saying, "My, you sound happy today!"

Aimee replied that she did indeed. The reporter went on, "You sound exactly like a bride, the way I thought you would."

"Oh, you've heard about it!" Aimee said. "Come on over, I want to talk to you."

The reporter went to her home and she told him about her plans to be married on Monday. Thinking quickly, he saw the opportunity for an exclusive story. He suggested that she should fly secretly to Arizona on Sunday morning, be married there, fly back, and announce the news to her congregation at the Sunday afternoon service. Aimee liked the drama involved; it was just her style. The reporter then called the operator of a charter air service and said, "Will you lend me an airplane Sunday if I promise to get the name of your air service on front pages all over the country Monday morning? I can't tell you why."

The flier agreed. The reporter took the evangelist, her bridegroom, and a photographer on a flight to Yuma, Arizona. The wedding ceremony was performed at the steps of the airplane, so the company's name showed in the photographs. En route back to Los Angeles the reporter wrote his story with the terse, attention-demanding lead, "Behold the bride—Aimee Semple McPherson!" His newspaper printed an extra edition with a blaring headline for sale to the crowds at a mammoth Sunday afternoon air show, at the same hour Aimee was presenting her husband to her tabernacle congregation. Editors of the opposition papers in town, caught empty-handed, fumed.

All of this was the result of a clever reporter's "fishing" questions, plus ingenuity by the reporter and cooperation by his city editor in making the arrangements. Sometimes a reporter must have a flair for salesmanship, too.

TAKING NOTES

The problem for the feature interviewer is to take sufficient notes during a conversation to provide accurate material when the story is written, but to avoid doing so in such an obvious manner that the conversational tone of the interview is destroyed. Excessive note taking may cause the person being interviewed to freeze up. Also, an interviewer who is extremely busy scribbling notes on everything that is said lacks time to absorb the atmosphere and observe the subject's personality and mannerisms. An experienced interviewer holds note taking to essentials, with emphasis on the need to get significant direct quotations recorded correctly. Keep your notebook discreetly out of sight during the preliminary conversational gambits. An easy approach, when the interview gets down to business, is to open the notebook and ask casually, "Do you mind if I take a few notes?"

An interviewer's notes should include descriptive touches of the person being interviewed. Little fragments jotted down inconspicuously while talking, just a few words at a time, can be expanded later when the story is written—notes such as "keeps lighting pipe," "fingers hair," "puts on, takes off dark-rimmed glasses," or "waves hands, gushy talker." Such impressionistic note taking is comparable to a painter's rough pencil sketches. Physical description and style of dress are important. These notes help the reporter to reconstruct an image of the interviewee when writing the story. Deftly inserted into the copy, these personality touches enable the reader to visualize the individual. Notice in the segment of the interview with Virgil Thomson quoted earlier how the single phrase "the little round man wearing a checkered jacket" brings the musician to life on paper.

THE TAPE RECORDER

Unless the interview subject objects, or is visibly nervous about having one in operation, use of a tape recorder is a desirable precaution. The interviewer may help put the subject at ease by saying something like, "If you don't mind, I'll use this tape recorder so we're sure we get everything straight." Should the subject keep eyeing the recorder uneasily, and it obviously is a barrier obstructing open conversation, quietly lean over and turn it off.

Again, the caution: Do not depend excessively on your tape recorder, because it might fail you. Not so long ago, the associate editor of a major West Coast

166 PART IV / INTERVIEWING AND PROBING

newspaper, the Portland *Oregonian,* found this out in an embarrassing and costly manner. After his exclusive interview with Governor Dixy Lee Ray of Washington was published, the governor protested that it contained quotations she had never uttered. She had her own tape recording of their interview to prove her contention. The editor admitted that he had fabricated some quotations because the tape recording he had made proved to be inaudible. Since his written notes were fragmentary and inadequate, he padded them out in his story with statements he erroneously believed the governor would have made. The *Oregonian* publicly apologized to Governor Ray, and the editor was suspended without pay for two months. The lesson for all interviewers is clear: Take sufficient written notes so you can do a complete story from them, and use the recorder as a backup supplement.

When conducting an interview by telephone from their office desks, some reporters hold the instrument to the ear with a telephone cradle and take notes directly onto a video display terminal, using a semishorthand. Then they get a printout of the notes. They find that note taking this way is faster and fuller than using handwritten notes. Others, less at home with the VDT, find the system cumbersome.

AN INTERVIEW WITH KIM NOVAK

In the following interview by Judy Klemesrud of the New York *Times* with Kim Novak, the semiretired film actress, observe how the writer extracted from their conversation the kinds of useful material we have been discussing. These include a provocative lead angle, descriptive physical touches, lively quotations, and a closing paragraph that rounds off the story.

Kim Novak Back After 11 Years

By JUDY KLEMESRUD
N.Y. Times News Service

Identifies Novak, states reason for interview

NEW YORK—Kim Novak, one of the country's best-known llama breeders, was in town the other day to talk about her avocation: movie acting. Or more specifically, her first feature film in 11 years, Agatha Christie's "The Mirror Crack'd," in which she plays an aging movie goddess who comes to Britain to co-star in a film with her bitter rival, played by Elizabeth Taylor. "Put the two of them in a tank with a killer shark," says one character in the movie, "and the poor shark would have an identity crisis."

"This film is so completely different from anything I've ever done," the reclusive actress said in her husky voice, when asked why she had left her mountaintop ranch in Carmel, Calif., to make the film. "My first thought was, 'It's not really for me, because it's not me.'

Quotations develop Novak personality

But the script was so good, and it had all those people I knew from the past, like Rock Hudson and Tony Curtis, and I was thrilled to work with Elizabeth Taylor for the first time."

And so Miss Novak accepted the part, even though she had promised her husband of five years, Dr. Robert Mallory, a veterinarian, that she would do no more lengthy feature films. "This one required only three weeks' work, and he said he didn't mind," she said. "Besides, it's the kind of movie my whole family could see—my husband has two children, 12 and 16."

Writer's observation

At 47, Miss Novak still looks as glamorous as she did when she was America's No. 1 box office attraction in 1956 after appearing in such films as "Picnic," "The Man With the Golden Arm" and "The Eddy Duchin Story." Her face is wrinkle-free, her green eyes are as smoldery as ever, her hair still platinum blond and her figure, in tight black corduroy pants, as trim as any fashion model's. "I keep in shape feeding the animals and cleaning the corrals," she said. "It's terrific exercise."

Miss Novak said that during her three weeks in Britain she did not get to know Elizabeth Taylor very well. "But we both had a lot of fun with our parts," she said. "We both had a lot of funny, bitchy lines to say to each other. In real life, that bitchiness rarely exists on a movie set, but actresses have certainly thought about it a lot. But they've never said it. That's why this movie was so much fun."

Meanwhile, back at the ranch, Miss Novak and her husband have 30 llamas, which they raise for sale, six horses, three goats, two raccoons, two dogs and one donkey. The door of the house, she said, is built high enough so the animals can wander in and out at will. "This way they realize that you respect them, and they respect you," she said. "If you only see your horse when you go out to ride, you don't know your horse."

Miss Novak says she is known as Kim Mallory in Carmel, and that she goes with her husband on most of his veterinary calls. "I'm his assistant," she said. "I feel very important to him, and I don't want to be replaced."

Novak answers reporter's prepared question

Develops llama lead angle

Let us go back to Klemesrud's lead. She caught our attention with a reverse twist device, alluding to Kim Novak not as the one-time top box office star but as "one of the country's best known llama breeders" for whom acting is now a hobby. Llama breeding in itself is mildly amusing, because it is so rare. Right from the start, the writer provides a focal point for the interview by showing Miss Novak's present set of priorities.

Film goers who remember the sleek, alluring Kim Novak on the screen naturally wonder what years in the barnyard have done to her beauty. How does she appear at 47? The interviewer tells us directly and emphatically: "Miss Novak still looks as glamorous as she did when she was America's No. 1 box office attraction in 1956 . . . Her face is wrinkle-free, her green eyes are as smoldery as ever, her hair still platinum blond and her figure, in tight black corduroy pants, as trim as any fashion model's." At another point, the writer alludes to Miss Novak's "husky voice." We can almost visualize the reporter jotting down these descriptive notes as she converses with the actress.

To reinforce the reader's perception of the actress as an animal breeder, the interviewer captures and employs such quotations as: "I keep in shape feeding the animals and cleaning the corrals. It's terrific exercise." And again, "If you only see your horse when you go out to ride, you don't know your horse."

As a way to give the story a strong ending, the reporter saved another quotation that reiterates the theme of the interview, how the former Hollywood star has changed her personal priorities. After reporting that Kim Novak accompanies her husband on most of his veterinary calls, she closes with the "kicker" quotation, "I'm his assistant. I feel very important to him, and I don't want to be replaced."

The interview is finished, and the reporter has gone as quickly as possible to a typewriter or a video display terminal to type out his or her expanded notes. Next comes the "manufacturing" job, turning the raw material into a finished product for publication.

STUDY PROJECTS

1. You have been assigned to interview an Oscar-winning dramatic film actress who is appearing on the campus. Prepare and submit eight questions you plan to ask her.

2. Clip an interview story from a newspaper. Underline in one color all personal descriptive touches used by the writer and all the direct quotations in another color.

3. Analyze a full-length interview story published in a newspaper. Discuss in 250–300 words its strengths and weaknesses.

READ MORE ABOUT IT . . .

John Brady, *The Craft of Interviewing* (Cincinnati: Writer's Digest, 1976).
Ken Metzler, *Creative Interviewing* (Englewood Cliffs, N.J.: Prentice-Hall, 1977).
Paul N. Williams, *Investigative Reporting and Editing* (Englewood Cliffs, N.J.: Prentice-Hall, 1978) includes material on interviewing techniques.

COMING UP NEXT . . .

The writer of a feature interview has two goals: to tell the reader what the subject has to say and to catch the essence of the subject's personality and experience. This chapter discusses how to achieve these objectives.

After determining a theme for the interview story, the writer must decide upon a lead. Should it be hard or soft? That depends upon what the subject said. Then comes development of the story in support of the lead—expansion of the theme and response to the reader's questions if a suspended interest or "come-on" introduction is used. Examples show how these writing problems can be solved.

Ways in which quotations, sometimes interwoven with the writer's observations, can be used to achieve the interviewer's two goals are explained. A breezy interview with an extroverted writer, Fran Lebowitz, that succeeds in its objectives, closes the chapter.

Chapter 15
Writing the Interview Story

CHOOSING A LEAD

The best interview stories are those with a theme. In writing them, the reporter should shape the material on hand to emphasize a distinctive point of view stated or demonstrated by the person interviewed. This is done by choosing direct quotations and summary comments from the conversation and organizing them into a cohesive whole. These nuggets may have been scattered throughout an hour of talk; the writer's craftsmanship lies in the ability to select the pertinent fragments, organize them, and weave them into a narrative pattern.

Before starting to write, the interviewer should analyze his or her notes and ask, "What has this person said that will interest my readers? What do I want to tell the readers about this person?" Some writers find that they can shape their interview stories more easily if they write down for their own guidance a theme sentence or two, then indicate those elements in their notes that develop the theme.

For example, in the interview with Kim Novak published in the preceding chapter, the writer might have framed a theme sentence something like this, "Kim Novak says she has made her marriage to a veterinarian and her interest in animals the primary concern in her life and regards an occasional film appearance as a change-of-pace novelty."

With the theme chosen, the reporter next selects the type of lead to use—the hard-news variety or the soft feature approach. This decision in turn influences how the rest of the interview story will be developed.

A hard-news lead is a head-on approach to the subject matter based on newsworthy statements made by the person interviewed, resembling the lead on a straight news story. It demands the reader's attention. When a soft feature lead is used, the tone is much different. This is a flank attack, like an army sneaking up on its objective from the side or rear. In it, the writer slides into the theme of the interview. This soft approach seduces the readers, luring them into the heart of the story with a provocative, often whimsical, opening paragraph. This "come-on" lead depicts an offbeat situation, a mood, or an intriguing aspect of the person interviewed.

When the interviewee has made genuinely newsworthy statements of significance to all readers, the hard lead should be used. Material about the subject's personality and background should be worked in as the story develops, or in a separate soft feature story, but it should not be allowed to obscure the news. The basic rule of spot news writing—Don't bury the lead!—applies equally to feature interviews that, perhaps unexpectedly, produce important information. Put it up front!

The following opening portion of an interview with former President Gerald Ford by an Associated Press reporter illustrates the hard-news approach to writing an interview lead.

Hard news lead	RANCHO MIRAGE, Calif. (AP)—Former President Ford says President Reagan is "naive" if he thinks budget cuts will be easier than tax cuts to sell Congress.	
Recommendation for action	And because of that, Reagan should hold off on the last two years of his three-year, 30 per cent tax cut program until there is "visible evidence" Congress will reduce the growth of federal spending, Ford says.	
Reason for recommendation	In an interview with the Associated Press at his home in the California desert, Ford said efforts to reduce federal spending always tend to generate formidable coalitions which band together to protect their own appropriations. "My own experience in Congress would lead me to the conclusion that the House and Senate would be more amenable to a reduction in taxes than they will be to an effort to reduce expenditures."	Quotation supports lead

Notice that the writer made clear early in the story the circumstances under which the former President offered advice to the incumbent chief executive—that it was during an interview in the relaxed surroundings of Ford's desert home. Ford's comments that were quoted later in the interview about financial and foreign affairs conveyed a more reflective, elder-statesman tone than if he had still been a decision-maker.

Compare that hard lead with this tantalizing soft lead on an interview with a

Polish survivor of Nazi prison camps during World War II. It contains no "news" in the traditional sense, but is so provocative that the reader automatically wants to know more:

> Till the day he died, Ted Tarnowski suspected that he was blessed with more luck than the average person.
> Since that day, he's never doubted it.

Immediately, the reader wonders how a man can be dead and still have his thought processes described in the present.

The writer, Walton R. Collins, quickly provides the answer, and in doing so begins to unfurl for the reader the reminiscences of a currently successful Polish-American chef whose wartime survival was truly miraculous:

> Tarnowski "died" in 1944 in the infirmary of a Nazi work camp in Steyr, Austria. Three days earlier a guard had caught him picking up a discarded cigarette butt and clubbed him viciously in the head with a gun. The wound, though superficial, turned gangrenous.
> If Tarnowski was not precisely dead when he was taken to the camp's infirmary, he was close enough by the primitive clinical standards of the setting. Judged too far gone to be worth treating, his body was flung on a pile of corpses awaiting transportation to a crematory at the Mauthausen concentration camp a few miles away.

By a lucky coincidence, Tarnowski was found by a doctor who detected vital signs in his body, brought him back to the infirmary, and eventually cured him. The writer used slight literary license by not putting quotation marks around the word *died* in the lead sentence, but the device was justified by the dramatic effect it produced. He explained the apparent contradiction immediately thereafter and so did not mislead the reader for more than a moment.

A vital point to remember about writing the feature interview is that the writer may use flexibility in narrative technique and judiciously inject personal observation that would not be acceptable in a straight news story.

Assigned to interview a woman artist who specializes in animal subjects, Hans Knight of the Philadelphia *Bulletin* wrote this lead:

> The other day, Joyce Gagen, a vibrant woman with honey-blonde hair and bright blue eyes, walked into Jack's Taxidermy in Burlington County, South Jersey, and asked if she could borrow a stuffed bear for a few days.

This lead attracts attention because it has physical action and novelty. Immediately, the reader wonders why Joyce Gagen needs a stuffed bear.

The writer answers that question within the next 100 words by reporting that Mrs. Gagen is "an up-and-coming wildlife artist, who, by her own admission, will stop at 'almost nothing' to obtain true models of what she paints."

It is not always easy to produce a brief soft lead on a feature story that tries to establish a mood, but it can be done. In just eight words, an Associated Press reporter who conducted a telephone interview in Oakland, California, "hooked" readers with this model of brevity.

> If you're going to sin, do it right.

What doors that opens for the reader's imagination! The interviewer draws the reader deeper into the story with a punchy second paragraph:

> Praying doesn't help. But as Sister Madeleine Rose Ashton can tell you, knowing the odds does.

Within 25 tantalizing words, the writer has mentioned sin, gambling, and a Catholic nun. Now comes the time to give the reader the answers:

> Sister Ashton—or "Mad Rose," as her math students call her—is well acquainted with casino odds, and is well known for her lecture entitled: "How to Gamble . . . If You Must."
>
> The prim Holy Name College instructor, a former president of the coeducational liberal arts school tucked away in the hills above San Francisco Bay, says although she'd rather spend her money on a ticket to the Oakland A's baseball game, she can beat the odds with the best of them.

Notice how the writer emphasized the incongruity of a Catholic sister teaching her students to gamble wisely by describing her as "prim"; yet she likes to attend major league baseball games. Having established the unusual personality of the interviewee, the writer then quotes her at length about which gambling games at Las Vegas offer the best and the worst odds; her practical advice included her assertion that there are only six good bets at the craps table and that keno has the worst odds.

Aware that many religious people believe gambling to be morally wrong, the reader inevitably wonders what Sister Madeleine Rose thinks about this. The interviewer saves the answer to that question for the final paragraph, as the "kicker":

> ... Sister Ashton said she has no moral objection to gambling—as long as the stake isn't the grocery money.

The three soft leads just examined share an important virtue—brevity. In addition, they share another element of writing technique that is vital to an effective interview story: After dangling a bit of mystery as an attraction, the writers did not wait long to let the readers know what the story was all about so they could decide whether to continue reading. Too much preliminary verbiage before getting into the core of the interview causes the reader to become impatient and bored, and probably to skip to another story.

A lead on an interview story that makes the reader feel involved emotionally —arousing sympathy or anger, for example—attracts readership. The following example not only stirs sympathy, but has the added strength of creating a sense of contradiction, somewhat like the Polish survivor story:

> SPRINGFIELD, Ore. (AP)— Laura Liberatore is crippled. She's also a junior varsity cheerleader, member of her school jazz choir, delegate to the student council and nearly a straight-A student.

A crippled cheerleader? The reader automatically wonders, how can that be? Soon we shall provide the answer.

DEVELOPING THE STORY

After creating a lead and deciding how to progress from it into the substance of the interview, the writer must plan how to develop the main body of the story and to round it off at the close. The type of material emerging from the reporter's conversation with the interviewee influences this planning.

Some interviews are purely informational and can be written on a question-and-answer framework, with explanatory and transitional passages worked in to provide an element of continuity. The goal of such interviews is clarity, not clever literary footwork. If the person being interviewed is an official of the Social Security Administration, and the purpose is to explain changes in Social Security benefits and filing procedures, this is no time for whimsy. The changes will affect the daily lives of millions whose income is at stake; they want a matter-of-fact explanation of the new rules, not entertainment. The lead should be based upon the official's description of the most significant change. The writer may inject a "plus" element by providing background on why the changes were made and by giving specific examples of how individuals with certain sets of circumstances will be affected. Although less fun to write than other kinds of interviews, the service feature is a challenge to the reporter's ability to explain sometimes complex material in terse, lucid language. The writing should be easily comprehended by readers who may be ill-informed about government procedures and worried about rumors that "They are going to take away our Social Security."

At the other end of the spectrum is the personality interview, sometimes poignant, sometimes frothy. Here the writer is free to employ some of the techniques the fiction writer uses—characterization, point of view, clever turns of phrase, suspense. Even that dangerous pronoun "I" may be used discreetly in some feature interviews when verbal interplay between interviewer and subject has an essential role in depicting the subject's personality. The body of some interviews may be developed in chronological style. In others, deft switching back and forth in describing the topics covered may be desirable if it helps to illuminate the basic theme. No rigid rules exist for writing the interview; much depends upon the situation, the type of person interviewed, and the writer's style.

Let us now look more closely at the interview with Laura, the crippled cheerleader.

Having been introduced to Laura by an intriguing opening paragraph, the reader has numerous questions. How did she become crippled? How badly is she handicapped? What does she think about her misfortune? What drives her to achieve the things the lead has listed for her, instead of surrendering in despair?

The writer answers these and other questions in a smooth-flowing style, alternating paragraphs of factual summary with direct quotations from Laura. Discussion of Laura's thoughts about her plight is almost entirely in direct quotations, projecting the story from her point of view.

Immediately, in the second paragraph, the interviewer summarizes the facts of Laura's accident and her present physical condition thus:

> The pretty, doe-eyed 17-year old Springfield High School student seemingly had the world on a string. But then, a little more than a year ago, she was left a paraplegic. She could not move from the neck down after an automobile accident in November 1979.

With the background spelled out, the writer moves into the most significant portion of the story—Laura's reflections about what the accident has done to her. The third paragraph gives the reader a quick insight into Laura, as she is today and as she perceives herself as having been before the accident.

> "I'm more patient now, I'm less cocky than before—not as mean and snooty," she says, sitting in a wheelchair in her bedroom.

After a summary of the extent of Laura's injuries and her four-month stay in a hospital bed, the writer switches back to Laura's comments about herself:

> "It gave me a lot of time to think and I guess that's when I set my values," she says. "When I felt depressed, I always thought of people who were worse."

Again the writer intervenes, explaining that Laura fantasizes about being able to walk someday and that when she dreams, she never thinks of herself as being in a wheelchair. Then comes another poignant quotation:

> "But in my dreams, I only see myself from the waist up," she says.

The reader begins to admire Laura and her determination. But still hovering unanswered is that question from the lead paragraph: How could a paraplegic girl become a cheerleader? By holding back the answer this long, the writer has legitimately used some mild suspense. Now comes the answer in the writer's words:

> . . . school officials decided she could be an extra member of the squad.
> So now, just as before, she's a familiar face at Springfield High games, performing arm movements of the routines and spending the rest of the time cheering on the sidelines.
> When squad members form a pyramid, her wheelchair is a part of the bottom of the formation.

After describing how Laura became a member of the cast for the school production of "Fiddler on the Roof" and kept right on singing after her wheelchair tipped over on stage, the writer ends the story with a strong, characteristic quotation from Laura:

> "I don't give up very easily," she says. "I have to work a little harder now, but being this way has given me a lot of patience . . . a lot of it. "I don't accept people telling me I can't do something."

This interview was well planned and written, with an attention-getting lead. Although arousing the reader's sympathy, it does not indulge in excessive pathos, dwelling instead on the girl's determination to improve her condition. It does, however, lack an important element, a physical description of Laura. The writer refers to her as "pretty, doe-eyed and 17" but nothing more. Is she blonde or brunette, short-haired or long? Does she speak slowly and reflectively or in a spirited manner? A few additional personality touches would have sharpened the reader's perception of her.

A feature interview whenever possible should have a consciously designed conclusion, such as those in the stories about the crippled cheerleader and the gambling nun. Editors rarely cut feature interviews from the bottom up, as they do spot news stories, unless the interview is exceptionally long. Thus the writer has an opportunity to wrap up the package and tie a literary ribbon around it. In a light personality story this conclusion may be a final humorous quotation that provides a twist, the way a clever comedian gets off the stage with a closing jest. The ending might also be a philosophical observation by the subject or a terse summary observation by the writer, provided the latter does not sound "preachy."

USE OF QUOTATIONS

From the preceding examples of interviews, the importance of lively, relevant quotations by the person interviewed is apparent. Quotations can be used by a skillful writer to depict character and, when interwoven with the writer's summary paragraphs, to provide a narrative flow.

Although the importance of accurate quotations has always been stressed by meticulous editors, newspapers traditionally protected those they interview by

---

Tips on Writing the Interview

1. Select a theme from your notes and build the story around it.
2. Decide between a hard-news lead and a soft feature lead.
3. Do not wait long to let readers know what the interview is all about; a lead that is too elaborately "featurish" may make the reader lose interest.
4. Work in descriptive touches of mannerisms, dress, and speech to build a sketch of the subject's personality.
5. Use direct quotations that tell what the interviewee wishes to convey and also those that illuminate his or her personality.
6. Since the feature interview is a less rigid form of writing than the straight news story, feel free to use such literary devices as point of view, suspense, crisp impressionistic style, and even, on occasion, the first person.

correcting their errors in grammar. If the interviewee actually said, "I ain't got no money," the statement came out in print, "I don't have any money." The editors' intention was to protect those persons who lacked the advantage of a good education from looking bad in print.

However, greater emphasis on naturalism in newspaper writing has caused a recent change in this practice. Increasingly, newspapers quote news sources exactly as they speak, including moderately strong profanity and obscenity. No firm pattern of practice has developed in this matter; individual newspapers have their own sets of standards. However, a profane laborer who barely got through eighth grade is much less likely today to sound in print like a college-educated Sunday School teacher than was the case 20 years ago. Minor slips in usage by usually well-spoken people should be corrected, under normal circumstances.

A BREEZY INTERVIEW

The value of lively quotations is evident in the following interview with a chatty, wisecracking New York author, Fran Lebowitz, by Steven Winn in the San Francisco *Chronicle*. Her comments on her career and her life in Manhattan are effusive, brittle, and consciously exaggerated. By interspersing his own wry comments about the author, the interviewer provides a brisk, perceptive portrait of Lebowitz. Notice how he pumps animation into his story with such touches as "was plopped down cross-legged on the bed in her hotel suite" and "One eyebrow went up, slightly, then dropped down again . . ." Although few interview subjects are as extroverted as Fran Lebowitz, a reporter's careful observation will discover distinctive mannerisms in every person; weaving allusions to these personality quirks into the story unobtrusively gives it a richer texture.

Another unusual aspect of this interview is that the reporter first talked with Lebowitz person-to-person and then attended a public performance by her. In his story, the reporter made the two episodes mesh, so that his report of her presentation reinforced the view of her he had gained in the personal contact. The final paragraph succinctly pulls together the impression the reporter wishes to give the reader.

By STEVEN WINN

Like most writers, Fran Lebowitz does not mind talking about herself. Nor, sharing another characteristic with others of her trade, does she avoid conversation about the promotion and sale of her work.

Last week, the night before reading from her forthcoming book at the College of Marin, the New York author was plopped down cross-legged on the bed in her hotel suite, recapping the extraordinarily sudden success of her first book, "Metropolitan Life," a collection of comic essays published in 1978.

"Literally, quite literally, my life

changed with one phone call," Lebowitz said. That 7 a.m. call from her agent, three years ago next month, brought news that the New York Times had just published a highly favorable review of "Metropolitan Life."

The book sold out at New York stores that day, and by dinnertime four Hollywood producers had made offers for the film rights.

"When the phone rang," Lebowitz recalled, "I naturally thought my entire family had been killed in a fire. In fact, I thought they *better* have been killed in a fire. No one ever calls me at 7 a.m." Lebowitz dropped her cigaret ash onto an already considerable mound in the ashtray, turned a contentedly glum face to the window and continued:

"Success didn't spoil me. I've always been insufferable. Besides, this whole idea that being a celebrity is so difficult offends me. The fact is, it's better being famous. More people like you; you can get better clothes. Look at it this way: what used to be a reasonable amount of money to live on for three years is now what I'd consider spending on an armoire."

One eyebrow went up, slightly, then dropped down again—a Lebowitz signal that she is seeking, but certainly not needing (and God forbid she should let on), an approving laugh.

There's a powerful sense about this 30-year-old woman that what she writes, the way she writes it, is what she *is*.

"I don't have a past," she deadpanned. "I'm from New Jersey. I moved to New York when I was 18 (and worked as a cabdriver, among other things, to support her writing).

"Before that there were two things I wanted to be: a toll collector and a cellist. I gave up on being a toll collector when I found out you didn't get to keep the money. The cellist was no good either: there's just no way to be a successful bad cellist, so I decided to be a famous writer instead."

Lebowitz may glide over the world of letters cynically, but it's obvious that her style—an original blend of epigram ("If your sexual fantasies were truly of interest to others, they would no longer be fantasies") and a kind of baroque formalism of language and syntax —is a hard-won source of pride.

Sticking to that style, she fended off a probe about what she thinks her work is all about. "I am social. And I'm certainly critical. Does that make me a social critic?"

Instead, she offered a more or less random series of sketches based on her life in New York—lines that might just as easily show up in her essays as in her speech.

"I don't go out in the day. In New York, when you go out in the day, you never get there—which actually isn't a bad idea.

"The apartment situation is so bad in New York that when I went on the 'Today Show' and said I was looking for a place, no one called.

"The only problem with my schedule is that it's hard to find people who will have lunch with you at 3:30 in the morning.

"I don't read newspapers," Lebowitz declared. "I mean I really don't read newspapers. I wouldn't know there was a nuclear war until the building melted."

Writing, which Lebowitz claims to religiously avoid ("I'd rather watch game shows"), nonetheless remains a principal topic of conversation.

Her kind of writing, she argued, is a kind of endangered species. "Look at this," she said, springing up and leading the way to the bathroom, "designer soap. How can you be a satirist in a world that actually has designer soap? Or Carl Sagan? Most of the things I've thought up as jokes turned out to be real."

If Fran Lebowitz is struggling, it didn't show at the College of Marin, where a disquietingly New Yorkish crowd of 400 showed up to hear her read from her new book, "Social Studies." (Lebowitz's contention that "there are really only about 80 people in the world, and I see them everywhere" was weirdly borne out by the audience: the College of Marin might just as well have been the New School for Social Research in Manhattan.)

Selections from the new book ranged over "People," "Places," "Things" and "Ideas"—the four modest divisions of "Social Studies." From the opening argument about human uniqueness (the only things that distinguish individuals from each other are the sizes of their feet and the exact way they like their eggs cooked), Lebowitz had the crowd glowingly responsive.

"The conversational overreacher is one whose grasp exceeds his reach. This is possible but not desirable," Lebowitz advanced. Then later: "Spilling your guts is just exactly as appealing as it sounds." And: "The opposite of talking is not listening. It's waiting."

Doting on her capsule autobiographies ("I'm not the type that wants to go back to the land. I'm the type that wants to go back to the hotel"), the audience peppered her with hey-lady-be-funny questions for a solid half hour after the reading. Lebowitz obliged.

"Nancy Reagan? Not my type exactly—sort of a richer Pat Nixon."

"I was on Castro Street today. Apparently people don't mind dressing alike."

"It's cheaper to eat out in Manhattan than it is to afford an apartment that's large enough for a kitchen."

A question about the new president drew a bemused hesitation, and then, with a self-delighted, got-it grin, this: "I think you should pick politicians solely on their looks. My objection to Ronald Reagan is not that he was an actor, but that he was a B-actor. I mean, America deserves Gregory Peck."

Beaming, Fran Lebowitz got what she was after: mad cheers, applause.

STUDY PROJECTS

1. Submit two newspaper stories based on interviews that contain hard news.

2. Paste up an interview story that lacks hard-news content; then write brief analytical notes concerning the story's structure alongside the relevant paragraphs.

3. In Steven Winn's interview with Fran Lebowitz, (a) list places in which the reporter subjectively interspersed comments on Lebowitz's personality; (b) cite ways in which the story might have been improved.

COMING UP NEXT . . .

Some facts are handed to the reporter on a platter—in police reports, news releases, and texts of speeches. For a good reporter, however, this is only the beginning. He or she must do research, must get in there and dig.

In this chapter, we show you how to search for facts and some of the best places to find them.

The first piece of advice is: Use the telephone! Alexander Graham Bell did journalism a tremendous service with his invention, but some reporters do not use it enough. The telephone book is a splendid source for the correct spelling of names and for addresses.

Among other sources waiting to be tapped are:

- The newspaper's library.
- Public records. Many revealing stories have been uncovered by persistent reporters searching through these accumulations of official paperwork.
- Standard reference works in libraries. This chapter includes a list of major ones.

Chapter 16
A Reporter's Research Tools

WHERE TO LOOK

At a civic reception, a coauthor of this textbook chanced to meet a man whom he had trained as a beginning reporter more than 35 years earlier in a press association bureau in London. The neophyte had been hired during a wartime manpower shortage because he happened to be an American civilian in the British capital. Later, after a successful career in corporate public relations, he became an attorney.

As the two men renewed acquaintance after the long interval, each thinking how gray-haired the other had become, the attorney said, "You taught me one thing I've never forgotten. One day a diplomatic story arrived from the Continent and you handed it to me with instructions to obtain reaction to it from the British Foreign Office.

"I asked, 'How do I reach the Foreign Office?' You replied, 'Look in the telephone book.'

"I've been using that advice ever since."

The telephone book is the most convenient and most frequently used of every reporter's research tools. Not only does it list the numbers of persons and organizations that may provide information for stories but it also spells their names correctly and gives their addresses. The more telephone calls a reporter makes, the more information he or she obtains for a story. The classified section of the phone book provides lists of companies, institutions, and services, conveniently indexed. If a reporter is assigned to obtain comments from local dentists about a newly announced form of anticavity treatment, for example, the Dentists category in the yellow pages provides a quick, handy list of sources.

Switchboards of most newspapers keep telephone directories of major American cities ready for use. Newsrooms usually have copies of phone books for all cities in their circulation area near the city desk. University and public libraries have collections of out-of-town phone books that will provide names, numbers, and addresses of distant sources a reporter may need to reach. The telephone company's directory assistance service will also aid the caller. In college, the campus telephone directory and student, faculty, and alumni directories are helpful.

What if the person you need to reach has an unlisted telephone or no telephone at all? You believe the person lives in your city, but have no idea where.

In most cities, the problem may be solved through another primary printed source of local information, the city directory. Most of these directories are published by the R. L. Polk Company. A Polk city directory lists local inhabitants alphabetically by address, occupation, home ownership status, and telephone number, if any. Another extremely valuable feature for the reporter is its cross-listing of residents by street and house number. Thus, under S. Elmore Rd., for example, each house number is listed, with the names of persons living at that location and telephone numbers. Having found the name of a resident at a desired number, the reporter can look up that person in the alphabetical listing. Another section lists phone numbers numerically, followed by the holder's name. Although city directories are usually quite accurate, they are not infallible; it is wise to double-check the information listed with the person involved.

Old city directories are kept on file at the public library or local historical society, and sometimes in newspaper and broadcasting station libraries. These are invaluable for a reporter doing a story involving local historical background, because they show details about the city at given times in the past.

The newspaper's editorial library is the starting place for a reporter searching out background for a story. In this library are clippings of published stories, filed by individual names and cross-filed by topics, such as School Board Elections or High School Football. When the accumulation of material under a general topic is large, it may be broken down into subsections or by dates. Files of past editions of the newspaper are kept, too, usually on microfilm. Electronic data storage is increasing in newspaper libraries.

Local historical museums and the local history and genealogical departments of the public library can provide valuable background about old families and situations.

Another published source of information about local individuals, often overlooked, is high school and college yearbooks, usually filed at school headquarters and libraries. Here is an example of how yearbooks can be used in research for a feature story.

You are assigned to write a story about a law school professor who has just been appointed a federal district judge. You know that he attended a local high school and that he received his bachelor's degree from the local university in a certain year. Count back four years to the date he graduated from high school, look up the class yearbook, find his senior photograph, and the listing of his activities. You discover that he played trombone in the school band, a casual fact that he had not mentioned in your interview with him. Armed with this information, you find in a follow-up interview that he helped pay his way through college and law school by playing in a campus dance band. Occasionally he picks up the old instrument and plays a little in the basement for relaxation. These details provide a lively contrast to his somber legal achievements. The vision of a trombone-tooting judge is intriguing. Class prophecies in high school yearbooks often provide surprising predictions about an individual's future, either accurate or ludicrously off base. The new judge's peers on the prophecy-writing committee guessed that some day he would be a famous comedian, because he did crazy stunts in school—another good angle. Make a copy of his photograph from the yearbook and include it in the photo layout with your story, an eye-catching contrast to the judge in his new black robes, with gavel. Digging out material of this kind is what makes research fun, and stories better.

PUBLIC RECORDS

The mass of printed records and electronically stored information accumulated in public offices holds a fortune in newsworthy information, waiting to be tapped. Tucked away in these public records is documentation for major front-page stories, as well as routine statistical information. Often the finest gems lie deep in the rows of file cabinets and stacks of record books. A persistent reporter can dig them out. Searching public records is often dull work, but immensely rewarding when the reporter discovers facts that make a story jell.

Reporters can freely inspect most public records at the local and state levels. Keepers of the records are usually pleased to assist reporters, showing them how material is filed and suggesting additional places to search; ask for their help when necessary. The precise systems of record keeping vary by states. Searches of federal files are often more difficult, as we shall discuss later.

Following is a list of public record sources that reporters commonly use, plus some less familiar sources that an investigative reporter might find helpful.

VITAL STATISTICS

The three traditional landmarks in the lives of individuals—birth, marriage, and death—are recorded for public inspection. Birth certificates and marriage licenses usually are filed with the county clerk. Death certificates may be filed with the county medical examiner or county clerk. Birth certificates in some instances may not contain the name of the father. Some newspapers publish a Vital Statistics column that includes lists of births, deaths, marriages, and divorces.

OWNERSHIP OF PROPERTY

Information about a piece of property is kept in county offices. Included are its owner of record, assessed valuation, and taxes. Assessed valuation generally represents about one-fourth to one-third of the presumed market price, depending upon the practice in various states.

Legal description of a property may be complex, reading something like this:

> Lot 10 of parcel 12 of the NW Sec of the SW quarter of Woodridge Gardens, T3S, range 9E, Lyons Township.

This needs to be translated into a street number for ordinary use. Map books and a tract index help the reporter to do this. A reporter planning to write about a certain piece of property should check the recorder's office, the assessor's office, and the tax collector's office. Filings of trust deeds show the size of loans made on properties.

Property records can be used by a reporter, for example, to develop a story about slum landlords in a city. Frequently, such an investigation shows that a large percentage of the rundown property belongs to absentee landlords. Documents tracing ownership of title may disclose interesting histories of buildings.

COURT RECORDS

In the court clerk's office are documents that trace the steps in every criminal and civil court action, from the original filing through the ultimate decision. Cases in which the attorneys make numerous legal moves on behalf of their clients build up voluminous files. (See Chapter 23, The Course of Justice, for organization of the courts.)

Divorces are granted by a county court and are part of the public record. Documents and testimony in divorce cases frequently contain lively story material.

A source sometimes overlooked is bankruptcy petitions filed with a federal court. These involve both companies and individuals, and state the amount of the petitioner's assets and liabilities.

Filings of federal and state tax liens against individuals and companies, including the amount owed, may provide valuable information to a reporter exploring an individual's financial history.

Documents pertaining to the probate of wills in the court files may contain newsworthy information.

BOARD MEETINGS

Minutes of public board meetings are transcribed and filed for inspection. These cover major news sources such as the city council, county board, school board, and planning commission. By checking the minutes of past meetings, a reporter may acquire background on controversial issues and perhaps find contradictions in the positions taken by board members at different times.

Records of hearings held by public utility commissions and licensing boards, such as alcoholic beverage control, also are open and contain potential story material.

LICENSES AND PERMITS

City and/or county licenses are required for operation of many kinds of sales and service businesses. These contain factual information about the applicant. Building permits provide facts about new construction projects, including their value.

VEHICLE OWNERSHIP

Records on motor vehicles are maintained by the state department of motor vehicles or the secretary of state's office. A reporter may check ownership of a vehicle either directly through the state office or through the local police department.

OTHER PUBLIC RECORD SOURCES

A reporter may find useful information in these additional places:

- **Campaign finance records.** Candidates for office must list contributions received and their sources, as well as campaign expenditures. These are available from election officials or the county clerk, depending upon the state. Although devices exist through which unrecorded contributions are made, these public lists can be revealing. By checking the list of contributors against the names of persons whom a successful candidate appoints to office, or who receive lucrative contracts from the winner, a reporter may uncover a highly illuminating story of political payoffs.
- **Charity records.** Financial reports by charitable and other nonprofit organizations must be filed annually with state agencies. Among the facts these disclose is how the money collected is spent and what percentage of the receipts is used for administration. Some charities of a dubious nature use such a high percentage of income for operating costs that little is left for the charitable purpose intended.
- **Expense account vouchers for public agencies.** How much did the mayor and city council members spend to attend a conference in a distant city? Did

three council members who, the reporter knows, drove in one automobile to an out-of-town meeting all turn in vouchers for mileage payment? It happens. Examination of expense accounts may produce a provocative story.

• **Audit and consultant reports.** Government agencies sometimes hire private firms to study their operations. When the results of these studies are favorable, they usually are announced in a press release. When unfavorable, the reports tend to become buried unless reporters watch for them. They are public records.

• **Military records.** Information on active service personnel may be obtained from the Pentagon. The Veterans Administration and the U.S. Army Personnel Center in St. Louis can help with ex-service personnel.

If a reporter digging for a story in the public records can enlist the friendly interest of clerks in the public offices, they may be able to lead him or her to obscure documents the reporter knows nothing about. In some cities, daily or weekly legal journals publish tabulations of many public record filings. These are worth checking.

(For an account of how a reporter, James Risser, uncovered a major national scandal by use of public records, see Chapter 17.)

GENERAL RESEARCH SOURCES

Frequently, a reporter needs to reach beyond local clippings and public records and obtain information from general research sources. An array of these is found in college and public libraries. Among the most important are the following:

• **Who's Who in America.** These volumes, published every two years, contain biographical summaries of prominent American men and women. Because persons listed check proofs of their own entries, accuracy of the content is high. For the same reason, *Who's Who* listings rarely contain anything derogatory about an individual. *Who Was Who* contains biographical sketches of important deceased persons.

• **New York Times Index.** All stories published in The *Times* since it began publication are summarized under subject headings, including date and page. For detailed information about a topic, the researcher turns from the index to microfilmed copies of the newspaper on file in most larger libraries.

• **Reader's Guide to Periodical Literature.** This monthly index of more than 150 general interest and nontechnical magazines lists published articles by subject and by author. This index will lead you to recent magazine articles on the topic you are researching.

• **Editorial Research Reports.** These include weekly background reports of about 6000 words each on topics in the news. The reports are later gathered into bound annual volumes.

- **Facts on File.** This is a weekly news digest with a cumulative index summarizing world and United States affairs. Issues are gathered into annual volumes.
- **Congressional Directory.** In this volume are listed members of Congress and Congressional committees, federal courts and judges, and agencies and offices of the executive branch.
- **Congressional Quarterly.** This weekly compilation, bound into annual volumes, describes the progress of legislation before Congress, summarizing committee actions, and recording the roll call votes of all Representatives and Senators. Most larger newspapers and libraries subscribe to this well-indexed service.
- **Moody's Manuals.** This authoritative source of information about large companies includes history, financial structure, organization, subsidiaries, and officers. These annual volumes available in most libraries are a quick and excellent service.
- **Paperback Almanacs.** *The World Almanac* and similar annual compilations are rich sources of condensed factual information. Ownership of one is a modest investment that pays rewards in information found and time saved.
- **Encyclopedias.** Every library has one or more sets. The *Britannica* contains the most detailed entries; other less comprehensive sets sometimes are quicker for checking simple basic facts on a topic.
- **Bartlett's Familiar Quotations.** You will find this handy for checking the accuracy of quotations used by speakers and of those you may wish to use in your own stories.
- **The Great Quotations, by George Seldes.** This volume is especially good for quotations by political and public figures and for those on free speech issues.
- **Current Biography Yearbook.** This contains objective biographies of prominent individuals published in monthly magazine form, and then is consolidated into annual volumes.

For assistance in research, ask librarians and government office clerks. They can find things for you and direct you to additional sources.

FREEDOM OF INFORMATION ACT

Obtaining access to certain federal government records long was like running an obstacle course that reached a final, insurmountable barrier. Classification of documents at various levels of confidentiality for alleged security reasons was a device the bureaucracy used to block their release. The instinct of the bureaucracy to conceal its mistakes and to make life easier for itself has traditionally been a major cause of obstructionism in record release.

Adoption of the Freedom of Information (FOI) Act in 1966 broke down many of the restrictions on public access to federal records. The Act, within certain limits, permits the media as well as individuals and organizations to obtain information from the files of agencies and departments of the Executive branch or from those of government-controlled corporations such as the U.S. Postal Service and Amtrak.

Nine types of information are exempted from disclosure to the public, such as trade secrets, personnel, and medical records. For reporters, perhaps the most important exemption covers investigative records compiled for law enforcement purposes if their release would interfere with enforcement proceedings or disclose the identity of a confidential source.

Application for release of information under the FOI Act can be in the form of a simple request letter addressed to the appropriate agency describing the desired material as specifically as possible. Charges are made for searching out and duplicating the material. Usually the person making the request must wait an extended period of time before receiving the material. So many requests have been filed with some agencies that long delays have occurred; the Federal Bureau of Investigation, for example, has taken more than a year to answer some requests. In practice, this situation makes the FOI Act of little value in obtaining material for spot news stories. By using the law, however, reporters have uncovered numerous significant stories that might otherwise have never come to light. The FOI Act became a "court of last resort" in instances in which normal reporting channels were blocked.

After taking office in 1981, the administration of President Reagan began a campaign for Congress to revise the FOI Act in order to block the release of some additional information. Administration leaders called their restrictive new proposals "fine-tuning" to eliminate abuses. Representatives of news media organizations called the proposals a dangerous attempt to restrict the public's right to information.

After the federal act became law, many state governments passed laws concerning release of their own records that were modeled after it.

STUDY PROJECTS

1. Submit a report giving a brief history of a newspaper group or broadcasting network, including the company's current officers and home office address.

2. Report how the member of Congress for your home district and the two U.S. Senators from your state voted on the sale of AWAC radar planes to Saudi Arabia. State where you obtained this information.

3. Submit a report stating:

a. Who won the World Series in 1925, who lost, and how many games were played.
   b. The name of the county in which Omaha, Nebraska, is situated.
   c. Who invented the following, and in what year?
      - Lightning rod
      - Phonograph
      - Passenger elevator
      - Telephone
   d. The electoral vote total James Buchanan received when he was elected President of the United States in 1856. Tell where you obtained your information.

READ MORE ABOUT IT . . .

Trudy Hayden and Jack Novik, *Your Rights to Privacy, An ACLU Handbook* (New York: Avon, 1980) contains a detailed discussion of the Freedom of Information Act.

David Anderson and Peter Benjaminson, *Investigative Reporting* (Bloomington: Indiana University Press, 1976) contains information about public records.

Philip Meyer, *Precision Journalism* (Bloomington: Indiana University Press, 1979).

COMING UP NEXT . . .

Every morning the mail courier dumps hundreds of news releases on editors' desks at a large newspaper. This stack of volunteered information is crucial to the daily news flow. Reporters simply would not have time to gather all the newsworthy information it contains. The usable material, however, must be plucked from a mass of uninteresting, self-serving announcements that an editor glances at, then chucks into a wastebasket.

In this chapter we examine the elements of a well-prepared news release, then show how a reporter, using the release as a starting point, should probe beyond it for the rest of the story. We tell how one who did so won a Pulitzer Prize.

The chapter warns reporters against falling prey to handout mentality, the state of mind that prevails among lackadaisical newspeople who forget that a news release is only a tool that rarely contains all the information they should have.

Chapter 17
The Handout—Tool and Trap

ROLE OF THE NEWS RELEASE

Using these essential editorial tools, a letter opener and a large wastebasket, a staff member on every newspaper spends part of the day burrowing through a stack of mail that each morning brings. This is the day's publicity deluge. It is submitted by organizations that have what they consider important news to announce or that wish the newspaper to publicize their projects, by individuals anxious to see their names in print, and by companies seeking free publicity for their products and services.

Those who send in these information sheets call them news releases or press releases. Editors and reporters usually refer to them as handouts. Digging through them for legitimate news is similar to panning for gold: a few valuable nuggets to be winnowed from a mass of debris.

The handout has become a standard ingredient of American journalism. Every newspaper edition contains stories developed from press releases; in the case of some thinly staffed publications, the releases are published verbatim. Larger newspapers often make it a matter of principle never to publish a press release exactly as they received it, to demonstrate their editorial independence. Even these carefully edited newspapers, however, are happy to receive releases; without them, their task of informing readers about what is happening in their communities would be far more difficult than it is.

Chapter 17 / The Handout—Tool and Trap

Even if heavily staffed, no newspaper can cover all newsworthy activities in its circulation area by the efforts of its reporters. It must depend in part upon information submitted to it voluntarily. This information may come through telephone calls from well-wishers and publicists or from personal visits. Both of these methods are time consuming for editors and reporters, as well as for the visitors and callers. When the information is submitted in written form as a news release, it can be digested and processed more rapidly; moreover, since it is on paper, the possibility of errors in names, dates, and other facts is minimized. The well-prepared release is an efficient tool for getting information from source to editor.

Despite their value, two major difficulties prevent handouts from being welcomed with unrestrained pleasure by editors and reporters: (1) Often they tell only part of the story, the part that the handout creator wants publicized; and (2) every publication is deluged with press releases of no redeeming news value, churned out by duplicating machines and dumped on the editor's desk to be opened.

Let us look on as the city editor of a medium-sized nonmetropolitan California daily newspaper plows through the day's pile of releases and listen to the flow of quick editorial decisions the process produces:

* City Recreation Department—Announcement of summer schedule . . . "Good story. Affects hundreds of local kids."

Paydirt from the first envelope! But see what releases come next:

* Society for Animal Rights—Founder of League Opposing Vivisection Experiments (LOVE) has written two songs opposing experimentation . . . "That's news? No, thanks!"
* California Department of Transportation—Director recommends allocation of $240,000 for improvements to the Palo Alto Multimodal Commute Station . . . "No, that's 250 miles from here. Our readers don't care."
* Alpha Beta Stores—"Alphylicious," the Alpha Beta "Munchy Monster," is zooming in from outer space with a Food Funtrition game . . . "Too commercial."
* Bank of America—Announces new manager for local branch . . . "Sure, we'll use this story. It's good local. But why didn't the release say what happened to the manager this one replaced? Was he fired, transferred, or is he working for a competitor? I'll have a reporter check on that."

On it goes.

* Nature Expeditions International—Prominent Himalayan naturalist who coauthored the classic *Birds of Nepal* will lead NEI's field trip into Kashmir and Ladakh . . . "No. Not many well-to-do birdwatchers around here."

- Carter Hawley Hale Stores—Announces appointment of product manager for junior sportswear . . . "They wasted their postage. Their nearest store is almost a hundred miles from here."
- California State Psychological Association—A Los Angeles psychologist gives his explanation for the rise in adolescent suicides . . . "Interesting topic. I'll give this handout to a reporter as background for a possible interview with a local psychologist. Better than using a canned release."
- Brush Poppers Riding Club—Local group will sponsor a gymkhana next Saturday . . . "Worth a brief. Plenty of horsey people around here."
- The Active Consumer, a release in the form of a column—Tells how to make your own taste test of beers . . . "It's just a sneaky plug for one brand of beer. Free publicity. Let them buy an advertisement."

Large newspapers receive hundreds of releases like these every day—some important to readers, some marginal, some good in one city, but nowhere else, many of no interest at all to general newspaper readers, others blatant or subtle attempts to obtain free commercial advertising.

THE WELL-PREPARED RELEASE

News releases most likely to receive an editor's attention contain four basic elements: identification, timeliness, accuracy, and information of interest to a substantial portion of the publication's audience.

At the top left of the sheet, the sender should list name, address, and telephone number. If it is a large organization, the name of a specific individual to call for further information should be included. Public relations (PR) firms prepare and distribute news releases for client companies. When this occurs, the name of the PR firm usually appears on the release.

Editors assume that the information in a release may be published immediately unless specified otherwise. On occasion, as when the text of a speech to be delivered at a certain hour is distributed in advance for the convenience of reporters, a specific release time is stated at the top of the first page. This is known as an "embargo." Although editors have no legal obligation to honor an embargo, they usually do so for everyone's convenience. If the embargo on an important story seems capricious or arbitrary, and appears to have been established by the news source to manipulate timing for propaganda or financial advantage, editors might use the story immediately. Usually they inform the source of the release of this fact, and why.

In some instances, news releases arrive too late for use. Producers of releases sometimes fail to consider postal delays and early newspaper deadlines; as a result their efforts land in the wastebasket.

When one of the media receives a news release from a properly identified source, it can reasonably assume that the routine facts it contains are correct, with accurate names and addresses. If such facts are wrong in the release, and are published in good faith, the publication gets the blame from the public. Remembering their embarrassment, the editors will be hesitant to use subsequent material from that source.

The danger of taking press releases at face value without checking them was brought home in an embarrassing way in Chicago a few years ago. Students at Knox College in Galesburg, Illinois, as an April Fool joke mailed an authoritative-looking press release to Chicago news outlets announcing that their 102-year-old private college had been sold to Saudi Arabian businessmen, who would use it as a tax shelter investment. Although most of the media rejected the story because they could not confirm it, a radio station and a wire service distributed the story, to the delight of the pranksters and the concern of the college administration. The media victims had forgotten an old axiom, "If your mother says she loves you, check it out."

Although most news releases are brief, on single sheets, those covering scientific, technical, and educational topics often are extensive because their subjects are complex. Preparation of such releases requires a high degree of skill and provides a valuable service to the media. It is unfair to place these in the same category with some of the publicity-seeking commercial handouts editors receive. For example, when the Rand Corporation issues a release summarizing results of a complicated research study that it has done for a governmental or private agency, the release has been prepared by a veteran newspaper writer and editor who know how to put the researchers' technical terminology into quickly comprehended language for the general reader; they also know how to find the most newsworthy lead the material provides without angering the scientists by sensationalizing their conclusions for popular consumption.

Editors and reporters who check the handout mail each day report another, less tangible value that offsets part of the drudgery: they absorb background information about a wide range of topics that may be helpful later. The late Associated Press columnist Hal Boyle wrote many entertaining columns under the heading, "Things I Didn't Know Until I Opened My Mail."

HANDOUT MENTALITY

We have examined the values and uses of the suitably prepared news release as a tool for delivering information for publication. At the same time, the system contains an inherent peril because it may make things too easy for the editor or reporter who is pressed for time or inclined to be lazy. Those who merely process news release material handed to them, without digging for the rest of the story, are victims of an occupational disease known as handout mentality.

When a cleanly written release containing legitimate news arrives, the easiest procedure for an editor is to copyread it, place a headline on it, and put it into print. That, of course, is precisely what the originator of the release hopes will happen. Some understaffed weekly newspapers in particular have inside pages filled indiscriminately with handout material. No particular harm results when small news releases announcing such routine events as civic meetings or club elections are handled in this corner-cutting manner, because there is not much more that needs to be done with them. They tell the story adequately. Publicity chairpersons often become skilled in providing precisely what the newspaper desires. Indeed, some publications hold training sessions to help volunteer publicity workers.

The peril arises when an editor or reporter treats a release about a significant news development in this "ho-hum" manner. Failure to ask the critical question "Why?" when reading it may result in a news story that is grossly insufficient.

Writers of commercial and political news releases naturally couch them in terms most favorable to their causes. They are paid to produce a favorable image of their employers. If elements in the news they are announcing are unfavorable to their employers, the writers slur over them with vague indirect references or omit them. This approach is reminiscent of the childhood taunt, "That's for me to know and for you to find out."

Handout mentality affects reporters on important beats, as well as those in the newsroom who handle the daily grist. A beat reporter may "get by" for a while by preparing stories only from material received in news briefings and official press releases. That approach, however, is not good enough for long.

From time to time critics accuse reporters covering the glamorous White House beat of suffering from handout mentality, because they work mostly from what the White House press office gives them. After the Watergate revelations dug up by Washington *Post* city staff reporters Bob Woodward and Carl Bernstein led to the eventual resignation of President Richard Nixon, the question was asked, "Why didn't the reporters working right there in the White House know about the illegal things that were happening under their noses and report them?"

No completely satisfactory answer to that question ever came, but the White House regulars defended themselves strenuously. They pointed out that they were so busy handling routine presidential stories that must be covered, and were required to be at press headquarters so constantly for this purpose, that they could not do the type of reportorial digging required to unearth such investigative stories.

FILLING THE GAPS

What should a reporter do when handed an important news release by the city editor with instructions to "develop this"?

First, the reporter should read the release with a certain amount of skepticism, especially if it comes from the public relations department of a corporation, or a public relations firm representing that company, or a government agency, or a political leader. The reporter's analytical ability is pitted against the skill of the news release writer. The reporter should think, "Everything they say in this is probably true. They are too wise to put out something that can be proven false. But what haven't they said?"

In a recent survey made by a unit of the J. Walter Thompson advertising agency, 55 percent of the business editors who responded criticized corporate press releases for burying important information.

The following example of how an energetic reporter may uncover a story bigger than the one a corporate news release discloses is hypothetical, to demonstrate how the digging process works. However, it closely resembles actual situations.

A major corporation with headquarters in the large local city issues a press release announcing the election of Samuel L. Jones as its new president. The release identifies Jones as a former vice-president of the firm, gives his biography, describes his career with the company, and includes an innocuous quotation credited to him, "I am sure that our company now is prepared to move ahead in the 1980s, ready to meet the challenges of new markets and new techniques."

Reading the release, the reporter wonders, "Where does it say whom Jones succeeded?" Buried at the end of the final paragraph is a brief sentence, "Jones succeeds William J. Grigg, who resigned for personal reasons."

Personal reasons? What personal reasons? An alert reporter senses that the real story may not be Jones's ascension to the presidency, but the unexplained departure of his former boss, Grigg. Similar suspicion arises when a release states that a leading executive has resigned "for reasons of health."

Former President Grigg had been active in civic affairs and was widely known as a local booster. He had been president of the company for nine years. Why did not the company's announcement at least contain an expression of gratitude for his services as its chief executive? The reporter sniffs a story of internal corporate warfare.

Following the trail, the reporter calls the corporate public relations officer who issued the release, seeking an elaboration. Why did Grigg resign, and why did the company gloss over the fact? The PR officer responds, "I'm sorry, but that is all I am authorized to say." This polite brushoff increases the reporter's suspicions. Obviously, the best source is the resigned president. The reporter calls his home and is told by a maid that Mr. and Mrs. Grigg have left town on a vacation, destination unknown. What other sources might there be? The new president, Jones, finally returns the reporter's phone call; he is polite but reveals nothing, blandly turning aside questions about a company crisis with a jovial denial.

Stymied by the orchestrated executive hushup, the reporter wonders who else might know what happened. From the corporation's annual report on file in the editorial library, she obtains names of the company's board of directors, the group that would have received the resignation and elected the new president. She begins telephoning them. One comments, "It was a nasty mess," but won't elaborate. At least the reporter's suspicions are confirmed. Finally, she reaches a director known to be a close friend of the former president. He is so angry that he is willing to talk.

The crisis arose, he discloses, because an executive committee recommended that corporate headquarters should be moved from the local city, where the company was founded, to another state in order to reduce labor costs and give the corporation a supposedly more glamorous "eighties" image. This put President Grigg on a spot. Approval of this recommendation would force him to take responsibility for laying off several hundred local workers and remove from the city a company that it regarded as a basic local institution—the very opposite of the booster role Grigg had long played in the community. He refused to accept the committee's recommendation. Aware of this and ambitious to reach the top of the corporate ladder, Jones conspired with several directors to raise the issue at the next board meeting. During the showdown session, the pro-Jones directors accused Grigg of being more concerned about protecting his well-publicized local image than about the financial welfare of the company. He accused Jones of being ruthlessly ambitious and sabotaging him. The animosity became intense. After 2 hours of acrimonious debate, the board decided by a one-vote margin to oust Grigg and install Jones as president.

The persistent reporter has uncovered a bigger story than she had anticipated, not only the corporate fight, but also very bad news for the community about the loss of jobs that could be expected to follow. Such a controversial story, however, needs more confirmation before it can be published. What if the director was grinding a personal ax and giving her a badly slanted version of what happened?

She reaches the new president by phone again and confronts him with the facts she has obtained, but without telling him from where they came. At first he refuses to confirm or deny the account. Then she asks, "Are any parts of the information I have just given you false?" Driven into a corner, he grudgingly replies, "No."

Next she asks another key question, "When will the headquarters be moved from here?"

He replies, "The new management team will draw up plans and present them to the board for approval within three months."

The next morning, the newspaper shocks the community with news of the upheaval within its leading corporation and disclosure that several hundred local workers could expect to lose their jobs.

This example, although partially hypothetical, illustrates how a reporter can go about digging behind a handout. Next, let us examine what happened when a reporter for a midwestern newspaper did precisely that and earned an array of prizes for his diligence.

FROM HANDOUT TO PULITZER PRIZE

James Risser of the Des Moines *Register* won the Pulitzer Prize for national reporting in 1976 for his series of articles revealing corruption in the inspection of U.S. grain shipments to foreign countries. His stories were a major factor in the conviction of more than 70 individuals and companies and the enactment of reform legislation by Congress—all because Risser's curiosity was stirred by a news release. Risser explained:

> Washington reporters are buried in press releases, which pour into our offices from every conceivable government agency and private-interest organization. Ninety-nine per cent of them are useful only as scratch paper.
>
> The package of press releases that arrives at the Des Moines *Register*'s Washington bureau each afternoon from the U.S. Agriculture Department is no exception. But on March 31, 1975, I found in the Agriculture Department package a short and blandly worded release that led me to the most interesting story I've worked on in my years of journalism.
>
> The release announced the suspension of five grain inspectors in Houston, Texas, because of their having been indicted by a federal grand jury for accepting bribes to certify that ocean-going ships were clean and acceptable for loading with grain to be shipped overseas. What struck me about the release was the fact that the inspectors, although federally licensed, were employees of a private inspection agency called the Houston Merchants Exchange.
>
> Judging by its name, it seemed likely to me that the exchange was some sort of business group and might very well be made up of people in the grain and shipping businesses. If that were the case, the regulators and the regulated might, in effect, be the same people—a serious conflict-of-interest situation.

Risser's suspicion proved to be correct.

He spent weeks studying how the grain inspection system worked. He interviewed federal officials who had not seen a reporter in years. On trips to New Orleans and Houston, the principal ports for grain shipments to foreign countries, he talked to dozens of persons involved in the grain trade. For many hours, he studied court records.

In his first story, published more than a month after he read the handout, Risser disclosed apparent widespread corruption in the grading and shipping of U.S. export grain. He reported that bribery of inspectors had become so common that some of the payments were being made by check, with the words, "gratuities for grain surveyor" on the check voucher. He said:

> Back in Washington I figured that if there were corruption in grain grading and weighing, there should be complaints from foreign buyers. At the Agriculture Department's Foreign Agricultural Service, I found that, indeed, foreign purchasers had been complaining for years, to little avail. They reported receiving dirty, weavil-infested, sub-standard grain, and less grain than they had paid for.

By laboriously checking records of one large elevator at New Orleans, comparing the tonnage of incoming and outgoing grain shipments, Risser discovered that during a three-year period the elevator company claimed to have exported 18.6 million bushels more grain than it had received. He found evidence that grain had been stolen.

Following other trails as he uncovered them, Risser wrote 68 stories about the grain corruption during the next eight months. Not only did he win a Pulitzer Prize, but also other major awards. Judges who gave him the distinguished service award from the Society of Professional Journalists, Sigma Delta Chi, praised him as "an outstanding example of a Washington correspondent acting as a watchdog for the public interest."

Beginning reporters, and experienced ones too, should heed Risser's statement, *"Much of the material I reported came from records which were available to anyone who asked for them and who took the time to study and analyze them."*

Risser, chief of the *Register*'s Washington bureau, won a second Pulitzer Prize in 1979.

A PRESS RELEASE DEBUNKED

Peter J. Boyer in his Hollywood column for the Associated Press illustrates the skepticism a knowledgable reporter shows toward a news release that seems too effusive. Remembering the old saying about killing a person with kindness, he wrote this column after reading a handout from the ABC television network:

Reading Between Lines of ABC Office Shuffle

By PETER J. BOYER

LOS ANGELES (AP)—ABC has moved Tony Thomopoulos, its post-Fred Silverman programmer, to Los Angeles in a move billed as a corporate streamlining and a major move up for Thomopoulos.

Oh, really?

In a press statement brimming with cheery words for Thomopoulos, ABC President Fred Pierce gave all the good reasons for moving Thomopoulos and ABC Entertainment from New York to Los Angeles (he didn't mention closer proximity to the ABC psychic as being one of them). Pierce even spoke of added responsibilities that Thomopoulos will assume out here . . .

Pierce spoke of the Thomopoulos reign in such glowing terms you might have thought these past three seasons had been hunky-dory for ABC.

"During the three years Tony has headed ABC Entertainment, ABC has enjoyed outstanding progress in its entertainment programming from early morning, through daytime, children's programs, prime time, our superb novels for television, miniseries and our late-night schedule," Pierce said. "He has assembled a talented staff of executives and this relocation will enhance our programming operations."

What Pierce could have said was this:

DURING THE three years Tony has headed ABC Entertainment, ABC has suffered through a nosebleed decline. When Fred Silverman left ABC for NBC's big bucks, ABC was No. 1 and folks there were very happy. Now ABC is No. 2 in the vital prime-time area, and grumpiness prevails. Instead of dogfighting with CBS, ABC's more realistic opponent is third-and-climbing NBC.

Thomopoulos' "talented staff of executives," talented as it may be, has provided ABC with television programs that viewers are greeting with indifference. The perception of ABC under Thomopoulos has changed from a powerful network champion to a struggling, hesitant contender on a cold streak....

As a columnist in the entertainment field, where appearances and posturing count for so much, Boyer has more freedom than most press association writers to speculate in print and to deflate flamboyant press releases.

Whenever reporters must handle a heavy load of routine work, they tend to fall into a pattern of operating and thinking that dulls the inquisitive instincts. That is when handout mentality takes hold. Every reporter should from time to time ask the self-searching question, "Is there more to this story, and am I doing enough to find out?"

STUDY PROJECTS

1. Bring to class six stories you believe were based on news releases. Be prepared to indicate why you believe so.

2. Rewrite a news story the source of which apparently was a press release by a large company. See if you can detect any favorably worded copy that may have come from this source.

3. The city editor has assigned you to develop a story from a brief news release in which Sophocles University announces that it has chosen the dean of students from your local university as its new president. List four sources to which you would turn and the kind of information you would seek from them.

READ MORE ABOUT IT . . .

Doug Newsom and Tom Siegfried, *Writing in Public Relations Practice* (Belmont, Calif.: Wadsworth, 1981).

David L. Lendt (ed.), *The Publicity Process* (Ames: Iowa State University Press, 1975).

Philip Lesly (ed.), *Public Relations Handbook* (Englewood Cliffs, N.J.: Prentice-Hall, 1975).

COMING UP NEXT . . .

At news conferences, reporters have the opportunity to question a newsmaker. Their task is to penetrate an evasive conferee's screen of defensive verbiage with questions that draw succinct, revealing answers.

Presidential news conferences are splendid examples of the tilting between newsmaker and questioners. This is the adversary relationship between government and press on open display. By watching a White House session on television, a young reporter can learn how to phrase effective questions and how to probe with follow-up queries.

This chapter provides tips on how to seek answers in press conferences: Do not be shy about asking difficult questions, and prepare yourself in advance as much as possible. Also, the chapter discusses what a reporter should do when requested by the newsmaker to keep information given at a news conference off the record.

Chapter 18
The News Conference

AN OPPORTUNITY FOR REPORTERS

A speech delivered at a meeting is a one-way street; the speaker tells listeners only what he or she wants them to hear and needs not justify statements made. In contrast, a news conference is two-way. The person who calls the conference usually opens it with an announcement of some kind, either orally or through distribution of a written handout, and then submits to questions from reporters. This gives the reporters an opportunity to obtain the additional information they desire.

At least, that is the theory of the news conference, or press conference as it often is called. Some political figures and corporate officials are so adept at evasive responses, however, that reporters leave their supposedly candid sessions frustrated by failure to obtain the information they seek. Since press conferences are among the most common methods of news dissemination, a reporter should know how to cover them effectively.

A news conference enables the host to give identical information to all the media simultaneously, thereby preventing the charge of favoritism and also saving time. From the reporter's point of view, this is both good and bad. Each reporter is protected from being beaten on the story by a competitor. For an enterprising reporter who has been working on an exclusive story, however, peril exists that the very material he or she has been collecting diligently will be "spilled" to everyone at the conference by the speaker. In such cases, the reporter should be careful not to ask certain questions, lest they tip off the competitors, and should try to obtain the answers privately.

Conferences are called for many reasons. In government, they may be held at regularly scheduled times, whether or not the agency involved has a specific piece of news to announce, in which case they frequently are known as briefings. The daily briefing for reporters at the State Department is an example. At the state level, governors may hold regular meetings with the press—at 10 A.M. every Tuesday, perhaps. Conferences by government officials, civic leaders, pressure groups, or business executives are called on an occasional basis, either when the person is involved in a current news situation or has an announcement to make.

During political campaigns, some candidates hold an excessive number of conferences, even when they have little to say, to get their names into print. A favorite ploy of candidates for statewide office is the "hippity-hop" news conference. The candidate flies from city to city in a private airplane. Reporters in each city have been invited to the local airport for a conference at a specified hour. The plane lands (late, more often than not) and the candidate meets the waiting reporters for a question period, then a half-hour later climbs aboard the plane and flies to the next city for a repeat performance. Thus, with a minimum expenditure of time, the candidate hopes to get his or her name into the newspapers, voice onto radio, and face on the television screen in eight or ten cities on the same day. Such excessive use of the news conference undercuts its news value and tends to make it a propaganda device rather than a useful exchange of information.

At a news conference, control of the situation lies in the hands of the person holding the meeting. An individual reporter has little opportunity to probe beyond the surface in group questioning. The larger the number of reporters present, the less opportunity each individual has. Shrewd newsmakers may exude an air of openness, whereas in fact they are trying to tell the press the least possible about a potentially embarrassing situation. They find that a tightly controlled news conference serves their purpose better than talks with individual reporters. A clever newsmaker often can manipulate a press conference so as to reveal very little beyond what he or she wants to say. Thus a press conference may be a defensive device rather than the open discussion it purports to be.

Reporters could improve their chances of obtaining valuable information at a news conference if they would plan a cooperative line of questioning. Occasionally this happens, with good results. The same is true in unpredictable situations, when reporters have no advance indication of what the conference is about, if two or three of them instinctively follow up each other's questions instead of jumping to new areas. But reporters at a press conference are competitors and at times personal rivals. Their newsgathering goals may vary. The needs of television and print reporters differ. Print media reporters complain that some newsmakers play so hard to the television cameras that the reporters cannot conduct concentrated

Chapter 18 / The News Conference   205

questioning. Since televised stories on news conferences are fragmentary, the public often fails to receive a report as comprehensive as it should be from a news conference.

For these reasons, experienced print media reporters regard press conferences in most instances as only a step in developing a story, not an end in themselves.

PRESIDENTS MEET THE PRESS

The most famous of all conferences are those held intermittently by the President of the United States on national television. Half a century ago, in the days of President Franklin D. Roosevelt, the White House press conference was a simple affair in which reporters assigned to the White House beat, and perhaps a few others, gathered around the President's desk for give-and-take questioning. Often the tone was jovial. This was an effective way for the President to exercise his charm on the reporters, to launch ideas for new laws as "trial balloons" through

President Reagan answers questions from White House reporters during a crowded news conference.

their stories, and at times to provide significant background information on news situations that could be published without the source being revealed.

From that format, the presidential news conference has developed into a theatrical production. Introduction of television cameras to these sessions by President Dwight D. Eisenhower in the 1950s was a major factor in the evolution, along with the growth in the number of reporters authorized to attend. Television and radio technicians also swell the crowd. During the Watergate investigation that led to President Richard M. Nixon's resignation, the atmosphere at his conferences bristled with hostility between the chief executive and some of his questioners. By the time of Jimmy Carter's presidency, reporters clamored so raucously to get the President's attention by standing up, waving their arms, and shouting "Mr. President!" that the conferences drew criticism from both inside and outside the media for their circus atmosphere. Certain reporters were regarded by their colleagues as camera hogs striving for attention. Guided by the recommendations of a commission appointed to examine the problem, President Ronald Reagan sought to create a calmer, quieter mood during the sessions.

Under today's circumstances, no president would dare attempt to disclose nonattributable background information at a news conference. Everything is on camera for the world to see instantly; as a result, presidents tend to give vague replies to the frequently difficult questions, unless they are stressing a point for their own policy reasons. Recent presidents have spent hours preparing for each news conference, being drilled by aides in answers to anticipated questions.

Any reporter can profit from watching and analyzing a televised presidential news conference. Observe how the questions are formulated: How some reporters ask direct, succinct ones, whereas others pose complex, multiple-part queries that invite evasive, partial responses; how certain reporters strive to put follow-up questions that will pin down an earlier vague presidential answer. Notice how frequently a president is not truly responsive to the question asked: How he begins as though to reply fully, trying to give viewers the feeling of candor, then skirts the issue with words that are not really relevant. All presidents use these tactics to varying degree, especially when things are not going well for them politically. Traditionally, presidential news conferences last 30 minutes and end when the senior press association reporter present says, "Thank you, Mr. President."

Although the news conferences most reporters cover are much smaller and less pressure-packed than presidential shows, the fundamental relationship between reporter and news source is the same. The reporter's role should be that of a diligent seeker of the whole truth, not that of an adversary straining to put the news source in a bad light.

HOW TO SEEK ANSWERS

Two pieces of advice will help a reporter to obtain maximum value from a news conference:

1. Don't Hesitate to Ask Tough Questions.

A person who summons a news conference lays himself or herself open to intense questioning in return for the opportunity to advocate a project or a point of view to the media. The reporter should not be timid about asking difficult and possibly embarrassing questions. This does not mean that the reporter has a license to behave in a browbeating, rudely aggressive manner. The most intensive questioning can be conducted in an aura of politeness; indeed, this is more likely to elicit useful answers than a resort to the shouting cross-examiner style.

2. Prepare Yourself as Much as Possible Before Going to the Conference.

Sometimes it is obvious what the person who called the conference will talk about. Even when that is not so, information about the individual involved may be available in the newspaper library, the files of the broadcasting station, or perhaps in the public library. The better informed in advance reporters are about the individual and probable topic, the easier it is for them to focus the questioning quickly on the substantive issues. Do not waste more time and questions than necessary on secondary points.

Human nature prompts all of us to put our best foot forward when presenting ourselves and our causes to the public. The person holding a news conference naturally concentrates on the positive aspects of the cause being advocated or defended. It is up to the reporters to uncover the other side of the story.

For example, a real estate developer invites reporters to a conference at which he shows an artist's elaborate renderings of a shopping center he plans to build. There will be two department stores and 75 smaller shops, he announces, to cost more than $6 million. Construction will begin "in the fall."

This appears to be good news for the city, which needs additional shopping facilities and the jobs the mall will create. But the experienced reporters present have been "burned" on real estate promotion stories before, so they begin probing.

Under their close questioning, the developer eventually concedes that he has not actually signed a contract with either "anchor" department store. Although he gives the impression that 63 other merchants have engaged space and will be in place for the grand opening, he acknowledges reluctantly that only 21 have signed leases. Finally, he discloses that although he has some construction financing, he will need to raise additional money before completion.

By their questioning, the reporters have put the story in perspective for their readers—that the glamorous-looking mall is highly speculative and underfinanced. The developer wants to use the publicity from the news conference to help promote his leasing activities. Announcement of his plans is a legitimate news story, but by including in it the negative facts they have elicited, the reporters make clear to the community that the project is far from certain and might never materialize.

Here is another case in which alert questioning by reporters at a news conference changes the complexion of a news story:

In a middle-sized city, an upsurge of crime has caused deep concern, especially in one area heavily populated by older citizens. They are too frightened to leave their homes at night because of assaults, robberies, and burglaries. Several murders have occurred. The mayor seeks reelection in the approaching municipal balloting and is being blamed by his critics for the outbreak of crime. Citizens demand that he do something. So he calls a news conference.

To the assembled reporters and television camerapeople, the mayor announces that he has taken two urgent steps. First, he has sent a special squad of 50 additional policemen into the high-crime area for intensive patrolling. Second, he has formed a citizens' anticrime street patrol to report seeing suspicious behavior and to investigate unusual incidents that may be connected with crimes in progress.

At first hearing, the mayor's program of action seems positive and responsive to the city's needs. He gives the cameras a sincere, determined, no-nonsense look.

Then the questioning begins. A reporter asks, "Where are those 50 policemen coming from? What other areas of the city will be deprived of their normal police protection to make this possible?"

The mayor responds, "No other section will be cut back. The patrol people in this special force are all volunteers, working on overtime."

This sends up a warning signal in one reporter's mind. "Sir, your controller's report to the city council last week stated that all the Police Department's overtime pay funds for the year have been used up. Where will the money come from?"

MAYOR: "We are drawing money from the Fire Department's overtime funds."
REPORTER: "Does this mean that in case of a major fire, you may not have enough money left to pay for all the fire-fighting hours that would be needed?"
MAYOR, reluctantly: "It might. But we hope that won't happen."

Another reporter, who took the time to study the newspaper library's clippings on the mayor and crime before coming to the conference, raises another issue.

"During your campaign for mayor, your opponent proposed a citizens' anticrime patrol and you denounced the idea. You said the volunteer patrol would become a vigilante group and endanger civil liberties. Now you have created exactly the thing you were against then. How do you justify that?"

MAYOR: (silence) "Well . . ." (more silence) ". . . Crime wasn't so bad then. After much thought, I have decided that the need for the patrol is greater than the problems it might create."
REPORTER: "If you had done what your opponent proposed when you took office four years ago, do you believe that crime in the city would be as high as it is now?"
MAYOR: "I don't know. Maybe I should have."

Thus, by sharp questioning and good preparation, reporters brought to light two aspects of the mayor's plan that he failed to mention and hoped would not be realized: that the city was dipping into its fire-fighting funds, perhaps dangerously, and that he had reversed himself 100 percent concerning volunteer patrols. Perhaps he acted wisely in both instances under the circumstances. That is for the voters to decide. The reporter's job is to dig out all the facts so the voters can be as well informed as possible in making their decisions.

THE OFF-THE-RECORD PROBLEM

Should reporters at a news conference agree not to publish information when it is offered to them off the record? That issue has been much debated. Politicians, in particular, sometimes attempt to keep potentially embarrassing material out of print by using the off-the-record ploy. Many city editors instruct their reporters to inform the hosts of news conferences who attempt to go off the record that they will not honor such requests. By agreeing to suppress material offered at a news conference, the editors reason, reporters may feel morally bound not to publish it even if they subsequently obtain it from another source. Thus, important legitimate news information may be kept from the public. Anything said at a news conference attended by a dozen or more reporters and photographers will not stay secret for long anyway. Those who do honor the request are placed at a competitive disadvantage if one person present does publish it. The general rule is that once a story has been broken, others are free to use it as well. If important information happens to come into a reporter's hands on an off-the-record basis, the reporter should without fail report it to the city editor. The editor might know of other sources who could confirm the information in publishable form.

At times, legitimate reasons arise for a news source to request that information be kept off the record temporarily, usually involving the public welfare or humanitarian concerns. If, for example, the police plan a series of narcotics raids and tell reporters so that they may accompany the raiders, advance publicity would make the raids useless. When someone is killed under tragic circumstances, reporters often are requested to withhold the victim's name until the family has been notified. Rarely, however, do situations of this nature arise in a news conference. Always, the city editor should be kept informed; the decision to publish or not to publish is made by the editor, not by the reporter.

STUDY PROJECTS

1. Clip or reproduce a story covering a presidential news conference. Submit a report analyzing the story—the types of questions asked, the relevance of the presidential replies, and other significant aspects (maximum of 300 words).

2. Attend a local news conference either on the campus or in the city. Submit a report on the performance of the person who held the conference and of the reporters who covered it.

3. Stage a mock news conference in the classroom in which a student or visiting speaker serves as the news source. After the source has announced a news development that he or she has prepared, have other class members acting as reporters subject the source to questioning.

READ MORE ABOUT IT . . .

Michael B. Grossman and Martha J. Kumer, *Portraying the President: The White House and the News Media* (Baltimore, Md.: Johns Hopkins University Press, 1981).

PART V
Legal and Ethical Responsibilities

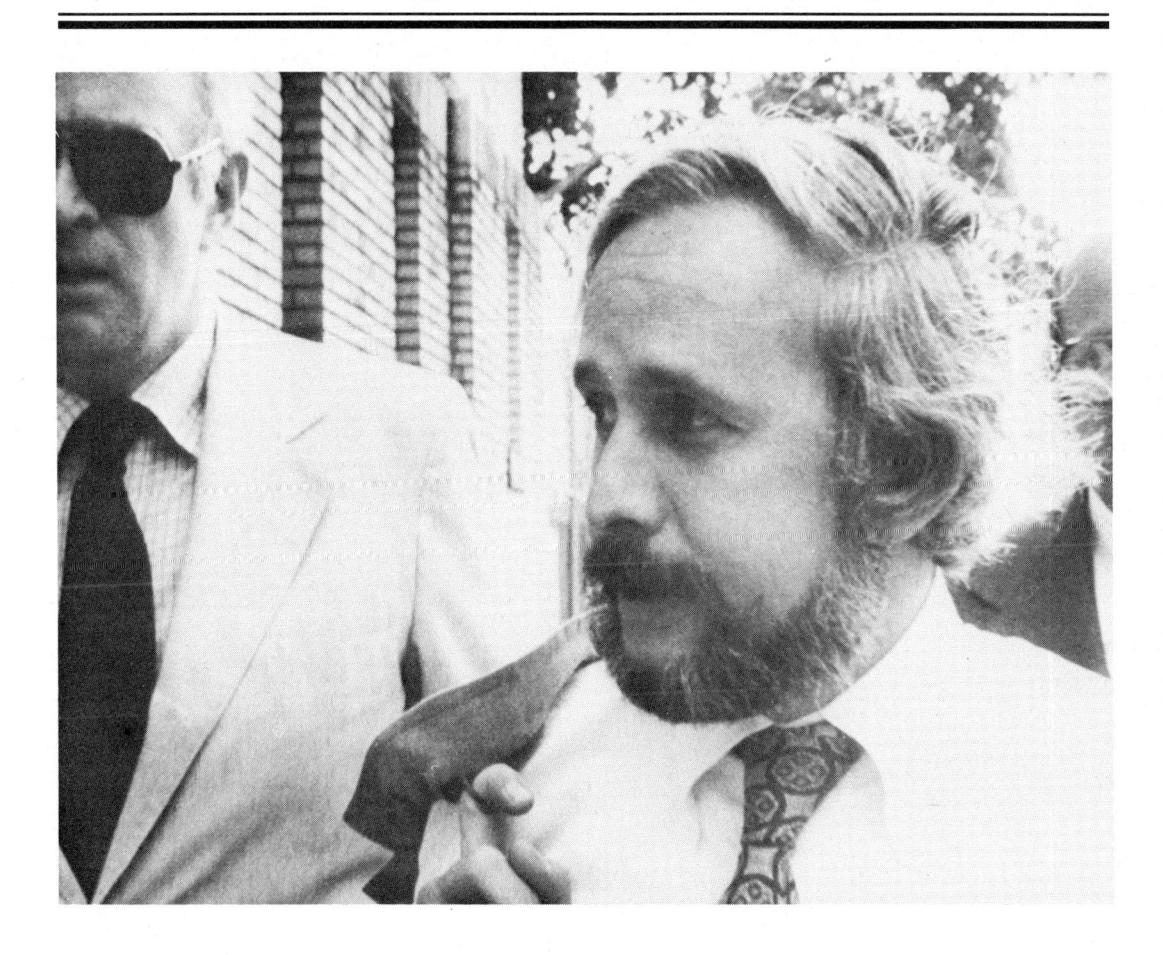

COMING UP NEXT . . .

Hanging over the head of every writer of news, and restricting what is published, are the laws against libel and invasion of privacy. Properly so, because the power of the press to inflict damage to a person's reputation is great. Society must have a way to protect its members from written and spoken defamation.

Every reporter needs to know what the laws of libel and privacy are. This chapter explains them. It describes the difference between civil and criminal libel and defines the defenses against allegations of libel. Knowing these, the writer has general boundaries within which he or she can work safely. Although libel law is complex, its principles are easily grasped.

Among provocative libel cases discussed in this chapter are those by actress Carol Burnett against the *National Enquirer,* Miss Wyoming against *Penthouse,* the landmark *New York Times* v. *Sullivan,* and *Mary Alice Firestone* v. *Time Inc.*

Chapter 19
Danger! Libel and Invasion of Privacy

REPUTATIONS ARE PRECIOUS

> Who steals my purse steals trash,
> 'Tis something, nothing.
> But he that filches from me my good name
> Robs me of that which not enriches him,
> And makes me poor indeed.
> —*Othello,* Act III, Scene iii

When William Shakespeare wrote those lines, he was expressing a belief as old as civilization—that a good reputation is a person's most cherished possession. "Thou shalt not bear false witness against thy neighbor" was one of the moral injunctions brought down by Moses from Mount Sinai. Every society has enacted laws protecting a person's reputation.

Reporters today bear a moral and legal responsibility to insure that no person is defamed in the stories they write. The press is powerful, and the damage inflicted through careless or malicious reporting can be tragic, both to the individual harmed and to the news media.

WHAT IS LIBEL?

Libel is broadly defined as *published defamation of character.* It is a false, malicious, and/or negligent publication that injures a person's reputation by lowering the community's regard for that person or by otherwise holding up him or her to hatred, contempt, or ridicule. Entertainer Carol Burnett was libeled when the *National Enquirer* falsely and maliciously reported that she had been drunk and disorderly in a Washington, D.C., restaurant. In court she was awarded damages in the amount of $1.6 million, which the judge subsequently cut in half.

Although awards of damages are rarely so high, juries are growing increasingly more sensitive to citizen complaints of libel as they consider approximately 500 libel suits filed against newspapers each year. Even when a newspaper wins a suit, its court costs may surpass $100,000. Thus reporters must be well aware of what constitutes libel and its defenses, and they must exercise extreme care in their handling of the news.

Slander is oral defamation. Because a person may be injured as greatly in a radio or a television broadcast as in a printed publication, the courts have come to treat broadcast defamation as libel. Reporters seldom encounter problems with slander.

There is much ambiguity in libel law. Interpretations vary from state to state, as do community attitudes and the circumstances under which suits are brought. In addition, there is no way to anticipate the findings of a jury. Four elements, however, must be present in an action in libel: defamation, identification, publication, and fault.

Defamation
The reporter can expect that it may be defamatory to:

1. Charge that a person has committed or has attempted to commit a crime, or that he or she has been arrested for the commission of a crime, has been indicted for a crime, has confessed to committing a crime, or has served a penitentiary sentence.
2. Impute that a person has committed an infamous offense, even though the words do not designate the particular offense.
3. Tend to diminish the respectability of a person or to expose him or her to disgrace or obloquy, even though the words do not impute commission of a crime.
4. Tend to disgrace, degrade, or injure the character of a person, or to bring him or her into contempt, hatred, or ridicule.
5. Tend to reduce the character or reputation of a person in the

estimation of his or her friends or acquaintances or the public from a higher to a lower grade, or tend to deprive him or her of the favor and esteem of friends and acquaintances or the public.
6. Impute that one has a perverted sense of moral virtue, duty, or obligation, or has been guilty of immoral conduct or has committed immoral acts.
7. Impute commission of fraud, breach of trust, want of chastity, drunkenness, gambling, cheating at play, violation of duties imposed by domestic relations, swindling, and so on.
8. Impute weakness of understanding or insanity.
9. Impute a loathsome pestilential disease, such as leprosy, plague, or venereal disorders.
10. Tend to expose a person in his or her office, trade, profession, business, or means of getting a livelihood to the hazards of losing office, or charge him or her with fraud, indirect dealings or incapacity and thereby tend to injure that person in his or her trade, business, or profession.

A newspaper also may commit a libel by insinuation, allegory, and irony, as well as through colloquialisms and connotations, if readers understand the statements in a derogatory sense. In addition, the newspaper may libel a person because of circumstances of which it is not aware. A classic example is that of an unmarried woman who fancied herself as married and who gave a Kansas newspaper a story identifying a bachelor as the father of her child. The court held that under the circumstances the plaintiff had stated a claim for relief for libel *per quod* (libel because of the circumstances involved).

Identification
If not named, the plaintiff must demonstrate that he or she was specifically identified in the defamatory publication, whether by inference or by having been included in a group or organization that was maligned. Generally, the larger the group, the less is the possibility of libel through identification.

Publication
Legally, a piece of writing is "published" when it is viewed by a single third person—in addition to the writer and the person being written about. For example, if William Reynolds dictates a letter to his secretary stating that Rosemary Smith is a thief and the letter is typed, a libel has been committed even though it may never have been mailed.

Fault
The plaintiff who is a public official or a public figure must prove actual malice to win any damages. Actual malice means that the defendant either knew that the defamatory statement was false or acted with a reckless disregard of the truth, such as entertaining serious doubts about the truthfulness of the charge or the

veracity of the informant. Under a recent U.S. Supreme Court ruling, the plaintiff, whether a public or a private person, may inquire into the state of mind of the defendant at the time the defamatory material was published. Punitive damages will be awarded only after a showing of actual malice, regardless of the status of the plaintiff. In addition, ill-will malice must be shown.

The U.S. Supreme Court has ruled that states have a right to select the standards under which suits brought by private individuals shall be adjudicated. Some states apply the actual malice test, and some others require proof of negligence, such as carelessness or deviation from normal standards of reporting.

Once the liability of the defendant has been established, a plaintiff then may seek punitive damages; or actual damages under which a specific monetary loss must be demonstrated; or compensatory damages, requiring proof of harm of an intangible nature such as emotional distress.

The two kinds of libel are *civil* and *criminal*. Newspapers seldom face state charges of criminal libel. This offense against society occurs when a published item causes, or tends to cause, a breach of the peace, such as insurrection or rioting. Civil libel, however, is common. In these cases, it is up to the offended person, not the state, to seek relief in court.

A newspaper is responsible for everything that it prints—stories, pictures, headlines, advertisements, letters to the editor, syndicated columns, and press association stories supplied to it by others.

Every person on the staff who knew or should have known of the defamatory material may be sued for libel—the reporter, rewrite person, copyreader, news editor, city editor, managing editor, publisher.

DEFENSES AGAINST LIBEL

The principal defenses against libel actions involving the press are provable truth, the privilege of reporting fairly and truly an official proceeding or statement, the right of fair comment, the constitutional defense, and consent.

TRUTH

The provable truth of a story is a complete defense in civil actions, although the law in a few states specifies that lack of malicious intent also must be proved. The best safeguard against a libel suit is to make certain before publication that any potentially libelous statement is true and, even more importantly, that it can be proved to be true. This is difficult, however, so newspapers—even though they print only stories believed to be true—generally rely upon other defenses.

PRIVILEGE

Journalists are privileged to provide a full, fair, and accurate report of a court proceeding, a legislative session, or what public officials say in the official discharge of their duties without incurring the risk of a libel suit. Both the press and the persons involved in these activities are protected. In Texas and California the protection is extended to public meetings. Care must be exercised, however, not to report a defamatory statement made by a public officer outside his or her official capacity.

A graphic example of privilege in reporting court proceedings occurred during the "palimony" trial in which Lee Marvin's former live-in girl friend, Michelle Triola Marvin, sued the actor for financial support. When she denounced a friend of Marvin's during her testimony, newspapers printed her outburst even though it was defamatory:

"Mr. Cabeen is a thief, he's a liar, he's a parasite. I did not like him after I saw him stealing (poker) chips from Lee when he was drunk."

Extracts from public records may be published even though the documents may contain libelous material. In some states, however, privilege does not include publishing the content of complaints or petitions before a public hearing has been held on them. There are other exceptions, including the contents of a warrant before it is served; information about arrests, unless a warrant has been served; and confessions to police. Reporters should make certain that the public record is one that is required by law to be kept; information reported on the police blotter or in other police records is not privileged in states where they are kept not because of a legal requirement but through custom or convenience.

Reporters quickly become alert to words that are libelous per se—that is, in themselves. These are words such as *swindler, immoral, coward, shoplifter,* and *incompetent.* Unless such an allegation can be proved in court or is protected by a privilege, it is actionable. Often reporters will use the word *alleged* in possibly defamatory stories. This means that the report came from a law enforcement officer or a public record, and the statement is privileged. If used with a report that is not privileged, the word *alleged* probably will not provide a defense if the statement is defamatory.

FAIR COMMENT

The right of fair comment by a newspaper extends to its reports on public performances by musicians, stage performers, football coaches and players, artists, writers, and any others who present their work or performance to the public. The principle is that all who offer their talents for public approval, especially for pay, expose themselves to criticism in print. This criticism must be limited to the performers' work and cannot be extended to their personal lives.

CONSTITUTIONAL DEFENSE

In 1964 the United States Supreme Court ruled that, in suits brought by public officials, state libel laws must yield to the First Amendment freedom of the press guarantee. This constitutional ruling of libel law will be discussed shortly.

CONSENT

If a person authorizes, requests, induces, or otherwise consents to the publication of material about himself or herself, the person cannot recover damages for injury if the matter is defamatory. Consent may be direct, either by oral or written authorization, or it may be implied or apparent.

Statutes of limitation, which vary from state to state and range from one to three years, provide another defense. No libel suit may be filed beyond that time period, which begins with the date of the first publication.

MITIGATORY DEFENSES

Proving the absence of malice helps to mitigate, or lessen, the amount of damages awarded. Chief among these defenses is showing that as soon as the defendant discovered an error had been made, a retraction, correction, or apology was published. To be most effective, such a statement should be published in a position in the newspaper equally prominent to that given the previously published libelous matter.

THE CONSTITUTIONALIZATION OF LIBEL LAW

In 1960 the New York *Times* published a full-page advertisement signed by 64 persons seeking financial support for Dr. Martin Luther King's Southern Christian Leadership Conference. Headed "Heed Their Rising Voices," the advertisement charged that a reign of terror prevailed against black students in Alabama. Contending that he had been libeled even though he had not been named in the advertisement, L. B. Sullivan, commissioner of public affairs for Montgomery, Alabama, sued the *Times* for libel. The Alabama Supreme Court awarded him $500,000 in damages. However, in a landmark decision in 1964, the United States Supreme Court for the first time invoked the First Amendment in a libel case and declared that a public official may not recover damages for defamatory statements relating to his or her official conduct unless it can be proved that the statements were made with "actual malice" with the knowledge that they were false or in "reckless disregard" of truth or falsity.

The decision was widely hailed by the news media, for it is difficult to prove actual malice. Normally, actual malice can be established only through a combination of findings such as failure to check the facts because of deadline pressure, failure to seek facts to ascertain accuracy even though there was ample time to do so, not heeding a warning that the information is false, fabricating quotations, doubting the truth of the matter, and basing material on overheard conversations.

In 1969, in *Curtis Publishing Co.* v. *Butts,* the Court stretched the application of the "actual malice" rule to public figures and, two years later, in *Rosenbloom* v. *Metromedia,* to include private persons involved in an event of public interest.

The evolution of the law of libel . . .

These U.S. Supreme Court cases are considered to be cornerstones in the evolution of libel law:

1964

• *New York Times v. Sullivan*, March 9, 1964: To recover damages for "a defamatory falsehood relating to his official conduct," a public official must show that the press acted with " 'actual malice'—that is, with knowledge that it (the published material) was false or with reckless disregard of whether it was false or not."

The case was brought by L. B. Sullivan, a city commissioner of Montgomery, Ala., who said he was libeled by a March 1960 full-page political advertisement in the Times called "Heed Their Rising Voices." The ad was placed by the Committee to Defend Martin Luther King and the Struggle for Freedom in the South. It told in part of an alleged incident—part of a series of events centering on the movement for black rights—in which Montgomery police "armed with shotguns and tear-gas ringed the Alabama State College campus" after students sang "My Country, 'Tis of Thee," on the state capitol steps.

The ad did not mention Sullivan by name, but because he was the city official in charge of police, he claimed defamation.

"It is uncontroverted that some of the statements" about the alleged Montgomery incident "were not accurate descriptions of events which occurred in Montgomery," the Supreme Court said in an opinion written by Justice William J. Brennan Jr.

But, the court added, ". . . we consider this case against the background of a profound national commitment to the principle that debate on public issues should be uninhibited, robust, and wide-open, and that it may well include vehement, caustic, and sometimes unpleasantly sharp attacks on government and public officials."

"Constitutional guarantees require, we think, a federal rule that prohibits a public official from recovering damages . . . unless he proves that the statement was made with 'actual malice,' " Brennan wrote.

Sullivan (above) and New York Times ad which he said was libelous.

1967

• *Butts v. Curtis Publishing Co.* and *Associated Press v. Walker*, June 12, 1967 Actual malice rule is extended to public figures.

The Saturday Evening Post, owned by Curtis Publishing Co., reported that University of Georgia athletic director Wallace Butts gave an opposing football team secrets about his plays and defensive patterns. The court found, however, that the magazine ignored "elementary precautions" in preparing the story and acted with actual malice; Butts won his suit.

In the same opinion, however, the court ruled that a former Army official could not recover damages against The Associated Press for its "hot news" report that he had "assumed command" of a group of students who "charged" federal marshals trying to uphold the admittance of a black at the University of Mississippi. The court held that even though the report was inaccurate, the public had a "legitimate and substantial interest" in the matter. "Negligence, it may have been; malice, it was not," the court held.

1971

• *Rosenbloom v. Metromedia*, June 7, 1971: Actual malice rule is extended to private individuals involved in matters of general and public interest.

George Rosenbloom was arrested by Philadelphia police for allegedly selling what a police captain called "obscene" material. Metromedia radio station WIP consequently reported that the city was cracking down on "smut merchants" and named Rosenbloom.

Rosenbloom was found innocent of "smut peddling" and, considering himself a private individual, sued Metromedia for libel.

Justice Brennan, again delivering the majority opinion, acknowledged that Rosenbloom was not a public official or public figure.

But, the Justice wrote, ". . . We think the time has come forthrightly to announce that the determinant whether the First Amendment applies to state libel actions is whether the utterance involved concerns an issue of public or general concerns."

There was no evidence that the radio station "in fact entertained serious doubts as to the truth" of the reports, Brennan stated.

1974

• *Gertz v. Welch*, June 25, 1974: A noted attorney who had defended a widely publicized case is considered not a public figure.

American Quarterly, a Robert Welch Inc. publication, described attorney Elmer Gertz as a "Communist fronter" and "Leninist."

Gertz sued, and American Quarterly argued that because of Gertz's involvement in a previous, unrelated but well-known case, he was a public figure who must show actual malice.

L. B. Sullivan and the New York *Times* advertisement that he claimed had libeled him. His suit resulted in the landmark *New York Times* v. *Sullivan* decision by the U.S. Supreme Court.

However, in *Gertz* v. *Welch* in 1974, the Court seemed to reverse its latter position. In a 5–4 decision, the Court held that a private person, regardless of involvement in a public event, might recover such actual damages as could be proved for injury or harm resulting from publication of a defamatory falsehood, without proof of actual malice by the libeler, but with proof of negligence as determined by a state standard.

After the Gertz decision, the American Newspaper Publishers Association warned that publishers "no longer have the protection of the New York *Times* Rule when libel is alleged by a private individual, involved in matters of public interest, who seeks to recover actual provable damages."

The definition of what constitutes a "public figure" was narrowed in 1976. The Supreme Court, in *Mary Alice Firestone* v. *Time Inc.,* ruled that the wife of Russell Firestone III, scion of a prominent industrial family, was not a "public figure" even though she was a pillar of Palm Beach, Florida, society and held press conferences during her celebrated divorce trial. She sued *Time* magazine for incorrectly reporting that her husband had been granted a divorce from her on grounds of extreme cruelty and adultery. "Negligence" and not "actual malice" was thus established as the standard of judgment despite the fact that Mrs. Firestone dropped the case rather than undergo a second trial ordered by the Supreme Court to determine *Time*'s degree of negligence.

The press suffered another blow when, in 1979, the Supreme Court ruled that engaging in criminal activity does not automatically make one a public figure, even for purposes of comment on issues related to the conviction. Because journalists had long operated under a "calculated risk" theory that a criminal cannot be libeled, this decision further greatly narrowed the definition of a public figure as expanded in *Sullivan.*

The case, *Wolston* v. *Reader's Digest Association, Inc.,* arose when a book author mistakenly identified Ilya Wolston as a Soviet espionage agent when in reality he had only been found guilty of criminal contempt for failure to appear before a grand jury in a case that had resulted in his aunt and uncle pleading guilty to espionage. This was an honest error, a United States district court ruled when Wolston sued for libel. The court asserted that because Wolston was a public figure, as a convicted criminal he had to prove actual malice. Therefore, the court granted a defense motion in behalf of the book publisher.

When the case reached the U.S. Supreme Court, however, Justice William Rehnquist wrote the reversal decision. He further limited the Gertz definition of a public figure, saying it included only those who voluntarily participated in public controversies over which the public itself was divided. Rehnquist's language seemed to have sounded the death knell for newsworthiness as a defense in libel actions.

Journalists were further troubled by a Supreme Court decision in 1979, in *Herbert* v. *Lando,* that permits pretrial discovery (the finding of facts before a trial commences) into the journalist's state of mind as a means of establishing the presence of actual malice in a libel action. The Court declared that such inquiries are valid and necessary in such cases.

The question of whether a person suing for libel is a public figure was central to several other recent cases that may be cited. In the Carol Burnett case, previously mentioned, Miss Burnett clearly was a public figure; therefore, she had to prove that the *National Enquirer* had reported the information about her with malice or a reckless disregard for the truth. She did so to the satisfaction of the jury.

A former Miss Wyoming, Kimerli Jayne Pring, sued *Penthouse* for libel in 1981. She contended that the magazine libeled her in a fictional story that related the sexual exploits of a baton-twirling beauty queen during a national pageant. Although the short story did not use Miss Pring's name, its chief character was called Miss Wyoming. Her attorneys listed 15 similarities between Miss Pring and the character, including the facts that both were the only baton twirlers at the pageant and both wore blue warmup suits. *Penthouse* claimed that Miss Pring was a public figure. A federal jury disagreed and awarded Miss Pring $26.5 million in damages.

After the Green Bay, Wisconsin, *Press-Gazette* published articles criticizing operations of the Brown County Juvenile Court, the court administrator, Wayne Walters, sued the newspaper for libel, seeking $3.7 million damages. The judge agreed with the newspaper's contention that Walters was a public figure and dismissed the case. He ruled: "There's not a scintilla of evidence to show that the paper had a serious doubt as to the truth of the story."

On the other hand, another newspaper, the Lake Charles, Louisiana, *American Press*, recently had to pay a $220,310 libel judgment to the former Lake Charles city attorney, Robert W. McHale, even though a federal court ruled that McHale was a public figure. An *American Press* editorial opposing McHale's reappointment as city attorney included the statement: "No bond buyer would buy a nickel's worth of securities on McHale's opinion." The court ruled that the statement was false and had been made with malice.

The court's opinion said: ". . . [I]t was made while the writer was surrounded by a multitude of facts and circumstances compelling the inference of knowledge" of its falsity, adding: "The court concludes that actual knowledge has been proved, or at least a reckless regard for the truth."

The Reporters Committee for Freedom of the Press reported in 1981 that a pattern of confusion was developing among federal and state appeals courts dealing with privately owned businesses and privately employed professionals who sue the media and claim they should be "private" rather than "public" figures. The committee noted that the U.S. Supreme Court had refused to review seven of the eight "public figure" cases that had been appealed during the previous 18 months, with the eighth case still pending at that time. In some cases the appellants won, in others the media. The Court's philosophy of not interfering with lower court decisions unless absolutely necessary seemed to prevail.

"Red Flag" Words

The following selected "red flag" words and expressions are typical of the numerous words and expressions that may lead to a libel law suit if not handled carefully in news stories. They are taken from a recently published Scripps-Howard paperback on libel law and the right of privacy, which may be obtained from the Newspaper Enterprise Associations, Box 91428, Cleveland, Ohio 44101.

- adulteration of products
- adultery
- altered records
- atheist
- attempted suicide

- bad moral character
- bankrupt
- bigamist
- blackguard
- blacklisted
- blackmail
- blockhead
- booze-hound
- bribery
- brothel
- buys votes

- cheats
- collusion
- communist (or Red)
- confidence man
- correspondent
- corruption
- coward
- crook

- deadbeat
- deadhead
- defaulter
- disorderly house
- divorced
- double-crosser
- drug addict
- drunkard

- ex-convict

- false weights used
- fascist
- fawning sycophant
- fool
- fraud

- gambling house
- gangster
- gouged money
- grafter
- groveling office seeker

- humbug
- hypocrite

- illegitimate
- illicit relations
- incompetent
- infidelity
- informer
- intemperate
- intimate
- intolerance

- Jekyll-Hyde personality

- kept women
- Ku Klux Klan

- liar

- mental disease
- moral delinquency

- Nazi

- paramour

- peeping Tom
- perjurer
- plagiarist
- price cutter
- profiteering
- pockets public funds

- rascal
- rogue

- scandalmonger
- scoundrel
- seducer
- sharp dealing
- short in accounts
- shyster
- skunk
- slacker
- smooth and tricky
- sneak
- sold his influence
- sold out to a rival
- spy
- stool pigeon
- stuffed the ballot box
- suicide
- swindle

- unethical
- unmarried mother
- unprofessional
- unsound mind
- unworthy of credit

- vice den
- villain

GUIDELINES FOR REPORTERS

1. Protect the reputation of others as you would your own.
2. Exercise extreme care in reporting possibly defamatory statements.
3. Make certain that there is a legal defense for statements of this nature.
4. Be careful what you write about the records of criminal defendants.
5. Know your state libel laws.
6. Remember that your use of the word *alleged* in a story provides no legal protection unless the statement comes from a privileged source.
7. Keep informed about court decisions in libel suits. The courts are narrowing the definition of public officials and public figures.
8. Know your rights and limitations in legal matters. Most newsrooms have manuals that can guide your reporting.
9. Call your editor's attention to possibly defamatory material in a story. If necessary, the editor will consult an attorney and decide what to publish.

THE RIGHT OF PRIVACY

Closely related to the question of libel is that of privacy: Under what circumstances does an individual have the right to keep his or her activities and photograph out of print? Persons unable or unwilling to sue for libel sometimes seek relief under the doctrine of the "right of privacy."

Louis D. Brandeis, who later became an Associate Justice of the U. S. Supreme Court, and attorney S. D. Warren enunciated the first authoritative legal statement on the right of privacy. In an article published in the *Harvard Law Review* in 1890, they wrote:

> Instantaneous photographs and newspaper enterprise have invaded the sacred precincts of private and domestic life; and numerous mechanical devices threaten to make good the prediction that "what is whispered in the closet shall be proclaimed from the housetops." For years there has been a feeling that the law must afford some remedy for the unauthorized circulation of portraits of private persons.
>
> The question whether our law will recognize and protect the "right of privacy" in the circulation of portraits and in other respects must soon come before our courts for consideration. . . .
>
> The principle which protects personal writings and other productions of the intellect or of the emotions is the right of privacy, and the law has no new principle to formulate when it extends this protection to personal appearances, sayings, acts and to personal relations, domestic and otherwise. . . .

Brandeis and Warren expressed the opinion, however, that the right of privacy should not extend to publication of matters of public or general interest nor to matter that is privileged under the laws of libel and slander. They argued that the right of privacy ceases with the publication of the facts by the individual, or with his or her consent; that the truth of the published material does not afford a defense; and that the absence of "malice" in the publisher does not afford a defense.

These principles gradually have been accepted, and the law of privacy is now recognized in more than 40 states: by statute in six states (California, New York, Oklahoma, Utah, Virginia, and Wisconsin) and by court decisions in at least 35 additional states. Where the public interest ends and the invasion of privacy begins, however, is difficult to ascertain and the Supreme Court has yet to issue a clear verdict.

Invasion of privacy is a tort—a wrongful act perpetrated by one person upon another. The late tort law scholar William L. Prosser pointed out that there are four kinds of invasion of privacy torts:

1. Appropriation to one's own advantage of the benefit of the name or likeness of another.
2. Unreasonable intrusion upon the privacy of private affairs of another.
3. Unreasonable publicity given to the private life of another, even though the facts are true.
4. Unreasonable publicity that places another in a false light before the public.

COMMERCIAL USE

Appropriation of a person's name or picture for commercial advantage is the oldest area of the tort of privacy. If a person's name or picture is to be used in an advertisement or for other commercial purpose, that person's specific written consent must first be obtained. A Texas court of civil appeals, for example, held that John Kimbrough, a former football player at Texas A&M University, had the right to sue for damages when his picture was used in a Coca-Cola advertisement without his specific consent. Newspeople need not be concerned with this violation since the courts have held that using such matter "for purposes of trade" applies to advertising, not to news copy, even though the publication in which it appears is sold for a profit.

INTRUSION

Intrusion upon a person's physical solitude is an invasion of privacy that may result in a lawsuit. It is closely related to trespassing upon one's property, a more clearly defined legal offense. Courts have ruled that reporters, and other persons, may be charged with trespass when they enter private places such as hospital rooms. Zealous investigative reporting may result in trespass or invasion of privacy suits. A California "healer" who practiced medicine without a license won $1000 in an invasion of privacy suit after *Life* magazine published an illustrated article titled, "Crackdown on Quackery." The story was obtained when a reporter and a photographer gained entry to the healer's home under false pretenses and relayed tape recordings to law enforcement officers waiting outside.

Generally, reporters and photographers may record and take pictures of what they hear and see in public places (except when forbidden in courtrooms and legislative chambers); however, 13 states prohibit the recording of a conversation without the permission of those involved. Photographers may not make nuisances of themselves in taking pictures of prominent persons; the "papparazo" who made a career out of photographing Jacqueline Kennedy Onassis and her children was severely limited in his actions by a circuit court judge and fined. A fashionable New York restaurant was awarded more than $250,000 in trespass damages after a local television station crew barged in unannounced to shoot film about possible health-code irregularities. In some states news organizations have won privacy cases on grounds that it is common practice for reporters to accompany officials into homes where a crime or tragedy has occurred. The prospect of suits under such circumstances, however, is always present.

EMBARRASSMENT

Many privacy suits have resulted from the public disclosure of embarrassing private facts about a person. If the publication offends the community's notion of the common standards of decency (known as the "unconscionability" rule), the plaintiff may gain a favorable decision. Such were the cases when *Time* magazine photographed a woman against her will and published a story proclaiming her as a "starving glutton"; when a woman's disfigured face was photographed without her consent while she was semiconscious; and when a woman was photographed with her skirt blown over her head as she entered a carnival "fun house." Most often, however, the defense of newsworthiness intervenes to protect the publisher. People may be photographed in public places with impunity, for example, while waiting in an unemployment line. Names and embarrassing information may be published if contained in a public record. If an event is newsworthy, even innocent bystanders lose their right to privacy. When an Atlanta television station revealed the name of a 17-year-old woman who died after being raped by six youths, the father sued for invasion of privacy. The U.S. Supreme Court, however, overturned the rulings of Georgia courts and found that, because the name had been part of a public record, the station could use it in a newscast without fault.

FALSE LIGHT

A publication may place a person in a "false light" through the coincidental use of names, fictionalization, or the misuse of names and pictures in otherwise legitimate news stories. In 1967 the U.S. Supreme Court invoked the First

Amendment right of press freedom in setting aside a lower court judgment against *Time* magazine. A family had argued that a Broadway drama based upon its own experience as the prisoners of three escaped convicts had invaded its privacy. The Court ruled that a "newsworthy person" could not collect damages for reports containing false information unless proof could be established that the errors were "knowingly and recklessly" published. In another case, however, the Court upheld a judgment in favor of the widow of a West Virginia bridge disaster victim on grounds of actual malice. A Cleveland *Plain Dealer* reporter and photographer had entered the home and talked with one of the woman's children while she was not at home. Inaccuracies and false characterization, such as the statement, "She wears the same mask of non-expression she wore at the funeral," were cited by the Court, which awarded the woman and her son $60,000 for suffering "outrage, mental distress, shame and humiliation."

FEDERAL PRIVACY LAWS

A growing concern about the right to privacy in an increasingly computerized and bureaucratic society resulted in the passage of several federal laws during the past decade. In addition to the Fair Credit Reporting Act, giving citizens the right to inspect and correct credit reports about themselves, they included the following:

1. The Family Education Rights and Privacy Act of 1974, which has sharply limited public access to records of students, thereby making the news reporter's job more difficult.
2. The Privacy Act of 1974, which stipulated types of information about individuals that could not be disclosed by federal agencies and provided means whereby persons could determine the nature of information about themselves in official files.
3. An act establishing the Law Enforcement Assistance Administration (LEAA), which in 1975 issued guidelines severely limiting the maintenance of, and the dissemination of information about, criminal justice records. The media argued that these provisions violated the principle of full disclosure of public information—"the people's right to know." As a result, some federal agencies relaxed their application of the guidelines and the LEAA decided to leave the matter up to individual states.

By 1979, laws sealing or expunging records in the criminal justice system had been enacted by 23 states. Media lobbying and editorializing, however, helped prevent the passage of such legislation in other states and helped bring about the repeal of laws previously enacted in Oregon, Hawaii, and Maine.

Debate over the important public policy issues involved will continue, for, as Arthur Miller, a Harvard law professor and an expert in privacy matters, says:

"Unfortunately, there is nothing more antithetical than the public's right to know and the individual's right to privacy."

STUDY PROJECTS

1. Clip from a newspaper five stories about criminal misconduct in which persons' names have been used. Attach these to a sheet of paper. Beside each item state whether, in your opinion, the persons involved have any grounds for a libel suit.

2. During a meeting of the state Legislature a member states that William Smith is a communist. No evidence is given that the charge is true. Can you safely print this allegation? Explain your answer in a brief report.

3. Under the heading, "Divorces Granted," a newspaper listed the following: "Irma and Don Stapleton, 1455 Alabama St." Actually, the couple had been listed in courthouse records as plaintiffs in a negligence suit. The reporter gathering items for the newspaper's legal records section had made a mistake. Do the couple have grounds for a libel suit? Explain your answer in a brief report and write a retraction.

4. A newspaper published a photograph of two children caught in a sudden rainshower. The caption identified the children. Two years later the newspaper darkened the photo to resemble a sketch and published it to illustrate a story about child abuse in the area. Is such an action libelous? What would the parents need to prove to obtain damages in a libel suit? Write a two-page, double-spaced report explaining your views.

5. A newspaper some years ago published the following review of a vaudeville act by the Cherry Sisters:

> Effie is an old jade of 50 summers, Jessie a frisky filly of 40 and Addie, the flower of the family, a capering monstrosity of 35. Their long skinny arms, equipped with talons at the extremities, swung mechanically, and waved frantically at the suffering audience. The mouths of their rancid features opened like caverns and sounds like the wailing of damned souls issued therefrom. They pranced around the stage with a motion that suggested a cross between the *danse du ventre* and fox trot—strange creatures with painted faces and hideous mien. Effie is spavined, Addie is stringhalt, and Jessie, the only one who showed her stockings, has legs with calves as classic in their outlines as the curves of a broom handle.

In a brief report explain whether, in your opinion, this review is libelous.

READ MORE ABOUT IT . . .

Don R. Pember, *Mass Media Law* (Dubuque, Iowa: Brown, 1981).

Marc A. Franklin, *The First Amendment and the Fourth Estate* (Mineola, N.Y.: Foundation Press, 1981).

The News Media & the Law, published six times a year by the Reporters Committee for Freedom of the Press, reports current libel cases.

COMING UP NEXT...

Undergoing severe public criticism on charges of irresponsibility and inaccuracy, the contemporary news media have subjected themselves to self-scrutiny. In some instances this has led to painful admissions of error.

This chapter examines the charges and cases of gross wrongdoing that support them, and also discusses the ethical standards newspapers have set for themselves and efforts being made by media leaders to live up to these standards.

Because newspapers and their staff members do not exist in a vacuum, they are faced constantly with problems of conflict of interest. They must decide such questions as, "Should our reporters break a law or engage in deceptive practices such as taking on a false identity in order to break a story that will serve the public good by revealing a criminal conspiracy?"

Questions of good taste arise frequently, too: Is this picture offensive? Should we print these "dirty words"? The answers involve judgment calls.

Chapter 20
Contemporary Issues of Ethics and Taste

RECENT ETHICAL PROBLEMS

Disclosures of a series of deceptive news accounts in 1981 focused news media and public attention once again upon the credibility of the press and the responsibility that society places upon its journalists to be truthful. In the span of only three months:

• Washington *Post* reporter Janet Cooke admitted that her sensational account of "Jimmy," an 8-year-old heroin addict, was a hoax. She resigned, and embarrassed *Post* editors returned the Pulitzer Prize she had just won for feature writing.
• The New York *Daily News* found that writer Michael Daly had used questionable journalistic practices in a story—techniques Daly said he had employed in "300 columns over two years."
• The National News Council, which considers complaints against the news media, sustained a charge that a *Village Voice* story by Theresa

Carpenter, who was given the Pulitzer Prize previously accorded to Cooke, gave a misleading impression.
- The New York *Times* questioned the accuracy of two stories about Polish unrest from free-lancer Harley Lippman which it had published.
- The Toronto *Sun* could not substantiate a stock manipulation story.
- Columnist Frank Saenz of the Oceanside (Calif.) *Blade-Tribune* resigned after plagiarizing an article by syndicated columnist Art Buchwald.
- WABC-TV, New York, dismissed five staff members after learning that letters read on news and public affairs programs had been fabricated.
- WBBM-TV, the CBS-owned station in Chicago, broadcast a hard-hitting documentary that raised questions about certain controversial techniques of investigative reporting on television. These included selective editing, the confrontation interview, undercover reporting, and preoccupation with dramatic pictures at the potential expense of accuracy and fairness. The documentary criticized a program on the ABC-TV newsmagazine "20/20," both for accuracy and the way it was reported.

The flurry of disclosures caused editors and critics to wonder how many other such stories had gone undetected and whether "playing fast and loose with the facts" was becoming more common.

Scurrilous newspaper stories and editorials were a national scandal in the "dark ages of journalism" soon after the Republic was formed. Hoaxes and other deceptive practices continued sporadically throughout the nineteenth century and into the twentieth century, but the integrity of the press has gradually improved during recent decades. The most notable progress was made during the 1970s, when gratuities and other conflicts of interest generally were banned from newsrooms, largely in response to national awareness of unethical practices in government and business culminating in the Watergate episode. Although gossip tabloids were flourishing and a resurgence of "peephole" journalism was evident, newspaper editors had become proud of the increasingly high professional standards of the press. Thus it was that the disclosures of 1981 came as a shock.

POSSIBLE CAUSES OF IMPROPER REPORTING

A number of reasons have been advanced by editors and observers of the press as to the possible causes of recent journalistic lapses.

THE "NEW JOURNALISM"

In the late 1960s the literature of the mass media began to herald a new journalism. Its reportorial and writing techniques were variously described as tell-it-as-you-see-it, impressionistic, saturation, humanistic, investigative—and even interpretive. Its second and most controversial characteristic was described as advocacy, activist, or participatory. The latter trend merely reflected the widespread frustration of the era and the demand that the conservative establishment give heed and power to others—youth, minorities, women. The mass media should be used, the argument ran, to further such reforms.

The movement subsided in the 1970s, but some reporters still confused the desirability of using fictional techniques in making stories appealing with the necessity of sticking to the facts. In a *Christian Science Monitor* story, Norman Isaacs, chairman of the National News Council, was quoted: "You have reporters who've adopted the thesis of [author] Tom Wolfe that a news story can't be explained unless a reporter gives vent to emotion . . . and instinct." The attitude, Isaacs continued, is that "attribution [to a named source] doesn't matter. It's 'Don't bother me about the facts. I know this is true. I have a feeling it's true.' " Janet Cooke's account of "Jimmy's" addiction no doubt expressed the truth of the tragic plight of many youngsters in Washington's ghetto neighborhoods. Her journalistic faults, however, lay not only in fabricating the story, but convincing her editors that she had to protect a nonexistent unnamed source.

David Shaw, media critic of the Los Angeles *Times,* echoed the observations of Isaacs, expressing his concern over: "Docudramas. 'Faction.' Nonfiction novels. Composites. Gonzo journalism. New journalism. The blurring of fact and fiction. . . ."

THE INFLUENCE OF TELEVISION NEWS

Many newspaper editors, some observers feel, put pressure on their reporters to write colorful stories to match the impact of television news.

THE INCREASING USE OF ANONYMOUS QUOTATIONS

Said *U.S. News & World Report:* "Ever since Washington *Post* reporters Bob Woodward and Carl Bernstein won acclaim for their Watergate stories, which relied heavily on unidentified sources, many editors say that resorting to anonymous quotes has been proliferating—sometimes needlessly."

THE URGE FOR FAME AND FORTUNE

There is an increasing drive, the magazine said, "by ambitious young men and women to make a big splash and win fame, six-figure book contracts and lucrative movie deals."

EDITOR AND REPORTER ATTITUDES

There is a great reluctance on the part of many newspaper editors to challenge or change a story presented to them, and also the refusal of some reporters "to concede any point, even a factual error," Isaacs charged. Too much local reporting, Isaacs observed, "is abominable and even slanted."

For more than a year, the fate of 52 American hostages seized at the U.S. embassy in Tehran by students with Iranian government backing dominated foreign news and stirred deep emotions among the American people. The hostages were set free early in 1981.

THE PUBLIC'S NEED FOR MYTHS

The public, surfeited by information, has a deep hunger for abstractions and myths, in the view of Lewis H. Lapham, editor of *Harper's* magazine. "If the media succeed with their spectacles and grand simplifications," he wrote, "it is because their audiences define happiness as the state of being well and artfully deceived."

THE DRIVE FOR IMPROVED PROFESSIONAL CONDUCT

CODES OF ETHICS

The model for modern-day codes of ethics is the Canons of Journalism established in 1922 by the American Society of Newspaper Editors. As revised in 1975, the statement of principles reads:

PREAMBLE: The First Amendment, protecting freedom of expression from abridgement by any law, guarantees to the people through their press a constitutional right, and thereby places on newspaper people a particular responsibility.

Thus journalism demands of its practitioners not only industry and knowledge but also the pursuit of a standard of integrity proportionate to the journalist's singular obligation.

To this end the American Society of Newspaper Editors sets forth this Statement of Principles as a standard encouraging the highest ethical and professional performance.

ARTICLE I—RESPONSIBILITY: The primary purpose of gathering and distributing news and opinion is to serve the general welfare by informing the people and enabling them to make judgments on the issues of the time. Newspapermen and women who abuse the power of their professional role for selfish motives or unworthy purposes are faithless to that public trust.

The American press was made free not just to inform or just to serve as a forum for debate but also to bring an independent scrutiny to bear on the forces of power in the society, including the conduct of official power at all levels of government.

ARTICLE II—FREEDOM OF THE PRESS: Freedom of the press belongs to the people. It must be defended against encroachment or assault from any quarter, public or private.

Journalists must be constantly alert to see that the public's business is conducted in public. They must be vigilant against all who would exploit the press for selfish purposes.

ARTICLE III—INDEPENDENCE: Journalists must avoid impropriety and the appearance of impropriety as well as any conflict of interest or the appearance of conflict. They should neither accept anything nor pursue any activity that might compromise or seem to compromise their integrity.

ARTICLE IV—TRUTH AND ACCURACY: Good faith with the reader is the foundation of good journalism. Every effort must be made to assure that the news content is accurate, free from bias and in context, and that all sides are presented fairly. Editorials, analytical articles and commentary should be held to the same standard of accuracy with respect to facts as news reports.

Significant errors of fact, as well as errors of omission, should be corrected promptly and prominently.

ARTICLE V—IMPARTIALITY: To be impartial does not require the press to be unquestioning or to refrain from editorial expression. Sound practice, however, demands a clear distinction for the reader between news reports and opinion. Articles that contain opinion or personal interpretation should be clearly identified.

ARTICLE VI—FAIR PLAY: Journalists should respect the rights of people involved in the news, observe the common standards of decency and stand accountable to the public for the fairness and accuracy of their news reports.

Persons publicly accused should be given the earliest opportunity to respond.

Pledges of confidentiality to news sources must be honored at all costs, and therefore should not be given lightly. Unless there is clear and pressing need to maintain confidences, sources of information should be identified.

These principles are intended to preserve, protect and strengthen the bond of trust and respect between American journalists and the American people, a bond that is essential to sustain the grant of freedom entrusted to both by the nation's founders.

Newspaper adherence to each of these principles of conduct has been severely questioned from time to time. The most stinging rebuke came in 1947, when the report of the Commission on the Freedom of the Press, headed by Robert Maynard Hutchins, at that time chancellor of the University of Chicago, found fault with many newspaper practices, including sensationalism. The commission's list of society's five requirements of the mass media remains pertinent today. They are: (1) a truthful, comprehensive, and intelligent account of the day's events in a context which gives them meaning; (2) a forum for the exchange of comment and criticism; (3) the projection of a representative picture of the constituent groups in the society; (4) the presentation and clarification of the goals and values of the society; and (5) full access to the day's intelligence.

In the early 1970s, largely because of Watergate, the public began to distrust all of its institutions much more strongly than before. Sensing the public mood, the Associated Press Managing Editors Association (APME), even before Watergate, began to look at influences on the probity of the press. The report of the APME professional standards committee in 1972 was the first salvo in what turned out to be a barrage of attention to the problem of media ethics.

The APME sent Carol Sutton of the Louisville *Courier-Journal* to report on the extent of gratuities for the press during three fashion events in New York and Montreal. Two weeks later she returned with a new canvas suitcase filled with what her newspaper colleagues termed "loot" and "goodies"—assorted cosmetics, jewelry, tote bags, and useless oddities—along with a report of countless other gratuities offered at these events. She returned all the gifts she could and gave others to charity, in line with the Louisville newspapers' long-standing policy against the acceptance of gifts by staff members.

The Detroit *News* discovered that during one year alone at least $56,000 worth of free gifts and services, including travel, was offered to its staff members. *New York* magazine reported on the news media staff members receiving free tickets to events at Madison Square Garden and on the influence of public relations people with the New York *Times*.

As a result of these disclosures, and continuing interest in the subject throughout the decade, most newspapers adopted rules barring gratuities, junkets, and other conflicts of interests by their news employees. Codes of ethics were adopted or revised by the Society of Professional Journalists, Sigma Delta Chi, and other organizations. The National Press Photographers Association, for example, adopted a code that stated, in part, that, "It is the individual responsibility of every photojournalist at all times to strive for pictures that report truthfully, honestly and objectively." The code ends with the statement: "No code of ethics can prejudge every situation; thus common sense and good judgment are required in applying ethical principles."

A Newspaperman's Credo

(The editors of *Editor & Publisher* magazine asked columnist Max Lerner to phrase his own code of journalistic ethics. It was printed in the magazine July 15, 1961, and again July 11, 1981. An editor's note accompanying its reprinting expressed the opinion that Lerner, "had he written it today, would have referred to newspaper people in general avoiding reference to 'newspaperman' exclusively. We prefer to let others edit it to that extent, if they so desire.")

1. I believe in the integrity of the newspaperman to the facts and events with which he is dealing. He must give the event as it actually happened, the facts as they actually are, to the best of his descriptive power. His obligation to what actually happened is as exacting as the obligation of a historian, and his regard for evidence must be as scrupulous.
2. He has also the obligation, whenever the facts or events do not speak for themselves, to give the frame within which their meaning becomes clear. This may be a frame of history, or a broader interpretative frame of fact. In doing this he must make clear the distinction between fact and event on the one hand and his own opinion on the other.
3. In deciding what to include or omit he must use to the best of his ability the test of what is newsworthy in the minds of his readers, and what is of importance in the flow of events. He must resist the temptation of including or excluding on the basis of what will help or harm whatever team he is on and whatever crowd he runs with.
4. This means that he must give a hearing even to unpopular causes, including those which he may himself detest. He has the obligation to keep the channels of the press open for a competition of ideas, since only through such a competition will the people be able to arrive at their own decisions of what is right and good.
5. In any contest of opinion he has the obligation to state, as fairly as he knows how, the opposing viewpoints. At the same time, if he is presenting opinion in an editorial or column, he has the obligation to set forth his own position honestly and forthrightly as his own, regardless of the consequences.
6. Beset as he inevitably will be by favor-seekers, special interests, press agents, public relations men, and operators of all kinds, he must keep himself scrupulously independent of their favors and pressures. This means that he must be strong enough to make himself unpopular with those who can smooth his path or make life pleasant for him.
7. He must resist all pressures from outside, whether they be from advertisers, government officials, businessmen, labor organizations, churches, ethnic groups, or any other source which has an effect on the circulation or revenue of his paper. This applies whether the newspaperman is a publisher, editor, reporter, reviewer, or columnist. Since the danger in many cases is that he will anticipate the pressures before they are exerted, and censor a news story, review, or opinion which may hurt circulation or revenue, he has the obligation to resist the voice from within which tells him to play it safe.
8. His responsibility is to his craft and to the integrity of his mind.

Surveys have shown that most journalists subscribe to the philosophy of *situation ethics,* meaning that they seek to follow a set of rules of conduct, but will break them when circumstances seem to dictate. In so doing, these journalists reject *absolutist ethics,* which is the rigid adherence to a fixed set of principles or rules, and *antinomian ethics,* which calls for the rejection of all rules. Journalists have mixed feelings about codes of professional conduct. Most seem to feel that codes are useful as standards against which to measure their own value systems; others, steeped in the individualistic tradition, take a cavalier attitude toward codes—supporting conscience and principle but disdaining formalized strictures.

CONFLICTS OF INTEREST

A far-ranging post-Watergate movement is under way among journalists—"from the publisher's suite to the pressbox"—to remove actual, potential, apparent, and even imaginary conflicts of interest. This movement media critic David Shaw of the Los Angeles *Times* discovered in a nationwide survey of reporters, editors, and publishers in 1978.

That is why the Louisville *Courier-Journal* told reporter Ben Johnson he had to resign from a neighborhood improvement association . . . why New York *Times* reporter John Kifner was taken off all political assignments when his wife began to work actively for a mayoral candidate . . . why the wife of former Los Angeles *Herald-Examiner* editor James Bellows did not plan to resume her public relations career in the city during his tenure . . . why Los Angeles *Times* editor William F. Thomas declined to serve on a school integration council.

It is why the New York *Times* fired reporter Laura Freeman when it was disclosed that she had been romantically involved with a politician while writing about him for the Philadelphia *Inquirer* . . . why reporter Jack Fuller worked elsewhere for a year before returning to the Chicago *Tribune* from a Justice Department post . . . why the Denver *Post*'s credibility in covering urban affairs suffered because of the paper's financial relationship with a foundation that was building an expensive cultural complex in the city . . . why Los Angeles *Times* coverage occasionally is criticized because of the Chandler family's assorted landholdings.

Shaw said the expression of journalistic outrage occasioned by disclosures that many American reporters worked for the Central Intelligence Agency abroad renewed ethical questions in many news quarters and engendered others as well:

> Should reporters (or editors) help their government? Should they participate in civic affairs? Join the PTA? United Way? Should they march in demonstrations? Make political contributions? Participate in political campaigns?
>
> Should they leave their jobs to work for the government, then return to journalism? Should journalists even make friends with prominent politicians and public figures?

How about journalists' love affairs? Their investments? The civic and political activities of their wives and husbands?

Do reporters and editors have essentially the same civil rights and civic obligations as other citizens? Or are they somehow "special"—subject to a different, more restrictive set of rules than their friends and neighbors?

In seeking answers to these questions, Shaw discovered "an enormous reservoir of virulent, often contrasting views on the entire question of the rights, privileges, responsibilities and limitations of journalists as public citizens."

Shaw seemed to agree with columnist Richard Reeves's statement that "We belong outside, like a cur with dirty feet" when he concluded: "Such conflicts—even the appearance of such conflicts—are intolerable."

DECEPTIVE PRACTICES

For decades many newspaper reporters and editors experienced few qualms about getting a news story through any means available, including deception. That these methods are still acceptable on some news staffs is evident from an article written for the *Saturday Review* by Nat Henthoff, a staff writer for the *Village Voice* and the *New Yorker*. Henthoff also teaches investigative reporting at New York's New School for Social Research.

In Henthoff's view, "few journalists" see anything wrong with bugging and wiretapping, printing intimate information of dubious value, adopting pretexts for interviews, and feeling free to "get" the citizen who replies, "No comment." Henthoff wrote: "[M]ost reporters think only of getting the story. The notion that they should be sensitive to individuals' privacy rights strikes them as a dangerous form of outside meddling with their special status. . . ."

Henthoff credited most of the journalist guest lecturers who appeared before his class with sharing these views. "I ask these reporters if they would bug and wiretap an uncooperative subject," Henthoff wrote. "Would they disguise their identities and infiltrate the subject's business or even family? The answer usually is affirmative, proudly so. After all, in order to satisfy 'the people's right to know' —the basic credo of our calling—a reporter has to be uncommonly resourceful, daringly inventive."

Henthoff cited as an example such stories as those that bring notoriety to a public official's son for living with another man. He referred to "the continuing, quasi-religious crusade of the press to be allowed to poke into all kinds of dossiers, from everyone's arrest records to reckless driving charges (later dismissed) against a public official." Is there any hope? "The press as a whole," he continued, "is no more likely to become more humane on its own than bill-collecting agencies."

The *Village Voice* staff writer may have been reflecting almost entirely the views of tough-minded metropolitan investigative reporters and their editors. For David Shaw, in another of his characteristically exhaustive examinations of sensitive press issues, found in a nationwide survey that employing deceptive means to obtain a news story is seriously questioned by newspaper editors.

This time Shaw posed a hypothetical situation to more than two dozen newspaper editors concerning a reporter's impersonation of a doctor. The replies reflected the heightened ethical consciousness of most editors in the post-Watergate era when, as Shaw put it, "journalists are so determined . . . to expose the deceptions and misrepresentations of others—in government, big business and elsewhere."

The reply of William Hornby, editor of the Denver *Post* and then president of the American Society of Newspaper Editors, was representative of the responses. Said Hornby: "We in the press are arguing for an open, honest society, demanding certain behavior from our public officials. We ought to be just as frank and straightforward in getting information as we claim other people ought to be in giving it to us."

Shaw said some editors see such proclamations as both unrealistic and self-righteous, and he quoted Michael J. O'Neill, at that time editor of the New York *Daily News:* "Sure, being the champions of truth and all that, you always have to be concerned about doing anything that appears to be misrepresentation. On the other hand, there are some situations where it's the only way to get the story."

When Chicago *Sun-Times* editors assigned a team of reporters to operate a Chicago bar, "The Mirage," incognito for four months in 1977, the resultant exposé might well have won a Pulitzer Prize a few years previously. Not so at that time, however, largely because several editors on the Pulitzer advisory board objected to the team's journalistic methods. (Nevertheless, the *Sun-Times* won eight major journalism awards, including the Sigma Delta Chi Distinguished Service in Journalism award for newspaper reporting for the Mirage series.)

"In a day in which we are spending thousands of man-hours uncovering deception, we simply cannot deceive," Benjamin C. Bradlee, executive editor of the Washington *Post* and a member of the Pulitzer board, said. "How can newspapers fight for honesty and integrity when they themselves are less than honest in getting a story? When cops pose as newspapermen, we get goddamn sore. Quite properly so. So how can we pose as something we're not?" (Bradlee later promptly returned Janet Cooke's Pulitzer Prize when she admitted that part of her story was fictitious.)

Shaw's survey found that most editors agree that misrepresentation is ethically sound only in extreme circumstances when the story would be of significant public benefit, and experience, common sense, and hard work had demonstrated that there was no other way to get the story.

OTHER ETHICAL PROBLEMS

The reporter encounters many other moral dilemmas in addition to those previously stated or alluded to: Is the journalist being "co-opted" by becoming too friendly with news sources? (Some newspapers regularly move their reporters from one beat to another to avoid such an eventuality.) Is the reporter unduly influenced by offers of free lunches and expense-paid trips? Do free tickets to movies, concerts, and sports events influence coverage? The answer to these questions, and others like them, can be found in the extent of the reporter's commitment to professional ideals.

SELF-CRITICISM

Reporters and editors alike mull over these and other ethical issues almost daily. When there is time, critiques follow each newspaper edition: Should we have run that photo showing the body of a dead youth being pulled into a boat? Did we give too heavy display to that financial story because we know the publisher has invested heavily in the firm's stock? Should we have refrained from running that story about the accused bank cashier until we got her side of the story? The answers may not be unanimous, but discussing the issues involved will help determine how future stories are handled.

On most metropolitan newspapers, and on many smaller ones, the assistant managing editor or other executive evaluates the reporting, writing, and display of each story, including headlines. Written critiques are circulated, containing praise, censure, or questioning, and individual conferences are likely as well.

Many newspapers employ *ombudsmen,* usually veterans of the newsroom, to handle complaints from the public and to see that corrections and responses are published in subsequent editions. On the Sunday after the Janet Cooke story disclosure, the Washington *Post* filled three and one-half pages with a remarkably frank and thorough explanation of how it happened, written by the newspaper's ombudsman, Bill Green.

GOOD TASTE

Reporters and editors are constantly faced with decisions as to whether to print possibly objectionable material. Newspapers are intended for reading by the entire family, including children; thus much of what appears in *Penthouse* magazine, for example, would never be published in a newspaper. Nevertheless, mores are constantly changing and what would have offended yesterday's generation may frequently be seen in print today, such as "syphillis" and "rape" for what formerly were identified euphemistically as "venereal disease" and "sexual assault."

THE PRINTED WORD

Obscenities, profanities, and vulgarities rarely appear in newspapers, and then, when adjudged necessary, often only with the approval of a top executive. At times, however, when an offensive word or expression is part of the verbatim testimony of an important trial, or otherwise is highly newsworthy, the matter may be printed.

Charles Alexander, editor of the Dayton (Ohio) *Journal Herald,* felt it necessary to print, from courtroom testimony, the words attributed to a Treasury Department agent just before the agent was slain during an argument. The language so infuriated the newspaper's publisher that Alexander was fired after he refused to admit that the decision was in error. Said Alexander: "It's a matter of truth. To me, the telling of that message from an incident in real life, including in one instance the raw vulgarity used by a man blind with rage, is a lesson that every man, woman and child should perceive in all its dimensions. It is shocking —it surely should be."

A key statement by President Richard M. Nixon in one of the Watergate tapes contained a four-letter word for defecation. Thirty percent of the editors responding to an Associated Press survey said their newspapers had printed all or nearly all of the story containing this and other vulgarities. More than half said the words were sanitized, and 15 percent of the papers edited out the offensive matter.

Similar editing attended the reprinting of a story attributed to then Secretary of Agriculture Earl Butz that appeared in *Rolling Stone* magazine. The Washington *Post* avoided the vulgarities, but made it plain what had been said by printing: "Coloreds only want three things . . . first, a tight (woman's sexual organ); second, loose shoes; and third, a place to (defecate)." Press associations paraphrased the language, but used it in full in a note for editors. The incident led to Butz's resignation, after which some newspapers printed the exact quote.

Virtually all newspapers printed President Jimmy Carter's challenge to Edward Kennedy: "If Kennedy runs, I'll whip his ass." Newspapers usually "write around" such language when used by nonprominent people or when the exact words are not germane to the story. A practice that many newspapers use is to print the first letter of the offending word, followed by "- - - ."

Another common newspaper practice, in order to avoid offending readers, is to eliminate as many gruesome details as possible from stories of that nature. In stories about traffic accidents, for example, it is sufficient to say that a victim suffered internal injuries, without describing them in detail. Similarly, a reference to third-degree burns makes the point sufficiently, without distasteful specifics.

PHOTOGRAPHS

An outcry from readers occurred about 30 years ago when a number of newspapers ran a photo of the body of actress Carole Landis, who had committed suicide, crumpled on a bathroom floor, with blood apparent nearby. This was one of the first such pictures printed in American newspapers. Readers are less squeamish today, in the wake of the Korean War, Vietnam combat, and similar scenes appearing in print and on their television screens. Recent polls, however, reveal that many readers strongly object to such photos.

Nudity seldom appears in newspapers. Only 4 of 138 editors responding to a survey said they used in full the photos transmitted by the Associated Press showing a bare-breasted Elizabeth Ray lying on a couch, at the height of a Congressional scandal. The Atlanta *Constitution* printed only in its first edition a picture submitted in its monthly amateur photography contest. Clearly visible were the genitals of male figures outlined in grillwork comprising the foreground of the scene. Embarrassed editors substituted another photo in subsequent editions.

A number of newspaper editors said they were uncomfortable about running a prize-winning photo showing Vice-President Nelson Rockefeller "giving the finger" to hecklers at a political rally. Few newspapers, however, failed to use the photo.

Because of their graphic nature, photographs generally are more heavily censored than the printed word. In both words and pictures, a guiding principle is as follows: Is there a compelling reason to publish this material?

GUIDELINES FOR REPORTERS

Establishing an absolute set of ethical rules for a reporter to follow is virtually impossible, because so many borderline situations arise. As this chapter has emphasized, the recent trend is toward much tighter enforcement of ethical standards.

These guidelines will assist a reporter:

GIFTS FROM NEWS SOURCES

Some newspapers forbid staff members to accept even the smallest gift, down to a cup of coffee. Others contend that this standard is unrealistically rigid; that any reporter who can be "bought off" with something as insignificant as a cup of coffee is not qualified to be a staff member, anyway. They recognize that reporters sometimes find themselves in situations where refusal of small gestures may offend the news source or be socially embarrassing.

When you start work for an organization, find out what its ground rules are and follow them precisely. If the rules allow some flexibility, ask yourself the questions, "Will the favor being offered cause me to give the source special consideration in stories I handle? Even if I know that it won't, will acceptance of it indicate to the would-be donor or others that I might be influenced?" If the answers are "yes," refuse it.

DECEPTION

In your reporting, do not pretend to be someone else. Never identify yourself falsely on the telephone as a police officer or other official, in hope that the false identity will cause the person you are calling to divulge information that would not be given to you as a reporter.

Newspapers sometimes send a reporter under false identity on an investigative assignment into places such as a mental hospital or nursing home to uncover wrongdoing. The decision to do this is made by upper level news management, never by the reporter.

COOPERATION WITH NEWS SOURCES

Remember that your obligation is to your employer, not to the news sources you cover. Deal with the sources in a friendly manner, but scrupulously avoid use of your reportorial power to do them a favor in print. On the police beat, when invited to accompany officers on raids and other incidents, make clear that you are present as an objective observer for the public, not as a potential witness for the prosecution.

PERSONAL INVOLVEMENT

Reporters are citizens, too, with the right in private life to participate in civic affairs and in fraternal, social, and religious organizations. However, if asked to take an executive or policymaking role in an organization, make certain that this does not create a possible conflict of interest with your job as a reporter. Discuss this and other questions of ethics with the editor to whom you are responsible.

STUDY PROJECTS

1. In Spokane, Washington, a rapist was sentenced to imprisonment for life plus 25 years. Later that day, a public defender who had represented the rapist in court drove her car off a bridge into the Spokane River. A photographer took a vivid picture of her, apparently resisting arrest after she was rescued. She was charged with negligent driving and driving while under the influence of intoxicants.

The *Spokesman-Review* published the photograph of the disheveled, struggling public defender in a dominant position on the front page, next to the story about the sentencing of her client. The newspaper received many critical letters from readers, accusing it of shameful sensationalism and a "cheap shot."

The managing editor published an explanation of why the picture was printed. Readers were invited to cast ballots approving or opposing the decision. Those who voted approved publication by more than 2–1.

Discuss whether you as an editor would have published this photograph large size on the front page, or in any form at all, specifying reasons for your decision.

2. The Chicago *Sun-Times* exposé of graft among Chicago municipal inspectors in its Mirage Bar series focused public attention on the weakness of the city's inspection system and led to a cleanup of abuses. State whether you agree or disagree with the Pulitzer Prize advisers who opposed giving the *Sun-Times* a Pulitzer award because it resorted to deception in newsgathering. Explain your reasoning.

3. A mass circulation tabloid morning newspaper in London publishes on page 3 each day large photographs of bare-breasted young women. No American newspaper does anything similar, including a New York newspaper owned by the same publisher. Is the London newspaper violating good taste? If not, should an American newspaper do the same thing? Why do you believe it is not done here, since such pictures are published in magazines sold in American supermarkets?

READ MORE ABOUT IT . . .

John L. Hulteng, *Playing It Straight, A Practical Discussion of the Ethical Principles of the American Society of Newspaper Editors* (Chester, Conn.: Distributed by The Globe Pequot Press, 1981).

National News Council, *After "Jimmy's World": Tightening Up in Editing* (New York: National News Council, 1981).

Warren K. Agee, Phillip H. Ault, and Edwin Emery, *Perspectives on Mass Communications* (New York: Harper & Row, 1982).

PART VI
Covering the Beats

COMING UP NEXT . . .

The core of the newsgathering structure maintained by newspapers and broadcasting stations is a system of beats. A reporter assigned to a beat is responsible for obtaining all news that occurs in the specified territory.

Beats are usually organized on a physical basis—police headquarters, the courts, city hall, for example—or by subject matter. Examples of subject matter are medicine, labor, and education. In outlying areas, large newspapers may place a reporter on a geographical basis; under this system, the reporter is responsible for all types of news originating in the assigned region.

In this chapter, we explain what a beat reporter seeks, using the education beat as an example, and describe how a reporter breaks in on a beat.

A veteran city hall reporter on a large daily tells in detail precisely how he covers his beat—an example of diligence and alertness for every young reporter to emulate.

Chapter 21
On the Beat

THE BEAT STRUCTURE

News stories do not fall into the hands of editors at random, like raindrops from heaven. They must be gathered systematically through a network of beats—that is, carefully delineated territories to which individual reporters are assigned. A reporter on a beat has a responsibility simply defined yet slightly awesome in scope: to find out and report everything newsworthy that happens in the appointed area.

Much, but not all, of the local news a newspaper publishes originates on the formally structured beats, or "runs," laid out by the city editor for general news coverage, and by the editors of special sections such as sports, family living, business, and entertainment. Every day brings stories, either anticipated or unexpected, that do not fall quite within the concept of any beat; these are handled by general assignment reporters. To use a military analogy, beat reporters are like troops posted at all the points in which action is anticipated, whereas general assignment reporters are reserves to be sent wherever and whenever needed.

On most newspapers, the basic beats are designed in a functional pattern to correspond with the operations of government and the most active nongovernmental portions of the city's social-economic-cultural structure. The scope of each beat and the number of beats a newspaper has vary with the size of its staff, the population of its primary city, and the way local agencies are organized. On smaller newspapers, a reporter may be responsible for a secondary beat that does not require full-time attention and thus can also handle general assignments. Or, a reporter may have two or more beats.

Traditionally, the fundamental general news beats are police and fire, city government, county government, the courts, education, social services, health, politics, business, and labor. These may be subdivided on large newspapers or combined in various ways on small ones. Metropolitan newspapers add specialized beats such as environment, minority organizations, and transportation. Because every city has its particular economic and social aspects, beats that are important for some newspapers are of little concern for others. For example, the Des Moines, Iowa, *Register* has no need for a reporter to cover the waterfront, but it gives much space to agricultural news. Conversely, a farm beat reporter on the New York *Post* would waste away from boredom. Outlying sections of a newspaper's circulation area often are covered on a geographical basis, with the reporter assigned to the region responsible for all types of news in the territory.

Another, quite different form of beat organization uses the anthropological approach. The principle is to assign reporters to cover each of humanity's basic needs, as anthropologists define them.

In their handbook, *The University City News Service,* John De Mott and Terry Hershey laid out an anthropological news beat structure for use by student reporters at Northern Illinois University. They believe that by dividing the entire range of human needs among reporters on a news staff, they are able to find stories that otherwise would be neglected and that can minimize the overemphasis in certain areas. Under the traditional beat structure, they contend, a sensational news event leads to the production of so many related stories that news balance is destroyed; overemphasizing an event results in failure to cover adequately other significant stories. An example of overemphasis, although it was not a local beat story, occurred in an afternoon newspaper of more than 100,000 circulation at the time of the assassination attempt against Pope John Paul II in 1981. Every story on the paper's front page, and the entire third page, dealt with aspects of the shooting. Little spot news space was available on page 2. Although the newspaper's circulation is heavily Catholic, and the shooting of the eminent church leader by a terrorist shocked the world, such enormous up-front emphasis on one event forced a severe cutback in space available for other important news.

Under the De Mott–Hershey theory, at least one reporter is assigned to each of these human-need areas, as described in their handbook:

- Food—The staff of life and the earning of one's substance.
- Trade—A market place for the exchange of one's labor.
- Shelter—A roof over one's head, and also planning the larger physical environment in the community around one's home.
- Sex—and marriage, the family, the care of children and larger social problems in the community.
- Physical Security—The public safety, government, the rule of law, enforcement of the law and the administration of justice.
- Health—Both physical and mental, private and public.
- Recreation—Relaxation, play and entertainment.
- Education—Preparation for more effective living and cultivation of the intellect.
- Beauty—The fine arts, "cultural" pursuits, etc.

- Faith—Religion, an answer to one's search for the good; as art is the answer to one's search for the beautiful and education a quest for the truth.

At first glance, the anthropological approach to news beats seems radically different from the usual functional assignments; closer scrutiny, however, shows that in many areas they are much alike although couched in different terminology.

The Physical Security category encompasses several standard beats: police and fire, the courts, city government, and county government. In the anthropological approach, each of these is a subarea under the general title Physical Security. Similarly, the category Trade involves assignments usually covered on the business beat. If a newspaper is large enough, the business beat may be a department with several staff members who specialize in finance and industry, employment, personnel and labor unions, and retail trade. Although the anthropological definition of education is broader than most city editors might apply to their education beats, coverage of school curriculum, administration, and student achievement is the core of both approaches. Many newspapers have religion editors, among

A photographer catches a moment of life-and-death drama as passengers leap from a China Airlines plane that burst into flames on landing at Manila International Airport. All 135 persons aboard escaped.

whom the able, energetic ones search out more significant material than the church service news releases that are thrown together to form a weekend religion page.

In other words, although few commercial newspapers are likely to commit themselves formally to this anthropological approach, many use it partially. In recent years, editors have been forced to recognize that readers want stories about a broader range of topics than the old familiar robberies, traffic accidents, and murder trials that pour in from the police and court beats. These continue to have a place in the newspaper, because they are news by any definition. But their frequency and abundance must be held down so that correspondingly larger space can be given to stories pertaining to contemporary human needs. As you analyze daily newspapers, notice how many stories concern such matters as finding a job, the cost of a typical market basket of food, improvements in the treatment of illness, ways to finance the purchase of a house despite inflationary prices, and the greatly liberalized sexual standards of the past two decades—topics that impinge directly on the daily lives of readers. Indeed, slowness to recognize the changing desires and needs of their readers cost many newspapers lost circulation until editors began to correct their shortcomings.

WHAT A BEAT REPORTER SEEKS

No matter how newspaper beats are organized, reporters should attempt to develop their potential to the utmost. A reporter should search within his or her beat for stories that expand the traditional boundaries of the assignment and seek news sources beyond the obvious ones. The stories are there. Reporters whose minds are unfettered by habit and who can recognize clues to such stories in the daily grist of material on their beats have an opportunity to give readers the kind of news that will help and please them.

What, for instance, does a reporter on the education beat do? Let us say that our hypothetical newspaper is situated in a city that has four high schools, an extensive system of elementary and junior high schools, and a four-year private college with 5000 students. The beat reporter is responsible for coverage of them all.

A fundamental responsibility of the reporter is to cover the administrative and policymaking functions of these schools.

This aspect includes attending meetings of the public school board—sessions that often are long and dull, but sometimes become heated and even acrimonious, especially when angry parents appear in a group to protest a policy they believe will harm their children's education. Because the private college is operated by a church, its board of directors meetings are not open to reporters. Although in theory school boards make policies and school administrations carry them out, in situations in which the superintendent is aggressive and the board passive the board may act as little more than a rubber stamp for the administration. A perceptive reporter soon can determine whether this is true. Frequent meetings between the reporter and the superintendent are desirable and usually can be arranged. The administrative office normally issues press releases announcing school schedules, personnel changes, building remodeling, bus schedules, and similar routine news. These releases are the basis for news stories. Advance stories listing the agenda for approaching board meetings are an important public service; thus parents can know what issues are coming up for discussion.

The college has a news bureau that issues frequent press releases about campus activities, including the appearance of prominent lecturers and other events of an intellectual or entertainment nature. The news bureau may also tip the reporter to story possibilities informally from time to time (but do not expect it to furnish a tip on any story that might reflect negatively on the college's image). Under normal circumstances, the education beat reporter is less concerned with operation of the college administration than with that of the public schools, because the latter are operated with taxpayers' dollars.

So far, we have discussed the surface aspects of the education beat—reporting of meetings, processing of news releases, and development of contacts with administrators. For a good reporter, this is only the beginning.

The easy news from public schools pertains to the mechanics of their operation, such as budget-making and appointments of administrators, more than to the teaching and learning processes. Here is where the reporter's intellectual curiosity comes into play. The perennial question among parents in every community is, "Just how good are our schools?" They hear horror stories about insolent behavior and rowdyism among students; boys and girls who are passed along from grade to grade without learning to read, write, and spell adequately; ill-prepared teachers; and the use of narcotics and alcohol on the school grounds. At the same time they are assured by administrators that the schools are better than ever and are giving students not only a textbook education, but lessons in social adjustment as well.

Where does the truth lie? In the role as a representative of the public's right to know, the reporter faces a formidable challenge in hunting the answers. Because in many respects education is an abstraction that cannot be reduced to a clearly defined column of results the way a bank statement is composed, the reporter must seek an objective path through a morass of self-serving assertions and emotional assumptions that may be false.

Here are stories that an alert reporter can unearth on the education beat to help parents understand the educational process their children are undergoing:

How high are the schools' test scores? These tests are the nationally standardized tests given to pupils at various grade levels to measure their progress. Is the achievement level of your schools in reading and mathematics above the national average, about average, or below? If reading results are poor, what does the school board intend to do about it? How do schools within the city compare with each other? If an extreme disparity exists, why? Similarly, some states have instituted a series of competency tests a student must pass before receiving a high school diploma. How many local high school seniors failed to receive diplomas last year because they did not pass the tests? In what areas were they especially weak? Obtain copies of the tests and publish sample portions of them so readers will see how difficult, or easy, they are.

The preceding are instances in which the scorecard technique is applied to education, a concept some educators dislike. Many stories without this aspect, however, can be done to illuminate the subject. Does the school system have a special program to stimulate its more talented students—a speed-reading program perhaps? What are the extra-bright eighth graders studying in science? The complexity of their projects, if reported, might surprise readers. At the other end of the spectrum—what kind of program does the system have for the mentally retarded children of the community? Do they attend classes in regular school buildings or are they concentrated in a special place? An interview with a teacher who has had unusual success in teaching the retarded would be informative and perhaps inspiring. Precisely what are the punishment procedures in the high schools? A story explaining the good conduct rules and telling how they are enforced would be instructive to parents. This should include the views of teachers and students about whether the system is fair and effective. Perhaps the education beat reporter can convince the newspaper to present annual Good Teaching Awards.

Stories about budgets occur frequently on many beats, especially those covering branches of government. Although stories on the budget-making process are rarely exciting, they are essential in keeping the public informed and must be handled with detailed accuracy. The size of local government budgets determines the county tax bill that a property owner must pay.

Every agency of government operates with a budget drawn up before the start of its financial year. The administrative officer in charge—the mayor or school superintendent at the local level, for example—submits a proposed budget to the appropriate legislative body for revision and approval. In these examples, that would be the city council or the school board.

The budget is filled with "line" items: so much for salaries, department by department; for installation of traffic signals; for a maintenance crew to clean city hall each night; and for the mayor's travel expenses to professional meetings.

Once approved, this budget becomes the financial chart under which the agency operates for the following year. Transfers of money from one account to another during the year must be approved by the legislative body.

A knowledgeable reporter may find significant stories buried in the column of figures. Compare the proposed budget with the one for the current year and seek reasons for increases. Funds for political favors may be buried as part of an innocent-looking item; so may funds intended to send a group of the mayor's favorite aides on a pseudobusiness trip to Hawaii. The reporter's queries to the administration about certain items may receive evasive answers. If this happens, the reporter might tip off a member of the legislative body, who can question the items in public session when the budget comes up for approval.

The list could go on and on. Researching some of these stories is time consuming and at times difficult, but the reporter can always be working on one or two of them while handling the day-to-day routine of meetings and releases.

At times the reporter is unable to develop a certain story in the territory for a valid reason, such as being too well known to the sources to handle an investigative story. In that event, the city editor may assign someone else on the staff to come onto the beat for that one story. Thus, the Albuquerque, New Mexico, *Tribune* had a woman staff writer work two weeks as a substitute teacher in the high schools and write a series of articles about her experiences. She had taught in the school system previously, but school officials did not realize that she was now a reporter. Her articles created a community controversy. She reported unruly students, low achievement, ineffective teaching, and a partylike atmosphere in which students were permitted to drink soda pop, and eat and talk at will in classrooms. The education beat reporter could not have spared the time for this provocative assignment, nor could that reporter have been effective after writing such subjective material that angered school administrators and board members.

The school officials contended that the reporter used deception to get her story; that she concealed from them her true role as a reporter while they accepted her in good faith as a teacher. The issue was whether her deception was justified in order to give the community an inside look at the schools, as she saw them. This is a specific example of a problem in journalistic ethics we discussed in Chapter 20.

Coverage of the local college provides the beat reporter an opportunity to interview eminent visitors to the campus, to dig up intriguing stories from the science laboratories, and to talk with faculty members about their views on national and international developments that fall within their special academic areas. For example, the college may have a professor who specializes in Latin American government, an excellent source for a story explaining the political and economic background of guerrilla warfare in Central America. Again, the field is as productive of stories as the beat reporter's time and ingenuity allow it to be.

BREAKING IN ON A BEAT

When you are assigned as a beat reporter, you first need to assemble the necessary tools. Establish a file of telephone numbers, addresses, and proper titles of sources on the beat. Set up a futures book in which you record the dates of scheduled events and reminders for follow-up stories. Although the city desk keeps a master futures book that includes some of the events on your beat, keep your own book. The city desk's reminders should be only a backup for you. Another device that will save you many future hours is a loose-leaf album in which to paste all your published stories with dates. You may wish to divide the clippings into categories for easier reference. This book of clippings is a quick reference file from which you can refresh your memory of what happened at an earlier meeting and confirm such information as the spelling of names and the titles of persons in the news. As you become established on the beat, accumulate your own desk library of background reports and other documents you acquire on the job. With these tools at hand, you will begin to feel confident that you have the beat assignment under control.

As the new person on the beat, you probably will be introduced to the primary news sources by your predecessor or by someone else on the staff. Be friendly and conversational on your first visits to the sources, but do not hang around them too long. Most of these people are busy. They are looking you over, like the new boy on the block, so do not come on too strongly. Remember that you must deal with them frequently, perhaps for a long time; your purposes are best served if you can develop a relationship of friendly cooperation. If your stories are fair and objective, even though probing and at times unfavorable to certain officials, the sources on your beat will come to respect your work. Even an adversary relationship with certain news sources, which circumstances may bring about, can be conducted in a polite if wary manner. Sources may flatter, cajole, or berate you about your stories, but they always are aware of the power your printed words have.

A VETERAN REPORTER TELLS HOW

Reporters develop many techniques for obtaining stories on their beats. In the following memo to the authors of this textbook, a long-time city hall reporter in a large midwestern city describes in detail, with candor, how he gets his news. He has seen numerous mayors come and go, along with their staffs, and he knows more about how municipal government operates than many of the city officials he covers. Like all good beat reporters, he has sought to maintain his independence as an unbiased reporter of what he sees and hears. In dealing with his sources, he has followed the basic rule for all beat reporters no matter how intimately they come to know the persons from whom they obtain news: You work for the newspaper, not for your friends on the beat. Never forget who hands out your paycheck.

Notice in the following memo how the reporter taps a wide range of sources and how he uses clues picked up from one source to obtain a story from another source.

>Each reporter develops a style and system for covering a beat. My aim always is to be the seeing eye and the big ear and pry into the most mundane things. Surprises never cease, even for me.
>
>On the beat I speak with anyone, from the custodian and guard right on up to the mayor, because casual remarks often lead to stories. And I read and inspect all available documents.
>
>Aside from known events that are on tap each day, scheduled meetings, press

Chapter 21 / On the Beat 255

Reporting social trends such as the phenomenal appeal of rock concerts is an important element of contemporary news coverage. This is a performance by the Rolling Stones at Philadelphia in September 1981.

conferences, etc., constant contact is required to become aware of routine developments. While still in the newsroom waiting for the city hall denizens to arrive for work at 8 A.M., I make a list of all the known events that will generate a story, and of possibles. Then I am on the phone as early as possible, confirming and probing. But telephone conversation cannot replace the personal contact, the eyeball to eyeball questioning and confrontation.

My usual itinerary at the city building is to say hello to the telephone operator at the Centrex system. She knows who is calling whom, sometimes why, and will tell if you have cultivated her.

On the way up to the mayor's office I touch base here and there: the city clerk's office, chat with a councilman if I see one, drop in on secretaries. By the time I get to the mayor I may have clues as to what is in the wind and can ask the right questions.

If the call on the mayor is impromptu, I simply begin asking what's new. I keep on the friendliest terms with the receptionist and the secretary, good sources for tips.

Mayors, being political animals, never want to announce bad news or anything that reflects on the administration, but most will not lie if asked a direct question. Suppose I already have some dope and the mayor hesitates. I imply that others have already given me part of the story, now what is your version?

A series of checklist questions must be asked to learn what is up on the mayor's schedule, whether he is planning a trip to Washington, etc.

The mayor's executives—the controller, the attorney, the chairmen of the Board of Public Works and the Board of Public Safety, and the mayor's administrative assistant—by the nature of their jobs are mother lodes of information and directly or inadvertently lead me to a story. What to them may seem routine may be a lively story. Often I will see them first and get briefed and backgrounded before seeing the mayor.

If I have time to kill I simply sit in the mayor's reception room to see who comes and goes. Visitors provide big clues on what may be transpiring. The mayor may say the meeting was of no consequence, so I call the visitor later at his office, comment to him that I had been chatting with the mayor about his visit, and the next thing he is telling me the nature of his call, assuming that the mayor already had told me. Nongovernmental visitors usually are not told to avoid the press and will talk. I've learned of a couple of mayoral appointments that way, before the mayor was ready to make the announcement.

Next stop is the city engineer's office and the Board of Works. The clerk of the board is a woman confidante who tips me off to brewing events. Then I see the engineer, who heads the department of public works, the traffic engineer and anyone else who may have something worthwhile to report.

Vigilance is imperative. I touch base every day, twice a day, with the principals in city government, even knowing that nothing is doing. Fail to do it and you miss a timely story or are scooped by the evening TV.

Tips may arise from anywhere—from casual overheard remarks in an elevator, from one end of a telephone conversation, from direct tips.

Official documents and records are there to read. The minutes of the city council, the works and safety boards, the water commissioners, claims for payment of bills, claims against the city, all are public records and a prime source of news. All they need is fleshing out with questions, and answers.

Bills and ordinances filed can be dry, forbidding stuff, but hidden in all that legalistic verbiage may be a clue that rezoning is being sought for a topless bar or something. Councilmen often will not read the ordinances they are acting upon and will quote the newspaper as the source of their knowledge about a bill.

Simply knowing the beat, all that it involves, such as the duties, operating procedures, funding, responsibilities of officials, is invaluable and necessary for covering and understanding the beat.

Follow the money. Budgets and how they are spent are major clues to what the city is doing. Politicians tend to disguise the purpose of a budget item, if it is embarrassing; even though budgets are boring, they reveal much.

Scrutinizing "in" and "out" baskets and documents on desks gives clues. Learning to read upside down helps. And there are always politicians, men and women, willing to blow the whistle on someone. The clerk's office, all women, is a hotbed of gossip and some fact. They are the keepers of the files for the city council and know what the council members are up to.

That upside-down stuff. For instance, I saw a letter on the desk of the mayor's secretary, recognized the name of a developer and guessed it was a proposal on a downtown development. Later I told the mayor that I understood he had received a proposal on the project (a shot in the dark). He acknowledged that it was correct and gave me the details.

The beat impinges on all aspects of city government, and while other reporters are assigned to various departments, such as redevelopment, public housing, public transportation, parks, what happens there ultimately affects my beat. So I maintain close liaison with those people, too.

Nothing should escape the attention of a reporter. One night, after attending a routine city council caucus that ended about 6 P.M., I saw the city controller still in his office, working. I got curious. What he was doing was helping the county auditor figure out year-end balances in city funds, on the last day, a task that belongs exclusively to the auditor's staff. Without the prompt posting of the figures, the city would have lost federal matching funds and been penniless for several months until taxes were distributed.

It became a page one feature on how the controller and his staff had worked over the holiday weekend doing the auditor's work. Until then the controller had uttered nary a word.

There are stories in every department every day; they need only be ferreted out. When things are slow on the beat I simply make calls to department heads and chat about their work. Or I will make a comment implying that I heard some action is imminent. To my surprise they will reveal something I had never heard of, but they think I already know.

Such chats with officials and employees turn up rich material for stories, learning what departments are doing. Things they consider mundane often are newsworthy.

The city council is easy to cover. Most of them want publicity on their favorite bills, but avoid you like the plague if they are in hot water. I call them at home, at their businesses, in city hall and play one off against the other to get information.

Tips on Covering a Beat

1. Develop a file of telephone numbers, addresses, and titles of news sources.
2. Maintain a futures book in which you record dates of scheduled events and reminders for follow-up stories.
3. Paste clippings of your published stories in a loose-leaf album for quick reference.
4. Make frequent contacts with the principal news sources on your beat. Be prepared with questions to ask about possible news stories.
5. Develop friendly contacts with secretaries, switchboard operators, and clerks in government offices; they can be good sources for news tips.
6. Read the official documents available on your run. These may look dull, but are the source for many stories.
7. Check with persons who come to see important officials. These visitors may provide clues to developing stories and often are willing to talk.

Bulletin boards: I read them all, in every department; many contain revealing tidbits. A notice on one board advised woman employees to go during work hours to a mall shop to see a model show and make work garment selections. The personnel director, a friend of the shop manager, arranged it. The story embarrassed her and the whole thing was called off. The mayor said it was all a mistake.

In the elevator I overheard an engineering underling make a remark that the downtown Pizza Hut had a notice posted on the restroom door that the facility was out of order and to go to McDonald's restroom a block up the street.

Pursuing it with the building department, I learned that the Pizza Hut when built had not been hooked up to the proper sewer line; raw sewage was on the surface outside. This had been going on for months. A health department inspector was aware of it but was withholding enforcement. The story resulted in the immediate shutdown of the Pizza Hut until a costly new sewer was installed, and the health inspector resigned. It seems that he was a friend of someone connected with Pizza Hut.

STUDY PROJECTS

1. Bring to class eight clippings of stories that originated on standard news beats and identify the beats from which they came.

2. Study the laws in your state pertaining to a reporter's right of access to cover meetings of public agencies. Discuss what steps you and your editors could take under state law if the city school board refused permission for you to cover a meeting in which it intended to discuss the closing of three elementary schools.

3. If, after the close of a county welfare board meeting you were covering, the board chairman gave you a list of persons whom he believed to be collecting welfare payments illegally, should you include the list in your story? Explain.

READ MORE ABOUT IT . . .

Henry H. Schulte, *Reporting Public Affairs* (New York: Macmillan, 1981).
Leon Sigal, *Reporters and Officials* (Boston: Heath, 1973).
George S. Hage, Everette E. Dennis, Arnold H. Ismach, and Stephen Hartgen, *New Strategies for Public Affairs Reporting* (Englewood Cliffs, N.J.: Prentice-Hall, 1982).

COMING UP NEXT . . .

Assignment to the police beat exposes the reporter to the sordid underside of a city that is full of violence, connivery, pathos, and occasional humor. At the same time, this beat is an exceptionally fine place to develop the basic reportorial skills of accuracy, ingenuity, and persistence. Time spent on the beat is a graduate course in human nature, too.

This chapter includes:

- A description of how a police department is organized along quasi-military lines.
- A list of news sources at police headquarters.
- Tips from a long-time police reporter on how to do the job better.
- The police signal code.
- A step-by-step description of how to develop a bank robbery story.
- Operation of a fire department, which usually is included in the police beat.
- Guidelines for writing police stories.

Chapter 22
Inside the Police World

THE POLICE REPORTER'S JOB

"The police beat? Me?"

Reporters out of college on their first jobs for a newspaper or a broadcasting station, expecting to handle feature interviews and in-depth stories of social significance, are frequently disappointed when assigned to the police beat instead. They should not be. City editors compare a reporter's time spent covering police with a young physician's service as an intern. Police news is bread-and-butter reporting, essential but rarely glamorous, routine but occasionally exciting—a testing ground in which a starting reporter's skills acquired in school are tempered by experience under pressure and time restrictions.

A reporter on the police beat must sort through the daily accumulation of crimes, tragedies, narcotics arrests, family quarrels, and accidents that emerges from the grim undersurface of contemporary life. Much of the local news in every edition of a daily paper comes from the police department, the fire department, which usually is included in the police beat, and the courts.

Police officers operate in a stratum of life that is often sordid and brutal. They deal with individuals in trouble as violators of the law or with victims of crimes, accidents, and emotional turmoil. The new reporter who has grown up in ordinary family circumstances and the relatively protected school surroundings usually knows little about the world in which the police function. His or her awareness may be limited largely to the sight of a police car speeding down the street with lights flashing and siren blowing, and to the often highly unrealistic police dramas on television. Assignment to the police beat may give the beginning reporter a jarring culture shock. It will also provide splendid training in the fundamentals of reporting that will be valuable later in all kinds of writing and broadcasting.

Accuracy. Awareness of news values. Techniques for the vitally important task of checking sources. Comprehension of how the legal system works, in practice as well as in theory. All of these basic tools the reporter needs are honed and sharpened by a period of police reporting.

The importance of accuracy cannot be overemphasized. Spelling of names, the sequence of events, and the roles played by various participants in a police incident need meticulous cross-checking by the reporter, because the episode may result in a criminal trial, a civil lawsuit, or insurance claims in which the news stories play a part. A carelessly written story may result in a libel suit against the newspaper, and the reporter as well.

Some young reporters approach the assignment with a negative attitude toward the police, acquired through hearing claims of police brutality, allegations of callous mistreatment of suspects, and charges of insensitivity to individual and racial rights. Such police misconduct exists, but to a far smaller degree than antiestablishment voices contend.

An able young black woman graduate of a major journalism school obtained her first reporting job on a newspaper with more than 100,000 circulation and was assigned to the police beat. This is her comment:

> As a black girl from Detroit, I had a poor view of police when I started the assignment. My opinion of them has risen as I came to know them as individuals. There are good police and bad police, as there are good and bad in everything. I'm glad I was put on the police beat, even though I never expected to be a police reporter. One of the most important things I've learned at police headquarters is the need to check facts and follow up and expand the basic facts in a police report.

HOW POLICE ARE ORGANIZED

The duty of the police department in our society is to keep the peace and to arrest persons charged with violations of the law. Responsibility for prosecuting and punishing those arrested lies with the prosecutor's office and the courts. Although police officers are frequently called upon to testify in court against alleged offenders, the police have no role beyond that in dispensing justice.

A police department usually is divided into two chief sections: the uniformed patrol division and the detective bureau, whose members work in civilian clothes. Uniformed officers patrol the streets; answer radio calls to the scenes of crimes, accidents, and disturbances; make arrests at the scene; and file written reports on the episodes. Detectives do the follow-up work by investigating crimes that have been committed, tracking down the perpetrators, making arrests, and assembling evidence for the prosecutor. The department has a record bureau as well as a dispatching staff, which receives calls from the public and assigns police cars by radio to the scene of the trouble. Large departments also may have a special uniformed traffic division and a juvenile bureau.

Never-ending police work functions on three 8-hour shifts a day, in which the midnight to 8 A.M. shift handles the heaviest load of killings and other violent crimes. A police department chain of command resembles the military with ranks rising through sergeant, lieutenant, and captain to the chief of police and assistant chiefs. Minor variations of this hierarchy exist in different cities. Fire departments have a similar structure.

In addition to the municipal police and fire departments, a police reporter's beat frequently includes the county sheriff's department, or a county police department, which has jurisdiction in unincorporated areas of the county, and the area office of the state police department. State police have traffic jurisdiction on highways and in some states have additional investigative functions.

If the city has an office of the Federal Bureau of Investigation, responsibility for covering it is normally included in the police beat. Generally tight-mouthed, FBI officers are a poor source for routine daily news stories, because their work consists primarily of investigation. When a big story involving violation of federal law occurs, however, the FBI frequently is the primary news source.

The FBI also collects and publishes national crime statistics. A study of these reports shows how well or badly your city is doing when compared with other cities in the amount of crime committed and the number of arrests made.

In its Uniform Crime Reports, the Bureau lists these eight major crimes as Part I offenses: criminal homicide, forcible rape, robbery, aggravated assault, burglary —breaking and entering; larceny—theft (except motor vehicle theft); motor vehicle theft; and arson. All other crimes, excluding traffic violations, are listed as Part II offenses.

SOURCES OF POLICE NEWS

Two basic sources for news stories exist at police headquarters:

1. *The preliminary written reports* filed by uniformed officers after they have returned from handling an incident.
2. *The coded radio calls* sent out by the dispatcher. A police radio is turned on constantly in the pressroom; reporters keep an ear attuned to it no matter what else they may be doing.

When a reporter goes to work in the morning at police headquarters in a city of 150,000, he or she may find an overnight accumulation of about 50 preliminary reports, frequently containing unique spelling that would make a copy editor twitch in dismay. A preliminary report includes the facts of the incident involved, the name of the officer who handled the call, the names and addresses of the persons involved, and other circumstances. These preliminary reports are official records and the information on them should be privileged for publication.

The reporter's task is to read these reports, looking for story possibilities—the dramatic, the significant, the unusual small incident that might be developed into a poignant human-interest item or a humorous quirk. Nowhere is the human condition more exposed under stress than in police work; a reporter with sensitivity and initiative will find unexpected stories and insights buried in these reports. Perhaps half a dozen reports out of the 50 appear to be worth pursuing. The rest are the dross of police work—family quarrels broken up, inconclusive reports of a prowler, a pair of drunks picked up for fighting outside a bar.

Newspapers and broadcast stations have individual policies regarding certain types of stories that guide the reporter in selecting the reports to develop. The larger the city, the less space a publication gives to routine crime, because there is so much of it. A small-city newspaper may publish a story on every burglary reported, a metropolitan paper none except those in which exceptionally large amounts of property, or unusual kinds of property, are stolen. Many newspapers report only automobile accidents that involve fatalities or serious injuries. Some do not report suicides, except briefly under exceptional circumstances. Newspapers withhold names of rape victims, but many publish relatively inconspicuous stories, vaguely stated, of rapes reported to the police, partly to make readers aware that such crimes happen in their city.

Small-city newspapers, especially weeklies, often publish lists of police reports in summary form, such as the following from the Dowagiac, Michigan *Daily News*. None of the items would have reached print in a large-city newspaper, but they hold interest for small community residents who may be acquainted with the individuals involved.

Police Log

Lightning strikes

A thunderstorm early this morning aroused one Dowagiac resident out of bed after lightning struck her home around 3 a.m.

According to the Dowagiac Fire Department, Jennett Howell of 703 Alma St. was awakened after lightning struck a television lead-in wire to her home.

As a result, a small fire broke out in her home, but was contained to the inside of a wall in the kitchen.

The fire department reported extinguishing the blaze within a half hour.

No estimate of the damage was given.

Bike theft

A bicycle, valued at $175, was reported stolen to the Dowagiac Police Department (DPD) yesterday from the home of Lyle Nichols of 803 W. High St.

According to Nichols, the bike had been parked on the front porch of the residence. He stated he was notified of the theft after a neighbor witnessed two white males with the bike.

Police are investigating.

Vandalism

Fred Culver of 415 N. Front St. told the DPD yesterday that someone damaged two storm windows on his home while he had been away.

According to Culver, the damage occurred sometime between March 3 and March 26 and was apparently done with a B.B. gun or a pellet gun.

The two windows were estimated at $50.

Tape theft

Rick O'Konski, of 410 Michigan St, reported to the DPD Tuesday the theft of 23 tapes and a tape case from his car.

According to O'Konski, the tapes and case were last seen in his car at 11 p.m. Monday. He stated that the vehicle was locked and when he returned to the car the next morning, the items were missing.

The tapes were valued at $195 and the case at $15.

A police reporter needs a keen eye for the exceptional. Unusual circumstances can turn an incident that normally would merit only a tiny routine story into front-page material. For example, take this bit of actual telephone dialogue between a police reporter in a midwestern metropolis and his city editor:

REPORTER: "I've got a leaper from the ninth floor of the Wilson Hotel."
CITY EDITOR: "Do one paragraph. Maybe we can use it as a filler."
REPORTER, laconically: "She had a kid under each arm."
CITY EDITOR: "What! Give me everything you can get on it. Why did she jump? Were they her children? Where'd she come from? Hurry it up!"

If a preliminary police report seems to have story possibility, the reporter checks with the detective to whom the case has been assigned for investigation, and possibly with the uniformed officer who responded to the call. The detective on a burglary case, for example, may be able to tell the amount of money taken. A telephone call to the victim may elicit the information that a rare item also had been stolen—something of little intrinsic value, but of news interest.

Tips from a veteran police reporter:

1. Check the sequence of serial numbers on the preliminary reports. If a number is missing, the watch commander may have withheld the report. The case may

involve rape, for example, or something that shows a police officer or prominent citizen in an unfavorable light. Ask the commander for the facts and why they have been withheld.
2. Check the booking records of the city jail to see what charges have been filed against persons held.
3. Include in your stories the names of officers who provide information. The favorable publicity may help their careers and should make them good sources for future tips.
4. Remember that a large percentage of homicides are committed by persons whom the victim knows, often family or friends. There are relatively few mysterious shootings. Question persons close to the victim for your story.
5. Make friends with the police and fire dispatchers. They often are excellent tipsters on stories.
6. Study the preliminary reports for patterns. Is there an exceptionally high number of purse snatches in one neighborhood? Perhaps a teenage gang is preying on elderly women. Ask an upper echelon police official for comment.
7. Use the telephone! That extra phone call you make may produce the details needed to make the story distinctive or to clarify it.

Here is a small example of this last tip. A preliminary report records a traffic accident in which a beer truck and a bakery truck collide. No injuries occurred. Not a story, by the usual rules of the newspaper involved. But the police reporter called the bakery manager to find out what his truck carried. The answer: pretzels. The reporter sensed a story angle and wrote a lead:

| Beer and pretzels were served at a street party in the 800 block of | Jefferson Ave. at twilight yesterday —unintentionally. |

The brief story of the collision provided a change-of-pace "brightener" in the day's otherwise grim police news, because an energetic reporter made an extra phone call.

Even in the midst of a crisis, individuals almost always will answer a ringing telephone, a psychological fact that every reporter should remember. A prime instance of this fact, which resulted in an exclusive story angle during a mass shooting, occurred in San Diego, California.

A 16-year-old high school girl who had bragged that she was going to do "something big to get on TV" opened fire from a window of her family home at children in a school playground across the street. During 15 minutes of shooting with a semiautomatic .22 caliber rifle, she killed the school principal and custodian as they attempted to rescue the children. Then she barricaded herself in her home for nearly 7 hours while police surrounded the house. She threatened to come out shooting.

While this was going on, a San Diego *Evening Tribune* reporter obtained her home phone number and called it. Hearing the phone ring, the girl halted in her life-and-death confrontation with the police to answer it. When the reporter asked her why she was shooting innocent people, she replied, "I don't like Mondays. This livens up the day. I have to go now. I shot a pig [policeman], I think, and I want to shoot more."

Eventually, after the newspaper's edition was on the street, the girl surrendered. The city desk's alertness gave police and the readers an important insight into the disturbed mentality of the deadly sniper. Occasions may arise in tense hostage situations, however, when telephonic intervention by a reporter might upset delicate negotiations between police and those holding the hostages. Thus, such phone calls by reporters should be made judiciously after consultation concerning the possible impact.

Police officers usually are cooperative when reporters seek information. As a reporter becomes acquainted with commanders, detectives, and patrolmen, and they see that the reporter's stories are accurate and fair, some of them will volunteer tips and information on stories. The police, however, cannot be expected to do the reporter's work. Their reports are written for official record purposes, not to provide news angles. That is up to the reporter's initiative.

The second primary source of story leads at police headquarters is the dispatcher's orders by radio to patrol cars, and radio reports back to headquarters from cars at the scene of incidents. Sometimes these codes report major newsworthy crimes in progress or just committed. This spot news must be handled by the reporter in a hurry. With deadlines approaching, the reporter needs to act quickly, gathering as much basic information as possible at headquarters and phoning it to the city desk. Depending upon manpower available at the moment, the city editor may order the reporter to go to the scene or may send another reporter, and usually a photographer as well, from the office.

Police radio calls are coded for brevity, clarity, and a certain degree of secrecy, using the National Police Radio Signal Code. The reporter should learn the most frequently used calls and have a full list at hand to check the more obscure ones when a dispatcher uses them. The code tells the patrol car assigned what kind of situation it will encounter. The patrolling officer acknowledges receipt of the call with the voice signal "10–4" and reports "10–23" upon reaching the scene. A listening reporter can tell from the code message whether the call has potential spot news value.

The following is a selection of the calls frequently heard on the police radio:

- 10–10 Fight in progress
- 10–16 Domestic trouble
- 10–29 Check records for wanted
- 10–31 Crime in progress
- 10–38 Stopping suspicious vehicle
- 10–39 Urgent, use light and siren
- 10–40 Silent run, no light or siren
- 10–90 Bank alarm
- 10–99 Records indicate wanted or stolen

Let us see what you as a police reporter should do upon hearing a 10–90 bank robbery alarm about an hour before the main edition deadline. First, inform the city desk of the alarm and the location. If the editor sends you to the scene, hurry! Once there, determine which uniformed officer is responsible for making the preliminary report; he or she is usually the best source of information. Try to catch a detective going in or out of the building. You probably will not be allowed inside immediately; do not get in the way of the police. Listen to the police talking among themselves. Observe the scene carefully.

Here are key questions the reporter should ask: What did the male robber look like? How was he dressed? Precisely what did he say or write to the teller who was held up? How was the robber armed? How much money did he obtain? Was anyone hurt? Did the silent alarm go off? Did the bank's hidden camera get a picture? How did the robber get away? Precisely what time did the robbery occur?

As soon as you are permitted to talk to the teller involved, ask for his or her reactions. And keep an eye on the clock! Probably you will not be able to get all the answers you need immediately, and the deadline must be kept. So get to a telephone as soon as you have fresh material and phone it to the city desk; the editor will have another reporter in the office take the facts and write the story. Then return to the scene, assemble the rest of the facts, and relay them to the office, before deadline if possible.

Working under deadline pressure is a challenging, often frustrating, experience for new reporters. They find that the clock and city editors will not wait. They cannot delay their stories until every detail is pinned down, but must "go" with what they have. Spot news reporting requires a well-organized mind, a quick grasp of details, and the readiness to plunge into a situation that is confusing and a little dangerous on occasion.

THE FIRE DEPARTMENT

Coverage of a fire department is similar to police coverage, but usually with less volume of business. The reporter works from the official preliminary report of a fire, filed at headquarters. Frequent routine checks of the department should be made. Arson investigators seek the origin of the fire. These officers are good sources for information about where and how the fire started, and whether it was of suspicious origin. Frequently, the reporter must track down the owner of the home or business to obtain details about loss sustained in a fire.

The amount of equipment dispatched to a fire in response to the first alarm is usually standardized in various cities by the type and location of the reported blaze. Tower trucks often "roll" automatically in response to first alarms in areas of high-rise buildings. Additional equipment is dispatched in response to requests for assistance from the first trucks to reach the scene. This makes the episode an extra-alarm fire. A four-alarm fire is the maximum turnout of equipment in most cities. A call from the scene for additional equipment automatically alerts the reporter to a potentially important story. When you go to cover a fire in person, always determine who is in command at the scene; he or she is your best source of information.

GUIDES TO WRITING POLICE STORIES

It is essential that a police story be written on the assumption that anyone involved in a possible violation of the law is innocent until proved guilty, or he or she pleads guilty, in court. A story about a person's arrest must carry no implication of assumed guilt in its phraseology, even though the circumstances when described objectively may lead a reasonable person to believe that guilt is self-evident. The facts should speak for themselves. Any implication or assertion of guilt by the reporter, or by anyone the reporter quotes except from an official record, is potentially prejudicial and libelous.

For instance, the preliminary police report of a burglary states that a patrol car answered a call from neighbors that a house had been broken into. The officers found the back door pried open and caught a man in the dining room. At his side was a bag containing silverware that the owners, upon their return home, identified as their property. These facts from the official report are privileged and may be reported in a straightforward manner. So may the fact that the man was arrested and booked into the city jail on a charge of suspicion of burglary. However, if the detective from whom the reporter obtained follow-up information commented, "He's guilty as hell," that opinion must not be reported.

In stories of traffic accidents, this nonjudgmental reporting also is vital. Only when the circumstances are obvious does a police preliminary report indicate apparent responsibility for the accident. The usual police report describes the movements of Car 1 and Car 2; the reporter should follow this description in the story, using the name of the driver to describe each car; thus stating that the two vehicles collided, not that one car ran into the other, unless the police report says it did. Seldom, except in fatal motor accidents, and not often then, does criminal prosecution result against one of the participants. Insurance company disputes over responsibility are frequent, however, sometimes leading to civil lawsuits. The reporter's account should not prejudice the course of these disputes.

Carelessness in reporting traffic accidents can result in garbled stories that hurt the newspaper's reputation for accuracy and force it to publish a correction. The following is an actual example of a sloppily handled story and the correction the newspaper published the following day:

| Damage to a Bureau of Streets vehicle struck by a car at Main and Swanson shortly before 3 p.m. Wednesday was estimated at $250. | According to city police, the truck, being driven south on Main by William A. Smothers, 25, of 67802 Valley, was struck by a car |

also traveling south on Main attempting to make a left turn.
The car was being driven by Sylvia Walters, 17, of 29432 Wright.
No injuries were reported.

The reporter who wrote the story from a preliminary report properly attributed the information to the city police, but carelessly misread the report and thus presented a false version of what happened. The newspaper published this correction:

In the report of an accident occurring on Nov. 8, The *Times* incorrectly stated that a car driven by Sylvia Walters, 17, of 29432 Wright, made a left turn in front of a city truck at Main and Swanson. The improper turn, according to investigating officers, was made by the driver of the city street department truck, William A. Smothers, 25, of 67802 Valley.

ETHICAL PROBLEMS ON THE POLICE BEAT

In the old days, police beat reporters working on a murder case brazenly trespassed into the homes of the victim and the alleged offender to obtain photographs, diaries, and other story material. Under pressure from their editors to "get the news, no matter what!," they were guilty of petty burglary and theft, not to mention invasion of privacy. In telephone calls they pretended to be police officers in order to obtain information. That raucous comedy of early Chicago newspaper days, *The Front Page,* by Ben Hecht and Charles MacArthur, revels in the amoral atmosphere of the old big-city police pressroom. Today, the rough-and-tumble approach is virtually gone. With heavy emphasis on ethical conduct being placed by editors and media managements, police reporters must handle their jobs differently.

Precisely what is ethical in police coverage, and what is not? Should a police reporter ever violate the law in order to obtain a story? How far should a reporter go in cooperating with police and being willing to serve as a prosecution witness? In return for news tips, should a reporter ever cover up misconduct by the police?

The National News Council sought answers to these and similar questions through a staff investigation and a questionnaire sent to a cross section of prominent editors and broadcasters. The results were contradictory. Although those questioned had thought deeply on the issues, they frequently disagreed among themselves about the proper policies.

The Council reported " . . . an absence of any evident consensus among journalists on the degree to which it was ever appropriate for newspapers or broadcasters to commit illegal acts . . . ." Some editors said, "Never, under any circumstances." Others said that violations under tight editorial control might be condoned if their purpose was to highlight public or private malpractices in need of reform. None of those responding, however, endorsed the discredited thievery and break-in practices once commonplace among police reporters.

Another ethical problem that plagues police reporters concerns their conduct when invited by police to accompany them on raids during which reporters and photographers observe criminal activity in progress. Should the newspeople offer to serve as witnesses for the prosecution and voluntarily turn over photographic evidence to help the state's case?

The editors who answered the questionnaire said a resounding "No!" to that. Even then, a few disagreed.

In its report, the Council said, "The overwhelming view was the one expressed by W. Vincent Burke, vice-president for news of Station WHAS-TV, Louisville, that invitations should be issued and accepted for the sole purpose of insuring accurate information to the public without any advance commitment on evidentiary cooperation." Generally, editors stressed to police reporters the need to maintain arm's-length relations with their news sources to avoid entangling alliances.

The police reporter's role sometimes arouses public emotions that may react unfavorably on the reporter for merely doing the assigned job. Such a situation occurred at Station KTRK-TV in Houston. While listening to police calls, a photographer learned that police were closing in on the kidnappers of a small child and the child's teenage babysitter in a shopping center. After the arrests were made and the victims were out of danger, the photographer took film with a telephoto lens from about 200 feet away. One bit of the film showed a police officer approaching one of the arrested men, who was standing quietly in handcuffs, and kneeing him in the groin. The incident was included in the footage shown on the air, without commentary.

The station received a heavy volume of critical telephone calls and letters, charging that it was a defender of criminals and an enemy of the police and law and order.

Reporting the incident to the National News Council, Walter W. Hawver, the station's manager of news operations, said, "We have no right to withhold from the public such information involving a public official. Our credibility would have been severely damaged if we were to make such a decision in any such case." Although the station's decision was wise, the unfavorable publicity for the police undoubtedly created a difficult atmosphere for the station's reporters working at police headquarters.

Whenever a police beat reporter encounters or anticipates an ethical question such as those mentioned above, he or she should consult immediately with the city editor or news director. As indicated, these problems are complex and the policy to be followed should be decided by the editorial management, not by the police reporter.

Another major guideline in writing police stories is careful attribution of published statements to the source from which they came. A story about the interrupted burglary cited previously should explain that "police stated" or "the arrest report showed" that these things happened. Never let the newspaper make statements of potentially criminal fact on its own authority.

When police arrest a person suspected of committing a crime, the legal machinery that eventually will either free or punish the suspect goes into operation immediately at the scene of the arrest. In the next chapter we shall examine how the administration of justice operates and how a reporter covers the courts.

A GLOSSARY OF COMMON POLICE TERMS

APB An all-points bulletin issued for the arrest of a suspect.

Arson Willful or malicious burning of a building or property of another, or one's own property for improper purpose, so as to collect insurance.

Booking The formal act of charging a suspect by police, including photographing and fingerprinting and placing the person in confinement.

Breathalyzer test Also called a drunkometer test. An at-the-scene test of the chemical content of a suspect's blood for intoxication.

Bunco A general term for swindles and cheating. Some large police department detective bureaus have special bunco squads.

Burglary The act of breaking into a building to commit a felony or a theft.

Desk sergeant The uniformed officer at a police station in charge of dealing with the public.

DOA Dead on arrival. Used when a crime or traffic victim is pronounced dead upon arrival at a hospital.

DUI Driving under the influence of alcohol.

Felony A major crime such as murder, arson, or armed robbery for which the penalty can be a prison term and/or a heavy fine.

Homicide The killing of one human being by another. Included under this general term are murder, the unlawful killing of one person by another, usually with malice aforethought, and manslaughter, the taking of a human life without premeditation. State laws specify varying degrees of murder and manslaughter.

Larceny The illegal taking of another person's property without consent, with the intention of depriving the person of the property. Grand larceny is theft that involves property above a certain value stipulated by state law, often $100. Petit larceny involves a theft below that amount.

Misdemeanor A lesser offense, such as violation of a municipal garbage ordinance, for which punishment is a small fine or possibly a short jail term. Most motor vehicle violations are misdemeanors.

Make sheet Sometimes called a rap sheet. The criminal history of a suspect, listing previous arrests and convictions. Usually not made available to reporters under current law.

Preliminary report The factual report of a crime or accident turned in by the uniformed officer who handled the case.

Robbery Taking another person's property from his or her person or in the person's immediate presence by the use of violence or intimidation.

Search warrant A document issued by a judge or magistrate directing a police officer to search a specified person or premises for stolen property or evidence.

Vice squad Plainclothes police officers assigned to making arrests for prostitution, gambling, and narcotics offenses. Some large departments have special narcotics squads.

STUDY PROJECTS

1. Bring to class two published news stories about major crimes committed in your city. Underline the sources given for the information contained in each story.

2. While you are on night duty at police headquarters, a preliminary report comes in that the bodies of two well-dressed men have been found on a lonely road outside the city. An hour later a report is received that the body of a young woman has been found in the apartment of one of the dead men. All three were shot from the rear, execution style. List five additional sources you would check to develop the story and describe the information you would seek.

3. Write a news story from the following set of facts:

  - Location: Broadway and Main, Springfield, Kansas.
  - Time: 6/22/82, 10:20 A.M.
  - Vehicle 1: Driver, Henry William Dean, 79, 1382 Woodridge Ave., Springfield. 1973 Chevrolet. Direction of travel: N-S on Broadway. Damage: Moderate, front end.
  - Vehicle 2: Driver, Bruce A. Stafford, 36, 591 W. Terrace St., Cambridge, Missouri. 1976 Dodge. Direction of travel: N-S on Broadway. Damage: Major, rear end, front end.
  - Vehicle 3: Driver, Nathaniel R. Thomas, 66, 1015 W. Barrett St., Springfield. 1968 Mercury. Direction of travel: N-S on Broadway. Damage: Moderate, rear end.
  - Injured: Bruce A. Stafford, distorted member, complaint of internal pain. Taken to Community Hospital.
  - Collision narrative: D-3 (Thomas) stated he was traveling northbound on Broadway in the number two lane of traffic and had stopped behind a line of vehicles that were stopped for the traffic control signal at the intersection of Main when all of a sudden he heard the squeal of tires, then a crash and then felt the impact of V-2 rearending his vehicle. D-2

(Stafford) stated he was traveling in the number two lane of traffic northbound on Broadway and had stopped for the traffic control signal behind a line of waiting vehicles when he heard brakes squealing and felt the impact when V-1 rearended his vehicle, which pushed the vehicle forward making it rearend V-3. D-1 (Dean) stated he was traveling northbound on Broadway in the number two lane of traffic and had stopped behind a line of vehicles waiting at the Main St. intersection for the traffic control signal when his foot slipped from the brake pedal and compressed the gas pedal and his vehicle jumped forward and rearended V-2, which in turn was pushed forward and rearended V-3.
- Cause: As evident by vehicle damages and statements, the T/C was obviously the result of V-1's unsafe starting of vehicle.
- Recommendation: None.

At the end of your paper state what additional information the reporter should obtain to make the story complete, and where it may be found.

READ MORE ABOUT IT . . .

National News Council, *Covering Crime: How Much Press-Police Cooperation? How Little?* (New York: National News Council, 1981).

Zay N. Smith and Pamela Zekman, *The Mirage* (New York: Random House, 1979). The story of how the Chicago *Sun-Times* exposed corruption by operating a tavern.

Henry H. Schulte, *Reporting Public Affairs* (New York: Macmillan, 1981).

George S. Hage, Everette E. Dennis, Arnold H. Ismach, and Stephen Hartgen, *New Strategies for Public Affairs Reporting* (Englewood Cliffs, N.J.: Prentice-Hall, 1982).

COMING UP NEXT . . .

The role of the courts is to mete out punishment to the guilty and to protect the innocent from false accusation. A reporter assigned to the courts must be familiar with the complicated manner in which they operate. Handling the court beat is a challenging assignment that involves diligent checking of records, careful follow-up work, and occasionally the stimulation of covering a big trial.

This chapter is a concise guide to a complex world of legal terminology and sometimes devious manipulation.

It describes the differences between criminal and civil law and between misdemeanors and felonies, the various levels of courts, and the procedures in a criminal trial. Other aspects of the justice system it discusses are constitutional guarantees, plea bargaining, the fight by the press against secrecy in the courtroom, and the handling of juvenile offenders.

Chapter 23
The Course of Justice

ORGANIZATION OF COURTS

Word from the city editor that "I want you to cover the court beat" often leaves a relatively inexperienced reporter uneasy. At first, the reporter feels lost in a morass of technicalities and complex language. The words printed in legal briefs and spoken in the courtroom often are strange. The documents look forbidding. Attorneys, judges, and court officials with whom the reporter deals have spent years comprehending, administering, and in many cases manipulating, the law. The newcomer worries about misunderstanding what is going on and committing blunders in stories.

The purpose of this chapter is to give a neophyte reporter basic comprehension of the administration of justice, so that he or she may approach a court assignment knowledgeably. Procedures vary from state to state and between state and federal law. But the principles of justice are the same throughout the United States: to give defendants a fair trial, with the presumption that they are innocent until proved guilty or they admit their guilt in court.

The first fundamental for a reporter to know is the division of court action into two types of law: criminal and civil. A reporter covers both types; the more exciting news stories, however, usually come from the criminal side.

Criminal cases involve a charge by the government—municipal, county, state, or federal—against an individual for violation of the law. Civil cases are legal contests between two parties to determine questions of rights and damages. For example, one individual sues another for breach of contract and demands payment of monetary damages for the harm allegedly done to him or her. After hearing evidence, the court decides whether the contract was violated, and if so how much the offending party must pay to the other.

The second fundamental is the division of criminal law into two categories of offenses: felonies and misdemeanors. A felony is a major crime such as murder, arson, or armed robbery for which the penalty can be a prison term and/or a heavy fine. A misdemeanor is a lesser offense for which the penalty is a fine or possibly a short jail sentence.

Several levels of courts exist to handle cases of varying severity. Although names of the courts differ among the states, the categories generally are as follows:

- Municipal courts (in some states)—Misdemeanors and preliminary steps in more serious cases.
- County courts—Felonies and serious misdemeanors that are violations of the state law; civil suits.
- United States district courts—Violations of the federal law, both criminal and civil.
- The old practice of having justice of the peace courts handle minor misdemeanor cases has largely died out.
- Small claims courts—Some states have courts in which civil cases involving small sums of money are heard by a judge without jury. Both accusers and defendants appear without an attorney.

When the result of a trial in the court of first jurisdiction is appealed by the loser to a higher court, cases from municipal and county courts go to the state courts of appeal; those from federal district courts go to the U.S. Court of Appeals and ultimately to the U.S. Supreme Court.

The third fundamental is that the Sixth Amendment to the Constitution guarantees all defendants in serious criminal cases the right to trial by jury and the right to have assistance of counsel. In practice, few jury trials are held in relation to the number of criminal cases processed by the courts—fewer than 1 in 10. A large percentage of criminal cases are settled before reaching the trial stage. In some others, the defendant chooses to be tried by a judge alone rather than by a jury.

Stories about legal actions should be written as much as possible in layperson's language. For example, when a defendant pleads nolo contendere, the writer should explain that this means "no contest."

CRIMINAL CASE PROCEDURES

In order to grasp the essentials of the criminal justice system, from the point of view of the reporter who covers it, we shall follow one case, that of an accused male burglar, from the time of his arrest until conclusion of his trial.

When the suspect is taken into custody, he is "read his rights" by the arresting officer; that is, he is informed that he may remain silent under questioning and has the right to be represented by an attorney. This is known as the Miranda Rule —a 1966 landmark decision by the U.S. Supreme Court in the case of Ernesto Miranda, in which the court ruled that this warning must be given to all suspects. Its purpose is to protect a defendant from confessing to a crime he or she did not commit—out of fear, duress, or misunderstanding of the charges and the law. At the police station the suspect is photographed, fingerprinted, and formally booked into the jail on the holding charge of suspicion of burglary. He can be held under this preliminary charge for only a relatively brief, specific period of time, after which he must be either charged formally or set free.

The form and the duration of the holding charge vary by states. Sometimes the police place as many charges as possible against a suspect, some of them quite technical, if the suspect has resisted arrest or otherwise given them trouble. The suspect may be released on bail by posting a bond, except in most capital offenses. The purpose of the bond is to assure his appearance in court when required; if he fails to appear, the money posted may be forfeited.

The procedure that follows varies by states. In the state in which our burglary suspect was arrested, the steps are these:

A police detective assigned to his case takes the information he or she has gathered about it to the prosecutor (sometimes called a district attorney). At this point comes the first step in the screening process. The prosecutor's office may:

1. Refuse to draw a formal charge of burglary because the evidence appears too weak, thus freeing the suspect.
2. Proceed against the defendant by drawing an affidavit that specifies the offenses with which he is charged. The prosecutor submits this affidavit to a judge; if the judge considers the evidence sufficient to show probable cause for trial, he or she issues a warrant charging the defendant with specific offenses and states the amount of bail the defendant must post. This warrant is read to the offender in jail or upon his subsequent arrest.
3. Turn the police information over to a grand jury. This body meets in secret and may call witnesses. It either indicts the defendant—that is, makes a formal accusation against him—on specific charges and orders him held for trial or it refuses to indict, thus ending the case. This procedure is always followed in capital cases, except those involving military personnel.

The prosecutor's affidavit includes details of the alleged crime. It is privileged as a public record and is an important news source for the reporter. Grand jury deliberations are not covered by the news media, although occasionally a witness before a grand jury will tell reporters later what his or her testimony was. Routine cases such as burglary charges rarely go through the grand jury process.

In addition, a citizen may go directly to the prosecutor with allegations of a crime. If the prosecutor is sufficiently impressed, he or she may draw up an affidavit for submission to a judge or refer the case to the grand jury. Such procedure is rare, but it gives the citizen an opportunity to circumvent the failure to act by an inept or corrupt police department.

In some states, after receipt of evidence from the prosecutor, a judge holds a preliminary hearing for the suspect, at which witnesses testify, to determine whether sufficient evidence exists for the defendant to be brought to trial. If the judge believes it does, the defendant is held to answer. If not, the case is dismissed. These hearings usually are open to the public and frequently provide lively news stories.

Thus, under either system, the strength of the government's case against the accused burglar whose fate we are following is tested by a judge during the preliminary stages.

ATTEMPTS AT SECRECY

Defense attorneys at times ask judges to hold hearings in secret, closed to the press and to the public. The usual claim is that for one reason or another, publicity resulting from a public hearing will prejudice the defendant's right to a fair trial. Disturbed by what they believe to be a growing tendency on the part of judges to conduct closed hearings, news media have fought to have all court appearances in the judicial process kept open to public scrutiny.

An important victory for the public and the media in preserving the right to an open trial occurred in 1980, when the U.S. Supreme Court ruled in *Richmond Newspapers* v. *Commonwealth of Virginia* that criminal trials will be open unless there is an "overriding interest" to close them. The decision does not, however, guarantee automatic access to pretrial hearings. Among reasons given for requesting a closed hearing are: (1) the claim that the defendant faces the substantial likelihood of being denied a fair trial, (2) imminent danger to the safety of persons involved, and (3) serious jeopardy to investigations in progress. Because judges in various states continue to permit closed preliminary hearings, sometimes for little apparent reason, it is obvious that the media have more battles to fight in their campaign for access to all stages of criminal proceedings.

If an attorney attempts to obtain a closed hearing, the court-beat reporter should notify the city editor or news director immediately, so the newspaper or broadcasting station management may undertake steps to protest the closure if it chooses.

In the event that the defendant has no attorney and cannot afford to hire one, the judge assigns a public defender as counsel.

We now continue with the burglary suspect who has been held to answer for the crime. In the next step he appears before a judge for arraignment. At this public hearing, the charges against him are read and the judge asks whether he pleads guilty or not guilty. If he says "Guilty," the judge sets a date for sentencing. If "Not guilty," a trial date is set.

Each of these pretrial stages in a criminal case may be worth a news story, especially if the case has caught the public interest because of its size or circumstances. A good reporter keeps his or her own log, and perhaps a scrapbook of clippings of stories printed about the case, for ready reference on each case being followed.

Between the arraignment and the date of trial, intense legal maneuvering frequently occurs, some of it in public but much backstage. The reporter needs to keep a close watch and to scrutinize court records regularly. Defense attorneys frequently attempt to delay trial dates as much as possible, hoping that witnesses may die or disappear and that public interest in a controversial case may dwindle. They may seek a change of venue (to move the trial to another city) or submit motions for dismissal, frequently on legal technicalities. Critics of the system contend that at times it more closely resembles a legal game between attorneys than proper administration of justice. Defense attorneys argue that they should use every legal maneuver possible to help their clients.

The most frequent type of legal maneuvering for which the court reporter must watch is plea bargaining.

Under this practice, the prosecutor's office and the defense attorney make a deal in which the defendant agrees to plead guilty to a lesser offense than the one charged against the defendant. Sometimes the judge in the case approves the deal in advance, at least informally. Thus the case does not come to trial; the defendant escapes with less punishment than he or she might have received if convicted on the more serious original charge. A variation of this, when a defendant faces several charges, is for the prosecutor to move for dismissal of all but one charge, usually a relatively minor offense, in return for a guilty plea to it. When several defendants are involved, a prosecutor may strike a deal with one of them, having him or her plead guilty to a lesser charge in return for acting as a prosecution witness against the fellow defendants.

A favorite ploy is for a defense attorney to get the charge reduced from a felony to a misdemeanor in return for a guilty plea. The misdemeanor carries less penalty and less stigma. As you read newspapers, notice how frequently civic leaders and politicians arrested for drunk driving escape being convicted on this charge. Usually, along the line the charge is reduced to something like reckless driving or failing to stop for a traffic sign, which does not involve suspension of the offender's driving license and carries a lesser fine.

When writing stories about court actions, the reporter should state whether plea bargaining was involved, citing both the original and reduced charges. This helps the public to know how often plea bargaining is practiced.

Critics of the American judicial system view plea bargaining as an insidious practice and wish to see it abolished or at least greatly reduced in scope. They contend that many defendants who have clever attorneys escape paying sufficient penalties for their crimes. In their view, many prosecutors use plea bargaining excessively to improve their records of successful prosecutions for political purposes, whereas others practice it as the lazy way out, especially when they know they have a weak case. Those who defend plea bargaining contend that it reduces the burden on the courts by eliminating many costly, time-consuming trials; they disagree that the practice weakens society's punishment of its offenders.

The following news story published in a midwestern newspaper shows how a routine court action in a criminal case is reported. It is written concisely, containing the basic facts including a plea bargain.

Tommie Olson Jr., 24, of Springdale, pleaded guilty in Superior Court today to a charge of attempted theft. He originally faced two counts of conspiracy to commit theft, but they will be dismissed according to a plea agreement.

Olson admitted to attempting to take a 1978 Jeep owned by Joseph Sanders, of 22577 Louise, on Jan. 7 from a parking lot at 382 Westmoor. He is free on bond awaiting sentencing.

Olson, his brother George Olson and Milton Jennings were apprehended by police after a security guard spotted the three allegedly trying to steal two vehicles.

The attorney for the accused burglar whose case we are following fails to make a satisfactory deal and has exhausted his list of motions to sidetrack the prosecution, so the case eventually comes to trial before a jury. Few people are present during the trial; only widely publicized cases draw much of an audience. A work table is provided for the press, but is vacant. News reporters can spend only limited amounts of their time attending routine trials, especially in larger cities where the case load is heavy. They obtain information about the outcome of the trial from the court clerk and, if unusual circumstances have developed, they may talk with the judge, the court stenographer who records testimony, and other personnel.

In the case of the burglar, the jury finds the defendant guilty. The judge sets a date for sentencing after an investigation by a probation officer, whose recommendation the judge considers in determining the sentence to be imposed. The guilty verdict provides one story, the sentencing another. Should he, having been found guilty, decide to appeal his case, the court record will be forwarded to a state court of appeal. Appeals courts do not hear witnesses, but make their decisions on the basis of the written record.

By using computers as research tools, diligent reporters sometimes can develop stories with a broad sweep concerning significant patterns in the administration of justice. The San Bernardino, California *Sun,* to cite one example, obtained from the local court the records of 7000 felony cases for review. Included were details of arrest, charges, disposition, pardon, and parole. This information was fed into a computer. The data that emerged showed that blacks and Hispanics had received tougher sentences than white offenders for comparable crimes.

Although an ordinary burglary case moves through the judicial process drawing little attention and only brief news stories, occasionally a sensational murder trial attracts reporters to the courtroom in hordes. They take down portions of the testimony verbatim, hasten to telephones and transmitting machines outside the courtroom to send periodic reports to their newsrooms, interview witnesses and attorneys in the corridors, and search for angles that will make their stories more appealing to readers than those of their competitors. It is cases of this nature that draw public criticism down upon the press for creating a circus atmosphere and for sensationalism.

When Jean Harris, headmistress of a girls' school, was tried at White Plains, New York, in the early 1980s for murdering her lover, Dr. Herman Tarnower, nationally known author of the *Scarsdale Diet,* 75 reporters covered the case. Some came from Great Britain, Canada, and Australia. On days when explicit sexual testimony was given, the press corps filled half the courtroom. During intermissions, Mrs. Harris mingled with reporters, offering tart comments on testimony by prosecution witnesses. The trial lasted 64 days, and the jury deliberated for eight days before finding her guilty of second degree murder. During the long wait for the verdict, reporters, television camera crews, and photographers clustered in the corridors, clamoring in vain to get a hint of what was happening in the jury room. Their editors demanded fresh stories, but nothing was happening, except in secret.

One Gannett reporter wrote in a "color article" about the waiting process, "It was feeding time at the zoo and for the second straight day there were only scraps. All the strange and wonderful creatures paced from side to side in their common cage, the county courthouse, squawking and growling. Poor beasts. There was such a large appetite to satisfy."

When they believe their cause can be helped by doing so, prosecution and defense attorneys at times feed tips and provocative comments about a case to reporters. If the attorneys' statements are not libelous or in contempt of court, newspapers frequently publish them to enliven their stories. This practice is known as "trying the case in the newspapers." To keep a rein on such maneuvering, the judge in a controversial case may order all parties involved not to make statements concerning it to the media.

A reporter covering the courts must bear in mind the possibility of contempt of court action against his or her employer, and possibly the reporter individually, if the reporter by writing or behavior willfully disobeys or disregards a court order or engages in misconduct in the courtroom.

Until recently, taking photographs was forbidden in American courtrooms during proceedings; this restriction is being relaxed. Both still and television photography are permitted in the courtrooms of certain states under controlled conditions, in some instances on an experimental basis. When photography is barred, as it was during the Harris trial, quick-sketch artists are employed by some television news programs to depict courtroom scenes and personalities during important trials.

Trial stories of a lurid nature are relatively rare. The reporter on the court beat spends far more time checking documents and talking with courthouse personnel than in recording graphic testimony from the witness stand that is likely to make front-page copy. Generally more restrained in tone now, the contemporary press gives less space to sensationalized murder trials than it did a half-century ago when the veteran Chicago *Daily News* reporter, Robert J. Casey, assigned to one more trial in a long line of lover's quarrel murder trials, wrote a cynical lead, "It is the same old plot, with a new blonde."

JUVENILE COURT HEARINGS

Reporters are forbidden to cover one type of criminal prosecution in any form —that involving offenses committed by juveniles. Cases of offenders under the age of 18 are assigned automatically to a juvenile court judge, who conducts informal proceedings in secret. Results of the cases are not announced publicly. In arrest reports involving juveniles, their names are deleted. The legal theory is that juvenile offenders are not fully responsible for their actions and that publicity about their youthful errors might unduly damage the rest of their lives. The goal of juvenile court justice is rehabilitation, not punishment.

Rarely, when a juvenile is charged with an especially grim murder or other grave offense, the case is transferred by the juvenile judge into an adult court, where it is handled like any other case and the defendant's name is made public.

A disturbing increase in major crimes by juveniles in recent years, especially homicides and assaults, has caused legislators to seek changes in juvenile laws. They wish to have youthful defendants in major crimes tried in adult courts almost automatically and subjected to the same sentences as those imposed upon adults. This movement has not gained much momentum, but continues to generate discussion. From the reporter's point of view, crime by juveniles is a closed book.

CIVIL COURT CASES

Cases tried under civil law run the gamut from petty disputes between neighbors to contests between giant corporations that involve hundreds of millions of dollars. Divorce cases are civil proceedings. So are disputes between insurance companies over damages in an automobile accident, suits by environmental organizations to prevent a power company from building a nuclear power plant, charges that one author stole material from another, claims for damages made by the families of victims in a hotel fire, libel suits, and hundreds of other causes. The list of reasons individuals and organizations find to file suit seems infinite. A governmental body may be either plaintiff or defendant in a civil suit. Plaintiffs may seek payment for actual damages suffered plus punitive damages.

Just as in criminal law, relatively few civil suits ever come to trial. Out-of-court settlements are made frequently during the course of pretrial proceedings. Many civil suits are filed for purposes of publicity and as "grandstanding" actions, such as during the closing phases of a political campaign when a candidate, stung by charges leveled by an opponent, files a million-dollar libel suit against the rival, then quietly drops the suit after election, no matter which of them was elected. Other suits are intended as a form of pressure, one party trying to force the other into making an agreement. Attorneys frequently handle civil cases involving damage claims on a contingency basis, receiving up to 50 percent of the damages awarded as payment for their work if the suit succeeds. This practice is especially prevalent in motor vehicle accident cases. Large companies at times settle cases that they regard as nuisance suits out of court for negotiated amounts, rather than go to the expense and trouble of a trial, even though they are confident that they would win.

The original filing papers by a plaintiff are a primary source for news stories. Not only do they state the basic cause of action, but frequently include substantial detail. They are privileged documents, once they have received some court recognition, as part of the official record. So are other documents that may be filed in connection with various pretrial motions by the plaintiff and countermoves by the defendant.

Some testimony in a civil case may be taken by deposition if it is impractical for the witness to be present in court. An example of this, encountered previously, occurred when Carol Burnett successfully sued the *National Enquirer* for libel damages over a story alleging that the entertainer had been boisterous in a restaurant and had picked an argument with Henry Kissinger, a fellow diner. The former Secretary of State did not testify in person, but stated in a sworn deposition made earlier that no argument occurred between them and her conduct was entirely circumspect. Depositions are made in the presence of attorneys for both sides. Additional forms of "discovery" of evidence in pretrial actions may be used, too. These maneuvers require submission of additional motions and briefs; the careful reporter reads all these filings in the court clerk's office in search of fresh news angles.

When a civil case comes to trial, before a judge alone or with a jury, reporters handle it just as they do a criminal trial, except that civil cases rarely send a reporter scurrying to a telephone with hot front-page headline material. In some cities, courts are so jammed with caseloads that civil suits may wait for several years before coming to trial.

A GLOSSARY OF COMMON COURT TERMS

Arraignment The appearance of a defendant before a judge to hear the charges against him or her and to enter a plea of guilty or not guilty.
Bail bond The amount of money a defendant may be required to post in order to remain free while awaiting trial, sentencing after conviction, or an appeal decision.

Bailiff Attendant who preserves order in a courtroom and has custody of prisoners during a trial.

Bench trial A trial before a judge without a jury.

Contempt of court Any willful disobedience to, or disregard of, a court order or any misconduct in the presence of the court. Punishable by fine or imprisonment.

Deposition A written statement made by a witness under oath for use in court in the witness's absence.

Grand jury A panel of citizens that investigates in secret the accusations against a person. If it finds the charges strong enough for the accused to face trial before a regular (petit) jury, it indicts the person.

Habeas corpus Order signed by a judge directing an official who has a person in custody to bring that person before the court to determine whether or not the person should be released from custody.

Parole Release of prisoners before their term has expired, on condition that they behave properly. If prisoners violate the terms of their parole, they may be returned to confinement for the remainder of their term.

Perjury The offense of willfully making a false statement when one is under oath to tell the truth.

Plea bargain Agreement negotiated between prosecuting and defense attorneys under which a defendant pleads guilty to a lesser offense than originally charged, before the case comes to trial.

Probation Suspension of a sentence given to a person convicted of a crime but not yet imprisoned, on condition of good behavior and regular reporting to a parole officer.

Public defender An attorney assigned by the court to defendants who cannot afford to hire their own counsel. The defender is paid from public funds.

Quash an indictment Action by a judge to set aside or annul an indictment presented by a grand jury.

Reading his rights A formal statement by a police officer to a suspect at time of arrest, informing him or her of the right to remain silent and to be represented by counsel. Known as the Miranda Rule.

Subpoena A written legal order directing a person to appear in court to give testimony or supply records.

STUDY PROJECTS

1. Bring to class four examples of stories reporting criminal trials and three examples reporting civil trials.

2. Collect a file of stories reporting the progress of a criminal trial. Underline important points of testimony by both prosecution and defense witnesses and significant admissions made by both sides under cross-examination.

3. Bring to class examples of news stories in which:

   a. A guilty defendant received a suspended sentence.
   b. A criminal case was settled by plea bargaining.
   c. An individual was indicted by a grand jury on a felony charge.
   d. An alleged offender was referred to juvenile authorities.

READ MORE ABOUT IT . . .

Henry H. Schulte, *Reporting Public Affairs* (New York: Macmillan, 1981).

George S. Hage, Everette E. Dennis, Arnold H. Ismach, and Stephen Hartgen, *New Strategies for Public Affairs Reporting* (Englewood Cliffs, N.J.: Prentice-Hall, 1982).

Ralph Izard, *Reporting the Citizens' News* (New York: Holt Rinehart and Winston, 1982).

COMING UP NEXT . . .

Even newsroom veterans who claim to have seen and heard everything feel a tingle in their blood when a big story breaks. That is the moment when all of a newspaper's resources, and the experience and ingenuity of its staff members, are thrown into a common cause—getting the story into print fully, quickly, and correctly.

In this chapter we look at two big stories, both unexpected and tragic, and see how the staffs of two metropolitan newspapers handled them.

The first story is the attempted assassination of President Reagan in Washington on a spring afternoon in 1981. The afternoon Washington *Star* did a remarkable job of covering the story and getting the news on the streets for the after-work crowds. Radio and television also provided swift, competent reports.

The other story covered the midair collision of a commercial airliner and a private plane over San Diego in which 144 died. For its coverage, which we examine in detail, the San Diego *Evening Tribune* won a Pulitzer Prize.

Chapter 24
The Big Story

ASSASSINATION ATTEMPT

When President Reagan stepped out of the Washington Hilton Hotel shortly before 2:30 P.M. on an early spring day in 1981 and was shot by a would-be assassin, the presses of the afternoon Washington *Star* a few blocks away were starting to print the final edition. In the *Star* newsroom, the atmosphere was relaxed. Editors and reporters routinely prepared for the next day's paper. Their work finished, some staff members had gone home.

Moments later, the newsroom became tense with action. A BIG story had broken, without warning. The manner in which the *Star* handled the challenge during the next few hours illustrates the intricate teamwork involved when a newspaper staff suddenly must cover a fast-breaking major story that is filled with confusion and immense significance. This splendid performance was an appropriate climax to the long and often brilliant life of the Washington *Star*, which was forced by excessive financial losses to cease publication five months later.

At such times, the sure hand of veteran editors and the esprit de corps found in a newsroom create a high level of swift, skilled, journalistic performance. Regular assignments are abandoned as the editor in charge moves reporters and photographers to crisis posts. Available staff members are assigned to unaccustomed slots as needed. Those who are off duty are summoned to work or hurry in voluntarily when they hear the news. Individual reporters, photographers, and editors function as parts of a cohesive whole, each contributing a bit to the unfolding story. A carefully structured organization exists in a metropolitan newsroom, honed so smooth as to be hardly apparent while it produces editions day after day. When an emergency arises, this organization demonstrates what it can do under extreme pressure. Dozens of staff members may contribute to coverage of sudden news that dominates everyone's mind. In Washington, where government and politics are the primary industry, the shooting of a president has an especially intense impact. Taking part in the coverage of a spectacular news event gives even old-timers a momentary tingle of excitement. Newcomers realize that this is the kind of drama they have read about; now they have a role in it.

George Beveridge, associate editor of the Washington *Star,* told his fellow professionals through an article in *Editor & Publisher* how the *Star* covered the Reagan shooting, demonstrating a lesson in reportorial speed and organization worth studying.

The first solid facts on the assassination attempt reached the *Star* newsroom in a call from the paper's White House correspondent, Lisa Myers. Immediately word was flashed to the pressroom: "Stop the presses!" No copies of the planned final edition left the pressroom. Instead, the front-page printing plate was removed. In the newsroom, work started immediately on preparation of a new front page. That required quick writing of a shooting story based on the skimpy facts available, and remodeling of the front page to make room for it.

Details of the shooting began to arrive by phone from the scene and from press association reports. Reporters covering the departure of the President from the hotel were eyewitnesses. They heard shots ring out. They saw Secret Service men push Reagan into his waiting limousine, which sped away to a hospital. On the sidewalk, fallen in the gunfire, lay Reagan's press secretary, James Brady. A police officer and a Secret Service agent also were wounded. A few feet away, spectators and Secret Service agents jumped on the young man who had fired the shots.

Reagan was still on his feet when he was shoved into the limousine. Nobody knew how badly he had been wounded.

In such a fast-breaking situation, the responsibility for assembling the fragments of fact into a coherent running account falls upon a rewrite man or woman. Handling rewrite is a job editors assign to a cool, fast, highly organized writer —a writer who can absorb information coming simultaneously from several sources that are often inconsistent and overlapping, who can mentally organize the jumbled material into news form and make it flow from the fingertips onto a keyboard without hesitation. A rewrite expert able to turn out crisp, accurate, smooth-reading copy at high speed under pressure is greatly prized in every newsroom.

In this instance, the rewrite task fell to the *Star*'s State Department reporter, Walter Taylor, who happened to be in the office.

Within minutes after the shooting occurred, the focus of the story changed. In fact, it fragmented in several directions. The wounded men were borne away to hospitals, and the assailant taken to FBI headquarters under heavy guard. While one set of reporters sent in eyewitness accounts from the shooting scene, others were dispatched to cover angles throughout the city.

Star reporters called in developments from police headquarters, from the two hospitals where the victims were taken, and from FBI headquarters where the arrested man was being questioned. At the White House, a *Star* staff member reported what was known and being done at the inner sanctum of government. Lisa Myers continued to report from the scene of the shooting. Inside the newsroom, the Pentagon reporter monitored the police radio. Another reporter watched television broadcasts for any late developments they might carry. The political editor provided background information to the rewrite man. Others checked news sources by phone from the office or went into the street for reaction comments.

In teams of two, the newspaper's photographers were dispatched to the crucial coverage points. The staff photographer who had covered the Reagan speech at the hotel rushed on-the-scene pictures to the newspaper plant. Another photographer covering an assignment in another part of the city heard a report of the shooting on the police radio in his car. On his own initiative he drove hurriedly to George Washington University Hospital and was able to take a picture of Brady being carried into the hospital.

Taylor, the rewrite man, sat in front of a VDT terminal and wrote the story, intermingling the material from Lisa Myers with other scraps of information being given to him. Soon he had put together enough facts under the Lisa Myers by-line for the *Star* to go to press with a replaced front page that proclaimed in large headline type: "President Reagan Shot."

While the first copies of this special edition were being sold on the streets, the front page was being remade again. Space was provided for additional portions of Taylor's story and for a photograph of the wounded President being pushed into his limousine. This new edition carried "EXTRA" in red ink at the top.

UNANSWERED QUESTIONS

A score of questions needed answers. How seriously had Reagan been shot? Who was John Warnock Hinckley Jr., the 25-year-old man under arrest? What was the motive for the shooting? Was it part of a conspiracy, perhaps international? What was the condition of Brady, who appeared to bystanders to be near death, and the two law officers? Where was Vice-President Bush? Who was in charge of the government during these critical hours? How had the assailant been able to get so close to Reagan? Reporters scrambled for answers, and Taylor's story grew.

The news editor, guided by a group of senior editors, ripped apart the front page and an inside page for still another EXTRA. Such multiple extra editions are a rarity in contemporary journalism; newspapers have almost quit issuing extras since the advent of television news. The *Star*'s editors and circulation managers knew that the huge force of government workers leaving their offices for the day would grab copies of the paper. The final edition press run was doubled.

This final extra had a dramatic sequence of three front-page photographs showing the President as he was shot and another photograph of Brady lying face down on the sidewalk, as well as additional newsphotos on the inside page. Across the top of the front page was a large two-line headline:

President Reagan Shot; Condition Called 'Stable'

Here is a portion of the shooting story published in that final extra. Observe the simple sentence structure, also the careful attribution of sources concerning the President's condition and the identity of the man arrested.

By LISA MYERS

President Reagan was wounded in an assassination attempt this afternoon outside the Washington Hilton Hotel.

Lynn Nofziger, a special assistant to the president, said Reagan was shot in the left side of his chest.

Nofziger said the president's condition was serious. Senate Majority Leader Howard Baker said Reagan would undergo surgery at George Washington University Hospital, where he was taken.

The White House said Reagan was in stable condition.

Reagan reportedly was conscious, and a witness said he walked into the hospital unaided, clutching his chest.

Three other members of Reagan's entourage also were shot.

Included among the wounded was White House press secretary James S. Brady, who reportedly suffered a head wound.

The other two injured members of the president's party were said to include a Secret Service agent and a Metropolitan policeman. The agent was tentatively identified as Tim McCarthy, 33, of Chicago. The identity of the policeman was not immediately known.

The policeman's condition was listed as critical, but the agent's condition was not immediately known.

Mrs. Reagan and top members of the White House staff went to the hospital to be with the president.

Immediately after the shooting, Secret Service agents and D.C. policemen took a suspected assailant into custody. He was identified by the Secret Service as John Warnock Hinkley Jr., 22, of Evergreen, Colo. . . .

At the end of the story, which ran about 450 words, the *Star* listed the names of 12 staff members who had contributed to it, in addition to Lisa Myers. The misspelling of the suspect's name as Hinkley instead of the less common Hinckley and listing of his age as 22 instead of 25 were the only errors, both minor, in a chaotic situation. This was newspaper reporting and editing of urgent spot news at its best, a model of teamwork, swift and orderly under severe tension.

The *Star*'s staff, however, could not sit back and rest after the extras. A newspaper staff always must think about tomorrow's paper. By the time the *Star*'s first edition appeared the following day, its staff had to try to find answers to those unanswered questions. The functioning of government during the crisis hours must be reported and analyzed, the political impact of the assassination attempt must be explored, Hinckley's background and personality must be investigated. Detailed medical reports on the President and the other wounded men must be gathered.

Immediately after the final extra came out, editors met to plan the next day's coverage. Reporters began work on their assignments. A national reporter in the Southwest on another story was diverted to Dallas to check on Hinckley's background, and another staff member flew from Washington to the home of Hinckley's parents in Colorado on the same mission. Jeremiah O'Leary, a White House correspondent who normally did not work on Monday, the day of the shooting, hurried to the White House. There he worked all night, covering developments, and was still dictating story material to the newsroom at midmorning the next day. A staff member wrote a profile of Brady, whom she knew well. Photographic layouts and drawings were prepared. On short notice, management enlarged the next day's edition by four pages to accommodate the mass of material. Approximately 30 members of the local staff contributed to the Tuesday coverage.

AMERICA A "GIANT NEWSROOM"

Radio and television broke the news quickly to Americans and within two hours, via satellite relay, to a worldwide audience. Erroneous, fragmentary, and accurate information alike was passed along as it arrived in the newsrooms. "As the story unfolded with all its fits and starts," wrote *Time* magazine, "American viewers caught a rare and instructive glimpse of the newsgathering process. In effect, they saw the news naked, before it is dressed up for the evening broadcasts and morning papers."

ABC cameraman Hank Brown kept his camera rolling throughout the horrendous scene, as did NBC cameraman Sheldon Fielman. The results were some of the most dramatic news shots ever made.

Dean Reynolds of United Press International dashed to a hotel phone and dictated the story to two rewrite men who took a sentence or two of dictation in rotation. CBS correspondent Lem Tucker ran across the street to a drugstore and shouted, "I'm from CBS News. I'll give you $100 to use your phone." Later he told an employee, "If I leave this phone, keep the line open. If anyone offers you more money, I'll double it." Tucker dictated the story standing on a Lipton soup case so he could watch the outside action.

The story broke in the following fashion:

• 2:30 P.M.—White House correspondent Sam Donaldson reported the news on ABC radio.

- 2:31 P.M.—UPI transmitted Reynolds's story.
- 2:32 P.M.—Tucker's story went out over CBS radio, and a moment later Cable News Network anchorman Bernard Shaw broadcast the first TV report.
- 2:33 P.M.—ABC-TV broke into a soap opera with a simple announcement, and a minute later anchorman Frank Reynolds went on camera. As Brown's film arrived, Reynolds told viewers: "You and I are going to look at this for the first time." Later, angered by conflicting reports as to whether Brady was still alive, Reynolds shouted to staff members: "Let's get it nailed down, somebody. Let's find out. Let's get the word here. Let's get it straight so we can report it accurately."

CBS anchorman Dan Rather, who had just finished lunch, began adlibbing on camera and remained on the air live for 6 hours.

NBC White House correspondent Judy Woodruff was 20 feet from Reagan when he was shot. Before the shooting, she was planning to run to the President's limousine to ask a question, but then realized her travel pool camera crew was not close enough to pick up the sound. Although shaken by the shooting, she spent 2 hours reporting developments at the White House.

Ross Simpson, a radio reporter for the Mutual Broadcasting System, walked unchallenged to the third floor of the hospital and gained detailed medical information about Reagan and Brady. He phoned in a series of reports for more than an hour before being evicted. ABC broadcast his briefing to fellow reporters.

Time also described some of the exhaustive newspaper coverage in the United States and abroad that was given the assassination attempt, then added:

"Thirty years ago, such comprehensive reporting would have been the talk of journalism. But last week its impact was dimmed by television's performance—often confused, sometimes wrong, but always breathtaking. For one draining afternoon, TV turned America into a giant newsroom."

DISASTER IN MIDAIR

Chaotic as it was, from a news coverage viewpoint the Reagan story did have an original focal point, the scene of the shooting outside the hotel. In addition, it had the advantage of having scores of reporters, photographers, and policemen as experienced close-up eyewitnesses. However, the midair collision between a Pacific Southwest Airlines 727 passenger jet and a Cessna 172 private airplane over central San Diego, California, on September 25, 1978, had neither. It was a terrible, incoherent jumble—scattered wreckage, scattered bodies of victims, and fragments of information for a news story spread haphazardly in dozens of places. Yet the San Diego *Evening Tribune* did such a fine job of making sense out of the chaos and producing exhaustive coverage at remarkable speed that it won a

Pulitzer Prize for spot news reporting. Significantly, the prize was awarded to the entire staff, not to any individuals.

At 9:02 A.M., the PSA jetliner from Sacramento and Los Angeles was descending on its approach to the San Diego airport, which lies close to the downtown area near the Pacific Ocean shore. The approach was routine, like those made by PSA craft and other airliners hundreds of times each week. Through a tragic mixup in air control information, a small private plane suddenly appeared in the same airspace. The planes collided several thousand feet in the air, in a clear sky, and plummeted to earth. Hundreds of persons on the ground saw the disaster occur.

News of the midair collision over the city reached the *Evening Tribune* newsroom quickly, just 28 minutes before the deadline for its first edition of the day.

A reporter at police headquarters was dictating a routine story by telephone to an editorial trainee in the *Tribune* newsroom when word of the crash came in. The trainee let out a shout that aroused the entire staff.

All available reporters and photographers were thrown into the coverage. Confusion prevailed. What planes had crashed? How many persons were killed? Did anyone survive? What happened to persons on the ground where the wreckage landed? How did the collision happen? What were the names of the victims? Those were the most urgent questions.

In a remarkably short time, by telephone or in person, reporters interviewed airport officials, residents at the crash sites, the Federal Aviation Authority, police, fire fighters, hospital personnel, officials of the airline involved, the owner of the private plane, and priests who anointed the dead. Staff members phoned in graphic descriptions of what they saw in the ruins. Photographers shot pictures and hurried back to the newspaper plant. In the newsroom, editors and rewrite specialists organized the mass of incoming information into a main story containing the primary facts. They also set up secondary stories, known as "sidebars," that covered in detail specific angles such as casualty lists, background of the PSA flight, and eyewitness reports from the main crash site.

Working swiftly, the *Tribune* hit the streets only 10 minutes later than its regular first-edition time with an accurate story on the basic facts of the crash. Expanded editions followed quickly.

Less than 90 minutes after the first bulletin reached the newsroom, the *Tribune* staff had reported, written, and edited a main story and six sidebar articles. Two hours after the collision, the newspaper had a spectacular and comprehensive edition on the street, including a large photograph of the main crash site. Across the full width of the front-page spread was the headline:

MIDAIR DISASTER
140 die, homes hit here
in deadliest U.S. collision

Below this comprehensive headline layout was a poignant one-column headline quoting an eyewitness that caught the drama of the moment:

"I looked and then— I screamed"

Throughout the day, in subsequent editions, the newspaper added further details, more names of victims, and additional photographs. Less than 6 hours after the crash, the final edition of the *Evening Tribune* contained a comprehensive layout that included ten stories on the disaster and a front-page color photograph of the crash site in flames.

Radio was on the air with bulletins and television stations broadcast action pictures from the site before the newspaper could reach the street. That is always the way in spectacular tragedy stories; the flexibility and immediacy of radio and the photographic impact of television give them a running start on coverage. The first word to the public usually comes from them. The newspaper's strength is its ability to cover a story in detail, to "swarm all over it," and to provide the background and perspective that the other media lack the time and often the facilities to present. When publications cover big spot stories with the speed, skill, and precision that the Washington *Star* and San Diego *Evening Tribune* displayed, they accomplish acts of professional skill that set a goal all newspaper people should try to emulate when a crisis situation arises.

STUDY PROJECTS

1. Find an account of how a newspaper or broadcasting network covered a major disaster story and bring it to class for discussion. Possible sources are *Editor & Publisher,* news magazines, newspapers, and books.

2. In a published account of a major disaster, underline the sources from which reporters obtained their information. List questions the story left unanswered and areas in which its information was vague and inadequate.

3. Write your own lead and the first 250 words of a story reporting one of the following historical events:

    a. The shooting of President Lincoln.
    b. The explosion of the German dirigible *Hindenburg* at Lakehurst, New Jersey.
    c. The great Chicago fire.

READ MORE ABOUT IT . . .

Carl Bernstein and Bob Woodward, *All the President's Men* (New York: Simon & Schuster, 1974).

Helen Thomas, *Dateline: White House* (New York: Macmillan, 1975).

John Jakes, *Great Women Reporters* (New York: Putnam, 1969).

Edwin Emery, editor, *The Story of America as Reported by Its Newspapers 1690–1960* (New York: Simon & Schuster, 1965).

PART VII
Interpreting the News

COMING UP NEXT . . .

"Just the facts, ma'am," as a stoney-faced television detective used to say, is not good enough in the coverage of many news stories. The reader needs to be told what the facts mean and to have them put in perspective. That is what interpretive reporting does.

An interpretive reporter gets beneath the surface of a situation to provide background information and explain the reasons why something has happened. In this chapter we examine examples of how reporters did this successfully with such diverse topics as the best-seller list, the uses of corn, street violence, and the shifts in the American population as shown by the 1980 census.

The chapter describes how the media cover Washington and examines the makeup of the capital press corps. It concludes with an explanation of investigative reporting and shows how to develop a specific investigative story.

Chapter 25
Interpretive Reporting

THE INTERPRETIVE DIMENSION

Contemporary reporting practice is a blend of the objective style that took root a century ago and the interpretive style increasingly in use since the 1930s. Interpretive reporting retains the crucial attribute of accuracy, which was the central concern of objective journalism, but adds the concept of fairness. The Commission on Freedom of the Press, in its 1947 report examining journalistic practice, called for "a truthful, comprehensive, and intelligent account of the day's events in a context which gives them meaning. . . . " This should involve reporting "the truth about the fact."

Objective reporting, as described historically in Chapter 2, offered a simple framework for reporting. Facts and opinions were to be reported accurately, and be attributed to sources, except in situations of eyewitness reporting of events. The reporter was expected to quote from all sides in a dispute, but to remain neutral in presentation of opposing views and conflicting factual claims. The reporter was not supposed to indicate the bias of the source, to question the accuracy of a statement made by a source, or to interject additional factual evidence challenging the facts or opinions supplied by the source. What began as a movement to reduce reporter bias and exalt the concept of accuracy became a barrier to comprehensive reporting. We now believe that the reporter, not the source, should determine the shaping of the news being offered the reader, listener, or viewer.

The rise of interpretive reporting meant that reporters were expected to sort out facts and opinions obtained from sources, to challenge or discard distorted accounts, and supply needed background and context for reader understanding of spot news events. Reporters were also freed to develop what are called enterprise stories. These offer readers background information about an immediate event, report trends perceived by the reporter in social or political situations, analyze a series of related events, or methodically explore an area of interest.

These are called nonevent stories, "think pieces," backgrounders, or depth reports, or are products of precision journalism, which involves the use of sampling, content analysis, or the sifting of large amounts of data. Editors in their newspapers put labels on interpretive stories, such as "Background," "News Analysis," or the *Christian Science Monitor's* "Trend" and "Focus." On the editorial page the label is "Opinion." In television, the product is the documentary-in-depth or the highly popular "60 Minutes" and "20/20." The identification may properly be "investigative journalism," which characteristically is adversary in nature. The investigative story will be described later.

At some point the interpretive news story may develop depths of analysis and challenge that bring it into the area of opinion writing and editorial comment. There are, however, fairly identifiable lines. The interpretive reporter avoids the expression of personal opinion permitted the columnist and the editorial page writer. The broadcast news analyst similarly avoids the voice style and opinion statements of the commentator. Yet many an explanatory or informational editorial, presented to give the reader some background depth of understanding, could well be transferred to a news page with appropriate labeling. And some "news analysis" stories could, with slight rewording to state the newspaper's opinion, become editorials.

The trend toward interpretive reporting began after World War I, which brought political, social, and economic changes ranging from dramatic to traumatic. Postwar crises in Europe were covered in the 1920s by a distinguished group of foreign correspondents, including Walter Duranty of the New York *Times* in the Soviet Union and the Chicago *Daily News* correspondents headed by Paul Scott Mowrer, Edgar Ansel Mowrer, Helen Kirkpatrick, and John Gunther. The same decade saw the first of the syndicated political columnists in Washington: David Lawrence of the *U.S. News,* Mark Sullivan of the New York *Herald Tribune,* and Frank R. Kent of the Baltimore *Sun.*

The years of the Great Depression and the rise of the New Deal made economics and labor two compelling fields for reporter specialization and interpretive writing. Vast increases in federal spending in public financing of such economic ventures as the Tennessee Valley Authority, in deficit spending, and in the federal budget made economics a major reporting area. Everybody learned together, in a fashion. As late as the 1940s the term *gross national product* (GNP) had to be explained each time a reporter used it—just as the term *supply side economics* needed explaining in the early 1980s to readers who took GNP for granted. The rise of "big labor" to challenge "big business" and the passage of the first collective bargaining law in 1935 brought the labor beat into full prominence with Louis Stark of the New York *Times* and John Leary of the New York *World* taking the lead.

Similarly, the advances in scientific technology made science writing an interpretive beat for William L. Laurence of the New York *Times* in 1930; it was Laurence who was selected by the government to describe the Hiroshima atomic blast to his fellow citizens. Federal involvement in stabilization of farm prices and regulation of crop plantings made agricultural specialists such as Theodore C. Alford of the Kansas City *Star* in demand. On metropolitan newspaper staffs these subjects and those of social work and education became interpretive areas.

The 1960s brought the urban writers, led by Ada Louise Huxtable of the New York *Times* and Wolf Von Eckhardt of the Washington *Post*. By 1968 so many dailies had urban reporters and writers that an Urban Writers' Society was formed. Environmental concerns became major news in the 1970s and reporters were involved in such subjects as environmental impact reports, nuclear power plants, air pollution, and ecology problems. Reporters such as Margaret Freivogel of the St. Louis *Post-Dispatch* and Paul Hayes of the Milwaukee *Journal* became known. On most newspaper staffs, reporters specialized in the women's movement and in the problems of minority racial groups and immigrants.

SOME INTERPRETIVE REPORTING EXAMPLES

The uses of interpretive reporting techniques in contemporary newspaper writing are legion. Eleanor Taniguchi of the Minneapolis *Star* took a minor incident in the world of book publishing and turned it into a smoothly reading, highly entertaining enterprise story by utilizing principles of depth reporting and data backgrounding. The story was of added interest to *Star* editors because their city is home base for the largest bookstore chain in the country, B. Dalton. But the headline would attract an army of movie viewers and readers. (The *Star* was merged into the Minneapolis *Tribune* after this story was published.)

007 Tripped up
Thriller knocked off best seller list by 001 digit

Suspended interest lead

It could be the plot for a whodunit—James Bond is resurrected by a new author in a new adventure, and the book hits the New York Times best seller list less than a month after being released.

Then, after just two weeks, the book mysteriously disappears from

States mystery

the list. Was it spirited off by the jealous ghost of Ian Fleming? Did enemy agents conspire to wipe 007 off the best seller list?

Solves mystery

Would you believe it was one digit too many on the book's computer registration number?

Believe it. "License Renewed," a spy thriller written by John Gardner about the late Ian Fleming's legendary secret agent, should have appeared on the Times list during June.

Instead, its reported sales kept it slightly below the cutoff point for the bottom of the best seller list until the end of June—all because the computer number identifying the book had 11 digits instead of 10, causing bookstore computers to record fewer sales of the book than actually occurred.

Factual background

The identifying number on the back of most books published in the United States is a 10-digit number, preceded by the initials ISBN. This stands for the International Standard Book Number, and in the many bookstores that use the ISBN system, that number identifies the country or publishing group, the publisher, title and the validity of the edition (meaning that it isn't a counterfeit copy).

When such books are sold, the store clerk punches the ISBN number into the cash register, causing the sales to be recorded by a computer. This helps the bookstore's buyer keep track of how many copies of a particular title were sold and how many should be reordered.

Transition

Enter the strange set of computer-age circumstances that kept James Bond and his author off the best seller list.

All major bookstore chains, including Waldenbooks and B. Dalton Bookseller, use the ISBN system for at least some management tasks, such as inventory, pricing and ordering stock. Smaller, independent bookstores are less likely to use the system because they don't sell as many books.

The New York Times best seller list is compiled from the computer-processed sales figures of 1,600 bookstores across the country, including several from the Waldenbooks chain.

Alas, poor 007, when the computers at these bookstores fail to register book sales, there isn't much chance of getting on the Times list.

"License Renewed" appeared on the New York Times list May 24 and May 31, then dropped from sight. Book editors at The Times surmised that the incorrect ISBN number on the book was preventing sales of the James Bond adventure from being registered. The novel reappeared on the list June 29, after the publisher, Putnam's and Sons, corrected the ISBN number.

Nobody at Putnam's or the subsidiary that issued the book, called Richard Merek, is sure how the ISBN number was misprinted.

However, Jeneanne Johnson, a spokeswoman for Merek, said she didn't think the author would lose any royalties as a result of the error. "There are a given number of books out there, and when they're sold out, the bookseller just orders more," she said.

Interview

The ISBN number, created in 1967 in Great Britain so that computers could be used for processing book orders and controlling book inventories, was introduced to the United States in 1969.

It is controlled here by the R.R. Bowker Co., a subsidiary of the Xerox Publishing Co. in New York. About 93 percent of all books published in the United States are labeled with an ISBN, according to Emery Koltay, Bowker Co.'s director.

Waldenbooks stores in the Twin

2nd interview

Chapter 25 / Interpretive Reporting   303

3rd interview	Cities area do not use the ISBN system because they aren't equipped with computerized cash registers, according to Eric Anderson, a cashier at the Calhoun Square store, 1115 S. Second Ave. He said, however, that the stores would be installing a computerized system of some type in the future. B. Dalton, the largest bookstore chain in the country, uses its own number system for recording sales	rather than the ISBN system. As a result, the misprinted ISBN number on Gardner's book had no effect on sales at B. Dalton stores, said Marilyn Pahl, a supervisor in the price control division. Gardner, a British writer of spy novels who lives in Dublin, Ireland, could not be reached for comment. James Bond, who was reported to be on assignment, also could not be reached.	Tongue-in-cheek ending

Not only are the readers entertained, but they learn a good deal about the book publishing business.

Our second example progresses in social consequence and economic importance, but is equally a model of effective writing. Ward Sinclair of the Washington *Post* wrote it as the opening installment of a five-part series, focusing on the seemingly prosaic subject of corn. Here is the article as it ran on page one of the St. Paul *Dispatch,* deep in the heart of the Corn Belt.

Corn: America's basic ingredient

Astonisher lead	Fanciful the thought might seem, but America will not make it through the rest of this day without corn.	meat, milk, eggs, meal, starch and sweeteners. Corn has become a great industrial generator, providing the basic ingredient of innumerable products and stimulating invention and ingenuity in the research laboratories. Beyond that, it will go abroad, bringing $7 billion or more in return, money that helps pay for the oil, the autos, the stereos and other things we cherish.	
Lead explained	We have nothing else like corn. Not oil. Not gold nor uranium. Not wheat nor soybeans. Not our assembly lines nor our high technology. Corn is our major foodstuff and our major agricultural export. It finds its way into thousands of common industrial products.		
	Across the nation, but principally in the rich black earth of the Midwest, the seeds are growing on millions of acres, soon to become a bounteous harvest that is the American equivalent of the petroleum wealth of the Persian Gulf. This is not the sweet corn that we eat off the cob, creamed or in kernels. It is field corn: dent corn to the farmer, maize to the Indian. It is far more than a staple of the American diet, converted as it is to	Other crops—wheat, for example—may be more prestigious. But corn is American, an extraordinary grain tracked through our history by romance and legend. Every schoolchild knows how the Spaniard found maize in the New World, how the pre-Columbian natives deified it, how the American pioneer thrived on it. We traded on corn, lived off it, boozed with it, embellished our language with it. But that glorified past doesn't	Historical background
			Transition

begin to reflect the bread-and-butter side of the humble kernel of corn.

Use of second person

You wake up on sheets of cotton, wearing pajamas of flannel, both woven with corn starch for sizing. You turn on the transistor radio—the dry cell batteries contain corn starch. You put on shoes with leather tanned from the lactic acid of corn. The plywood and the wallboard in your bedroom contain corn starch. Your bath powder contains corn; your cosmetics, a corn ingredient.

Breakfast begins with corn flakes. The milk came from a cow fed with corn; the eggs, fried in corn oil, from a chicken who got her energy from corn. The pig that became the sausage and bacon grew up on corn. The English muffin is rolled in corn meal. You spread it with margarine, made from corn oil, or butter from that corn-fed cow, then smear it with corn-sweetened jelly.

Your car may be driven by gasohol, made from corn distilled to alcohol. Your soft drink is sweetened with a powerful corn syrup, colored by a caramel from the corn and carbonated by the carbon dioxide from the corn distilling process. The penicillin you're taking for that infection is made possible by another corn distillery byproduct.

Lunch is a hamburger, from a corn-fed steer. The bun has a wheat base, but it contains corn syrup. The paper wrapping was produced with a corn starch.

At midafternoon, you mail a birthday card to mother. The card was treated with a corn derivative to hold the ink, the stamp and the envelope have a glue made from corn.

For dinner, you don a clean shirt or dress, gently stiffened with corn starch. The cocktail began in a cornfield—the bourbon is distilled from corn mash, and the mix that made it a whiskey sour is sweetened with corn sugar and blended with a dextrin from the corn.

You dine on ham (from the corn-fed hog), sweet potatoes (candied with corn syrup), sweet corn, cornbread (from cornmeal) and salad doused with dressing that flows easier because of a gum extracted from corn. The beer and wine contain corn ingredients. Dessert turns out to be an imitation tapioca, made from corn starch, sweetened with corn syrup, blended with milk and eggs.

Transition

Impressive as this inventory might be, it only begins to describe the place of field corn in the American economy.

U.S. Department of Agriculture economists calculate that last year's drought-stricken harvest from 73 million acres was about 6.6 billion bushels of corn. It will be used in two principal ways: 4.1 billion bushels fed to livestock; 2.5 billion to be exported.

About 750 million bushels will be used for human food and for seed and industrial purposes. That corn is available from the reserve of around 1.6 billion bushels left over from the record 1979 crop and a tiny flow of imports.

These numbers keep changing, but the wet-milling industry that makes starch, sweeteners, alcohol and animal feed will use about two-thirds of the 750 million bushels. The rest will go to ethyl alcohol (for gasohol), for seed, for flour, meal, grits, flakes; for pet foods, beer and distilled spirits.

The largest overall use of corn, obviously, is for food. The American farmer markets his corn through the meat, eggs and milk he produces.

The center of this prodigious harvest is the Corn Belt, composed of six midwestern states: Iowa, Illinois, Minnesota, Nebraska, Indiana and Ohio, which last year grew about 4.8 billion bushels, or roughly 72 percent of all the nation's corn.

Iowa, with 1.46 billion bushels, and Illinois, with 1.06 billion, were far and away the leaders, together outproducing all other major corn-growing countries in the world. Minnesota's production falls next in line with 610,130,000 bushels harvested last year. A record 670 million bushel harvest was forecast for this season before the late June storms in southern Minnesota.

| Transition

Once that grain leaves the farm, an impressive ripple effect begins, spilling all across the American economy in ways seldom perceived. The USDA estimates that 20 percent of all the country's jobs are related to agriculture, which means that corn, as the principal crop, plays a vital role in turning over the dollar.

There is no reliable dollar figure on the place of corn among commerce and industry, but it may be in the multibillions.

Just as the corn spreads its wealth through the economy, it generates scientific inquiry and stimulates ingenuity that leads industrial processors into flights of technological fancy. Each new process leads to two more, and the future possibilities seem infinite.

The Archer-Daniels-Midland Co. at Decatur, Ill., for instance, the country's major producer of alcohol from corn, has found a way to use the heat and excess carbon dioxide from its corn-refining operations.

The carbon dioxide from its alcohol fermentation is captured, processed and sold—200 tons of it a day —for the fizz in soft drinks, for fire extinguishers, for fast-freezing of food. Waste heat is channeled into two half-acre experimental greenhouses, where garden vegetables are grown hydroponically and sold in local supermarkets. Archer-Daniels foresees huge potential for commercial hydroponics, using the waste heat and carbon dioxide to stimulate plant growth.

Not far away, at the USDA's Northern Regional Research Center at Peoria, scientists have made formidable discoveries by probing deeper into the potential of corn.

The Peoria researchers discovered xanthan gum in the corn, which is now used widely in processed foods and by dozens of industries to make paint pigments, ceramic glazes, insecticides and herbicides, cosmetics and fire retardants. They found a way to convert corncobs into low-grade methane gas for drying grains, a major expense for farmers using petroleum products.

But the basic corn component they are exploring is the starch, which USDA scientists like Dr. William M. Doane say one day could help pry America away from its dependence on petroleum. "We think we have just scratched the surface of new technologies with starch," Doane said.

The array is impressive already: urethane plastics, for example, as well as a biodegradable plastic film for packaging that replaces plastics derived from petroleum, and a product called Super Slurper, a dust that can absorb 2,000 times its weight in water.

"Technologically, from plant materials we could make all the products we now make from petroleum," Doane said. "The cost still is not feasible, but we continue to search . . ."

Which is a long way from the traditional notion of corn as a mainstay of the American pantry. But then, maybe it isn't at all.

| Interview

| Interpretive summary

Note how the latter part of the article utilizes USDA data and a variety of interviews in the Corn Belt. Even so, the story maintains its pace.

This example of a nonevent story, involving analysis of data from the 1980 census and of computer maps affording the reporter a visual perception of his subject, illustrates some of the techniques of precision journalism. John Herbers of the New York *Times* wrote the story from Columbia, South Carolina. It won play in the Minneapolis *Tribune* for understandable reasons.

Study shows amenities lured Americans

Interpretive summary lead

The areas of the United States that have experienced the most rapid growth recently are mostly places that offer outdoor recreation, a pleasant climate or natural beauty, according to a recent analysis of the 1980 census.

Interview

One significance of that finding, said one of the analysts, Ronald Briggs, a geographer, is that millions of Americans apparently did not feel constrained to locate close to their employment and did feel free—being financially able—to live in areas with the amenities they wanted.

Supports the lead

The analysis, made by computer maps drawn at the University of South Carolina, showed large population increases from 1970 to 1980 along seashores, inlets, lakes, rivers, mountainsides, ski resorts, hunting preserves and other such places, as well as in picturesque towns and villages.

Population movement to those areas took place in every region, as part of a general dispersal of population from urban centers to outlying areas. After decades of moving toward large cities, Americans in the 1970s reversed the pattern and the nonmetropolitan areas grew faster than metropolitan areas.

More interview

Briggs, of the University of Texas at Dallas, said the population increases in places offering outdoor recreation and natural scenery first showed up in the 1960 and 1970 censuses, but seemed tentative. "In the 1970s it just exploded," he said. He was assisted by David Cowen, also a geographer, who is director of the Social and Behavioral Science Lab at the University of South Carolina.

These are among the reasons for this growth, according to a number of studies:

Analytical conclusions

• Of the millions of Americans who retired in the 1970s, a significant portion had enough money to move to resort areas or to communities that offered pleasant surroundings and recreational pursuits.

• Because of changes in technology and transportation, many industries and other employers left the cities and set themselves up in or near areas providing outdoor recreation and reasonably priced housing and land.

• Despite the increase in energy costs in the 1970s, there also was an increase in long-distance commuting, in part because of improved highways.

• Areas built in the 1950s and 1960s chiefly for retirements acquired an economic base that attracted younger working people who were eager for the amenities that had brought in the older people.

"The story of the '70s appears to be the amenity-rich versus the amenity-poor, not Sun Belt versus

Published report quoted

Frost Belt," the authors said in a report prepared for the magazine American Demographics.

The computer maps showed that although the Northeast and Middle West did lose population to the South and West, as widely reported, the changes were more complex than that.

More interview

The growth in the mountain states of the West and in Appalachia was based largely on expansion of mining and other energy-related developments. But Briggs said the analysis showed that the population drawn to the new jobs tended to settle where the amenities were, even though that might be miles from the jobs.

For example, Sweetwater County, Wyo., is enjoying a boom in mining on its dreary, windswept deserts. But most of the new population is settling near the Flaming Gorge National Recreation Area.

And, whether or not they have a strong industrial base, the counties that are growing the fastest are usually the ones with coastlines, lakes, mountains and attractive scenery. Thus, even though the industrial North lost population to the South and West, mountain regions of upper New York, Vermont, New Hampshire and southern Maine showed substantial population growth, as did central Michigan, Wisconsin and Minnesota.

Thirty-nine counties more than doubled in population during the 1970s. While most started from a very small base, their growth nevertheless showed what is happening. Some are on the fringes of large metropolitan areas. Douglas, Summit and Park counties near Denver, for example, all offer spectacular scenery and winter and summer sports.

Interpretation of statistics

But others are far removed from large cities. San Juan County, Wash., is made up of offshore islands near San Juan National Park. Kalkaska County in Michigan is a wildlife and scenic area more than 100 miles north of Lansing.

In Florida, the most rapid growth took place between the big metropolitan centers, in areas with the most lakes, best coastlines and cooling breezes.

Since the census was completed, there has been considerable speculation whether this kind of movement is continuing under changed economic conditions. Government analysts are predicting that population dispersal will continue for some time.

Outlook for future

Markedly more interpretive is this final example, involving a "trend" report, background analysis, use of interviews, data, and news developments to knit together a typical *Christian Science Monitor* interpretive story. It was written by Ward Morehouse III, a staff correspondent, under a 1981 New York dateline.

U.S. cities riot-free this summer: can simple courtesy keep them calm?

Interpretive lead

So far, this summer has been relatively free of street violence in the cities of America despite dire predictions about the effect of Reagan administration budget cuts on the urban poor.

Supports lead	Only recent sporadic clashes between police and minority demonstrators and construction workers here in New York have marred the picture, unlike last year when rioting erupted in Miami, Tampa, and other US cities—and unlike Britain, whose old industrial cities are beset by similar trouble at the moment.
Transition	Can common courtesy and brotherly love help defuse racial tensions and prevent minority unrest?
Conclusions from interviews	An emphatic yes, declare some authorities on social problems, such as Steve Klein of the Martin Luther King Center for Social Change in Atlanta, which holds annual conferences on nonviolent means for social change.

But other leaders stress just as emphatically that additional concrete steps have to be taken to avoid the possible recurrence of the kind of strife that has shaken American cities in the past. Street crime, which is on the rise, these leaders say, is only a more subtle form of minority unrest.

According to Mr. Klein, Columbia University sociologist Herbert Gans, and other authorities whose views were solicited, these are the main reasons why minority communities have not reacted so far, despite the considerable "economic crunch":

• By improving minority hiring practices and working more closely with neighborhood leaders, many police departments throughout the nation have not generated the kind of "sparks" (such as shootings of blacks by white officers) that have triggered much of the urban violence in the past.

• When such incidents have taken place—inadvertently or otherwise—reason often has prevailed over emotion. Even in Philadelphia, which has a long history of black unhappiness with police brutality, "There have been some shootings of blacks by white officers [in the past year], but there has been an opportunity for reason," says civil rights lawyer Anthony Jackson.

• "There may be a perception within the minority community that we're on a conservative crest right now and this may not be the most propitious time to go out in the streets and demonstrate," says Bernard McDonald, an expert on minority community affairs with the Ford Foundation.

Mr. McDonald, who is black and has been a community activist himself for many years in Brooklyn, also believes "there is more common sense and understanding within the minority community, which indicates that urban unrest has not been that useful in producing lasting results. . . ."

• More blacks and other minorities now are working within the system to attain their goals.

However, some experts like Klein believe the lack of widespread unrest this summer could well be "the lull before the storm," unless greater efforts are made to stem rising black unemployment and other critical needs. Specifically, Klein warns that the fact that 314,000 CETA (Comprehensive Employment and Training Act) jobs will be eliminated locally by Sept. 15—half of which are held by blacks—could generate new unrest.

(Others contend that the schools, which will have resumed for a majority of young people by then, will help channel the restlessness that might have been caused, had the CETA cuts come earlier.)

Nationwide, however, the job picture for blacks seems to be worsening. According to the latest US Department of Labor figures, black unemployment has risen over the last year, while white unemployment has fallen. Total black unemployment has gone from 14.5 percent in June, 1980, to 15.5 percent last month. Many minority leaders contend that black unemployment is even higher, especially in urban areas. White unemployment, on the other hand, has dropped from 6.7 percent to 6.4 percent in the same period.

Transition — Meanwhile, the Reagan administration contends that its economic package is a prescription that will eventually reduce minority unemployment as the entire economy improves and more workers are needed.

Interview — "Obviously, lots of things have been done since the 1960's," Professor Gans said in an interview. "One of the things is that you have a larger black middle class and a larger black upper-middle class that is much less threatened than poor blacks. On the other hand, with the economic crunch, the whole atmosphere is becoming leaner, and the signals for that are coming from Washington."

As a result, he continued: "I think that delinquency and juvenile crime will go up. It has to if the unemployment figures go up. Mugging is an individualistic kind of protest, in a way. It's not necessarily a conscious one, but I'm not sure that riots are always conscious protests."

2nd interview — Mr. McDonald says one has to be careful in trying to link unemployment to racial unrest: "Simply because there is high unemployment [among minorities], I don't think one should expect automatically for there to be urban unrest. These incidents usually result from some precipitous act, whether it relates to the criminal justice system [or] police handling of a sensitive situation."

WASHINGTON: POLITICAL NEWS CENTER

Not only is the capital of the United States the world's leading news center, and the focal point for our national political events, but it is also a major center for interpretive reporting. Under its dateline, hundreds of news dispatches flow daily to all corners of the nation and every country abroad reporting spot news, but more importantly interpreting the policy decisions and actions of the White House and the government, in terms of the lives of people everywhere.

A Washington job is the goal for many reporters who hope to find satisfaction in being close to the source of global decisions and in recording the interplay of forces that produces our national policy. This is a viable goal for talented young men and women who are interested in politics and public affairs and who prepare themselves for a role in the Washington press corps. Stephen Hess, in a Brookings Institution publication, *The Washington Reporters,* offers a profile of that press corps.

Hess found that there are 1250 reporters covering the national government for commercial news media (this excludes editors, broadcast producers, photographers, columnists, local staffs of the capital's press, and more than 500 correspondents of foreign media based in Washington, as well as thousands of information and public relations people). Of these reporters, 38 percent work for newspapers, 14 percent for news services, 13 percent for the broadcast media, and 10 percent for magazines. The remaining 25 percent are reporters for specialized publications, such as newsletters, magazines, and newspapers that provide data and trends analyses for business and social groups. They are all a well-educated group of professionals; one-third of the 1250 have graduate degrees. Most of them find satisfaction in their work.

What are the reporting assignments available to the Washington press corps? General assignment status in a news bureau was the title of 20 percent. Reporting regional news for newspapers was the job of 14 percent. Twelve percent covered one or more of the domestic agencies (agriculture, civil rights, consumer affairs, education, health, labor, transportation, and urban affairs). The Congressional press galleries claimed 8 percent. Economics (Treasury, Federal Reserve) and business reporting were the specialty of 7 percent. What Hess called diplomacy (State Department, embassies, Defense Department, and national security) was the beat of 7 percent. Five percent were in the White House press corps. Other specializations reported on were law, including the U.S. Supreme Court, 5 percent; politics, 4 percent; energy, 4 percent; and science, 2 percent.

In the eyes of Washington correspondents responding to questionnaires in depth, the most prestigious beats are State and Defense. Next best jobs, in order, are self-directed general assignment, the Supreme Court and law, politics, the White House, and Congress. But White House correspondents, who see themselves as interpreters rather than beat reporters, know that nearly all reporters have a deepseated, if secret, desire to be a part of the group that covers the President and the mainsprings of national and global policymaking found in the executive offices.

The innermost circle of influence is that formed by the correspondents for the three networks (ABC, CBS, NBC), the two press associations (AP, UPI), three newsmagazines *(Newsweek, Time, U.S. News & World Report),* and three newspapers (Washington *Post,* New York *Times, The Wall Street Journal*). Next in influence among the press corps are the Los Angeles *Times,* Baltimore *Sun,* Boston *Globe, Christian Science Monitor,* Chicago *Tribune,* and Knight-Ridder newspapers. Individuals such as John Osborne of the *New Republic* and Elizabeth Drew of the *New Yorker* win recognition. So do the correspondents of such great overseas news organizations as Reuters, the *Times,* and the BBC of Britain; Agence France-Presse and *Le Monde* of France; and the large press contingents from Germany, Japan, and Latin America.

COVERING THE WHITE HOUSE AND CONGRESS

More fast-breaking major stories come from the White House in a year than any other single Washington source. The pressroom in the White House is staffed by some of the best-informed and most experienced reporters in Washington. They are called upon to handle stories full of complexities and nuances, and the way they handle them has a strong impact upon public opinion both in this country and abroad. A misconception of American policy, coming from a poorly handled news story, can have serious repercussions.

The president's press secretary frequently meets the reporters as a group to give them news of developments in the Executive branch. Such news is usually labeled "the White House said" or is attributed to the press secretary by name. Between group meetings, the secretary undertakes to obtain answers to questions submitted by individual reporters. When the White House has a story of special interest coming up, it frequently puts out advance notification to enable attendance by other reporters in addition to the crew of regulars. The White House reporters also obtain important stories by interviewing prominent visitors who come to talk with the president.

At stated times or at indefinite intervals, depending upon his schedule and inclination, the president holds a news conference. There is no legal obligation for him to do so, but this long-established custom makes him more available for personal contact with reporters than any other major government leader in the world. These conferences are attended by scores of reporters who hold White House credentials, in addition to the regular men and women on the beat, whose number varies from 35 to 45.

Frequently a president will discuss so many subjects in a single news conference that it will produce several stories. There might be a story on a critical development in Soviet-American relations, another on his plans for the political campaign, and a third about problems of the federal budget. The press associations carry a single dispatch including all these angles plus separate stories on the most important topics.

When the president travels, he is accompanied by reporters for the press associations, the newsmagazines, the networks, and, within the limits of available space, by reporters of individual newspapers. They follow the president in separate automobiles or a press plane. Rarely are the White House correspondents out of close touch with the president and his staff, no matter where he goes.

Coverage of Congress falls into two categories. The first is news the reporters obtain while attending public debates and committee hearings of the Senate and House of Representatives. The second is the material they gather in personal conversations with the lawmakers and their staffs. If a reporter develops good contacts and shows that he or she can be trusted, there will be stories and news angles from these politicians, most of whom are publicity conscious.

Some Senators and Representatives are the key figures in party strategy and in directing the movement of legislation through Congress; others are specialists in such fields as foreign affairs, atomic energy, and finance. Like one on any beat, the experienced Congressional reporter learns where to turn for certain kinds of information, which sources are the best informed and most reliable, and which are merely trying to use the press for their own purposes.

Both houses of Congress have press galleries in which reporters can watch the floor debate and take notes. All statements made in the debate are privileged. Behind the galleries are long, bustling pressrooms in which the reporters have their typewriters, telephones, and telegraph and broadcast facilities.

Many of the biggest Congressional stories come from committee hearings held in special rooms some distance from the main debating chambers. Some of these sessions are closed to reporters, especially when members are discussing matters involving national security. However, by talking to committee members after the meetings, reporters at times can obtain printable information about the general trend of discussions. Edited transcripts of the testimony, with secret material deleted, are sometimes made public later.

Public hearings on controversial bills and investigations held to determine the need for legislation are fast-breaking, exciting stories to cover. Among the spectacular ones in recent years are those involving Watergate, unethical influences in government, foreign affairs, and alleged subversion. The hearing rooms are jammed with reporters, photographers, and spectators. What the witnesses testify before the committee is privileged, but what they say to reporters in the corridors is not. Some refuse to answer questions from the committee, pleading the protection of the Fifth Amendment against incriminating themselves. At times this refusal leads to indictments for contempt of Congress.

INVESTIGATIVE REPORTING

If a newspaper is to fulfill its role in a community, it must do more than report the surface, easy news from routine sources. As a force for civic good it must search for the concealed stories—those the public should know about, but which have been unwritten either through neglect or a calculated effort by someone to hide them. If the news media do not do this job for the public, who will? Development of such stories is called investigative reporting.

Articles disclosing conditions in slum areas, health hazards, insufficient school facilities, and other such civic ills fall within this category. Such "situation" stories can often be developed by an enterprising reporter without encountering any opposition more serious than lethargy, although the stories when published may create a strong reaction. When reporters dig into unsavory situations involving possible criminal offenses, they face a more serious problem. Every year there are examples of editors and reporters, on large papers and small ones, whose tenacity and courage bring to light unethical conduct by public figures and sometimes outright criminal actions. Occasionally, a reporter on such work suffers a physical beating at the hands of criminals, and in rare instances, death. An example is the 1976 murder of Don Bolles of the *Arizona Republic* in Phoenix, solved largely by the efforts of the national organization called Investigative Reporters and Editors, Inc. These episodes are so unusual that they attract much attention, but every day the investigative reporter must show moral courage in the face of social and economic threats of a type seldom encountered by reporters working on more orthodox stories.

Investigative reporting requires a special set of news talents, of which relentless tenacity is foremost. A reporter assigned to a difficult investigation may go weeks without seeing a line of copy in print. He or she may have to fight off a feeling of frustration when leads fail to develop and there is not printable evidence to support suspicions. Yet if the reporter is convinced that those suspicions are justified, he or she will keep plugging away, hoping for a break. When that break comes, as it often does, the story may be on its way to a Pulitzer Prize.

The attention riveted on the media during the Watergate crisis and in its aftermath by the book and movie, *All the President's Men,* did more than win fame and fortune for Bob Woodward and Carl Bernstein of the Washington *Post.* Their investigative reporting, complete with the suspense of a presidential resignation and the mystery of a "Deep Throat," spurred reporters everywhere to adopt adversary positions. They also had the examples of Dan Rather of CBS and Clark Mollenhoff of the Des Moines *Register,* who dueled with President Nixon in his press conferences. And of columnist Jack Anderson, who broke the "Pakistan tilt" story, or reporter Jack Nelson of the Los Angeles *Times,* who began the revisionist estimate of J. Edgar Hoover. But equally important were the local investigative stories.

ASSIGNMENT: SLUM CLEANUP

Here is an assignment that a city editor might give you with instructions to develop it into a series of stories.

Your city has an unsightly area of cheap rooming houses, bars, dubious hangouts, and rundown homes. Several murders and a number of teenage hoodlum gang fights have occurred there. The city editor wants the story behind the headlines. Just how bad is the area, and why? The purpose of the series is to point the finger at the basic causes and to propose some course of civic action.

How would you go about developing the series from the start of the assignment until the stories are ready to print?

Here is the procedure that has been used on several metropolitan newspapers in preparing similar stories. The first step is to define the scope of your investigation. What is the exact geographical area to be investigated? Does it have a commonplace local name such as the West Side, the Valley, or Skid Row? Then comes a list of aspects to be covered. Some of the main ones are the health situation, crime records and police costs, property ownership, the schools and churches, racial problems, municipal and recreation facilities, housing, and juvenile delinquency.

With this list in hand, the reporter determines where he or she can go for information in each field. Official statistics will provide the foundation upon which to develop the articles.

HEALTH

The city health department has figures that may be very revealing. A blighted area usually has an exceptionally high tuberculosis rate. Is that true here? Get figures comparing this area with other sections of the city. What about pest control? Does the department have a greater problem in this section? Check the coroner's death statistics. How do hospital facilities compare with the rest of the city? Talk with two or three doctors to get anecdotes and personal experiences that will personalize the statistics.

PROPERTY OWNERSHIP

The neighborhood is conspicuous for its rundown buildings. Is this because the residents have little pride, or are they too poor to afford the upkeep? The reporter can go to the city building department for answers that should be in the inspectors' reports. How many of the buildings have records of fire, health, and building code violations? How much effort have these departments made to enforce the municipal ordinances, and how well have the courts backed them up? Have the departments instituted condemnation proceedings against the worst health traps and firetraps or merely filed their inspectors' reports with a shrug? The latter has happened in some cities until a newspaper has turned the publicity upon the situation. The reporter goes to the worst buildings and interviews the residents and the managers, but discovers that the owners do not live there. Who does own the property? Again he or she can get the answers from the records—this time in the county's land files where the deed for every piece of property is registered. Checking a dozen typical buildings, the reporter may find that in ten cases the owner lives in another, perhaps wealthy part of the city or in another city entirely. This may establish a pattern of absentee ownership that frequently leads to neglect. To put teeth into the stories, the reporter can get in touch with the owners of the buildings most frequently cited for municipal code violations and print the list of offenses along with the owners' excuses.

CRIME RATE

Is there really more crime in the neighborhood than elsewhere, or is it, as some residents contend, that the papers just play up crimes in this area? Check the police statistics. How do offenses such as robbery, homicide, narcotics, and drunkenness compare with those in other neighborhoods? Many cities have a breakdown of police costs per individual resident by police precincts. How much more does it cost the taxpayer to police this blighted area than other parts of the city? Spend some time at the police station in the neighborhood, if there is one, to hear the officers' stories of what they are up against. Must they patrol the streets in pairs at night? Do they have enough plainclothes detectives to check vice? Are they vigorous in trying to keep down petty crime, or do they blink their eyes at some of it? Do you detect any hints of police protection for gambling and vice? If possible, talk to the men who run the gambling games and to the prostitutes, questioning them about payoffs. If they claim that they are "paying off," demand specific information of time, place, and amounts. This information should be cross-checked as carefully as possible before publication; few editors will accept the testimony of one or two petty criminals as conclusive. But if you find a substantial pattern of reports, you have run across an important spot news story.

RACIAL PROBLEMS

Frequently, blighted areas attract mixed racial strains, including nonwhite groups who have difficulty in finding housing in the better neighborhoods because of prejudice. The recent pattern in large cities is population movement toward the suburbs, leaving an area of once-attractive houses into which low income and transient groups move. Racial and other barriers go down. Sometimes this leads to serious stresses. Does this situation exist here?

EDUCATION

How do school facilities compare with other parts of the city? Go to the Board of Education for statistics on average class size, teacher load, age of buildings, and other criteria to determine whether the pupils are receiving below-standard treatment because they live in a poor neighborhood. Talk to the principals and teachers in the neighborhood schools about truancy rates and pupil turnover. How does the transient nature of the school population affect discipline? What special steps have been taken to control teenage delinquency? Talk to the district's ministers and the police juvenile division about the same problem.

RECREATION FACILITIES

Does the neighborhood have its share of playgrounds and other supervised facilities where youths can gather? What do recreation leaders say they need—more help, equipment, places to meet? Does the city recreation department have any plans for providing these?

A reporter who has checked all these sources will have more facts about the neighborhood and its problems than anybody in town. All the material is there for the asking, but nobody has ever had a reason to assemble it all before. From roaming the streets, listening to conversations in corner bars, and talking to residents of all sorts, the reporter will have a "feel" for the area. If he or she shows a sympathetic attitude, there will be no difficulty in getting the residents to talk. And no matter how broken down and impoverished the section may be, there will be a strong strain of neighborhood pride among many of its residents—men and women who seem to be truly happy and content.

The facts are all in hand. Now how does all this get into such news story form that people will want to read it? Newspaper readers do not want sociological textbooks. To hold their interest the stories must be not only factual and constructive, but also written so they are attractive to readers.

The answer lies in human beings. The reporter who can translate all the statistics and official reports into terms of the men and the women who live in the neighborhood has captured the art of the storyteller. For example, the police records report 30 cases of auto hubcap thefts from the area in the past three weeks. Do any of the reports mention a witness? If so, look the person up and get the story. Perhaps he is an old man who was sitting on his front steps when a gang of a half-dozen youths worked their way down his block one night, prying hubcaps off one car after another. He called to them to stop, but two of the gang threatened him and forced him to stand in the dark corner of his porch until the thefts were finished. If the reporter starts the article about juvenile crime by describing the episode through the old man's eyes, the reporter has captured an audience. Then statistics can be used to show how commonplace such incidents are, with the explanations by the police about their efforts to control the thefts. A lead paragraph with statistics has a deadening effect.

Reporters must organize their stories. The editor, after hearing a verbal report on the material, suggests a series of six articles. A logical first step in organization is for the reporter to list the conclusions—the significant facts that investigation has established, and the recommendations, partly personal and partly those of persons interviewed, on steps that can be taken to improve the situation. These should form the concluding article. The first five articles should be so arranged that a factual background is laid for all the major conclusions to be reached in the last article. The opening installment must be sufficiently colorful and closely enough related to the general news situation to catch the reader's attention. It should give the reader an indication of the aspects to be covered in the subsequent articles. But it should not be overloaded with "teaser" material; on a major series of this type the reader expects solid information from the start.

Occasionally, news stories based on personal investigation by a reporter are written in the first person. More common is the report with a by-line in regular news story form, with perhaps an interjection of the "I" approach where the reporter's own experience adds substantially to the story's meaning.

STUDY PROJECTS

1. Using an interpretive news story from Washington about foreign affairs, underline all the places where the writer expressed a judgment, suggested future developments, or sought to tell the reader the meaning of a set of facts.

2. Bring to class examples of three of the following types of stories:

a. A significant trend or development in medicine.
b. An interpretation of the president's economic policies and their possible impact on individuals or groups of citizens.
c. An explanation of a development in the women's movement.
d. Efforts to restrict operation and expansion of nuclear power plants in the United States.

3. You have been assigned to write a series of articles about the use of drugs in your local high schools. Discuss the types of material you would seek and the sources from which you would obtain them.

READ MORE ABOUT IT . . .

Clark Mollenhoff, *Investigative Reporting* (New York: Macmillan, 1980).
Lou Cannon, *Reporting, An Inside View* (Sacramento: California Journal Press, 1977).
Winthrop and Frances Neilson, *What's News—Dow Jones, The Story of the Wall Street Journal* (Radnor, Pa.: Chilton, 1973).
Stephen Hess, *The Washington Reporters* (Washington: Brookings Institution, 1981).

COMING UP NEXT . . .

A reporter who also can take news photographs possesses an extra skill that helps to open the door for job opportunities, especially on middle-sized and small newspapers.

This chapter describes the kinds of photographs a reporter who doubles as a photographer usually has to handle and gives suggestions from professionals on how to take them, including things to avoid. The principles of news photography are explained.

The rights of a photographer differ somewhat from the rights of a reporter, especially in courtrooms. A set of 11 guidelines for police-press relations adopted by the National Press Photographers Association, printed here, will help the reporter-photographer fill the role to the fullest possible extent.

Concluding the chapter are instructions on how to write cutlines, those important words under a picture that help to give it meaning.

Chapter 26
The Reporter as Photographer

A SUPPLEMENTARY SKILL

In the old days of vaudeville shows, the violinist in the pit orchestra who could also play the trombone during the loud music was referred to as "doubling in brass." Much the same can be said of the reporter who takes photographs on story assignments. This supplementary skill is a valuable asset. Editors of smaller newspapers in particular consider a reporter's ability to use a camera an important work tool.

Large newspapers have staffs of full-time photographers who record in pictures the news that reporters record in words. A metropolitan paper may have 15 or more "photogs," as they are commonly called in newsrooms. When assigned by the photo editor, a photographer either accompanies a reporter on a story, the pair of them working as a crew, or goes out alone to get the desired picture. Reporters on large newspapers generally take photographs only when assigned to a territory so far removed from the home office that sending a photographer on every picture possibility is impractical. Some large newspapers therefore assign combination reporter-photographers to these outlying beats. In the event of a major story, such as a natural disaster, one or more full-time photographers would be sent to the scene.

When a reporter and photographer are sent on a story as a two-person team, they work as equal partners in deciding how to approach the assignment and in gathering information. A beginning reporter fortunate enough to be paired with an experienced photographer on an assignment can learn much from the veteran. Most long-time photographers are happy to give the newcomer a hand, if they sense that the young reporter is anxious to learn.

On small daily newspapers and weekly papers the situation is much different. The daily may have one or two full-time photographers, or none at all. A weekly rarely has a professional staff photographer and thus the responsibility for picture taking falls upon the reporters. Usually the small newspaper's staff includes one or two darkroom technicians, often working part time, who develop the rolls of film turned in by the reporters and make prints from which editors choose the pictures for publication. Because personnel emergencies arise on small staffs, from illness or vacations, the reporter who can step into the darkroom and handle the processing task is especially appreciated.

Newspapers generally provide picture-taking reporters with suitable cameras and, of course, with the necessary supplies. Some reporters prefer their own cameras to those owned by the company.

KINDS OF PHOTOGRAPHS

The reporter doubling as a photographer cannot fairly be expected to produce work that rivals the pictures taken by skilled photo specialists. With some practice, however, he or she can take publishable news pictures of routine subjects, occasionally coming up with a shot that causes readers to say, "That's a good picture!"

The reporter on a small newspaper can expect to take pictures in three general categories:

1. Spot news shots such as those of fires, serious automobile accidents, and high school football games.
2. Photographs to illustrate feature stories the reporter has written. These provide an opportunity for distinctive pictures, because the writer-photographer is less pressed for time than on spot news assignments.
3. Set-up shots.

This third category is the most humdrum and in a sense the most troublesome. It consists of pictures recording such situations as the ceremonial presentation of a check to an organization from a donor, two officials shaking hands, installation of a civic organization's officers, and the meeting of a committee planning a charity dance. These and similar situations occur so frequently in small-city life, and are so difficult to present in innovative form, that they result in trite "waxwork museum" poses. Photographic purists abhor them. Large newspapers refuse to publish certain types of stilted photographs, such as the check-presentation scene. Yet small-city newspaper editors often publish such photos, knowing well that they are trite, because their audience expects them. Their readers are more interested in "getting our picture in the paper" than in the higher levels of photographic art. Such community service photographs in many instances publicize approaching civic events to stimulate attendance and to provide an ego-flattering payoff to volunteers who work on the project. If a newspaper in a small city bans such pictures, as some do, it can anticipate charges that it does not care about the community's welfare.

Anyone who doubts the attention such photographs receive should watch the presiding officer at a local men's service club hold up a newspaper photograph. He announces that Joe Johnson had his picture in the paper last week being installed among officers of Friends of the Library. "That will cost you a $5 fine for getting free publicity, Joe!" Loud hoots of laughter from the audience—and everyone present is reminded that the newspaper publishes local pictures.

In this classic shot, the late Nelson Rockefeller confronts his hecklers.

If the reporter-photographer works for a paper that publishes such photographs, the best he or she can do is to strive for a slightly different approach. The cliché form shows two men facing the camera, each with one hand holding onto the check that one is presenting to the other. The check is the important element. So why not shoot from an angle, rather than from straight ahead, showing the face of the check, not its back? Were Joe Johnson and his fellow officers lined up in rigid formation, as though waiting for a firing squad to pull the trigger? Instead, why not photograph them paging through a stack of new novels the library has just received? That is what Friends of the Library is all about. By inventing some kind of "business" or finding a suitable prop to keep the subjects looking less posed, you will make your pictures far more interesting. Use the same ingenuity in setting up a picture as you do in creating a "different" lead on a feature story.

TAKING THE PICTURE

Photography is far too complex for its techniques to be covered in this short chapter. If possible, student journalists should enroll in a course in news photography. They can find in photography magazines valuable information about camera exposures, lighting methods, and attractive photographic composition that involves both individuals and objects. These magazines are available on newsracks and in libraries as are books on photography. Another way to improve the technique is to join a camera club.

Most news photographs the reporter takes involve black and white film. The 35-millimeter single-lens reflex camera is favored for newspaper work, because it is light and flexible. Wide-angle and telescopic lenses may be added for more elaborate work.

When they function as photographers, reporters should remember: Do not get so preoccupied with taking pictures as to neglect the reportorial duties. As a reporter, get the facts for the story, and as a photographer, take down full information for the picture captions. Be especially careful to check the spelling of names for persons in each picture you take and make certain that the names are listed in correct left-to-right sequence.

Also, avoid embarrassment by learning at least the rudiments of the news situation involved before preparing to take a picture. John J. McPhaul recalls in *Deadlines & Monkeyshines* what happened to a Chicago newspaper photographer of limited scientific education who was assigned to cover the tenth anniversary of the first self-sustaining nuclear chain reaction at the University of Chicago. Gathering several of the world's eminent nuclear scientists before his camera, he told them he had a series of three pictures in mind: "First, you guys putting the atom in the machine. Then splitting the atom. And finally all of you grouped, looking at the pieces."

Certain principles of news photography should be mentioned here, because they are basic.

- **Anticipation.** The photographer must be prepared to cover spot news quickly by having the proper equipment in ready-to-shoot condition. Exciting news shots can vanish while you fumble with the camera.
- **Instinct.** In every spot news situation, a critical moment exists. Try to sense when that moment will arrive. When it does, shoot!
- **Direction.** When handling groups of individuals, the photographer must function much like a film director by controlling their movements and shaping them into attractive informal poses. Chat with them to get them relaxed as you prepare their position. Always place the most important individual in or near the center of the group. Thus, if space for the picture on the newspaper page is limited, the print can be cropped from one or both sides without losing its point. Notice how a camerawise politician gravitates to the center of a group when it is about to be photographed, so that his or her face will not land in the wastebasket.

Some newspapers have a rule against showing more than five persons in a group photograph. More than that, their editors contend, creates an unattractive mass. This rule helps the photographer avoid embarrassment when everyone wants to get into the picture. By inviting the head of the organization to select the five persons, and perhaps providing discreet suggestions, the photographer avoids having to be arbitrary and offend someone.

- **Composition.** Photographic composition follows the basic rules of design in painting. Instead of putting the subjects in a straight horizontal line, group them sometimes in circular fashion or in a triangular arrangement. Or place them in a rising vertical position so the picture can be published in long, narrow form instead of the usual horizontal. If you feel uncertain about the results you will obtain with these variations, take a protective additional shot in a more traditional pose. Because of newspaper column width limitations, group your subjects closely enough to eliminate "dead" space between them.

When photographing a scene, include a person whenever possible. A picture of a victim poking through the wreckage from a tornado is more eyecatching than one merely showing the debris.

YOUR RIGHTS AS A PHOTOGRAPHER

In most places where you go as a reporter, you are free to function as a photographer as well, but this privilege is not universal. Courtrooms in particular are uncertain ground. Until recently, the use of cameras during court proceedings was forbidden everywhere. That ban is breaking down. Still photography and television shooting are permitted during court proceedings in a number of states, under controlled conditions. The trend toward courtroom photography is growing. Be sure to learn the local rules before attempting to use your camera in a court.

Law enforcement officers usually cooperate with press photographers on spot news pictures, to the point that some police radio dispatch systems include coded calls indicating that an incident under investigation by police has picture possibilities. Occasionally, however, antagonistic police officers or public officials give photographers a difficult time and unjustly try to prevent them from taking pictures. This occurs most frequently in moments of extreme tension, or when the picture might embarrass the police or the official involved.

The National Press Photographers Association has adopted a set of 11 guidelines for police-press relations. These were developed after extensive discussion with journalists and law enforcement officials. Although these guidelines pertain primarily to photography, they are couched in terms that apply to reporters as well. They are:

1. Journalists may not resist, obstruct, or oppose an officer in the lawful execution of a legal duty. The presence of a photographer or a reporter at an accident, crime, or disaster scene, and the taking of pictures or the asking of questions relative to the incident do not constitute unlawful interference, and should not be restricted.
2. Journalists may be asked to show their press credentials.
3. Journalists have the responsibility and the right to photograph and to report events that transpire on public property.
4. It is the long-standing custom of public safety agencies to invite journalists upon private property where an event of public interest has occurred. Journalists are required to enter in a peaceful manner, and not to cause any physical damage.
5. No journalist should be denied access on the basis of public safety. In those circumstances where the general public has been denied access to an area on this basis, photographers or reporters should be granted access after first being cautioned of the risks, and after the officer has received acknowledgment that the journalist understands the risk. The decision to assume the risk of danger remains with the journalist.
6. Denial of access to crime scenes is sometimes necessary to an investigation because of crime-scene processing or the collection of evidence. The reasons for such a denial should be explained to the journalist, and access granted as soon as is practical under the conditions.
7. A police officer should not restrict a journalist from taking pictures or asking questions, even though the officer may disagree with the nature of the pictures or questions. It is the journalist's obligation to take pictures and to ask questions, and it is solely the editor's responsibility to determine which photos or what information will be run.
8. When journalists are present, either on their own initiative or by being granted access to an area under police control, officers will not attempt

to restrict any of their actions, unless their actions are clearly interfering with an ongoing investigation.
9. Journalists apprehended for violating the law will be dealt with in the same manner as any other violator.
10. A police officer should realize that a journalist has the responsibility to collect as much information about an incident of public interest as quickly as possible. This requires meeting deadlines for distribution of the news, and sometimes requires the collection of information that may seem irrelevant, unimportant, or even improper to the officer. As long as the journalist does not violate the law or directly interfere with an investigation, the police officer should not impede the journalist.
11. Police officials should neither encourage nor discourage the photographing of suspects or defendants when they are in public places. Officers should not deliberately pose a person in custody for the press.

WRITING CUTLINES

"I need lines for this page-one art."

Requests such as this are common in newsrooms. "Lines" refers to the cutlines—or captions as they are sometimes called—that accompany newspaper photographs, graphs, and charts, usually referred to simply as "art." Writing cutlines is an integral part of a reporter's job.

Cutlines explain and identify the scene, objects, or people depicted in the accompanying art. The name is derived from the letterpress process of etching a picture on a zinc plate, which is then cut to a specified size. Cutlines may consist of a single identifying name or phrase, a one-line sentence, or a series of sentences, usually preceded or followed by a line showing the source, such as "Staff Photo by Irene Weatherby" or "UPI Photo."

The essential requirements are thoroughness and brevity. If the lines accompany a story, the reporter should not repeat any more of the salient facts provided there than is absolutely necessary and, if possible, should avoid repeating key words and phrases. If the art is to be run without a story, the cutlines likely will be longer, though not excessively so.

Because the photographer has caught a moment in time, the lines usually are written in present tense.

Canadian Prime Minister Pierre Trudeau shows off on a trampoline during the Canada Day celebration in Ottawa on Wednesday.

At times future tense may be indicated.

> Brookwood Mall will be the scene of fireworks Friday night.

Infrequently, past tense is used, as in these cutlines accompanying a three-photo spread:

> The Red Sox had that down-and-out feeling yesterday—and for good reason. Rick Miller was forced to hit the dirt (top) to avoid a Pete Vuckovich pitch; Dwight Evans (above) arrived just a bit too late to snare Ted Simmons' single; and Dave Stapleton (right) misplayed Robin Yount's grounder to short for an error, setting up a Milwaukee run in the first inning.

People in a photograph are identified left to right. In a group shot, the form usually is: top row, middle row, bottom row (or the reverse). When the positioning is irregular, other means must be found to identify each person correctly.

A reporter should never write cutlines "cold"—without first viewing the picture. Often the notes that he or she has taken, or have been provided by others, fail to reflect the photo accurately, as could easily happen in an action shot. The caption of one recent newspaper photo stated that a girl was crying at the funeral of her brother, but no tears were visible.

Improper identification not only lessens the credibility of the newspaper, but also may lead to a libel suit, for example, when a person is erroneously described as a convicted murderer. For these reasons identification must be positive. Because similar photos may be confusing or attached information lost, it is common practice for identifying information to be written in soft pencil on the back of each photograph.

After writing cutlines in which a number of people are identified, the careful reporter will check to insure that no name has been omitted. Haste in writing lines can lead to such an error and to others much more embarrassing, such as when a Georgia newspaper caption writer, working hurriedly past the regular deadline, described Pope John Paul II as "the first non-Catholic Pope" (he meant "non-Italian").

In years past, many newspapers printed large headlines, either above the photograph or below it, to help attract attention. This practice has largely been abandoned; instead, most editors prefer to "let the picture speak for itself." On some papers, however, the caption will appear below the photo in this form:

> **Record Cantaloupe**
> A cantaloupe grown by Gene Dautridge (R), of Route 3, Rocky Mount, N.C., is said to be a world's record, weighing in officially at 43 pounds,

8 ounces. The seeds were developed by Ed Weeks (L), of Greenville, N.C. (AP Laserphoto)

More commonly, a headline phrase will be imbedded within the cutlines paragraph itself, set either in all-capital letters or in boldface type.

LEGION POST BURNS—Boston firefighter mans post at hydrant while others battle two-alarm blaze which heavily damaged Wolcott street headquarters of Readville American Legion Post early yesterday. Officials estimate damage at $20,000.

Violence in Liverpool—Three ranks of policemen, taking cover behind riot shields, protect themselves from flying objects thrown by West Indian rioters in the English port of Liverpool. Almost 200 policemen were injured in the disturbances, which have been going on for two nights. Strife there follows an outbreak of racial violence in West London, where Asian immigrants clashed with white gangs.

Because no story accompanied these two photographs, the lines ran longer than they would have otherwise. When a story is used, the lines may read simply:

Wayman Stewart works on dormitory repairs

A combination of an all-capital line and a phrase set in regular body type often is employed.

ATHLETIC, 'REDDISH-BLOND HAIR
Police Composite of Suspect

At times a phrase extracted from the story will enliven cutlines.

Williams: "The White House Has Been Too Slow"

As can be seen from these examples, the style with which cutlines are prepared varies from newspaper to newspaper.

A good checklist to follow in writing captions is the following, which the Associated Press provided for its staff members:

1. Is it complete?
2. Does it identify fully and clearly?
3. Does it tell when?

4. Does it tell where?
5. Does it tell what's in the picture?
6. Does it have the names spelled correctly with the proper name on the right person?
7. Is it specific?
8. Is it easy to read?
9. Have as many adjectives as possible been removed?
10. Does it suggest another picture?
11. Never write a caption without seeing the picture.

The New England Press Association offered these guidelines to help photographers take better, more lively pictures:

1. Change the angle—show readers something they could not see for themselves.
2. Show incompleted action—readers will subconsciously complete the action.
3. Use props—they help tell the story.
4. Tighten composition—avoid unnecessary space.
5. Focus on one subject.
6. Limit people—use a representation of groups.
7. Add people—to show sizes of objects and add life to photos.
8. Capture moods of people—find the peak of emotion.
9. Shoot action and reaction—turn the camera the other way.
10. Strive for technical excellence—know shooting conditions and use supplemental lighting equipment when needed.

READ MORE ABOUT IT . . .

Ken Kobre, *Photojournalism: The Professional Approach* (Somerville, Mass.: Curtin and London, 1980).
Harold Evans, *Pictures on a Page* (Belmont, Calif.: Wadsworth, 1979).
Phil Davis, *Photography* (Dubuque, Iowa: Brown, 1979).

COMING UP NEXT . . .

Writing for the ear differs from writing for the eye. So do reporting techniques for radio and television news, as compared with newspaper reporting. This chapter examines those differences and explains the operations of broadcast news departments.

All forms of news reporting share the need for accuracy, clarity, objectivity, and fairness. These are basics. The differences arise from the technical requirements of the media.

Radio reporters in the field ply their craft with microphones and tape recorders; in the studio they use tape splicers and other electronic gear. Television reporters in the field must think visually as well as aurally and move about with accompanying camera crews. The newspaper reporter is not burdened by equipment, nor so slavishly tied to the requirements of the second hand of the clock.

The chapter also shows how to write copy for broadcasting. Stories are shorter than newspaper accounts and more conversational in tone, with less detail and more broken sentences.

Chapter 27
Reporting and Writing Broadcast News

DIFFERENCES IN METHODS

Broadcast and newspaper journalists have much in common: They gather news from essentially the same sources; share a knowledge of what makes news; seek to observe the precepts of accuracy, clarity, objectivity, and fairness; and must respect the laws of libel and right of privacy. Distinctive differences exist, however, primarily in respect to reporting techniques, deadlines, and the writing style and length of stories.

REPORTING FOR RADIO

Just as with large, medium-sized, and small newspapers, reporting procedures vary according to the size of radio stations. Some established metropolitan stations have newsrooms, staffs, and beat systems that correspond to a considerable extent with those of large newspapers. There is far greater competition in radio, however, and most staffs consist only of the news director and from one to three reporters.

What do these people have to work with? Radio newsrooms are equipped with a teletype service provided by a press association, and some receive audio news services as well. Equipment is available for the constant monitoring of local police, fire department, and highway patrol (state police) radio calls. Many stations receive 24-hour U.S. Weather Service teleprinter service or frequent audio reports.

Also generally available are a battery of telephones; tape recorders; two-way radio control panels; tape splicers to edit and repair audio tape; one or more large wall clocks with sweep-second hands; a wide range of maps; AM and FM radio receivers; newspaper files; informational records; reference books; a date book noting future events; and other assorted materials. The most frequently used reporting aid, of course, is the telephone.

At a typical small station, the early newsperson (perhaps even the news director) will begin the day with a quick check of the press association machines, followed by telephone calls to the nerve centers of the station's coverage area. These include the police, fire, sheriff's or county police departments, and local and area hospitals and funeral homes. Calls to correspondents (stringers, as they are known) may produce additional news. Local and area morning newspapers are searched for tips about stories, which must be followed up or simply verified. As time permits, television and radio newscasts are monitored.

After quickly writing and perhaps delivering the early morning newscasts, the reporter, and possibly others, will leave the station to visit courts and other public offices, cover community and area events, and conduct interviews. Because newscasts are hourly occurrences at most stations, reports must be called in frequently to be written and put on the air. The reporter will deliver, in person or by carrier, tape-recorded actualities—the "actual" sounds of news in the making—for incorporation into the major noon broadcasts and others that follow. This routine will continue until sign-off time.

On larger stations, these procedures are multiplied, for many persons are involved in reporting, writing, and delivering the news on a continuing basis. On both large and small stations, no day's work ends until a tentative schedule for the next day has been prepared.

The radio reporter encounters several problems not faced by his or her colleague in the world of print journalism.

Although a great many judges have opened their courtrooms to television cameras, most still exclude the use of a tape recorder in court proceedings. The recorder is vital to good broadcast newsreporting; judicious use of taped excerpts greatly enlivens newscasts. Judges generally are fearful that jurors allowed to return to their homes in the evenings will hear actualities that may prejudice their decisions. Barring a tape recorder from a courtroom, however, severely hampers radio news reporting.

Security officers pounce upon the assailant moments after his attempted assassination of President Reagan outside a Washington hotel.

There are other problems involving the tape recorder. Interviewees often "freeze up," speak in an artificial manner, ask that a faulty statement be rerecorded, or hem and haw in such a fashion that editing the tape becomes a chore. In order to elicit terse responses that will consume only a few seconds of air time, radio reporters also must be very careful to phrase their questions properly.

Persons called by telephone for quick responses to questions just before air time often want to think about their answers before replying, and must be called back. During any recorded telephone interview, Federal Communications Commission regulations require that the interviewee be informed of that fact.

For identification and promotional purposes, many radio stations mark their vehicles with their station's call letters. The presence of these vehicles at a civil disturbance will often single out the news team for abuse, whereas the pencil and notebook newspaper reporter (although not always the photographer) may go unnoticed.

Another problem of the radio news reporter, not shared equally with the newspaper reporter, relates to the frequency of radio newscasts (up to 48 or more in a single day on some stations). This is one of the strengths of radio. If no one takes his or her place, however, the radio reporter must often leave a news scene to call in the story. On the other hand, although the radio reporter generally must sit through a lengthy meeting to insure that no significant news is missed, the headline character of radio news reports at times permits early departure.

WRITING NEWS FOR RADIO

Brevity, clarity, accuracy, and interest are the hallmarks of good radio newswriting. The 5 minutes allotted to a newscast may be taken up with a 15-second opening, a 15-second closing, and 90 seconds of commercials, leaving time for only 3 minutes of news. Because most newscasters read copy at the rate of about 15 or 16 lines a minute, only six to nine stories, covering about 45 lines, can be written for this time period. In a 15-minute newscast about 11 minutes are filled with news.

Consequently, the reporter must be highly selective. In sharp contrast with most newspaper stories, only one or two main points can be made in each news item. The listener must get details from other sources.

Here are some recommendations for the radio newswriter:

Write in informal, conversational style, as though you are talking to a listener; in effect, you *are* "talking"—with your typewriter. Avoid the more formal style of newspaper writing. For example, a newspaper lead might read:

```
Temperatures in Iron City soared to a record 100 degrees
Wednesday, and forecasters predict that at least five more such
days are in prospect.
```

The radio story might begin:

```
The July heat wave. It's still with us. The mercury soared to 100
degrees this afternoon. And there's no relief in sight.
```

Note the short sentences and even a phrase in the radio news lead. A "sentence" without a verb is permissible occasionally if the principal idea is conveyed. There is an easy conversational flow to the writing. Numerous variations are possible, of course, and because the news should be rewritten for each succeeding newscast, listeners may hear a number of fresh approaches to the story.

For the most part write short, declarative sentences, but vary this style if necessary to avoid a choppy effect. Without crowding, include the essential five Ws and, if possible, the "how" in the story. Avoid clutter. And emphasize human interest elements whenever you can.

In contrast with most newspaper stories, begin sentences with attribution and, because immediacy is important, stress the "today" element. For example, a morning newspaper might report:

New water rates approved last week by City Council will go into effect immediately, Mayor John Smith announced Wednesday.

Updating the story and beginning with the attribution, the radio reporter, who has gained this information independently or verified the newspaper account, likely would write:

Mayor John Smith has announced that the new water rates approved last week by City Council will go into effect immediately.

Both present and present perfect tenses may be used in radio newswriting. If the morning newspaper had reported that "Governor Wayne Smith called on legislators Wednesday to return for a special session," the radio news reporter would likely write: "Governor Wayne Smith *is calling* for a special session of the Legislature," or "Governor Wayne Smith *has called* for a special session. . . ." Including "yesterday" in the lead will date most stories. Using present or present perfect tense also will eliminate the frequency of "today" in the several stories of a newscast, saving precious words for other purposes. Sometimes, however, the time must be clearly stated to avoid confusion.

Note the use of yesterday, today, and tomorrow in radio copy—not Wednesday, Thursday, and Friday.

When you identify a person by title, put the title first unless it is too lengthy; that prepares the listener for who the person is. Examples: City Council President Susan Adams; William Smith, president of the State Board of Examiners.

Use direct quotations sparingly, and do not begin a story with a direct quotation—listeners may misunderstand. Unless a direct quote is striking, paraphrasing is much better. If a utility company president told you, "We'll appeal the commission's ruling," the statement is too trivial for direct quotation. But if the president said, "There's too much hankypanky going on to suit me," that statement is controversial and colorful, and should be quoted.

By inflection the newscaster may clearly indicate the direct quotation when it is read. To insure that the quotation is read properly, however, the reporter might write: "The president put it this way: 'There's too much hankypanky going on to suit me.'" Or: "Said the president: . . . " Or: "The president said—and these are his words: . . ." Other variations are possible. In years past newscasters often said, "quote . . . unquote," but the practice has been abandoned—no one talks that way.

Do not lead with unfamiliar names—most listeners will not retain a name in their minds long enough to identify it with the rest of the story. Instead, begin with a general identification and provide the name later. Examples:

A 20-year-old Lawrenceville man has been killed in a highway accident east of Rome. Roger Smith was pronounced dead upon arrival at an area hospital last night.

A Watkinsville attorney—Mary Jones—has been elected president of the Georgia Bar Association.
A t h e n s   h a s   a   n e w   F i r e   D e p a r t m e n t   c h i e f .   H e   i s   E r n e s t   W i l l i a m s . . . .

Generally avoid newspaper style in reporting names and ages. A newspaper story likely would read: "Ernestine Wheeler, 15, of 1010 Downey Road, is the youngest person...." Radio news copy probably would read: "Fifteen-year-old Ernestine Wheeler...," or "At 15, Ernestine Wheeler is...."

Because radio news is conversational, contractions may be used judiciously. There is a danger, however, in writing such contractions as "can't" or "wouldn't" because the negative may not be heard.

Avoid the use of slang, dialect, and colloquialisms.

When the meaning is clear, use general rather than specific expressions. For example, it is better to write "a broadcast employees' union" than "the National Association of Broadcast Employees and Technicians."

When inserting an actuality into a news script, select about 15 to 20 seconds of the most significant portions of the audio tape. Skillfully blend the actuality into what precedes and follows it, but never repeat the exact words of the insertion.

Here are some tips on preparing news copy:

Unless your newsroom prefers all-capital letters (the form in which news service copy traditionally has been provided), type all copy in capital and small letters (known as upper- and lowercase); studies have shown that such copy is easier to read than all caps.

According to your station's practice, type on standard-size paper or half-sheets, but on one side of the paper only. Observe normal margins.

Write your name, a one- or two-word slug line, and the page number in the upper left-hand corner. Skip about 14 lines before writing. Use normal paragraphing. Do not split words or hyphenated phrases from line to line. And do not continue a paragraph from one page to the next.

Except for roundups of related items, headlines of stories to come, or closely related stories, place individual stories on separate pages. If more than one story appears on one page, separate the items with marks such as -O-. Place a mark such as XXX at the end of each story. Stories are written on separate pages to permit newscasters to rearrange their order if desirable.

Provide phonetic spelling in parentheses after names that may be difficult to pronounce; these are known as pronouncers. Example: "Juan Martinez (Wahn Mahr-<u>tee</u>-ness)." In local copy underlining of accented syllables indicates emphasis; in news service copy an apostrophe is used. Follow this guide:

- AH—a in arm.
- A—a in apple.
- EH—ai in air.
- AY—a in ace.

- E—e in bed.
- EE—ee in feel.
- I—i in tin.
- Y—i in time.
- OH—o in go.
- OO—oo in pool.
- UH—u in puff.
- KH—a gutteral sound.
- ZH—g in rouge.
- J—g in George.

Vowels are pronounced alike in all languages except English and German.

Use local, state, and national pronunciation guides available to you. Repeat the pronouncer each time the unfamiliar name or phrase is used in copy.

Abbreviate rarely. Mr., Mrs., Ms., and Dr. are acceptable, as are time designations such as A.M. and P.M., although "this morning" and "tonight" are preferable (do not use both P.M. and tonight). If initials are to be read as such use hyphens: S-O-S, C-I-O, N-B-C. When the initials are to be pronounced as a word, omit the hyphen: NATO.

Do not use symbols such as: %, $, ¢. Write: percent, dollars, cents. Spell out decimals: 7 point 6. Use figures for numbers 10 through 999. Round off large and detailed numbers: a thousand two hundred, instead of a thousand two hundred and four.

Use traditional punctuation most of the time, but seldom use question marks, quotation marks, colons, and semicolons. To make reading easy, write: The former city manager—Sarah Bush—said.... Use three dots in a row for dramatic effect and to indicate a pause: She stopped ... too suddenly ... and the chain reaction of crashes began.

When you have finished, read the copy aloud to eliminate any problems. Corrections may be inserted in pencil, but if a single letter in a word is incorrect, rewrite the entire word. If your copy is messy, retype it. If time is available and you can improve the copy, rewrite the entire story. Almost all stories can be strengthened by rewriting.

REPORTING FOR TELEVISION

Gliding ever nearer to the forest fire raging 1200 feet below, the helicopter hovers momentarily as the camera operator focuses out the window. Almost simultaneously, thousands of television viewers in the area see and hear the report.

In a nearby city, another member of the station's staff focuses a miniature, hand-held camera on the mayor as the mayor makes an important announcement. The sound and pictures may be transmitted from a microwave dish atop the station's van nearby to the tallest building in the city, where one of four "horns," placed to pick up signals from all points of the compass, beams the story back to the station. Or the signal may simply be "bounced" off a building.

At the studio, tapes are edited on machines that transfer selected segments of the mayor's talk from original to final form. Because the forest fire report is being aired live, the mayor's remarks are transferred to a 1-inch tape "cart" or to a ¾-inch cassette tape, to be inserted later into the same newscast or into another later in the day.

Meanwhile, the producer and others watch critically as newspeople, technicians, and engineers follow the script to effect a smoothly coordinated newscast. Most of the program consists of "tell" stories—brief summaries read by the anchorperson, often illustrated with drawings or other graphics on the screen. Interspersed also are excerpts from previous network newscasts, meteorological reports, sports accounts, and commercials.

The preceding is a typical newscast by a major television station—one of almost 100 in the United States that own or lease helicopters to provide live or taped coverage of, and to transport staff members quickly to, scenes of developing news events. Few stations can afford a helicopter, which may require $250,000 to purchase or $150,000 a year to lease; all, however, have "mini-cams" even though they may not have set up facilities to transmit reports live.

The revolution in communications technology has greatly improved the quality of news programming in recent years and put broadcasters in a better financial position in covering news as well as in other operations. The developments include new videotape technology, satellite communication, instant-replay techniques, portable film and tape equipment, the use of jet aircraft to transport tape or film when satellites are not used, and efficiently packaged, high-capacity switching gear. A tremendous growth has occurred in recent years in the distribution of news to and from stations by satellite. For example, Cox Broadcasting Corporation has installed a system that links all its stations by satellite and Cable News Network beams 24 hours of news reports daily to millions of viewers.

Other than its pictorial elements, the newsroom of a television station is much like that of a radio station or a newspaper. Reporters gather the news in person and by telephone, work in press association dispatches, and prepare scripts for each newscast. Daily assignment schedules are followed, interrupted only by unexpected developments that often add excitement along with feverish work to get the news on the air as quickly and accurately as possible. Newspeople, however, now have the tools they need for the job—a far cry from the days of cumbersome equipment when Fred Friendly, former CBS radio-TV producer, wryly described television as a "two-ton pencil."

On field assignments the reporter gathers notes and works with camera personnel to make certain that all visual elements are covered. The reporter generally will tape the opening and closing of the report on the scene. As each cassette is

338 PART VII / INTERPRETING THE NEWS

```
SLUG:    HOME OF THE BRAVES              PAGE:  5
ACTION
NEWS 2   DATE: 4/21/82   WRITER: N. DAVISON
ATLANTA
              DORSEY READS           The Atlanta Braves
                                     have made Baseball history!
                                       Before a crowd of
                                     more than 37-thousand last
                                     night...the team broke the
                                     major league record for most
                                     consecutive wins at season
                                     open.
              VO/SONY____   ____       Fans poured onto the
                                     field...wild with excitement
         CG# 300-Fulton County        ...after the team downed the
              Stadium/last night     Cincinnati Reds...4-to-2.
                                       "Braves Fever" has
                                     definately reached a fever
                                     pitch.
              SOS          ____     in:.."the team is simply...
         CG# 301- Braves Fan         out:...I just love em.."
              VOS          ____        The Braves picture
                                     perfect record now stands at
                                     12 and 0.
                                       And with a record like
                                     that...who knows?..."this
              ENDS         ____     really could be the year."
              PAD          ____
```

The script for a television news story, ready for feeding through the station's Telesync prompter system. Anchorwoman Joselyn Dorsey of station WSB-TV in Atlanta, Georgia, read the copy on the right side as technicians worked in the videoshots and screen superimpositions noted on the left side. "VO/SONY" and "VOS" instructed Dorsey to read copy while pictures and sound from a Sony Company-manufactured videocassette *(Continued)* removed from the camera, it is carefully labeled. If the footage is to be sent back to the station, the reporter will write an explanation of what has been taped—called a "dope sheet"—so that producers and writers may assemble the components into a story. Often, however, the reporter will return to the station to edit and write the story personally.

WRITING NEWS FOR TELEVISION

Many television news stories, of course, are written for delivery without accompanying pictorial elements. When working with illustrative material, however, the reporter prepares a script to be voiced over maps, still photographs, film, or videotape recordings. This is known as voice-over (V/O), with the reporter endeavoring to insure that the words and pictures complement each other.

In working with tape or film, the writer first screens the footage, examines the accompanying notes, and, if necessary, obtains additional information by telephone, by reading press association reports and newspaper accounts, and by examining reference books. The reporter then refers to a "spot" sheet, noting the sequence and the length of each edited scene. This information generally is typed on the left side of the script and the timed narration is provided on the other side.

The writer must make sure that the spoken words will not exceed the length of the tape, that all necessary identification and interpretation are provided, and that there are no redundancies. Good writers will insure that the words do not "fight" the pictures and that the script is written, insofar as possible, to match the personality and the preferred cadences of the anchorperson.

Achieving clarity, accuracy, and high viewer interest in television news is not easy, but can be perfected in time. As the late Carl E. Lindstrom said: "The news writer is an artist. In its simplest terms, art is the business of selecting for effect —plus skill. The writer is the creative manipulator of the most plastic, the most resistant, the most mercurial and yet the stickiest substance known to man—the written word."

---

were being shown. "CG# 300" and "CG# 301" cued technicians to superimpose words on the screen. "SOS" (sound on Sony) and the "in" and "out" designations on the same line cued the tape editor that the video excerpt (also known as a "sound bite") began with the phrase, "the team is simply," and ended with the words, "I just love 'em." "PAD" at the end instructed the tape editor to add three to five seconds of video after the "end" time for the anchor. The added video kept the tape picture from "hitting black" in the event the anchor had read slower than originally timed.

STUDY PROJECTS

1. Rewrite a newspaper story of 400 words or more into a 100-word story intended for use in a radio news broadcast.

2. Listen to a 5-minute radio newscast, either a network program or a local one. List the stories it covered. Then indicate the pages of that day's newspaper on which the same stories were published and note any that did not appear in the paper.

3. Watch an evening television network news program. List the stories covered in it and how many minutes or seconds were devoted to each. Indicate whether each story had picture coverage or was merely told by an anchorperson or a correspondent in the field.

READ MORE ABOUT IT . . .

Martin Maloney and Paul Max Rubenstein, *Writing for the Media* (Englewood Cliffs, N.J.: Prentice-Hall, 1980).
Irving Fang, *Television News* (St. Paul, Minn.: Rada Press, 1980).
Broadcasting is the weekly trade magazine of television and radio.

COMING UP NEXT...

This book has given you a sound grounding and extensive practice in the principles and techniques of journalism. You enjoy the work and desire a job in the media. What faces you when you move from the campus into the professional field?

Internships provide an excellent opportunity for the transition from classroom to professional work. Those who desire them should apply early because competition is intense.

In this final chapter we offer a realistic report on what editors expect from their new staff members, including a proper attitude toward learning on the job, as well as what newcomers may expect in working conditions, salaries, and assignments.

Differences between work on a daily and a weekly are explained, as are the opportunities for members of minorities.

Chapter 28
What to Expect on the Job

PREPARING FOR THE JOB

A college student whose ambition is a career in the media should begin preparing for it as early as possible, not only by taking courses in communications, but by seeking parttime work in the media while in school. Nothing equals personal experience in helping a student to decide whether the multifaceted field of mass communications is what he or she really wants.

Those who have worked on their high school newspapers already have some realization of what journalism involves when they enter college. Jobs on campus newspapers, magazines, and broadcasting stations provide invaluable experience. Commercial newspapers and broadcasting stations in college towns frequently hire students as parttime help. Even if these jobs are clerical and nonprofessional in nature, they open doors for the student to become acquainted with a professional operation.

Those students who are fortunate enough to obtain internships on publications or at broadcasting stations have a head start toward landing a good job after graduation. As interns they see what commercial media work is like and can participate in it.

An intern not only receives on-the-job training, but, in most cases, is paid for doing so. More and more newspapers and stations have well-developed internship programs; some magazines, publishing houses, advertising, and public relations companies do, too. Employers use the internship system to obtain replacement staff power during the vacation period and to observe the ability of students whom they might wish to hire after graduation.

Thus, students hoping for media careers should vigorously seek out internship possibilities with media within their own states or elsewhere. Early application is essential, because competition for internships is intense.

It is easy to see why. The Newspaper Fund, Inc., in 1980, through a questionnaire to 124 randomly selected newspapers in a circulation range from under 10,000 to above 100,000, found that 50 of the 295 young men and women hired by those newspapers in the past year had previously held internships on the papers that hired them.

Some newspapers with extensive internship programs assign editors to work closely with the interns. In addition to doing simple reporting and editing tasks, interns on some newspapers choose and develop a group project for publication at the end of the summer. Social activities for the interns often are part of the program.

Mary Anne Dolan, editor of the Los Angeles *Herald Examiner,* is among the women who hold high level newspaper management positions. She confers with Joseph Farah, executive news editor, and James Roark, photo editor.

Not all internships go to students enrolled in journalism schools; some are granted to students with majors in fields such as history, English, political science, and economics who are interested in media careers. The bulk of internships, however, is assigned to journalism school students. Similarly, The Newspaper Fund study found that 82.5 percent of the starting openings in the 124 daily newspapers surveyed were filled by journalism school graduates.

Most interns report that their experience was extremely helpful and stimulating, and the usual comment from editors who have coached them is, "They were a fine bunch!" Even blasé newsroom old-timers concede that having enthusiastic young men and women around enlivens their working lives, and they find pleasure in introducing the interns around on their beats.

THE PROPER ATTITUDE

The college graduate who is fortunate enough to be hired for a media job immediately after commencement enters the working world with reason for confidence; he or she has taken journalism courses, including extensive study of the theoretical and ethical problems of the media, and probably has worked for the school newspaper and/or broadcasting stations. The graduate has had the opportunity for a good general education as well and has been trained in the processes of thought and analysis. Those who have had internships have an added advantage.

Each year's supply of graduates is a vital resource for the media and their supporting fields, such as public relations and advertising. From the graduates is drawn new talent to fill gaps in the professional ranks left by retirement, resignation, dismissal, and death. Employer and recruit have a mutual interest in the newcomer's success.

Despite this fact, young journalists sometimes find the path more difficult than they anticipated. The fault lies on both sides. Management often fails to be sufficiently helpful and thoughtful toward the newcomer, who is discovering the difference between working for grades in school, with faculty members providing guidance, and working for a city editor or other media boss who demands and expects work that meets professional standards. Graduates on the other hand may arrive on the job with expectations that are unrealistically high and an attitude that, seasoned workers sneer, they are "God's gift to journalism." A few older staff members, dissatisfied with themselves and perhaps uneasy about their jobs, may resent the talented newcomer. Most experienced staff members are generous in their readiness to help the beginner, however, if they sense that the newcomer shows a desire to learn.

Graduates moving from the campus into their first professional jobs can profitably heed the comments by the main recruiter for a large national newspaper group. In a discussion with other professionals, he said that on the whole he was pleased with the beginners he hired but cited four elements starting journalists need to comprehend in order to succeed:

1. Journalism students should become aware that the ways things are done on a newspaper are neither all right nor all wrong (some find only fault).
2. The you-owe-me attitude evident among some beginning reporters must go; journalism students should be reminded that nobody owes them anything.
3. Some journalism students need to possess a stronger work ethic, an appreciation of "drudgery with excitement."
4. Students need orientation on the realities of newsroom life—peer groups, use of power, pettiness, and other aspects of group behavior.

Looking back after a year or two of professional experience, youthful reporters questioned by the authors also offer the newcomer advice. Some of their observations are criticisms of the editors in charge and others are warnings of realities the newcomers must recognize.

1. Most city editors don't spend time going over stories with new writers, pointing out good work as well as mistakes, as their instructors did. The editors agree that they should do more of this and function in part as teachers, but point out that conflicting pressures for their attention are intense. Beginners should watch how staff veterans handle stories. If you aren't offered help, ask for it.
2. Time pressure is heavy, perhaps the single biggest difference a beginner will find compared with the pace in college. Deadlines don't wait.
3. Editors notice initiative by new reporters. Do more than the stories assigned to you; be on the lookout for story ideas of your own to propose to the city editor.
4. Expect pressures, including flattery, from persons and organizations anxious to get their names into the paper or to influence the way you write a story so that it is favorable to them. Be prepared for angry phone calls, some of them nasty, from readers protesting a mistake in one of your stories. The power of the printed word on people's emotions can be intense.

WHAT KIND OF SALARY?

Naturally, the beginning reporter wants to know not only what opportunities a job offers but the salary it pays and the prospects for advancement.

Newspapers pay their senior executives well, but starting salaries for beginning reporters and photographers are not especially high compared with other fields of work. A Newspaper Fund survey in 1981 showed that some senior editors on metropolitan newspapers earned more than $50,000 a year. Among smaller city newspapers, managing editors of those in the 10,000 to 24,999 circulation category averaged $25,000. A similar survey by the Newspaper Fund in 1980 showed the median salary paid to graduates starting work on daily newspapers was about $190 a week, not quite $10,000 a year. These amounts have increased gradually since the surveys were taken, keeping pace with inflation. On most daily newspapers carefully structured scales provide increases in salary as the individual's experience grows, assuming that job performance is satisfactory. Medical insurance, pension plans, and other benefits usually are provided.

Salaries in general are higher on larger newspapers, especially the metropolitan dailies, than on the smaller ones. Salaries approaching $700 a week went into effect for reporters and photographers on the huge circulation New York City daily newspapers in the early 1980s. Larger newspapers in particular often have contracts with The Newspaper Guild that specify salaries and working conditions. Non-Guild newspapers of comparable size tend to pay approximately at Guild levels.

Pay for beginners on weekly newspapers tends to be lower and more varied than on the dailies, depending upon the size and financial strength of the weekly. Many of these publications are prosperous, with strong circulation and advertising revenue; others, however, are marginal operations barely providing a living for their proprietors, who have little money available to pay their staff reporter, or reporters, the kind of salaries they wish they could. Work on a weekly newspaper, unless shoddy practices are permitted, provides splendid experience, giving the beginner an opportunity to learn more aspects of reporting, editing, and newspaper management simultaneously than is possible on a beat assignment for a large daily. Reporters who get their professional training on weekly papers may transfer to dailies after a year or two, or decide to remain in the weekly field and eventually acquire a publication of their own.

Because public relations firms offer higher salaries to beginners than do newspapers and many broadcasting stations, graduates frequently seek starting jobs with PR firms. The Newspaper Fund survey found median pay in 1980 for beginners entering public relations to be in the $231–$240 range, as compared with the newspapers' $190.

Against this lure of higher salaries, many newspaper and broadcasting executives—and some public relations executives—contend that a person whose long-range goal is public relations work will succeed better in that field if he or she first has a few years of professional reporting and editing experience. This teaches the young professional the problems and demands of the print and broadcast media in intimate form; with this knowledge, these executives believe, the public relations practitioner can deal with the media more effectively.

THE BEGINNER'S ASSIGNMENTS

Newcomers on newspapers who expect to receive choice assignments from the start, because they achieved outstanding college records, will be disappointed. A city editor wants to watch a recruit's on-the-job performance for accuracy, reliability, and initiative. Every staff has its star writers and solid veteran reporters who have proved themselves and earned advancement to their present roles; the newcomer cannot expect to step into their positions immediately.

The beginner on a newspaper may be kept in the office at first, doing such small tasks as going through press releases in search of usable stories, taking notes on telephone calls from outside reporters and the public, checking on facts in the editorial library or by telephone for the editor, handling short rewrite assignments, and perhaps writing obituaries. This routine may seem unglamorous, but the editor regards it as a period of testing. For the alert newcomer, this is a time to get the "feel" of a newspaper office, to become acquainted with fellow staff members, and to adjust to the tempo of deadlines.

After a break-in period, or perhaps immediately on smaller dailies, the newcomer may be assigned to a beat, most likely the police run. Especially on smaller papers, the city editor has personal acquaintances among the news sources and can check on the reporter's performance not only from stories turned in, but also from private reports from the beat. A beat reporter's performance is constantly being compared with that of competitors in the print and electronic media. Missed stories and conflicts in story versions in which the reporter is shown to be incorrect are weighed by the editor against good writing and initiative in digging up extra stories and occasional important exclusive stories when considering a young reporter for advancement. So is the reporter's ability to get along with news sources, neither irritating them unnecessarily nor doing unwarranted favors in print for them.

If the beginner is assigned to the sports department of a larger daily, the work at first probably will include taking results of high school games by telephone, covering secondary games, and editing routine news service copy and statistics, such as the daily major league baseball standings. On a sports staff of several people, eventually a young man or woman reporter will be assigned to a particular sport and begin to develop a specialty, such as football or basketball. Small dailies may have a one-person sports department, aided in game coverage by reporters from the general news staff and by "stringers." This is a relatively common place for a beginner to break in.

Perhaps the newcomer is assigned to the life-style section, once known as the women's section and now usually called Family Living or something similar. At first this assignment means such tasks as editing syndicated copy, taking club notices, and handling recipes. Soon the section editor may assign the novice to a feature story, leading to the first by-line.

For some newcomers who show a flair for language, the break-in period is followed by assignment to the copydesk. Here staff members polish the reporters' copy and write headlines under the supervision of the copydesk chief. While doing this, the newcomer becomes involved in techniques of newspaper production that do not directly concern a reporter. Staff members who rise to editorial management positions usually have both reportorial and desk experience.

When graduates take jobs with weekly newspapers, they find themselves doing a bit of everything, because most weekly staffs are too small to permit specialization. The weekly reporter may cover both a school board meeting and a high school football game, lay out pages and write headlines, take women's club meeting notices on the telephone, and perhaps deliver bundles of newspapers to the post office on the way home after work.

A basic precept for reporters is to keep their supervising editors aware at all times of what they are working on and where they can be reached. If a news crisis arises, the desk editor may wish to rearrange assignments in a hurry. The editor wants to know the sources from which story material is obtained, especially when it is of a controversial nature, even if the reporter has been given the information in confidence. Editors are old hands at keeping confidences and judging the validity of sources. They need to know because they have responsibility to see that nothing is published that is false, misleading, or libelous. From their broader view and their awareness of what other reporters are working on, editors may find that one reporter's information fits into a bigger picture than he or she realizes.

Writing memos to the supervising editor is good practice for a reporter to follow. These can report on the progress of stories being developed, dates of future events on the beat, rumors the reporter is checking, and possible story ideas. Memos keep the editor informed and strengthen a reporter's reputation for awareness and initiative.

Especially on small dailies and weeklies, young reporters (older ones, too) must expect evening work. City council meetings, civic dinners, and organization meetings are frequently held at night. Some of them drag on interminably. Yet the reporter who covers them must be on the job the next morning. On weeklies, these time demands build to a climax on publication day and the night before; then comes time at the weekend when the schedule is lighter. Management should provide overtime pay or suitable time off to balance the workload. A reporter has a right to expect fair treatment in this respect, although willingness to put in a few extra hours occasionally without making a fuss for compensation makes a good impression on an editor who is operating with a low budget.

At one time, before newspaper managements realized that feminine staff members can cover every assignment as well as male reporters do, they were reluctant to assign women to some of the more strenuous beats for fear of subjecting them to situations they might find physically difficult or distasteful. That overly protective attitude has vanished, as women have come to make up a large segment of news staffs. Although the number of women in decision-making editorships is rising, some feminine journalists complain that they still are not given equal opportunity for promotion. In their own defense, senior newspaper executives reply that length of service must be considered in a promotion policy and contend that it would be unfair to pass over a competent, experienced man for promotion in favor of a less senior but otherwise equally qualified woman. The present inequity will diminish as the large number of able female journalists who have come into newsrooms fairly recently acquire seniority.

In fact, slowness of promotion is a complaint heard from youthful journalists of both sexes. Although obtaining starter jobs is relatively easy, they say, they cannot advance to important positions as rapidly as they believe they should because too many persons with longer experience are ahead of them. Part of the problem lies in the fact that the number of higher echelon positions in the ordinary newspaper table of organization is relatively small in relation to the size of the staff.

Members of minorities have been obtaining jobs in steadily if not swiftly growing numbers. In 1981, according to Jay T. Harris, formerly of Northwestern University's Medill School of Journalism, about 2400 of the 45,500 daily journalists in the United States belonged to a minority race, a sixfold increase since 1968. Competent black reporters have gravitated rapidly to the large circulation newspapers, which offer top salaries and are eager to increase their minority representation. Editors of many smaller newspapers say they wish to hire additional qualified minority reporters, but complain that a shortage of applicants exists. Able young black and Hispanic reporters are watched with particular attention by their superiors as candidates for promotion. The only qualities most editors demand of their young staff members today are competence and reliability.

Appendix A
Writing Electronically

A reporter who has learned to use an electric typewriter will have little trouble in composing stories on the video display terminal (VDT). The basic keyboard is the same, but in addition numerous auxiliary keys are available to expedite the preparation of copy.

Turning on the machine, the reporter enters a password (perhaps his or her last name) and a page format appears on the screen, along with a square blip of light called a cursor. Pressing an auxiliary key, the reporter moves the cursor to the point at which he or she wishes to begin typing. A slugline identifying the reporter and story is entered. A few lines below, the reporter inserts a paragraph symbol and begins writing.

If a mistake is made, the reporter simply moves the cursor to that point and types the correct word or phrase, obliterating the previous copy. The paragraph symbol is inserted at the end of each paragraph. If necessary, entire paragraphs may be deleted or moved elsewhere in the story.

When the story has been completed, the reporter may type an explanatory note to the city editor (it will not be printed) before pressing a key that inserts the story into the editor's file. An unfinished story may be placed in computer storage, in the reporter's file, for additional work later.

The city editor reads the story on the screen and then holds it in his or her file, returns it to the reporter with a query, or passes it along to the news editor or copydesk. After a headline is written and printing instructions are given, the story is sent to the phototypesetting machine, which sets it into type at the rate of about 150 column-wide lines per minute.

A set of auxiliary keys on the VDT carries abbreviated instructions such as the following:

PAGE UP SCROLL	PAGE DOWN SCROLL	PREV WORD	PREV SENT	PREV PARA
DEL CHAR	INS CHAR	RTS	PREV LINE	WRTE
↑	↓	TOP	SWAP	L/C
←	→	NEXT	KEEP	DONE
¶				

Machines often carry additional keys across the top of the keyboard with such notations as: HELP, SAVE, SAVE & ERASE, INSERT, USER ONE, USER TWO, USER THREE, CANCEL, GO.

One of the authors of this text wrote the following, in part, for a trade magazine after a summer of work at the Atlanta *Constitution:*

> The VDT is as far removed from pencil, paper and pastepot as a Cadillac from a Henry Ford flivver.
>
> The terminal, umbilically linked with its life-giving computer, almost miraculously is transformed from a fire-breathing monster to a purring kitten after only a few weeks' work. You gotta know the strokes!
>
> Despite your most determined efforts, copy CAN be lost in the bowels of the computer, though rarely. Beware of nearby electrical storms and purges! The storms can ripple, garble, freeze or obliterate your electronic copy. The purges occur—often with only a half-minute warning—when the computer's technical masters decide to remove all the previous copy to make room for more.
>
> The news, wire, copy and city desks are still the nerve center of the universe. A seat on computer row, within eye- and ear-shot of the pressure-tense news desks, provides a priceless front-row view of the reporting of mankind's furor, foibles and frolics. No TV set can match it!

OPTICAL CHARACTER RECOGNITION

At many newspapers, reporters prepare copy on special sheets that can be read by the optical character recognition (OCR) machine. They use electric typewriters (usually IBM Selectrics) equipped with special command keys. After editing, the copysheets are fed one by one into the scanner, which reads the copy at the rate of about 1200 words per minute and either produces punched paper tape for the phototypesetting machine or places the story directly into computer memory.

Extreme care must be taken in preparing the copy. Here are the instructions given at one newspaper:

Setting the Typewriter

1. Set the paper edge guide (the movable metal guide at left behind the platen) even with the first white line.
2. Set the left-hand margin guide at 10 and the right-hand guide at 70. This is important, because your margins must be at least half an inch on each side of the copy.
3. Set the multiple copy control lever (the lever on the left side on top labeled A through E) on position A.
4. Take care to insert copy paper evenly so that your typewritten lines go straight across the page at a 90-degree angle from the edge of the paper. If the lines are askew, your story will be garbled in print.
5. Use white bond paper or carbon books only and take care that the paper is clean and free of smudges before you begin and after you finish.
6. The ribbons on your typewriter can be used only once. They do not reverse, so learn how to change the ribbon.
7. Your copy must be triple spaced so that it can be edited. . . .

Writing Your Story

1. Just as you have done, put your name at the very top left-hand corner of the page. This violates the two-inch rule for the top margin, but it doesn't matter because the line will be edited out before the copy moves to the scanner.
2. Move the copy paper through your typewriter at least two inches. Type #ED on your copy against the left-hand margin. This tells the scanner that the material is editorial matter.
3. Hit the carriage return button on your typewriter twice (to triple space) and type b against the left-hand margin, space over five spaces, and type in the tag line for your story. For example:

    b   STORY TAG

4. Move the copy paper through your typewriter another two inches. If there's a chance your story will be by-lined (even an outside chance), type in #BF on the left-hand margin. Then space over five spaces and

type in your by-line, followed by five more spaces and #C. For example:

```
#BF        BY YOUR NAME         #C
```

5. Hit the carriage return button twice again and type #PD against the left margin. This defines the paragraph indentation for the scanner. Begin your story on the same line. The TAB key on your typewriter should be set to move the small red arrow over to the number 25 for paragraph indentation. It is important that all paragraphs begin equidistant from the margins, so you must use the TAB button. If the paragraphs are not equidistant from the margin, your story may appear in print as one long paragraph. Example:

```
#PD             Now is the time for all good men

to come to the aid of their party.

                The quick brown fox jumped over

the lazy dog's back.
```

6. Type your story as you normally would, remembering to triple space. Remember to stop typing at least an inch from the bottom of the page.
7. Type #ET against the left margin at the bottom of the page. Begin the second page at least one inch from the top of the paper with #ED. Triple space and type #BF, space over five spaces, and type the tag line for your story and Take 2. Example:

```
#ED



#BF       STORY TAG Take 2
```

8. Follow the procedure outlined in steps 6 and 7 for all subsequent pages of your story. Number the takes consecutively, ending each page on a paragraph and typing the code #ET at least one inch from the bottom of each page.
9. Use a paper clip to keep the pages of your story together. DO NOT paste your story together.

Editing Copy

1. Copy deletions can be made only with black felt-tip pens. A single *vertical* line beginning above a character and extending down through it will delete the character. For example:

    ```
    Yoϕur  would be read by the scanner as  Your.
    ```

2. A horizontal line extending through several characters, words, phrases, or lines will delete all characters touched by the line. For example:

    ```
    Your copy ms̶ m̶t̶ u̶s̶ ; m̶s̶t̶u̶ must be clean and

    neat.
    ```

    The scanner would read this line as: `Your copy must be clean and neat.`

3. Additions to copy must be typed below the line in which they are to be inserted. They also must be made exactly halfway between lines, which means you hit the carriage return button once (1½ spaces) before your insertions. The number of words or phrases that can be inserted into one line is limited only by the length of a typed line. But, words and phrases can be inserted in a line only where one or more deletion marks have been made.

4. Words or phrases to be inserted into a line must be preceded by a slash and a space and followed by a space and a slash. For example:

    ```
    The quick brown fox jumped over the lazy b̶r̶o̶w̶n̶
                            / green /
    dog.
    ```

    The scanner would read this as: `The quick brown fox jumped over the lazy green dog.`

    When you are inserting letters within a single word, however, you do not use a space after the first slash and before the second slash, that is: /c/.

5. The scanner inserts words and phrases into a line of copy on a one-to-one basis with deletion marks in the copy and in the same sequence as the deletion marks appear in the line of copy. For example:

> The quick ~~stupid~~ fox ~~stumbled~~ over the pretty
>   / brown /   / jumped /
> green dog which ~~happened to be~~ sleeping at the
>   / c /   / was /
> time.

These lines would read: The quick brown fox jumped over the green dog which was sleeping at the time.

6. A long paragraph can be forced into two smaller paragraphs by inserting the code #P into the long paragraph. For example:

> Combat veterans who previously shrugged off
>
> rocket attacks by the Communists nervously
>
> joked about last-minute shellings and openly
>
> admitted they didn't want to be the last to
>
> die. Two nights before the war officially
>   / #P Two /
> ended, more than two dozen Communist rockets
>
> landed, killing one American and wounding a
>
> number of others.

The scanner would automatically begin a second paragraph at: Two nights before. . . .

CODES

Writing and editing your story will require the use of a few codes. The codes actually are instructions to the computer and it is imperative that they are used properly. All codes will begin with the pound symbol: # followed by one or more letters. There are hundreds of codes, but, as a reporter, you will use relatively few of them, including:

#ED Tells the scanner that the copy is for the news columns. It is used on all news copy.
#BF Tells the scanner that the copy following the code is to be set in boldface type. This code is used to set the tag lines and by-line for your story.
#C   Tells the scanner to center the line in the column of type. It is used following the line to be centered and is primarily for by-lines, but has other applications such as subheads.
#PD Defines the starting point for all paragraphs. All subsequent paragraphs must start at the same TAB stop or the scanner will not recognize them as paragraphs.
#P   Tells the computer to force a paragraph at the point this code is used. (See *Editing Copy*, item 6.)
#ET Tells the computer that this is the end of a take or page. Must be used at least one inch from the bottom of the page.

A CAUTIONARY NOTE

Be careful how you make corrections with the black pen. Do not mark out words and lines ~~like this~~ like this. Just use a single, light stroke ~~like this~~ like this. Same goes for marking out single letters. Do not do it lik~~k~~e this; do it with a single stroke lik~~k~~e this.

The scanner does a good job, but it is very sensitive—probably overly so. It will try to read every mark on a page and try to make something out of it. So we must edit with extreme care and keep copy as clean as possible.

A SAMPLE STORY

The following is a typical story, ready for the scanner:

```
Your name


#ED


#BF     TYPICAL STORY
```

#BF   By YOUR NAME   #C

#PD   This is the first paragraph. Any successive line on this page starting at the same TAB position will automatically be treated as a paragraph.

          This is the second paragraph. No paragraph indication is required because it began at the same TAB stop as the first paragraph.

          This is not a paragraph, because it did not begin the required distance from the left margin. So the scanner would treat this as the third sentence of the second paragraph.

          If you ~~sea~~ see that you've misspelled a ~~lone line~~ word or used the wrong word, it is much easier to start over again and type it ~~corr e~~

correctly than to make corrections between the

~~words~~ lines.

#ET

Appendix B
Excerpts from The Associated Press *Stylebook*

The following entries from The Associated Press *Stylebook* provide writers of news stories with a useful guide to style and punctuation:

abbreviations and acronyms A few universally recognized abbreviations are required in some circumstances. Some others are acceptable depending on the context. But in general, avoid alphabet soup.

The same principle applies to acronyms—pronounceable words formed from the initial letters in a series of words: *ALCOA, NATO, radar, scuba,* etc.

Some general principles:

BEFORE A NAME: Abbreviate the following titles when used before a full name outside direct quotations: *Dr., Gov., Lt. Gov., Mr., Mrs., Rep., the Rev., Sen.* and certain military designations. Spell out all except *Dr., Mr.* and *Mrs.* when they are used before a name in direct quotations.

AFTER A NAME: Abbreviate *junior* or *senior* after an individual's name. Abbreviate *company, corporation, incorporated* and *limited* when used after the name of a corporate entity.

In some cases, an academic degree may be abbreviated after an individual's name. See **academic degrees.**

WITH DATES OR NUMERALS: Use the abbreviations *A.D., B.C., a.m., p.m., No.* and abbreviate certain months when used with the day of the month.

Right: *In 450 B.C.; at 9:30 a.m.; in room No. 6; on Sept. 16.*

Wrong: *Early this a.m. he asked for the No. of your room.* The abbreviations are correct only with figures.

Right: *Early this morning he asked for the number of your room.*

IN NUMBERED ADDRESSES: Abbreviate *avenue, boulevard* and *street* in numbered addresses: *He lives on Pennsylvania Avenue. He lives at 1600 Pennsylvania Ave.*

ACCEPTABLE BUT NOT REQUIRED: Some organizations and government agencies are widely recognized by their initials: *CIA, FBI, GOP.* On second reference, let the context determine, for example, whether to use *Federal Bureau of Investigation* or *FBI.*

AVOID AWKWARD CONSTRUCTIONS: Do not follow an organization's full name with an abbreviation or acronym in parentheses or set off by dashes. If an abbreviation or acronym would not be clear on second reference without this arrangement, do not use it.

Names not commonly before the public should not be reduced to acronyms solely to save a few words.

academic degrees If mention of degrees is necessary to establish someone's credentials, the preferred form is to avoid an abbreviation and use instead a phrase such as: *John Jones, who has a doctorate in psychology.*

Use an apostrophe in *bachelor's degree, a master's,* etc.

Use such abbreviations as *B.A., M.A., LL.D.* and *Ph.D.* only when the need to identify many individuals by degree on first reference would make the preferred form cumbersome. Use these abbreviations only after a full name—never after just a last name.

When used after a name, an academic abbreviation is set off by commas: *Daniel Moynihan, Ph.D., spoke.*

Do not precede a name with a courtesy title for an academic degree and follow it with the abbreviation for the degree in the same reference:

Wrong: *Dr. Sam Jones, Ph.D.*

Right: *Dr. Sam Jones, a chemist*

When in doubt about the proper abbreviation for a degree, follow the first listing in Webster's New World Dictionary.

addresses Use the abbreviations *Ave., Blvd.* and *St.* only with a numbered address: *1600 Pennsylvania Ave.* Spell them out and capitalize when part of a formal street name without a number: *Pennsylvania Avenue.* Lowercase and spell out when used alone or with more than one street name: *Massachusetts and Pennsylvania avenues.*

All similar words (*alley, drive, road, terrace,* etc.) always are spelled out. Capitalize them when part of a formal name without a number; lowercase when used alone or with two or more names.

Always use figures for an address number: *9 Morningside Circle.*

Spell out and capitalize *First* through *Ninth* when used as street names; use figures with two letters for *10th* and above: *7 Fifth Ave., 100 21st St.*

Abbreviate compass points used to indicate directional ends of a street or quadrants of a city in a numbered address: *222 E. 42nd St., 562 W. 43rd St., 600 K St. N.W.* Do not abbreviate if the number is omitted: *East 42nd Street, West 43rd Street, K Street Northwest.*

capitalization   In general, avoid unnecessary capitals. Use a capital letter only if you can justify it by one of the principles listed here.

Many words and phrases, including special cases, are listed separately in this book. Entries that are capitalized without further comment should be capitalized in all uses.

If there is no relevant listing in this book for a particular word or phrase, consult Webster's New World Dictionary. Use lowercase if the dictionary lists it as an acceptable form for the sense in which the word is being used.

As used in this book, *capitalize* means to use uppercase for the first letter of a word. If additional capital letters are needed, they are called for by an example or a phrase such as *use all caps.*

Some basic principles:

PROPER NOUNS: Capitalize nouns that constitute the unique identification for a specific person, place or thing: *John, Mary, America, Boston, England.*

Some words, such as the examples just given, are always proper nouns. Some common nouns receive proper noun status when they are used as the name of a particular entity: *General Electric, Gulf Oil.*

PROPER NAMES: Capitalize common nouns such as *party, river, street* and *west* when they are an integral part of the full name for a person, place or thing: *Democratic Party, Mississippi River, Fleet Street, West Virginia.*

Lowercase these common nouns when they stand alone in subsequent references: *the party, the river, the street.*

Lowercase the common noun elements of names in all plural uses: *the Democratic and Republican parties, Main and State streets, lakes Erie and Ontario.*

POPULAR NAMES: Some places and events lack officially designated proper names but have popular names that are the effective equivalent: *the Combat Zone* (a section of downtown Boston), *the Main Line* (a group of Philadelphia suburbs), *the South Side* (of Chicago), *the Badlands* (of North Dakota), *the Street* (the financial community in the Wall Street area of New York).

The principle applies also to shortened versions of the proper names for one-of-a-kind events: *the Series* (for the World Series), *the Derby* (for the Kentucky Derby). This practice should not, however, be interpreted as a license to ignore the general practice of lowercasing the common noun elements of a name when they stand alone.

DERIVATIVES: Capitalize words that are derived from a proper noun and still depend on it for their meaning: *American, Christian, Christianity, English, French, Marxism, Shakespearean.*

Lowercase words that are derived from a proper noun but no longer depend on it for their meaning: *french fries, herculean, manhattan cocktail, malapropism, pasteurize, quixotic, venetian blind.*

SENTENCES: Capitalize the first word in a statement that stands as a sentence.

In poetry, capital letters are used for the first words of some phrases that would not be capitalized in prose.

COMPOSITIONS: Capitalize the principal words in the names of books, movies, plays, poems, operas, songs, radio and television programs, works of art, etc.

TITLES: Capitalize formal titles when used immediately before a name. Lowercase formal titles when used alone or in constructions that set them off from a name by commas.

Use lowercase at all times for terms that are job descriptions rather than formal titles.

colon The most frequent use of a colon is at the end of a sentence to introduce lists, tabulations, texts, etc.

Capitalize the first word after a colon only if it is a proper noun or the start of a complete sentence: *He promised this: The company will make good all the losses.* But: *There were three considerations: expense, time and feasibility.*

EMPHASIS: The colon often can be effective in giving emphasis: *He had only one hobby: eating.*

LISTINGS: Use the colon in such listings as time elapsed *(1:31:07.2)*, time of day *(8:31 p.m.)*, biblical and legal citations *(2 Kings 2:14; Missouri Code 3:245–260).*

DIALOGUE: Use a colon for dialogue. In coverage of a trial, for example:
Bailey: What were you doing the night of the 19th?
Mason: I refuse to answer that.

Q AND A: The colon is used for question-and-answer interviews:
Q: Did you strike him?
A: Indeed I did.

INTRODUCING QUOTATIONS: Use a comma to introduce a direct quotation of one sentence that remains within a paragraph. Use a colon to introduce longer quotations within a paragraph and to end all paragraphs that introduce a paragraph of quoted material.

PLACEMENT WITH QUOTATION MARKS: Colons go outside quotation marks unless they are part of the quotation itself.

MISCELLANEOUS: Do not combine a dash and a colon.

comma The following guidelines treat some of the most frequent questions about the use of commas.

For more detailed guidance, consult "The Comma" and "Misused and Unnecessary Commas" in the Guide to Punctuation section in the back of Webster's New World Dictionary.

IN A SERIES: Use commas to separate elements in a series, but do not put a comma before the conjunction in a simple series: *The flag is red, white and blue. He would nominate Tom, Dick or Harry.*

Put a comma before the concluding conjunction in a series, however, if an integral element of the series requires a conjunction: *I had orange juice, toast, and ham and eggs for breakfast.*

Use a comma also before the concluding conjunction in a complex series of phrases: *The main points to consider are whether the athletes are skillful enough to compete, whether they have the stamina to endure the training, and whether they have the proper mental attitude.*

WITH EQUAL ADJECTIVES: Use commas to separate a series of adjectives equal in rank. If the commas could be replaced by the word *and* without changing the sense, the adjectives are equal: *a thoughtful, precise manner; a dark, dangerous street.*

Use no comma when the last adjective before a noun outranks its predecessors because it is an integral element of a noun phrase, which is the equivalent of a single noun: *a cheap fur coat* (the noun phrase is *fur coat*); *the old oaken bucket; a new, blue spring bonnet.*

WITH INTRODUCTORY CLAUSES AND PHRASES: A comma normally is used to separate an introductory clause or phrase from a main clause: *When he had tired of the mad pace of New York, he moved to Dubuque.*

The comma may be omitted after short introductory phrases if no ambiguity would result: *During the night he heard many noises.*

But use the comma if its omission would slow comprehension: *On the street below, the curious gathered.*

WITH CONJUNCTIONS: When a conjunction such as *and, but* or *for* links two clauses that could stand alone as separate sentences, use a comma before the conjunction in most cases: *She was glad she had looked, for a man was approaching the house.*

As a rule of thumb, use a comma if the subject of each clause is expressly stated: *We are visiting Washington, and we also plan a side trip to Williamsburg. We visited Washington, and our senator greeted us personally.* But no comma when the subject of the two clauses is the same and is not repeated in the second: *We are visiting Washington and plan to see the White House.*

The comma may be dropped if two clauses with expressly stated subjects are short. In general, however, favor use of a comma unless a particular literary effect is desired or it would distort the sense of a sentence.

INTRODUCING DIRECT QUOTES: Use a comma to introduce a complete, one-sentence quotation within a paragraph: *Wallace said, "She spent six months in Argentina and came back speaking English with a Spanish accent."* But use a colon to introduce quotations of more than one sentence.

Do not use a comma at the start of an indirect or partial quotation: *He said his victory put him "firmly on the road to a first-ballot nomination."*

BEFORE ATTRIBUTION: Use a comma instead of a period at the end of a quote that is followed by attribution: *"Rub my shoulders," Miss Cawley suggested.*

Do not use a comma, however, if the quoted statement ends with a question mark or exclamation point: *"Why should I?" he asked.*

WITH HOMETOWNS AND AGES: Use a comma to set off an individual's hometown when it is placed in apposition to a name: *Mary Richards, Minneapolis, and Maude Findlay, Tuckahoe, N.Y., were there.* However, the use of the word *of* without a comma between the individual's name and the city name generally is preferable: *Mary Richards of Minneapolis and Maude Findlay of Tuckahoe, N.Y., were there.*

If an individual's age is used, set it off by commas: *Maude Findlay, 48, Tuckahoe, N.Y., was present.* The use of the word *of* eliminates the need for a comma after the hometown if a state name is not needed: *Mary Richards, 36, of Minneapolis and Maude Findlay, 48, of Tuckahoe, N.Y., attended the party.*

NAMES OF STATES AND NATIONS USED WITH CITY NAMES: *His journey will take him from Dublin, Ireland, to Fargo, N.D., and back. The Selma, Ala., group saw the governor.*

Use parentheses, however, if a state name is inserted within a proper name: *The Huntsville (Ala.) Times.*

WITH YES AND NO: *Yes, I will be there.*

IN DIRECT ADDRESS: *Mother, I will be home late. No, sir, I did not do it.*

SEPARATING SIMILAR WORDS: Use a comma to separate duplicated words that otherwise would be confusing: *What the problem is, is not clear.*

IN LARGE FIGURES: Use a comma for most figures higher than 999. The major exceptions are: street addresses *(1234 Main St.)*, broadcast frequencies *(1460 kilohertz)*, room numbers, serial numbers, telephone numbers, and years *(1976)*. See separate entries under these headings.

PLACEMENT WITH QUOTES: Commas always go inside quotation marks.

numerals A numeral is a figure, letter, word or group of words expressing a number.

Roman numerals use the letters *I, V, X, L, C, D* and *M*. Use Roman numerals for wars and to show personal sequence for animals and people: *World War II, Native Dancer II, King George VI, Pope John XXIII.*

Arabic numerals use the figures *1, 2, 3, 4, 5, 6, 7, 8, 9* and *0*. Use Arabic forms unless Roman numerals are specifically required.

The figures *1, 2, 10, 101,* etc. and the corresponding words—*one, two ten, one hundred one,* etc.—are called cardinal numbers. The term ordinal number applies to *1st, 2nd, 10th, 101st, first, second, tenth, one hundred first,* etc.

Follow these guidelines in using numerals:

LARGE NUMBERS: When large numbers must be spelled out, use a hyphen to connect a word ending in *y* to another word; do not use commas between other separate words that are part of one number: *twenty; thirty; twenty-one; thirty-one; one hundred forty-three; one thousand one hundred fifty-five; one million two hundred seventy-six thousand five hundred eighty-seven.*

SENTENCE START: Spell out a numeral at the beginning of a sentence. If necessary, recast the sentence. There is one exception—a numeral that identifies a calendar year.

Wrong: *993 freshman entered the college last year.*

Right: *Last year 993 freshmen entered the college.*

Right: *1976 was a very good year.*

CASUAL USES: Spell out casual expressions:
A thousand times no! Thanks a million. He walked a quarter of a mile.

PROPER NAMES: Use words or numerals according to an organization's practice: *20th Century-Fox, Twentieth Century Fund, Big Ten.*

FIGURES OR WORDS?

For ordinals:

—Spell out *first* through *ninth* when they indicate sequence in time or location: *first base, the First Amendment, he was first in line.* Starting with *10th,* use figures.

—Use *1st, 2nd, 3rd, 4th,* etc. when the sequence has been assigned in forming names. The principal examples are geographic, military and political designations such as *1st Ward, 7th Fleet* and *1st Sgt.*

SOME PUNCTUATION AND USAGE EXAMPLES:
—*Act 1, Scene 2*
—*a 5-year-old girl*
—*DC-10* but *747B*
—*a 5-4 court decision*
—*2nd District Court*
—*the 1970s, the '70s*
—*The House voted 230–205.* (Fewer than 1,000 votes)
Jimmy Carter defeated Gerald Ford 40,827,292 to 39,146,157. (More than 1,000 votes)
Carter defeated Ford 10 votes to 2 votes in Little Junction. (To avoid confusion with ratio)
—*5 cents, $1.05, $650,000, $2.45 million*
—*No. 3 choice,* but *Public School 3*
—*0.6 percent, 1 percent, 6.5 percent*
—*a pay increase of 12 percent to 15 percent*
Or: *a pay increase of between 12 percent and 15 percent*
Also: *from $12 million to $14 million*
—*a ratio of 2-to-1, a 2-1 ratio*
—*a 4-3 score*
—*(212) 262-4000*
—*minus 10, zero, 60 degrees*

OTHER USES: For uses not covered by these listings: Spell out whole numbers below 10, use figures for 10 and above. Typical examples: *The woman has three sons and two daughters. He has a fleet of 10 station wagons and two buses.*

IN A SERIES: Apply the appropriate guidelines: *They had 10 dogs, six cats and 97 hamsters. They had four four-room houses, 10 three-room houses and 12 10-room houses.*

semicolon In general, use the semicolon to indicate a greater separation of thought and information than a comma can convey but less than the separation that a period implies.

state names Follow these guidelines:
STANDING ALONE: Spell out the names of the 50 U.S. states when they stand alone in textual material. Any state name may be condensed, however, to fit typographical requirements for tabular material.
EIGHT NOT ABBREVIATED: The names of eight states are never abbreviated in datelines or text: *Alaska, Hawaii, Idaho, Iowa, Maine, Ohio, Texas* and *Utah.*
Memory Aid: Spell out the names of the two states that are not part of the continental United States and of the continental states that are five letters or fewer.

Appendix B / Excerpts from The Associated Press *Stylebook* 367

ABBREVIATIONS REQUIRED: Use the state abbreviations listed at the end of this section:

—In conjunction with the name of a city, town, village or military base in most datelines.

—In conjunction with the name of a city, county, town, village or military base in text. See examples in punctuation section below.

—In short-form listings of party affiliation: *D-Ala., R-Mont.*

The abbreviations are:

Ala.	Ariz.	Ark.	Calif.
Colo.	Conn.	Del.	Fla.
Ga.	Ill.	Ind.	Kan.
Ky.	La.	Md.	Mass.
Mich.	Minn.	Miss.	Mo.
Mont.	Neb.	Nev.	N.H.
N.J.	N.M.	N.Y.	N.C.
N.D.	Okla.	Ore.	Pa.
R.I.	S.C.	S.D.	Tenn.
Vt.	Va.	Wash.	W. Va.
Wis.	Wyo.		

PUNCTUATION: Place one comma between the city and the state name, and another comma after the state name, unless ending a sentence or indicating a dateline: *He was traveling from Nashville, Tenn., to Austin, Texas, en route to his home in Albuquerque, N.M. She said Cook County, Ill., was Mayor Daley's stronghold.*

MISCELLANEOUS: Use *New York state* when necessary to distinguish the state from New York City.

Use *state of Washington* or *Washington state* when necessary to distinguish the state from the District of Columbia. (*Washington State* is the name of a university in the state of Washington.)

time element Use *today, this morning, this afternoon, tonight,* etc., as appropriate in stories for afternoon editions. Use the day of the week elsewhere.

Use *Monday, Tuesday,* etc., for days of the week within seven days before or after the current date.

Use the month and a figure for dates beyond this range. See **months** for forms and punctuation.

Avoid such redundancies as *last Tuesday* or *next Tuesday*. The past, present or future tense used for the verb usually provides adequate indication of which *Tuesday* is meant: *He said he finished the job Tuesday. She will return on Tuesday.*

Avoid awkward placements of the time element, particularly those that suggest the day of the week is the object of a transitive verb: *The police jailed Tuesday.* Potential remedies include the use of the word *on*, rephrasing the sentence, or placing the time element in a different sentence.

time of day The exact time of day that an event has happened or will happen is not necessary in most stories. Follow these guidelines to determine when it should be included and in what form:

SPECIFY THE TIME:
—Whenever it gives the reader a better picture of the scene: Did the earthquake occur when people were likely to be home asleep or at work? A clock reading for the time in the datelined community is acceptable, although *predawn hours* or *rush hour* often is more graphic.

—Whenever the time is critical to the story: When will the rocket be launched? When will a major political address be broadcast? What is the deadline for meeting a demand?

DECIDING ON CLOCK TIME: When giving a clock reading, use the time in the datelined community.

If the story is undated, use the clock time in force where the event happened or will take place.

The only exception is a nationwide story or tabular listing that involves television or radio programs. Always use Eastern time, followed by *EDT* or *EST,* and specify whether the program will be broadcast simultaneously nationwide or whether times will vary because of separate transmissions for different time zones. If practical, specify those times in a separate paragraph.

ZONE ABBREVIATIONS: Use *EST, CDT, PST,* etc., after a clock time only if:

—The story involves travel or other activities, such as the closing hour for polling places or the time of a televised speech, likely to affect persons or developments in more than one time zone.

—The item involves television or radio programs. (See above.)

—The item is undated.

—The item is an advisory to editors.

CONVERT TO EASTERN TIME? Do not convert clock times from other time zones in the continental United States to Eastern time. If there is high interest in the precise time, add *CDT, PST,* etc., to the local reading to help readers determine their equivalent local time.

If the time is critical in a story from outside the continental United States, provide a conversion to Eastern time using this form:

The kidnappers set a 9 a.m. (3 a.m. EDT) deadline.

titles In general, confine capitalization to formal titles used directly before an individual's name.

The basic guidelines:

LOWERCASE: Lowercase and spell out titles when they are not used with an individual's name: *The president issued a statement. The pope gave his blessing.*

Lowercase and spell out titles in constructions that set them off from a name by commas: *The vice president, Nelson Rockefeller, declined to run again. Paul VI, the current pope, does not plan to retire.*

FORMAL TITLES: Capitalize formal titles when they are used immediately before one or more names: *Pope Paul, President Washington, Vice Presidents John Jones and William Smith.*

A formal title generally is one that denotes a scope of authority, professional activity or academic accomplishment so specific that the designation becomes almost as much an integral part of an individual's identity as a proper name itself: *President Carter, Gov. Ella Grasso, Dr. Marcus Welby, Pvt. Gomer Pyle.*

Other titles serve primarily as occupational descriptions: *astronaut John Glenn, movie star John Wayne, peanut farmer Jimmy Carter.*

A final determination on whether a title is formal or occupational depends on the practice of the governmental or private organization that confers it. If there is doubt about the status of a title and the practice of the organization cannot be determined, use a construction that sets the name or the title off with commas.

ABBREVIATED TITLES: The following formal titles are capitalized and abbreviated as shown when used before a name outside quotations: *Dr., Gov., Lt. Gov., Rep., Sen.* Spell out all except *Dr.* when they are used in quotations.

All other formal titles are spelled out in all uses.

ROYAL TITLES: Capitalize *king, queen, etc.,* when used directly before a name.

TITLES OF NOBILITY: Capitalize a full title when it serves as the alternate name for an individual.

PAST AND FUTURE TITLES: A formal title that an individual formerly held, is about to hold or holds temporarily is capitalized if used before the person's name. But do not capitalize the qualifying word: *former President Ford, deposed King Constantine, Attorney General-designate Griffin B. Bell, acting Mayor Peter Barry.*

LONG TITLES: Separate a long title from a name by a construction that requires a comma: *Charles Robinson, undersecretary for economic affairs, spoke.* Or: *The undersecretary for economic affairs, Charles Robinson, spoke.*

UNIQUE TITLES: If a title applies only to one person in an organization, insert the word *the* in a construction that uses commas: *John Jones, the deputy vice president, spoke.*

Appendix C
The Language of Journalism

Reporters and editors have a vocabulary of their own, partly technical terms and partly slang. This is a guide to expressions and words frequently heard in the newsroom.

Ad   Advertisement.
Add   Addition to a story, such as "first add."
Advance   A story about a future event.
Agate   Small type used in box scores and similar tabulations. 5½ points deep (72 points to the inch).
AM   A morning newspaper.
Angle   The approach emphasized in a story's lead.
AP   The Associated Press, a cooperative news service.
Art   A term to describe all types of newspaper illustrations.
Attribution   Identification of the sources for information in a news story.
Backgrounder   A story giving the background of a spot news situation.
Banner   Large headline running the width of a page. Also called *streamer, line,* or *ribbon.*
Beat   (1) A reporter's assigned territory, sometimes called a *run.* (2) A story that is exclusive or published ahead of the opposition.

bf Abbreviation for boldface type.
Blurb A piece of promotional copy, usually brief.
Body type The type in which most news stories are set, frequently 9 point or 10 point.
"Boil it down" Shortening of a story, eliminating nonessential matter.
Boldface Darker, heavier body type used for emphasis.
Break The point at which a story continues in another column (sometimes called a *wrap*) or on another page.
Brightener A brief, humorous change-of-pace news story.
Budget Daily listing of anticipated stories compiled by an editor. AP and UPI open their news reports with budgets.
Bullet A large round dot used as a typographical device to introduce items in a list.
Bulletin Brief first announcement of a major news development, used especially by the press associations.
By-line Name of the reporter at the top of a news story.
Camera-ready type Paste-up type that is ready to be photographed for a printing plate.
Caps Capital letters.
Caption Headline or descriptive type accompanying an illustration. Also called a *cutline*.
clc Abbreviation for capitals and lowercase letters.
Column (1) Width of a line of type. Most newspapers are 6 or 8 columns wide. (2) An article of opinion or comment.
Copy Material prepared for use in a newspaper.
Copy editor A person who edits stories for publication and writes headlines for them. Also called a *copyreader*.
Copydesk The place where copy editors work.
Copywriter One who writes material for advertisements.
Correspondent A reporter based at some distance from the home office. Sometimes a part-time writer who is paid by the story.
Credit line A type line stating the source of a picture or story.
Crop To eliminate unnecessary portions of a photograph.
CRT Cathode-ray tube, used in electronic editing. See *Video display terminal*.
Crusade A newspaper campaign with stories and editorials to obtain a reform.
Dateline The place where an out-of-town news story originates, shown at the start of the copy.
Deadline The minute at which all work of writing and editing stories must be finished for an edition of a newspaper.
Deck A secondary element of a headline. Known also as a *bank, readout,* or *drop head*.
Double truck Two facing pages of a newspaper made up as a single unit in the center of a section.

Down style A newspaper style using a minimum of capitalization.

Dummy Diagram of a newspaper page on which placement of stories and advertisements is marked.

Ear The front-page space on either side of a newspaper's nameplate in which promotional matter or weather forecasts sometimes appear.

Editorial (1) An expression of opinion by the newspaper, published on the editorial page. (2) Sometimes used to describe all nonadvertising content of a newspaper issue.

Editorialize To inject the writer's opinion into a news story.

Em Typographical measurement used in describing column width. A pica em is approximately one-sixth of an inch.

Embargo A restriction against immediate publication of news material. It usually states the precise hour at which publication is authorized.

Face A variety of type. Bodoni, for example.

Feature (1) A story written with a "soft" or nonspot news approach. (2) As a verb, to play up a story or an angle.

Filler A brief minor story to fill an odd corner of space on a page.

Flak Slang description of a publicist.

Flash First urgent words announcing a major news break on press association wires. Rarely used.

Folio A line of type stating page number and date, usually at top of the page.

Folo A story updating an earlier one. Short for follow-up.

Font Type of one size and style, such as 18-point Bodoni.

Futures book A dated file kept by editors and reporters with reminders and information about stories to be done in the future.

Guideline Word or phrase identifying a story, placed at its top for quick identification. Also called the *slug*.

Gutter The white space between the type on facing pages.

Halftone Metal or plastic engraving of a photograph in which the image is created by raised dots.

Head shot Also called a *mug shot*. Photograph of the subject's head, often including shoulders.

Headline schedule List of the headline combinations used by a newspaper.

Hold for release Story material withheld from publication until authorized by an editor. Often called *hfr*.

Hole (1) News space available in an edition, the *newshole*. (2) An open space on a page that needs to be filled by type or illustration.

HTK Abbreviation for "head to kum," used on a news story to indicate that a headline must be written for it.

Input Story material typed into a computer. Also as a verb: to *input* a story.

Insert Additional material to be placed at a designated place within a news story.

Italics A type style used for emphasis, in which the letters slant to the right. The opposite of *roman*. Abbreviated as *itals*.

Jump To continue a story from one page to another. The material that is jumped is called the *runover*. The headline on the runover material is a *jump head*.

Kicker A small headline, usually underlined, placed above another head with supplemental information. Sometimes called an *eyebrow*.

Kill To throw away copy and/or type that has been prepared for publication, but no longer is needed.

Layout A completed page dummy, showing where stories and advertisements should go. As a verb, to *lay out* a page.

lc Lowercase letters of the alphabet.

Lead First paragraph of a news story. Pronounced *leed*.

Legman A reporter who gathers news, then phones it to the office instead of writing it. Some of the best *legmen* are women.

Letterpress Traditional printing process in which the image is transferred to paper by a raised surface, such as type.

Line drawing An illustration such as an editorial cartoon in which no shaded matter appears.

Logotype A newspaper's nameplate or *flag*. Sometimes called a "logo."

Makeover The new version of a newspaper page after fresh material has been added and some old material removed.

Makeup The process of placing stories and advertisements on a page.

Masthead Short body of type listing the newspaper's ownership. Place of publication and other facts of its organization.

More A slug word placed at the end of a block of copy, indicating that additional copy will follow.

Morgue Old-time slang word meaning *newspaper library*.

Must A slugline giving the editor's instruction that the story MUST run.

Newsprint The large rolls of paper on which a newspaper is printed.

Obit Abbreviated form of *obituary*, widely used to refer to a story about the death of a person.

OCR Short for *optical character recognition*, a machine used for feeding typewritten material into a computer or a phototypesetting machine.

Offset printing Printing process in which a rubber roller takes an impression from a surface and transfers it to the paper.

Off the record Material given to a reporter with a request from the news source that it not be published.

Op-ed page Short for *opposite editorial page*, on which columns and other opinion material are published.

Output Material transmitted from a newsroom computer into a phototypesetting machine. Also as a verb, to *output* a story.

Pad To make a story longer by adding minor information.

Paste-up The act of pasting photoset type onto a cardboard sheet. When the paste-up is complete, the sheet is photographed by a platemaking camera.

PM An evening newspaper.

PR Public relations.

Precede A brief late news development placed above the main story, just under the headline.

Press release An information sheet provided by a source desiring to have the material published. Known also as a *news release* or *handout*.

Print-out The printed form of a news story stored in the computer, used for reference purposes.

Proof A copy of a story or page that has been set in type, used for checking and correction purposes.

Revise As a verb, to make changes in a story. As a noun, pronounced ree-vise, the altered story.

Rewrite (1) To write a new version of a story that needs improvement or one that has appeared in another newspaper. (2) As a noun, the task of taking information from a field reporter by telephone and putting it into story form.

Rim The outer rim of the desk around which copy editors sit.

Roundup A story in which several related events are combined for simplicity of reading and economy of space.

Rule A printed line to separate portions of type, such as a column rule.

Running story One in which new developments occur for two or more days.

Satellite dish The saucer-shaped instrument on which news stories and photographs are received from a relay satellite in space.

Scanner See *OCR, optical character recognition*.

Schedule A list of stories planned for publication. Often called a *sked*. As a verb, to *sked* a story.

Short A brief story.

Sidebar A story supplementing a main story in which a special angle is developed.

Situationer A story, often without a spot news element, in which a news situation is discussed and analyzed.

Slug See *Guideline*.

Slot The place at the head of the copydesk occupied by the copy chief, who is said to be "in the slot."

Standing head An identifying headline such as "Obituaries" used repeatedly without change.

Stet Mark used by copy editors to indicate that corrections should be ignored and original copy used.

Stringer A part-time newspaper correspondent who is paid fees for work done; not a staff member.

Stylebook A newspaper's guide to style in such matters as capitalization and punctuation. Many newspapers use the AP or UPI *Stylebook*.

Subhead Small headlines inserted between paragraphs of a news story to improve readability.

Tabloid A newspaper whose pages are half the size of a standard-size newspaper.

Time copy Stories without a pressing time element that can be held for later publication.
Typo A typographical error.
Update Revise a story to include new information.
UPI United Press International, a press association.
Video Display Terminal An electronic typesetting machine with televisionlike screen and a keyboard on which stories are composed and edited, then dispatched into a computer. Known also as a VDT, "the tube," and CRT.
wf initials for *wrong font,* meaning incorrect use of a typeface.
Widow A line of type too short to fill out a column, leaving awkward-looking white space. Especially evident in cutlines.

Index

Abbey, Donald and Barbara, 46
Abbreviations, 336, 360–362
Absolutist ethics, 237
Accuracy, 9, 55–56, 146, 234, 236, 261
Acronyms, 336, 360
Actual malice, 218–221
Addresses, abbreviation for, 361–362, 367
Advertising department, 4
Advocacy reporting, 20
After "Jimmy's World": Tightening Up in Editing, 244
Agee, Warren K., 20, 244
Agence France-Press, 310
Airplane crash, 292–294
Alabama, 218
Albuquerque *Tribune,* 253
Alexander, Charles, 241
Alexander, Peter W., 15
Alford, Theodore C., 301
All the President's Men, 295, 313
Alpha Beta Stores, 193
Alternative journalism, 19
American Broadcasting Company (ABC), 200–201, 231, 291–292, 310
American Newspaper Publishers Association, 219, 220
American Press Institute, 72
American Society of Newspaper Editors, 26, 59, 115, 233–235, 239
Amtrak, 189
Analogy, 137
Anderson, Clark, Jr., 46
Anderson, Clark, Sr., 47
Anderson, David, 190
Anderson, Jack, 313
Andreas, Charlie, 46
Andrews Air Force Base, 46
Angle, of story, 76–77, 151–154
Announcements. *See* Press releases
Anonymous quotations, 232
Antinomian ethics. *See* Ethics

AP Log, 59, 120, 126, 153
APME News, 59
APME Red Book, 59
Arizona Republic, 312
Art of Readable Writing, The, 128
Ashkinaze, Carole, 28
Ashton, Sister Madeleine Rose, 173–174
ASNE Bulletin, 59
Associate editor, 4
Associated Press, 18, 19, 45, 58, 95, 101, 115, 116, 120, 126, 131, 133, 152, 153, 162, 171, 173, 195, 200, 241, 242, 310, 327, 370
Associated Press Managing Editors Association, 104, 235
Associated Press Stylebook and Libel Manual, 65, 360–369
Athenian dramatists, 13
Atlanta, Georgia, 225
Atlanta *Constitution,* 15, 28, 242, 352
Atlanta *Journal,* 149
Attitude, 232, 344–345
Attribution, 40–41, 56, 125–126
Auburn University, 26
Audiences, 30
Ault, Phillip H., 20, 244

Background material, use of, 78–79
Bagdikian, Ben H., 11
Baker, Howard, 290
Baltimore *Sun,* 300, 310
Bank of America, 193
Bartlett's Familiar Quotations, 188
Beats
  breaking in on, 253–254, 345
  courts, 275–284
  coverage of, 254–258
  development of, 250–253
  fire department, 267–268
  kinds of, 247–250
  police department, 260–272, 324–325

Bellows, James, 237
Benjaminson, Peter, 190
Bennett, James Gordon, 14
Berger, Meyer, 89
Berner, R. Thomas, 111
Bernstein, Carl, 19, 196, 232, 295, 313
Bernstein, Theodore, 100
Beveridge, George, 288
Blacks, employment of, 261, 349
Block, John, 45
Block paragraphing, 38
Boccardi, Louis D., 58
Bogart, John B., 24
Bogart, Leo, 33
Boise, Idaho, 27
Bolles, Don, 312
Boston, Massachusetts, 14
Boston *Globe,* 100, 310
Bowman, William W., 21
Boyer, Peter J., 200–201
Boyle, Hal, 195
Bradlee, Benjamin C., 239
Bradley, Ed, 19
Brady, James, 288, 290–291
Brady, John, 168
Brandeis, Louis D., 223
Brando, Marlon, 161–162
Brighteners. *See* Human interest
British Broadcasting Corporation (BBC), 310
British Foreign Office, 182
Broadcasting, 340
Broadcast news
  compared with print news, 330
  crisis reporting, 291–292
  influence on newspaper reporting, 232
  interns, 342
  radio, reporting for, 330–333
  radio, writing for, 333–336
  television, reporting for, 336–337, 339
  television, writing for, 338–339
  television news script, sample of, 338–339

377

378 Index

Brookings Institution, 309
Brown, Hank, 291–292
Brush Poppers Riding Club, 194
Buchanan, James, 190
Buchwald, Art, 231
Budgets, government agencies, 252–253, 256
Bureau of Land Management, 27
Burke, W. Vincent, 270
Burnett, Carol, 214, 221, 283
Bush, George, 289
Business editor, 4
Butz, Earl, 79–80, 81, 241

Cable News Network, 337
California, 27, 217, 224
California Department of Transportation, 193
California Polytechnical State University, 79
California State Psychological Association, 194
Callihan, E. L., 111
Cannon, Lou, 317
Capitalization, 42, 362–363
Capote, Truman, 161–162
Cappon, Jack, 95, 120, 121, 153
Carmel, California, 166–167
Carpenter, Theresa, 230–231
Carroll, Jan, 45
Carter, Jimmy, 206, 241, 369
Carter Hawley Stores, 194
Casey, Robert J., 282
Cassopolis, Michigan, 132
Cassopolis (Michigan) *Vigilant*, 101
Catledge, Turner, 24
Central Intelligence Agency (CIA), 19, 237
Chadwick, Henry, 15
Charleston, West Virginia, 153
"Charley's Angels," 29
Charlotte *Observer*, 115
Cherry Sisters, 227
Chicago, 89, 195
Chicago *Daily News*, 282, 300
Chicago Press Club, 16
Chicago *Sun-Times*
  Mirage bar series, 239, 243–244, 273
Chicago *Tribune*, 24, 123, 237, 310
Chicago Tribune Press Service, 140
China Airlines, 248
Christian Science Monitor, 232, 300, 307–309, 310
Christie, Agatha, 166
Chronological stories, 46–47
Circulation department, 4
City directory, 183
City editor, 3, 4, 9, 20, 109, 165, 201, 209, 247, 260, 313, 347, 351
Civil War, 15, 37
Clarity, 103, 113–114, 333
Clark, Roy Peter, 26, 100, 115
Clemens, Samuel, 118

Cleveland *Plain Dealer*, 226
Cliché, 123
Coaches, of writing, 100
Coca-Cola, 224
Colesanti, Donna, 47
Colesanti, Frank, 47
College of Marin, 178
Collins, Walton R., 172
Colloquialisms, in broadcast news, 335
Colonial period, 18
Columbia Broadcasting System (CBS), 42, 291–292, 310, 313, 337
Columnists, 200–201
Commercial use, invasion of privacy, 224
Commission on Freedom of the Press, 33, 235, 299
Communist Party, 143
Comprehensive Employment and Training Act (CETA), 308
Compton, California, 27
Conciseness, 116–118
Congress, 27, 31, 90–91, 171, 189, 199, 310, 311–312
Congressional Directory, 188
Congressional Quarterly, 188
Consent, as libel defense, 218
Consequence, news value element, 31
Considine, Bob, 87, 89
Cooke, Janet, 57, 230, 231, 232, 239, 240
Copley News Service, 101
Copper Development Association, 139
Copple, Neale, 143
Copydesk, 4, 347
Copy preparation
  optical character recognition, 61, 352–359
  traditional method, 61–65
  video display terminal, 61, 351–352, 352–359
Corantoes, 32–33
Corn, 303–306
Courts
  cameras in courtrooms, 323–324
  civil cases, 282–283
  criminal cases, 276–282
  glossary, 283–284
  organization of, 275–276
Covering Crime: How Much Press-Police Cooperation? How Little?, 273
Cox Broadcasting Corporation, 337, 339
Craft of Interviewing, The, 168
Cramer, Richard Ben, 119
Creative Interviewing, 168
Crime reporting. *See* Courts; Police reporting
Crippen, Robert L., 120
Current Biography Yearbook, 188

Curtis, J. Montgomery, 72
Curtis, Tony, 167
Curtis Publishing Company v. *Butts*, 218

Dallas, Texas, 291
B. Dalton Bookseller, 301–303
Daly, Michael, 230
Dana, Charles A., 15, 16, 24
Dangling modifier, 103
Dateline: White House, 295
Davis, Phil, 328
Davis, Richard Harding, 16
Day, Benjamin, 14–15
Dayton *Journal Herald*, 241
Deadline Every Minute, 31
Deadlines, 3, 5
Deadlines & Monkeyshines, 322
Decency, standards of, 225
Defamation, as libel element, 214–215
Defense Department, 310
DeFontaine, Felix Gregory, 15
DeMott, John, 248
Dennis, Everette E., 258, 273, 285
Dental X-rays, 29
Denver *Post*, 237, 239
Department of Agriculture, 199, 304
Department of Health and Human Services, 88
Department of Justice, 237
Department of Labor, 308–309
Depositions, 283
Depth Reporting, 143
Des Moines *Register*, 198–200, 248, 313
Desmond, Robert W., 14, 21
Details, in stories, 114–116
Detroit *News*, 235
Deukmejian, George, 134–135
Dial, The, 15
Dialect, in broadcast news, 335
Diamond, Jack (Legs), 89
Dickens, Charles, 113
Dillinger, John, 89
Dim, Stuart, 115
Direct quotations, 124–125
Disaster reporting, 292–294
Divorce cases, 282
Doctor Perry's drugstore, 16
Documentaries, 19
Dolan, Mary Anne, 343
Donahue, Phil, 57
Donaldson, Sam, 291
Dooley, Vince, 31, 33
Dorsey, Joselyn, 338
Dowagiac (Michigan) *Daily News*, 263–264
Drew, Elizabeth, 310
Duranty, Walter, 300

Earthquakes, 158–159, 163
Editing, 4, 61–65, 347
Editing in the Electronic Era, 65
Editor, 4

Index

Editor & Publisher, 11, 72, 102, 236, 288, 294
Editorial Research Reports, 187
Eisenhower, Dwight D., 206
Electronic journalism. *See* Broadcast news; Optical character recognition; Video display terminal
Elements of Style, The, 116, 128
Embarrassment, invasion of privacy, 225
Emery, Edwin, 20, 244, 295
Emery, Michael, 20
Employment
   attitudes on job, 344–345
   beginning assignments, 67–72, 342–349
   internships, 342–343
   minorities, 261, 349
   preparation for, 342–344
   salaries, 345–346
   women, 20, 343, 348
Encyclopedias, 188
Entertainment editor, 4
Equal Rights Amendment, 76, 77
Ethics
   absolutist, 237
   antinomian, 237
   codes of, 233–236
   conflicts of interest, 237–238
   deceptive practices, 238–239, 242–243
   gratuities, 235
   guidelines for reporters, 242–243
   obscenity, profanity, vulgarity, 178, 240–241
   other problems of, 239–240
   photographs, 241–242, 321
   police coverage, 269–271
   possible reasons for abuses of, 231–233
   recent problems, 230–231
   situation, 237
Evans, Harold, 328
Event-centered stories, 28
Evergreen, Colorado, 291
Executive editor, 4
Extra edition, 5

Facts on File, 188
Fair comment, as libel defense, 217
Fair Credit Reporting Act, 226
Fairness, 56, 58, 234
False light, invasion of privacy, 225
Family Education Rights and Privacy Act of 1974, 226
Family life editor, 4
Fang, Irving, 340
Farah, Joseph, 343
Faulkner, William, 113
Fault, as libel element, 215
Fawcett-Majors, Farrah, 30
Feature stories
   interviewing for, 157–158
   writing of, 130–143

Federal Aviation Authority, 293
Federal Bureau of Investigation (FBI), 19, 89, 189, 262, 288
Federal Communications Commission, 332
Felony, 271
"Fiddler on the Roof," 176
Fielman, Sheldon, 291
Fifth Amendment, 163, 312
Fire department, coverage of, 267–268
Firestone, Brooks, 95
Firestone, Russell III, 220
First Amendment, 217, 218, 225–226, 234
First Amendment and the Fourth Estate, The, 228
Five "Ws" and how, 10, 38–40, 51
Fleming, Ian, 302
Flesch, Rudolf, 128
Ford, Gerald, 80, 171
Ford Foundation, 308
Foreign correspondents, 14, 16, 18, 32
Forrestal, James, 150
Franklin, Benjamin, 14
Franklin, James, 14
Franklin, Marc A., 228
Free and Responsible Press, A, 33
Freedom of Information (FOI) Act, 188–189
Freedom of the press, 234
Freeman, Laura, 237
Freivogel, Margaret, 301
French Revolution, 14
Friendly, Fred, 337
Front Page, The, 269
Fugger newsletter, 13
Fuller, Jack, 237
Fuller, Margaret, 15
Futures book, 253

Gagen, Joyce, 172–173
Galesburg, Illinois, 195
Gallagher, Jim, 140–143
Gallup (New Mexico) *Independent,* 101
Galway Race Track, 126–127
Gardner, John, 302
George Washington University Hospital, 289–290
Georgia, 225
Georgia Center for Continuing Education, 43
Gertz v. *Welch,* 220
Gibson, Martin L., 65
Gilbert, Mrs. Ginny, 48, 50–52
Gilboy, Robert, 111
Glenn, John, 369
Glossary, 370–375
Goepp, Dr. Robert A., 29
Goodbye Gutenberg, The Newspaper Revolution of the 1980s, 11
Grady, Henry W., 15
Grammar, 10, 76, 93–95, 99–109, 177–178

Grammar for Journalists, 111
Great Quotations, The, 188
Great Women Reporters, 295
Greeley, Horace, 15
Green, Bill, 240
Green Bay (Wisconsin) *Press-Gazette,* 221
Greenwich, Connecticut, 139
Grossman, Michael B., 210
Gross national product (GNP), 300–301
Groth, Dr. David, 28
Gunther, John, 300

Hage, George S., 258, 273, 285
Hagerstown, Maryland, 46
Hallett, Carol, 80
Handouts. *See* Publicity releases
Harper's, 233
Harris, Jay T., 349
Harris, Jean, 281
Hartford *Courant,* 110, 150
Hartgen, Stephen, 258, 273, 285
Harvard Law Review, 223
Hawaii, 226, 252
Hawver, Walter W., 270
Hayden, Trudy, 190
Hayes, Paul, 301
Healion, James V., 139
Hearst, William Randolph, 16, 20
Hecht, Ben, 269
Helicopter, use of, 336
Hemingway, Ernest, 113
Hendrickson, Molly and Dean, 139–140
Hentoff, Nat, 238
Herbers, John, 306
Herbert v. *Lando,* 220
Hersh, Seymour, 19
Hershey, Terry, 248
Hess, Stephen, 309, 317
Higgins, Marguerite, 16
Hinckley, John W., Jr., 138, 289–291
Hiroshima atomic explosion, 301
Hoaxes, 148
Hoffa, James, 162
Hollywood, 179
Holy Name College, 173
Hoover, J. Edgar, 313
Hornby, William, 239
Hostages in Iran, 233
Housing coverage, 313–316
Houston Merchants Exchange, 199
Hudson, Rock, 167
Hulteng, John, 244
Human interest, 14–15, 29, 31–32, 46, 49
"Hunger in America," 19
Huntsville (Alabama) *Times,* 365
Hutchins, Robert Maynard, 235
Huxtable, Ada Louise, 301

IBM Selectrics, 353
Idaho, 27

Index

Identification
  in broadcast news, 324
  in cutlines, 326
  delayed, 43–44
  immediate, 42
  as libel element, 215
  in obituaries, 146
I. F. Stone's Weekly, 19
Indianapolis, Indiana, 45
Indio (California) *Daily News,* 100
Information Machines: Their Impact on Men and the Media, The, 11
Information Process: World News Reporting to the Twentieth Century, The, 21
Intelligencers, 13
International News Service, 89
International Standard Book Number, 302–303
Internships, 342–343
Interviews
  conducting of, 160–168
  note-taking, 165
  preparation for, 158–160
  role of interviewer, 157–158
  spot news, 157–158
  tape recorder, use of, 165–166
  tips, 159
  writing, 170–180
Introduction to Mass Communications, 20–21
Intrusion, invasion of privacy, 224–225
Invasion of privacy. *See* Privacy
Inverted pyramid, 37, 131
Investigative Reporting, Anderson and Benjaminson, 190
Investigative Reporting, Mollenhoff, 317
Investigative Reporting and Editing, 168
Ireland, 126
Irwin, Will, 16
Isaacs, Norman, 232
Iserman, Theodore, 122
Ismach, Arnold H., 258, 273, 285
Israeli, 119
Izard, Ralph, 285

Jakes, John, 295
Japan, 161
Jensen, Gregory, 123
Jobs. *See* Employment
Johnson, Ben, 237
Johnson, Jeneanne, 302
Johnstone, John W. C., 21
Jones, Rev. Jim, 32
Jonestown, Guyana, 32
Journalese, 100
Journalism Educator, 152
Journalist. *See* Reporter
Julian (California) *Sun,* 138
Juvenile offenders, 282
J. Walter Thompson advertising agency, 197

Kaltenborn, H. V., 18
Kansas City, Missouri, 162
Kansas City *Star,* 301
Kendall, George Wilkins, 15
Kennedy, Edward, 241
Kennedy, John F., 118
Kent, Frank R., 300
Kifner, John, 237
Kimbrough, John, 224
King, Dr. Martin Luther, 218
King, Peter, 134–135
Kirkpatrick, Helen, 300
Kissinger, Henry, 283
Klemesrud, Judy, 166–168
Knight, Hans, 172
Knight-Ridder Newspapers, Inc., 72, 100, 310
Knox College, 195
Kobre, Ken, 328
Koltay, Emery, 302
Koppinger, John, 91
Korean war, 241
KTRK-TV, Houston, 270
Ku Klux Klan, 222
Kumer, Martha J., 210

Lait, Jack, 89
Lake Charles (Louisiana) *American Press,* 221
Landis, Carole, 241
Language Skills for Journalism, 111
Lapham, Lewis H., 233
Las Vegas, Nevada, 123, 173
Laurence, William L., 301
Law, Caroline, 136
Law Enforcement Assistance Administration (LEAA), 226
Lawrence, David, 300
Leads
  abstract language, 91–92
  astonisher, 87
  complex story, 88
  contrast, 85–86
  descriptive, 87
  dialogue, 90
  direct address, 87
  editor's advice about, 95–96
  flat, dull, 93
  historic, 89
  interview, 170–174
  literary allusion, 86–87
  obituary, 147
  other poor, 94–95
  parody, 86
  question, 88
  quotation, 89–90
  say-nothing, 90–91
  speech, 71
  ungrammatical, 93–94
  varieties of, 85–90
  writing of, 35–44, 51, 75–77
Leary, John, 301
Leary, Warren E., 29
Lebanon, 119
Lebanon (Kentucky) *Democrat,* 47

Lebowitz, Fran, 178–180
Le Monde (France), 310
Lendt, David L., 201
Lerner, Max, 236
Lesly, Philip, 201
Levi Strauss & Company, 134–135
Libel law
  constitutionalizing of, 217–221
  defenses, 216–218
  definition of libel, 214–216
  guidelines for reporters, 223
  "red flag" words, 222
  reporter responsibilities, 9, 213–214, 216
Liberatore, Laura, 174, 175–177
Library (morgue), 183
License Renewed, 302
Liebling, A. J., 161
Life, 225
Life on the Mississippi, 118
Lindstrom, Carl E., 339
Lippman, Harvey, 231
Lippmann, Walter, 18
Lloyds of London, 13
Localizing, 44
Loh, Jules, 116
London, 13, 14, 123, 182, 244
London *Morning Chronicle,* 14
London *Morning Herald,* 14
London *Sunday Express,* 136
Los Angeles, 27, 293
Los Angeles *Herald-Examiner,* 237, 343
Los Angeles *Times,* 100, 101, 102, 108, 151, 232, 237, 310, 313
Lost Dutchman gold mine, 23
Louis-Schmeling fight, 87, 89
Louisville *Courier-Journal,* 235, 237
Lufkin, Texas, 121

MacArthur, Charles, 269
McCarthy, Tim, 290
McCarthyism, 19
McCoy, Tim, 72
McDonald's, 258
McGrory, Mary, 123
McHale, Robert W., 221
McPhaul, John J., 322
McPherson, Aimee Semple, 164
McWilliams, Carey, 19
Madison Square Garden, 235
Magazines, 19, 310
Maine, 226
Making News, 33
Mallory, Dr. Robert, 167
Maloney, Martin, 340
Managing editor, 4
Manila International Airport, 249
Martin Luther King Center for Social Change, 308
Mary Alice Firestone v. *Time Inc.,* 220
Marvin, Lee, 217
Marvin, Michelle Triola, 217
Mass Media Law, 228

Index 381

Mawby, Dr. Russell, 101
Medieval ballad singers, 13
Mercantile press, 18
Metropolitan Life, 178–179
Metzler, Ken, 168
Meyer, Philip, 190
Miami *Herald,* 100
Milford (Utah) *Beaver County News,* 101
Miller, Arthur, 226
Miller, Lee, 143
Milwaukee *Journal,* 100, 301
Minneapolis *Star,* 301
Minneapolis *Tribune,* 301, 306
Mirage, The, 273
Miranda, Ernesto, 277
Miranda Rule, 277, 284
Misdemeanor, 271
Mitchell, David and Cathy, 7
Mitigatory defenses, in libel law, 218
Modern Media Institute, 26, 100
Mollenhoff, Clark, 313, 317
Montana Bureau of Investigation, 91
Montreal, 235
Moody's Manuals, 188
Morgue (library), 183
Morris, Joe Alex, 31
Moscow, 141
Moses, 213
Moses, J. Roy, 152
Mount Sinai, 213
Mowrer, Edgar Ansel, 300
Mowrer, Paul Scott, 300
Mullen, William, 123
Mulligan, Hugh, 126–127
Murrow, Edward R., 18
Mutual Broadcasting System, 292
Mutz, John M., 45
Myers, Lisa, 288–290
My Lai massacre, 19
Myths, public need for, 233

Napoleon, 14
Nashville *Tennessean,* 47, 86–87
Nation, 19
National Association of Broadcast Employees and Technicians, 335
National Broadcasting Company (NBC), 201, 291, 310
National Enquirer, 214, 221, 283
National Institute for Occupational Safety and Health, 28
National News Council, 230, 232, 244, 269–270, 273
National Police Radio Signal Code, 266
National Press Photographers Association, 235, 324
National (telegraph) editor, 4
National Weather Service, 151, 154, 331

Nature Expeditions International, 193
Nazi, 172, 222
Neenah, Wisconsin, 46
Neilson, Winthrop and Frances, 317
Nelson, Jack, 313
New Deal, 19
New-England Courant, 14
New England Press Association, 328
New Journalism, 18, 20
Newman, Edward, 100
New Orleans, 96, 199
New Orleans *Picayune,* 15
New Republic, 310
News
  accuracy, 9, 55–56, 234, 236
  attribution in, 40–41, 56, 125–126
  broadcast, 291–292, 330–339
  chronological treatment of, 46–47
  conferences, 203–209
  definitions of, 23–26
  editing of, 61–65, 347
  elements of, 30–33, 55–59
  fairness, 56, 58, 234
  "hard" and "soft," 26–30, 130–143
  identification in, 42–44, 146, 215, 324, 326
  interpretive, 19, 30, 299–309
  investigative, 7, 19–20
  leads, 35–44, 51, 71, 75–77, 85–96, 137, 147, 170–174
  localizing, 44
  objective, 58–59
  opinion in, 20, 59
  photographic, 319–328
  pyramid style, 37
  radio-television, 330–339
  rewriting, 48–52
  sense of, 8, 13–14, 26
  sentences, 102–104
  sexism in, 51
  structure, 35–37, 121–122
  style, 10–11, 64–65, 113–127, 333–336, 338–339
  writing tips, 50
New School for Social Research, 180, 238
News conferences
  off-the-record problem in, 209
  opportunities during, 203
  presidential, 205–206
  questioning in, 206–209
Newsday, 115, 137–138
News Editing, 65
News editor, 4
Newshawkers, 13
Newsletters, 310
News Media & the Law, The, 228
Newsom, Doug, 201
Newspaper Enterprise Associations, 222
Newspaper Fund, Inc., 343
Newspaper Guild, 20, 346

Newspapers
  daily, 3–7
  mercantile, 18
  penny press, 18
  political, 18
  weekly, 6–7, 14, 320, 346–348
News People, The, 21
News photography
  cutlines, 325–328
  guidelines, 328
  kinds of, 289, 320–322
  principles of, 322–323
  reporter involvement in, 319–320, 322
  restraints, 225, 241–242
  rights, 323–325
News releases, 71. *See also* Publicity releases
Newsroom
  changing, 61
  during crisis, 287–294
  operation of, 3–7
New Strategies for Public Affairs Reporting, 258, 273, 285
Newsweek, 11, 310
New York, 138, 224, 235
New York *Daily News,* 127, 230, 239
New Yorker, The, 161, 238, 310
New York *Herald,* 14, 15
New York *Herald-Tribune,* 16, 24, 300
New York *Post,* 16, 248
New York *Sun,* 14, 15, 16, 24
New York *Times,* 15, 16, 17, 18, 24, 89, 100, 102, 166, 179, 187, 218–219, 220, 231, 235, 237, 300, 301, 306, 310
New York Times Index, 187
New York *Tribune,* 15
New York *World,* 16, 24, 301
Nixon, Patricia, 180
Nixon, Richard, 19, 25, 80, 196, 206, 241, 313
Nobel Prize, 159
Nofziger, Lynn, 290
North Texas State University, 152
Northwestern University Medill School of Journalism, 349
Note-taking
  condensing word, 69
  shorthand, 69
  tape recorder, 70–71
Novak, Kim, 166–168, 170
Novik, Jack, 190
Nudity, 241
Numerals, 365–366

Oakland A's, 173
Obituaries, 145–150
Objectivity, 18–19, 58–59
O'Boyle, Thomas A., Jr., 149–150
Oceanside (California) *Blade-Tribune,* 231

382 Index

OCR. *See* Optical character recognition
Offset printing, 6
Off-the-record, 209
Oklahoma, 224
O'Leary, Jeremiah, 291
Omaha, Nebraska, 190
Ombudsmen, 240
Onassis, Jacqueline Kennedy, 225
O'Neill, Michael J., 239
On Writing Well, 128
Optical character recognition (OCR), 61, 352–359
Oregon, 226
Organization of Petroleum Exporting Countries (OPEC), 152
Originality, in phraseology, 122–123
Orr, Robert D., 45
Osborne, John, 310
Othello, 213
Overcrowding, in stories, 120–121

Palestine Liberation Organization (PLO), 119
Palm Beach, Florida, 220
Paperback almanacs, 188
Paragraphs, 36–38
Parallel construction, 103
Paraphrasing, 42–43
Partial quotations, 124
Pasadena, California, 27
Passive voice, 49
Peck, Gregory, 180
Pember, Don R., 228
Pennsylvania Gazette, 14
Pentagon, 187
Penthouse, 221, 240
Pepsi-Cola, 86
Perry, James, 14
Persistence, in interviewing, 163
Personality interview, 175–177
Personalized approach, to stories, 132–134, 137
Perspectives on Mass Communications, 244
Pett, Saul, 162
Philadelphia, 69, 255, 308
Philadelphia *Bulletin,* 172
Philadelphia *Inquirer,* 119, 237
Photography, 328
Photojournalism. *See* News photography
Photojournalism: The Professional Approach, 328
Phototypesetter, 4
Pickett, Calder M., 21
Pictures on a Page, 328
Pierce, Fred, 200
Pittsburgh Pirates, 131
Pizza Hut, 258
Playing It Straight, A Practical Discussion of the Ethical Principles of the American Society of Newspaper Editors, 244
Plea bargaining, 279
Point Reyes (California) *Light,* 7
Police department
  coverage of, 263–272
  functions of, 262
  organization of, 261–262
  radio codes, 266
Police reporting, 260–272, 324–325
Political press, 18
Pope John Paul II, 126–127, 248, 326
Portland *Oregonian,* 166
Portraying the President, the White House and the News Media, 210
Precision Journalism, 190
Press and America: An Interpretive History of the Mass Media, The, 20
Press and Public: Who Reads What, When, Where and Why in American Newspapers, The, 33
Press conferences. *See* News conferences
presstime, 219
Prince Charles, 123
Pring, Kimerli Jayne, 221
Privacy
  invasion of, 224–226
  laws, 226–227
  right of, 223–224
Privilege, as libel defense, 216–217
Process-centered stories, 28
Production department, 4
Prominence, news value element, 31
Pronouns, 101
Pronunciation, in broadcast news, 335–336
Prosser, William L., 224
Proximity, news value element, 30–31
Publication, as libel element, 215
Public figure, 220–221
Publicity Process, The, 201
Publicity releases
  development of, 196–201
  handout mentality, 195–196
  role of, 192–194
  well-prepared, 194–195
Public opinion polls, 30
Public records. *See* Sources
Public relations
  news preparation for, 346
  publicity releases, 192–201
  salaries, 346
  Washington, D.C., practitioners, 309
Public Relations Handbook, 201
Publisher, 5
Pulitzer, Joseph, 16, 18, 20, 24
Pulitzer Prize, 7, 118–119, 162, 198, 200, 230, 231, 239, 244, 313
Punctuation, 363–366, 387

Purdue University, 80
Putnam's and Sons, 302
Pyle, Ernie, 16

Quotations, use of, 68–72, 77–78, 89, 124–126, 177–178, 334

Radio news. *See* Broadcast news
Rancho Mirage, California, 171
Rand Corporation, 195
Rather, Dan, 19, 292, 313
Ray, Dixy Lee, 166
Raymond, Henry J., 15
Reader's Digest, 29
Reader's Guide to Periodical Literature, 187
Reagan, Nancy, 180, 290
Reagan, Ronald, 41, 79, 80–81, 138, 171, 180, 189, 205, 206, 287–292, 332
Reagan administration, 28, 91, 307–309
Reasoner, Harry, 19
Redundancy, 101
Reeves, Richard, 238
Rehnquist, William, 220
Reid, Whitelaw, 15
Religious terminology, 148
Reporter
  current role of, 7
  historical role of, 13–20
  minorities, 349
  power of, 20
  twentieth century, 16–17
  woman, 15–16, 20, 343, 349
Reporters and Officials, 258
Reporters Committee for Freedom of the Press, 221, 228
Reporting
  advocacy, 20, 231–232
  airplane crash, 292–294
  alternative, 20, 231–232
  background material, use of, 78–79
  clichés, use of, 123
  courts, 275–284
  development of, 13–20
  foreign, 14, 16, 18, 32
  historical development of, 13–20
  improper practices in, 231–233, 238–239, 242–243
  interpretive, 19, 28–30, 299–309
  investigative, 7, 19–20, 312–316
  note-taking in, 68–71
  objective, 18–19, 299–300
  photographic, 319–329
  planning of stories, 71–72
  presidential assassination attempt, 287–292
  qualifications for, 7–11
  radio-television, 291–292, 294, 330–339
  science, 301
  specialized, 19
  speeches, 72, 75–80

sports, 16, 131–132, 347
standards, 18
style, development of, 113–127
tape recorder, use of, 70–71, 165–166, 225, 331–332
themes, development of, 77–78
Washington coverage, 14, 309–312
women in news, 51
Reporting, An Inside View, 317
Reporting Public Affairs, 258, 273, 285
Reporting the Citizens' News, 285
Reston, James B., 18
Reuters, 310
Rewrite, 16, 288–289
Rewriting, 48–50
Reynolds, Dean, 291–292
Reynolds, Frank, 292
Richard Merek, 302
Richmond Newspapers v. *Commonwealth of Virginia,* 278
Richter scale, 159
Riis, Jacob, 15
Risser, James, 187, 198–200
R. L. Polk Company, 183
Roark, James, 343
Robbins, Dr. Anthony, 28
Robinson, Henry Crabb, 14
Rochester, New York, 115
Rockefeller, Nelson, 242, 321
Rolling Stone, 241
Rolling Stones, 255
Roman news posters, 13
Roosevelt, Franklin D., 69, 205
Rosenbloom v. *Metromedia,* 218
R. R. Bowker Company, 302
Rubenstein, Paul Max, 340
Ruehlmann, William, 143

Sacramento, California, 27, 115, 293
Saenz, Frank, 231
Safer, Morley, 19
Safire, William, 100
Sagan, Carl, 180
St. Louis, Missouri, 187
St. Louis *Post-Dispatch,* 16, 301
St. Paul *Dispatch,* 303
St. Petersburg *Times,* 26, 100, 101
Salaries. *See* Employment
Salisbury, Harrison, 16
San Bernardino (California) *Sun,* 280
Sanders, Carl, 149
Sanders, Marlene, 42–43
San Diego *Evening Tribune,* 266, 292–294
San Francisco, 7, 16, 27
San Francisco *Chronicle,* 123, 178
San Francisco *Examiner,* 134–135
San Jose *Mercury-News,* 100, 101
San Luis Obispo County *Telegram-Tribune,* 79
Santa Barbara *News-Press,* 101
Santa Maria Arts Council, 91

Santa Maria (California) *Times,* 101
Satellite, 337
Saturday Review, 238
Saudi Arabia, 189, 195
Scanner. *See* Optical character recognition
Scarsdale Diet, 281
Scene-setting, 126–127, 135–137
Schulte, Henry H., 258, 273, 285
Scripps, Edward Wyllis, 16
Scripps-Howard Newspapers, 221
Seattle, Washington, 96
Second-day stories, 131–133, 145, 151–154
Seldes, George, 188
"Selling of the Pentagon," 19
Sentences, 101–104, 333
Sexism, 51
Shakespeare, William, 213
Shaw, David, 100, 101, 102, 108, 151, 232, 237, 238–239
Shibutani, Tamotsu, 24
Shields, Brooke, 88
Siegal, Allan, 100
Siegfried, Tom, 201
Sigal, Leon, 258
Sigma Delta Chi Distinguished Service in Journalism Award, 239
Silverman, Fred, 200–201
Simpson, Ross, 292
Sinclair, Ward, 303
Situation ethics, 237
Sixth Amendment, 276
"60 Minutes," 19, 300
Slander, 214, 224
Slang, 335, 370
Slawski, Edward J., 21
Smith, Anthony, 11
Smith, Merriman, 69, 118–119
Smith, Zay N., 273
Social Security, 31
Social Security Administration, 174–175
Social responsibility. *See* Ethics
Social Studies, 180
Society for Animal Rights, 193
Society of Professional Journalists, Sigma Delta Chi, 200, 233
Solana Beach, California, 134
Solvang Municipal Improvement District, 92
Sony Company, 338
Sources
computer, use of, 280
library, 187–188
obituary news, 148–150
public records, 184–189
verification of, 9
where to find, 182–184
South Bend *Tribune,* 100, 101, 110, 132
Southern California, 163
Southern Christian Leadership Conference, 218

Soviet Union, 142, 300
Speech stories
covering, 67–72
writing, 75–80
Spelling, 99–102, 104–111, 148
Spell It Fast: The Quick Way to Spell Using 60 Stimulating Word Lists, 111
Spencer, Lady Diana, 123
Spokane *Spokesman-Review,* 243
Sports editor, 4
Sports reporting, 16, 131–132, 347
Springfield, Oregon, 174
Stalking the Feature Story, 143
Stanley, Henry M., 15
Stark, Louis, 301
Starr, Douglas P., 152
State editor, 4
Steffens, Lincoln, 15
Stone, David, 138–139
Stone, I. F., 19
Stoneleigh, England, 29
Story of America As Reported by Its Newspapers 1690–1960, The, 295
Story of Ernie Pyle, The, 143
Strunk, William, 128
Style
broadcast news, 333–336, 338–339
editing, 62–65
how to develop, 113–127
inverted pyramid, 37–38
techniques, 10–11
Subject and verb agreement, 101
Suicides, 150
Sullivan, L. B., 218–219
Sullivan, Mark, 300
Summers, Jerry Wayne, 47–48
Supply side economics, 300–301
Suspended interest stories, 47–48
Sutton, Carol, 235
Sutton, Willie, 36
Swissheim, Jane Grey, 15
Synanon, 7

Taniguchi, Eleanor, 301
Tarbell, Ida M., 15
Tarnower, Dr. Herman, 281
Tarnowski, Tod, 172
Taylor, Elizabeth, 166–167
Taylor, Walter, 288–289
Tekulve, Kent, 131
Telegraph, use of, 16
Telegraph (national) editor, 4
Telephone, use of, 148, 157, 183, 291
Television news. *See* Broadcast news
Television News, 340
Tellico Dam, 101
Tempo
in sentence structure, 121–122
in stories, 114
Tennessee Valley Authority, 300
Texas, 217, 224

Index

Thatcher, Margaret, 29
Theme, 77–78, 170–171. *See also* Unity
Thomas, Bob, 161
Thomas, Helen, 18, 295
Thomas, Lowell, 18
Thomopoulos, Tony, 200–201
Thompson, Dorothy, 16
Thomson, Virgil, 162, 165
Thoroughness, 146
Thurtell, Joel, 132
Time, 11, 19, 225, 226, 291, 292, 310
Time element, in stories, 367–368
Timeliness, news value element, 31, 33
Times of London, 14, 310
Titles, 42, 334, 368–369
Today Show, 179
Town criers, 13
Treasury Department, 241
Trimborn Farm, 85
Trudeau, Pierre, 325
Truth, as libel defense, 216
Tuchman, Gaye, 33
Tucker, Lem, 291–292
Tupperware, 102
Twain, Mark. *See* Clemens, Samuel
"20/20," 231, 232
Tyler (Texas) *Telegram,* 24

Underground press, 20
Union Bag-Camp Paper Corporation, 122
United Press, 31, 69
United Press International, 18, 27, 101, 118, 123, 139, 152, 162, 291–292, 310, 325, 375
United Press International *Log,* 59
U.S. Army Personnel Center, 187
U.S. Court of Appeals, 276
U.S.-Mexican War, 15
U.S. News, 300
U.S. News & World Report, 232, 310
U.S. Postal Service, 189
U.S. Secret Service, 288, 290
U.S. State Department, 204, 310
U.S. Supreme Court, 216, 217, 218, 219, 220, 221, 223, 224, 225, 226, 276, 277, 278, 310
United Technologies, 117
Unity, 44–46, 102–103. *See also* Theme
University City News Service, The, 248

University of Chicago, 29, 235, 322
University of Georgia, 31, 33
University of Missouri School of Journalism, 24
University of South Carolina, 306
University of Texas at Dallas, 306
Urban Writers' Society, 301
Utah, 224

Vacaville, California, 27
Valdes, Anne C., 149
Variety
  in writing features, 130–132
  in writing leads, 85–90
VDT. *See* Video display terminal
Ventura (California) *Star-Free Press,* 101
Verbs, use of, 118–120, 125
Veterans Administration, 187
Video display terminal (VDT), 3–4, 61–62, 74, 166, 289, 351, 352, 375
Vietnam, 19, 241
Village Voice, 230, 238
Villard, Henry, 15
Virginia, 224
Vital statistics, 184
Voices of the Past, 21
Von Eckhardt, Wolf, 301

WABC-TV, New York, 231
Waldenbooks, 302
Wallace, Mike, 19
Wall Street Journal, 117, 310
Walker, Stanley, 24
Walter, Wayne, 221
W & J Sloane, 140
War coverage, 18, 119
Warner, Dudley, 150
Warren, South Dakota, 223
Washington, D.C., 18, 29, 214
Washington Post, 19, 46, 57, 100, 101, 196, 230, 232, 239, 240, 241, 301, 303, 310, 313
Washington reporting
  assignments, 309–310
  Congress, 311–312
  during crisis, 287–292
  White House, 310–311
Washington Reporters, The, 309, 317
Washington Star, 123, 287–291, 294
Washington, State of, 166
Watergate scandal, 25, 80, 123, 196,
206, 231, 232, 235, 237, 239, 241, 312, 313
Wayne, John, 369
WBBM-TV, Chicago, 231
Weather stories, 145, 150–151
Welfare and health stories, 28
Westley, Bruce, 65
West Virginia, 226
WHAS-TV, Louisville, 270
What's News—Dow Jones, The Story of The Wall Street Journal, 317
Wheeling (West Virginia) *Daily News,* 72
White, E. B., 127
Whitechapel Club, 16
White House, 196, 205, 289–292, 310–311
White Plains, New York, 281
Who's Who in America, 78, 187
Wight, John, 14
Williams, Paul N., 168
Williams, Walter, 24
Winn, Steven, 178
Winners & Sinners, 100
Wisconsin, 224
Wisner, George, 14
Wolfe, Tom, 232
Wolston, Ilya, 220
Wolston v. Reader's Digest Association, Inc., 220
Women, 15–16, 20, 51, 343, 349
Woodruff, Judy, 292
Woodward, Bob, 19, 196, 232, 295, 313
Word usage, 100–109
World Almanac, 188
World Series, 190
World War I, 300
World War II, 172
Writing for the Media, 340
Writing in Public Relations Practice, 201
WSB-TV, Atlanta, 338

Xerox Publishing Co., 302

Young, John W., 120
Your Rights of Privacy, An ACLU Handbook, 190
Yuma, Arizona, 164

Zekman, Pamela, 273
Zinsser, William, 128